BRITAIN'S
CENTURY

BRITAIN'S
CENTURY

Year by year from 1900 to 2000

A Dorling Kindersley Book

Dorling DK Kindersley

LONDON, NEW YORK, SYDNEY, DELHI,
PARIS, MUNICH, JOHANNESBURG

Editor in chief: Derrik Mercer
Editor: Henrietta Heald

Original edition produced by Jacques Legrand

© 1992 Chronik Verlag, im Bertelsmann Lexikon Verlag GmbH,
Gütersloh/München

This edition © 2000 Dorling Kindersley Limited, London

Most of the material in this book originally appeared in *Chronicle of Britain*,
first published in 1992 by Chronicle Communications Limited, Farnborough

Revisions to this edition by Amber Books Limited, London

2 4 6 8 10 9 7 5 3 1

A CIP record for this book is available from the British Library

ISBN 0 7513 2172 9

Printed in Portugal by Printer Portuguesa

see our complete
catalogue at
www.dk.com

Contents

A Century of Challenges

During her long reign, from 1837 to 1901, Queen Victoria presided over an astonishing expansion of British commercial and industrial power.

As THE 20TH CENTURY DAWNED, Britain held sway over the largest empire in history. Queen Victoria, aged 80 and monarch for more than 60 years, was Empress of India and ruled territories from Canada to Australia, from the West Indies to the South Pacific; one in four human beings lived within the empire. Britain also ruled the waves for, despite challenges from other nations, the Royal Navy was still without equal across the globe; its mastery of the seas guaranteed the security of the land territories.

Within two years of the start of the new century, Queen Victoria was dead; the Victorian era, that potent symbol of British prosperity, power and pride, was at an end. The confidence of Victoria's reign, which left an enduring legacy in the monumental architecture of buildings such as the Royal Albert Hall, appeared to waver as her son Edward's reign progressed and divisive social conflicts became increasingly common. Following the creation of the Women's Social and Political Union in 1903, the women of the suffragette movement pursued a vigorous campaign for the right to vote. The unrest of the working classes became increasingly apparent, despite a raft of social legislation delivered by the 1906 Liberal government that included free school meals for poor children in 1906, old age pensions in 1908, and in the same year a statutory eight-hour working day for miners. Trade unionism became more and more militant and there were a series of often violent strikes in 1911-12. A number of socialist organisations had been created at the end of the 19th century, including the Fabian Society (1883-4) and the Independent Labour Party (1893). In 1900 trade unionists and socialists founded the Labour Representation Committee, precursor of the Labour Party, to sponsor candidates for the House of Commons. With Liberal support, LRC candidates won 29 seats in the 1906 general elections that returned a Liberal government. In Ireland, meanwhile, where the new nationalist party Sinn Féin was formed in 1905, the tensions between demands for home rule in the south and the Unionist determination in the north to remain part of the United Kingdom were increasing to such a pitch that many foresaw civil war.

These issues were essentially unresolved in the summer of 1914 when Britain entered the general European war. The four years of this brutal, slogging conflict, in which three-quarters of a million Britons and almost a quarter of a million subjects from other parts of the Empire were killed, transformed Britain. The effectiveness of wartime government control of industry and the railways was remembered in the peace. Working class deference to its "betters" virtually disappeared, partly because of the disproportionate slaughter of the "officer class" during the trench warfare, but more importantly because of the ever increasing power of the trade unions and the improved economic standing of industrial workers due to the demand for labour. Many women were socially and economically emancipated by leaving the home to work in wartime munitions factories. Years of campaigning by the women's suffrage movement had its reward in autumn 1918 when MPs voted to extend the vote to women over 30 (and to all men over 21). In the December election that followed, the wing of the divided Liberal party that remained loyal to Herbert Asquith rather than to David Lloyd George was virtually annihilated, taking only 28 seats while the emerging Labour Party won 63. In 1924 the first Labour government was voted into power. The country had been brought close to economic ruin by the war. Many of the industries that had powered Britain's 19th-century prosperity were weakened or had been overtaken by foreign competition. Moreover, the harsh financial reparations imposed by the victors on Germany guaranteed that that country, which had been Britain's prime foreign customer, would be economically depressed for years. Britain entered a period of severe economic difficulties that lasted with few respites until the outbreak of World War II. Lloyd George's November 1918 rallying cry to build in Britain "a fit country for heroes to live in" must have seemed a distant dream.

The interwar years saw the empire change character. Under the 1931 Statute of Westminster part of it was redefined as the "British Commonwealth of Nations" and the larger Dominions – Australia, Canada, South Africa and New Zealand – were granted independence as "autonomous communities within the British Empire". Most of Ireland won independence from Britain in 1921, under a treaty that partitioned the country into the Irish Free State in the south and six largely Protestant northern counties that remained in the United Kingdom as Northern Ireland. This treaty led to a bitter civil war in the Free State in 1922-3 as some southern nationalists refused to accept partition.

At the end of the 1930s Britain entered World War II a less confident and prosperous nation than she had been at the start of the last great global conflict in 1914. Nevertheless in 1940, following the fall of France and facing imminent defeat at the hands of the seemingly unstoppable German army just 21 miles away across the Channel, the nation exhibited under Prime Minister Winston Churchill a seemingly unbreakable resolve. During the heroic autumn of 1940, when the country had no allies save the Dominions, the RAF withstood the might of the Luftwaffe in the Battle of Britain, and subsequently the British people stoically endured the bombing onslaught of the Blitz. With America's entry into the conflict in 1941, and when it became clear that Russia was fighting back against the German invaders, the miraculous prospect of eventual victory sustained the country's spirit.

Curiously, Churchill's domestic political touch deserted him in the 1945 peace. In a bitter campaign for the first post-war election he misjudged the national mood in his attacks on the socialists who had worked alongside him in the wartime government, and the Labour Party was returned with a landslide 146-seat majority, the first independent majority in its history. Under Prime Minister Clement Attlee, the government set about an industrial nationalisation programme and the creation of the welfare state. Victory in World War II had come at a heavy price, for the war left Britain economically crippled, forced to sign up for United States aid under the Marshall Plan of 1947 and uncertain of its role in a new world order

The Dome at Greenwich in southeast London was built as the centrepiece of Britain's celebrations of the start of the third millennium.

in which the US and the Soviet Union loomed large as "superpowers". Britons endured austerity measures in many cases worse than those they had suffered on the home front during the war. On the international stage Britain embarked on a swift but dignified retreat from empire. India became independent in 1947, Burma and Ceylon in 1948; Britain withdrew from Egypt (save the Suez Canal Zone) and from Palestine in 1948. The Gold Coast and Malaya gained their independence in 1957, and by the end of the 1960s only a very few scattered parts of the world remained under British control.

In the second half of the 20th century the two most pressing problems for Britain were probably its relations with continental Europe and the future of Northern Ireland. When the European Economic Community (EEC) was founded under the 1957 Treaty of Rome Britain elected to stand aloof, and although she did eventually join in 1973 the question of further British integration in Europe remains a live and politically divisive issue. In January 1999, when the European currency, the euro, was launched, Britain once more held back, and even the avowedly pro-European Labour government that swept to power in May 1997 has not unambiguously committed itself to joining at a later date.

Despite continuing puzzlement about national identity and role in the world, the country nevertheless gathered itself for the millennium celebrations of December 1999 in a state of relative harmony and prosperity. The devolved assemblies in Edinburgh and Cardiff showed signs of satisfying Scottish and Welsh nationalism, while in Northern Ireland the implementation of the 1998 Good Friday agreement seemed, after 30 years of bloody conflict, to give a stronger chance of peace than many had dared believe possible. Britain faced the future with a spring in its step and a confidence that it could rise to the challenges of a new era.

As prime minister from 1940 to 1945 Winston Churchill inspired the country to resist doggedly until victory was eventually achieved. At one time this had seemed an impossibly distant prospect.

	1900–1909	**1910–1919**	**1920–1929**	**1930–1939**	**1940–1949**

Politics and Society

1900–1909

Empire thrives
One in four people worldwide live in the British Empire, which covers one-fifth of the global landmass.

End of Victorian era
Queen Victoria dies in 1901 and is succeeded by her eldest son, Edward VII.

South Africa
Britain defeats the Boers in 1902. In 1910 the Union of South Africa is created.

New political parties
In England the Labour Party (1900) and in Ireland nationalist Sinn Féin (1905) are formed.

Suffragette movement
Women fight for the vote.

Scouts
Baden-Powell launches the Scouting movement in 1907.

1910–1919

Edward VII dies
The popular king is succeeded by his son, George V, in 1910.

Great War 1914–18
Three-quarters of a million Britons and 200,000 from the Empire go to their deaths on the battlefields of Europe.

Working class poverty
In 1914 20 per cent of Dubliners are reportedly living in squalid tenements.

Easter Rising
In 1916 the Irish Republican Brotherhood leads an insurrection against British rule.

Women in politics
In 1918 women are for the first time eligible to vote. Nancy Astor (pictured above, third from left) becomes the first woman MP in 1919.

1920–1929

Birth pangs of free Ireland
A 1921 treaty creates the Irish Free State but sparks a civil war in Ireland.

Family planning
Britain's first birth control clinic opens, in London, in 1921.

Labour in power
James Ramsay MacDonald heads the first Labour government in 1924.

General Strike
The TUC calls Britain's first general stoppage in 1926.

Preserving the countryside
In 1929 Britain's first "green belt" is approved – a five-mile-long stretch of countryside near Hendon to be protected from development.

1930–1939

Holidays for the young
In 1930 the Youth Hostels Association opens its first cheap hostels for young hikers.

Labour government falls
In 1931 Labour prime minister Ramsay MacDonald forms a 'National' government, which is mostly Conservative.

Depression
By 1932, 3 million – one in four members of the British workforce – are out of work.

Abdication
After the death of George V in 1936, Edward VIII abdicates for love of American divorcee Wallis Simpson.

New era in Ireland
In 1937 a new constitution creates Eire.

Appeasement and war
Negotiation fails to avert another world war. Prime Minister Neville Chamberlain declares war on Germany at 11.15am on 3 September 1939.

Evacuation
Fear of enemy bombing leads to mass evacuation of children from major cities in 1939.

1940–1949

Battle of Britain
In 1940 the RAF defies the might of the attacking German Luftwaffe.

Dad's Army
Veterans enlist in the Home Guard, so named in 1940.

World War II
The British–American–Russian alliance defeats Nazi Germany in May 1945 and Japan in August 1945, after atom bombs are dropped on Hiroshima and Nagasaki.

Welfare state
After its 1945 landslide victory, Labour sets about creating the welfare state. Its flagship, the National Health Service, begins operation in 1948.

End of empire
India and Pakistan become independent in 1947.

Education
The school leaving age rises to 15 in 1947; the first comprehensive schools are established in 1948.

State control of railways
From 1948 all Britain's railways are owned by the state.

Ireland a republic
In 1949 Eire leaves the Commonwealth, becoming the Republic of Ireland.

Technology and Culture

1900–1909

Wireless shrinks world
Italian wireless pioneer Guglielmo Marconi works in Britain. His invention sends a Morse code message from the Lizard peninsula, Cornwall, to St John's, Newfoundland, in 1901.

Rolls-Royce
Motor-racing pioneer Charles Rolls teams up with Manchester engineer Henry Royce in 1904 to manufacture and sell cars.

National theatre
The Abbey Theatre in Dublin opens in 1904.

Heavy hitter
HMS *Dreadnought* is the world's fastest and most powerful battleship (1906).

Tube travel
London's Central Line (1900) and Bakerloo Line (1906) are the country's first deep underground railways.

First flight
In 1908 American Samuel Cody makes the first powered aeroplane flight in Britain.

Modern style
Glasgow School of Art's library building, designed by Charles Rennie Mackintosh, is opened in 1909.

1910–1919

Modern novel
D.H. Lawrence, Henry James and Joseph Conrad pioneer the "modern" novel.

Titanic disaster
The "unsinkable" SS *Titanic* sinks after striking an iceberg in 1912.

War poets
First World War soldier-poets protest at the inhumanity of war.

Aces high
The aeroplane proves its worth as a weapon in World War I.

Armoured vehicle
The first tanks are used by the British at the Somme in 1916.

DAILY GRAPHIC
£1,000 INSURANCE
ACCIDENT
TUESDAY, APRIL 16, 1912

TITANIC SUNK: APPALLING LOSS OF LIFE

1920–1929

Broadcasting giant
The BBC is created in 1922.

Wembley triumph
In 1923 Wembley Stadium hosts its first FA Cup Final: Bolton Wanderers beat West Ham 2-1.

Imperial Airways
Britain's first national airline takes to the skies in 1924.

TV pioneer
John Logie Baird demonstrates his television in 1926.

Life saver
Alexander Fleming discovers penicillin in 1928.

Modernism
Irish novelist James Joyce is at the forefront of this literary movement.

Cinema boom
Britons flock to the "pictures" to see stars such as Charlie Chaplin and Mary Pickford.

Flying Scotsman
A fast, non-stop London–Edinburgh train service is inaugurated in 1928.

High street revolution
Chain stores such as Woolworth's change the face of British shopping.

1930–1939

Long-distance heroine
Briton Amy Johnson is the first woman to fly solo across the world (1930).

Atomic discovery
In 1932 James Chadwick identifies the neutron, a particle in the atom which has no electrical charge.

Mandatory driving tests
The Road Traffic Act 1934 makes new drivers face a test of competence.

New telephone kiosks
In 1934 the red public phone box, designed by Sir Giles Gilbert Scott, appears.

Penguin paperbacks
Allen Lane produces the first paperback books in 1935.

Tracking device
Scientists directed by Robert Watson-Watt develop radar.

TV on air
The BBC launches the world's first public TV service in 1936, but suspends it in 1939 when war breaks out.

Bank holidays
The 1938 Holidays with Pay Act gives workers paid holidays. Resorts and holiday camps are booming.

Jet breakthrough
Frank Whittle does pioneering work on the jet engine.

1940–1949

Home front
Britons endure rationing and enemy bombing. Women are called up to work in industry.

Dambuster
Barnes Wallis's "bouncing bomb" is used in a 1943 RAF raid on German dams.

Wonder drug
By 1943 penicillin, first used in Britain two years earlier, is employed in military hospitals, though supplies are still imported from the US.

GI brides
In 1946 many of the 50,000 British women who got engaged to or married US servicemen they met during the war emigrated to the US.

Transatlantic trips
In 1946 BOAC begins twice-weekly flights to New York.

Nuclear power
Britain's first atomic reactor, at Harwell, starts up in 1947.

Movie mania
Britons make 30 million cinema visits a week.

New Towns
Basildon and Harlow are among the new settlements built to boost housing stocks.

Dance-hall fever
US-style "jitterbugging" is the latest dance craze.

1950–1959

Lifting the gloom
The 1951 Festival of Britain temporarily dispels the clouds of postwar austerity.

Coronation
Following the 1952 death of George VI, his eldest daughter is crowned Elizabeth II on 2 June 1953.

Atomic blast
Britain explodes its first atom bomb in October 1952. The Campaign for Nuclear Disarmament is born in 1958.

Suez crisis
In 1956 military action misfires in the Suez Canal zone; invading British and French troops withdraw.

Immigration
People from the West Indies, India and Pakistan arrive to make a new life in Britain.

De Havilland Comet
Britain launches the world's first passenger jet airliner in 1952.

Life's building blocks
In 1953 Briton Francis Crick and American James Watson discover the structure of the genetic material DNA.

ITV
In 1955 independent television is launched, with the first British TV adverts.

Calder Hall
The world's first large nuclear power station connected to the public electricity supply opens in 1956.

Rock 'n' roll
In 1957 Tommy Steele and skiffle star Lonnie Donegan provide Britain's answer to Elvis Presley and Bill Hailey.

Hi-fi
The first long-playing 33rpm records and "stereophonic" record players appear in Britain in 1958.

Riding on air
Suffolk boat-builder Christopher Cockerell unveils the hovercraft in 1958.

Motoring booms
The first British motorway, the M1, opens in November 1959, three months after the launch of the Mini motor car at £500.

1960–1969

National service
The call-up for military training ends in 1960.

Lady Chatterley trial
In 1960 D.H. Lawrence's novel *Lady Chatterley's Lover* is prosecuted under the Obscene Publications Act; an Old Bailey jury declares that it is not obscene and can go on open sale.

Profumo affair
War secretary John Profumo quits in 1963 after lying to MPs about his part in a high-society sex-and-spying scandal.

Great Train Robbery
Thieves seize more than £1 million in used notes in a 1963 raid.

Hangman hangs up noose
In 1964 MPs vote to abolish the death penalty for murder.

Wembley triumph
England hosts the 1966 World Cup – and wins, beating W. Germany 4-2 in the final.

Troops in
British troops are deployed in Ulster in 1969 to quell Catholic–Protestant fighting.

Fab Four
The Beatles erupt into the British consciousness in 1963.

Swinging Sixties
From late 1965, women's skirts get shorter while men's hair gets longer.

Jet-powered *Bluebird* crashes
Donald Campbell dies in 1967 attempting to break his own world water speed record.

Electric revolution
Britain's last steam-hauled passenger trains are withdrawn from service in 1967.

Flower power
The hippy movement hits Britain in 1967 with rock festivals, cannabis and LSD.

Speed of sound
The first supersonic passenger aircraft, Concorde, developed in a British–French partnership, takes to the air in 1969.

1970–1979

Shoppers get the decimal point
In 1971 Britain goes decimal, abandoning shillings and pence.

Bloody Sunday
30 January 1972: British troops open fire on civil rights marchers in Derry, killing 13.

Direct rule
In 1972 self-government in N. Ireland is suspended. The province will be ruled directly from Westminster.

Common Market
Britain joins the European Economic Community in 1973.

Three-day week
Britain's economic difficulties force the government to impose a three-day working week in 1974.

Silver Jubilee
1977 sees celebrations for the 25th anniversary of Queen Elizabeth's reign.

Winter of discontent
Strikes hit public services in winter 1978–9.

Iron Lady
Margaret Thatcher becomes Britain's first woman PM in 1979 and launches the "enterprise culture".

The Beatles split
Quarrels send the pop icons their separate ways in 1970.

Black gold
In 1970 British Petroleum discovers oil under the North Sea.

Number cruncher
Clive Sinclair's pocket calculator, using a silicon chip microprocessor, is launched in 1972.

Radio rivalry for BBC
New stations LBC and Capital Radio go on air in 1973.

Curtain up
The National Theatre in London opens in 1976.

Punk rock
The Sex Pistols lead a rock revolution in 1976.

Test tube baby
Louise Joy Brown, who grew from an implanted lab-fertilized egg, is born in July 1978.

1980–1989

Royal fairy tale
Prince Charles marries Lady Diana Spencer in July 1981.

Street fighting
In 1981 riots erupt in Toxteth (Liverpool) and Brixton (London).

Britain at war
The 1982 conflict in the Falkland Islands ends in British victory over Argentina.

Conference bomb
In 1984 an IRA bomb at the Tory conference fails to kill the PM, Margaret Thatcher.

Papal peace message
Pope John Paul II visits the Irish Republic and begs for peace.

Miners' strike
In 1984–5 British miners take on the Conservative government – and lose.

Anglo-Irish Agreement
The 1985 agreement between the UK and Ireland sparks fierce protests from Unionists.

Cross-Channel link
In 1986 Britain and France agree to dig a Channel Tunnel.

Triple winner
In 1987 Margaret Thatcher becomes the first PM of the 20th century to win three successive elections.

Personal computers
The microchip revolution brings PCs into British homes.

TV transformation
Britain gains a fourth TV channel in 1982; breakfast TV, satellite dishes and video recorders soon transform viewing habits.

Compact discs
The CD quickly displaces the vinyl record.

Feed the world
Bob Geldof leads rock stars in Band Aid (1984) and Live Aid (1985) to aid famine victims.

School tests
The government imposes a national curriculum and tests for children at 7, 11, 14 and 16.

Post-modernism
A new, sometimes playful style can be seen in architecture and literature.

1990–1999

Thatcher resigns
After 11 years in power, Mrs Thatcher is ousted by her fellow Conservatives in 1990.

Gulf War
In 1991 Britain, the US and others launch Operation Desert Storm after Iraq invades Kuwait.

Poll tax
The "community charge", replacing rates, proves widely unpopular and is abandoned.

Princess Diana
The death of Diana, Princess of Wales, in a Paris car crash in 1997 plunges the nation into mourning.

Labour landslide
Labour returns to power in 1997, ending 18 years of Conservative rule.

Good Friday Agreement
In 1998 Republicans and Unionists agree a deal to end 30 years' bloodshed in N. Ireland.

Lords reforms
In 1999 the Labour government removes the voting rights of hereditary peers in the House of Lords.

Devolution
Assemblies open in 1999 in Edinburgh and Cardiff.

Channel Tunnel
In 1994 the Channel Tunnel is opened, linking Britain and continental Europe.

Internet
The world wide web links British homes and businesses to "websites" across the globe.

Globe Theatre
A £30 million recreation of William Shakespeare's Globe Theatre opens in 1996 beside the Thames in London.

Clone sheep
In 1997 Dolly the sheep is the first mammal to be cloned from an adult rather than an embryo cell.

Millennium Dome
The £780 million Millennium Dome opens in Greenwich on 31 December 1999 as the centrepiece of Britain's millennium celebrations.

London, 9 January 1900. A nationwide influenza epidemic is taking 50 lives a day here alone (→ 17/2/05).

USA, 18 February 1900. The Briton Harry Vardon is the world golf champion.

South Africa, 28 Feb 1900. Ladysmith is relieved after 118 days of siege (→ 18/5).

Dublin, 4 April 1900. Strict security is in force as Queen Victoria begins a three-week visit to Ireland which will also take her to Cork and Galway (→ 19/1/01).

Brussels, 4 April 1900. The prince of Wales is shot at by a 15-year-old "anarchist".

Europe, 7 April 1900. Britain, France, Germany and the US warn China to suppress the Boxer rebellion or be invaded (→ 14/8).

South Africa, 28 May 1900. Britain annexes the Orange Free State (→ 25/10).

London, 22 June 1900. The Wallace collection of art is opened to the public.

England, 27 August 1900. The first weekly long-distance bus service in Britain begins; the journey between London and Leeds takes two days.

Britain, 31 August 1900. Coca-Cola goes on sale for the first time.

South Africa, 25 Oct 1900. Lord Roberts, the British commander-in-chief, claims that the Boer War is over as the Transvaal is formally annexed by Britain (→ 29).

Suffolk, September 1900. At Newmarket the prince of Wales's horse Diamond Jubilee adds the St Leger to victories in the 2,000 Guineas and Derby this year.

London, 24 October 1900. Members of the National Union of Women Workers hold a meeting about drunkenness and illness.

London, 29 October 1900. Huge crowds greet returning Boer War troops (→ 14/6/01).

Cumbria, 9 November 1900. The world's biggest battleship, the 15,150-ton Japanese *Mikasa*, is launched at Barrow-in-Furness.

Lancashire, 1 December 1900. Four people die and 2,000 are ill from drinking beer treated with arsenic.

Isle of Wight, 19 Jan 1901. Queen Victoria is gravely ill (→ 22/1).

Mafeking siege relieved in Boer War

The battle for Mafeking was long and hard; the joy of victory was intense.

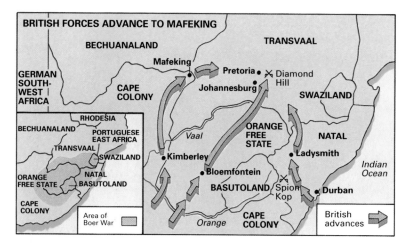

London, 18 May 1900

Mafeking has been relieved. The news that the seven-month-long siege was lifted two days ago was broken tonight by a Reuters news agency dispatch, and the whole of London is celebrating. Rarely has there been such a spontaneous outburst of joy. Even the government's reluctance to confirm the news has not disheartened crowds thronging the capital, singing patriotic songs. Special editions of the newspapers have been printed, and the prince of Wales led the festivities at Covent Garden opera house when the news was shouted from the gallery.

Viewed dispassionately the fervour is hard to understand, for the loss of Mafeking, an insignificant stop on the railway line to Rhodesia, would have had little effect on the outcome of the war. The siege has, in fact, cost the British 160 casualties and the Boers twice that number, a small bill to pay in the context of a war which has proved altogether more bloody than Britain had anticipated.

Yet, under the charismatic Colonel Baden-Powell, the defence of Mafeking has come to represent, in the words of *The Times*, "the fundamental grit of the breed". But the war is far from over; the Boers are turning to guerrilla tactics in their bid to resist the imperial ambitions of Britain in South Africa (→ 28).

A 'Labour Party' is created by unions

London, 27 February 1900

Trade union leaders meeting in London today resolved to abandon the old rather loose alliance with the Liberal Party and to sponsor their own candidates for the House of Commons. They set up a special action group, to be known as the Labour Representation Committee with James Ramsay MacDonald of the Independent Labour Party (ILP) as its secretary.

The move was opposed at first by the miners' union, whose strength has enabled it to force its candidates on the Liberals. But most union leaders had found the party unwilling to adopt working men as candidates. With the ILP making little headway outside the north of England, union leaders have looked enviously at the German socialists, who won 50 seats in the 1898 Reichstag elections.

Delegates representing over half a million trade unionists attended today's meeting in London, along with societies such as the Marxist-orientated Social Democratic Federation. However, socialist dogma took second place to practical politics. Moves to confine policy to "class war" issues and candidates to the working classes were rejected; a levy on union members to fund Labour candidates was accepted. James Keir Hardie, the ILP leader, said that the aim was to develop "a distinct Labour group in parliament" with freedom to shape its own policy. It poses a great challenge to existing parties (→ 3/9/02).

The friendship of actress Lillie Langtry with the heir to the throne shocked Britain. Now she is the talk of Washington as a dissolute heiress in a new drama.

An era ends as Queen Victoria dies

Tories win power in the 'khaki election'

London, 17 October 1900
Lord Salisbury's Tories have been returned to power with an overwhelming House of Commons majority in what is being called the "khaki" election. With only one result still to come, the Tories and their Unionist allies have 402 MPs; the Liberals, Irish Nationalists and other opposition parties have 268.

The Liberals have been deeply divided by the Irish home rule issue, with MPs breaking away to join the Tories as Liberal Unionists. Tory popularity plummeted when the war in South Africa opened badly, but after the tide turned the government seized the opportunity to call a snap election attacking the Liberals as "unpatriotic" (26/2/02).

Wilde dies in exile and still in disgrace

Paris, 30 November 1900
The writer Oscar Wilde has died in Paris aged 44. Once the toast of London and renowned for his wit and humour as a dramatist, he was convicted of homosexual offences in 1895 and sentenced to two years' imprisonment with hard labour. He drew upon his experiences in *The Ballad of Reading Gaol* which was published anonymously. Since his release in 1897 he had lived in Paris under the name of Sebastian Melmoth. The cause of his death is thought to have been cerebral meningitis. None of his plays has been performed since his disgrace.

Oscar Wilde: a genius disgraced.

The British Empire mourns a great monarch; Victoria's reign began when royalty's popularity was at a low ebb.

Isle of Wight, 22 January 1901
Queen Victoria died peacefully today at Osborne House, her seaside home near Cowes. She was 81. Most of her large family were gathered at the bedside, among them the new monarch, King Edward VII. They each kissed her hand in farewell as the end approached, and the closing words of the blessing were pronounced by the bishop of Winchester: "The Lord lift up his countenance upon thee and give thee peace."

An extraordinary era in British history had ended. Victoria became queen at 18 and ruled for over 63 years, nearly 40 of them as a lonely widow following the death of her beloved husband, Prince Albert from the duchy of Saxe-Coburg-Gotha. He died of typhoid in 1861. The couple had nine children.

Victoria's reign started with the monarchy held in very low esteem; it ended, owing in large measure to her formidable character, with it as a revered institution. She presided over a burgeoning empire which she saw develop into the greatest in history; she lived through an industrial revolution at home that enabled Britain to become the world's pre-eminent producer of manufactured goods; and she oversaw reforms that made the country a model of constitutional government.

Her ministers at the heart of these great changes were never lacking in trenchant advice from their sovereign, who had a shrewd insight into government at home and abroad. In the last quarter of her reign Britain's strength was beginning to be challenged abroad, and at home there was much poverty. But it was then that her popularity reached its peak (→ 23).

British forces lead Chinese rescue mission

Peking, 14 August 1900
British troops were in the forefront of an international force which today ended a 56-day siege of Europeans here in the Chinese capital. The allied column of 10,000 men had met fierce and determined resistance, but the so-called "Boxer rebellion" appears to be over; both the emperor and the empress dowager are reported to have fled the city. The Boxers are members of what started as a patriotic society devoted to martial arts. This grew into a popular movement against foreign influence generally; a German minister in Peking was murdered, and other foreign diplomats were besieged in their embassies. Diplomats and their families in the British embassy had less than a week's supply of food when their rescuers arrived. More than 1,500 foreigners elsewhere were killed.

Irish Nationalists in bid to heal the rifts

Ireland, 1900
The Irish Nationalist Party, which has been split since the scandal linking its former leader, Charles Parnell, to Mrs Katharine O'Shea, has been reunited into one party with John Redmond as chairman. New life has been injected by William O'Brien, the founder of the United Irish League (→ 5/3/01).

London, 27 January. Edward gives Kaiser William of Germany, his nephew, the rank of field marshal in the British Army (→ 8/11/02).

Windsor, Berkshire, 4 Feb. Victoria is buried beside Albert, her beloved consort.→

Westminster, 5 March. Police eject Irish Nationalists from the House of Commons (→ 6/10).

London, 25 March. The first diesel motor goes on public display.

England, 27 April. Tottenham Hotspur, a non-league club, win the FA cup, beating Sheffield United 3-1 after a replay at Bolton; the first match, played at the Crystal Palace, ended in a 2-2 draw.

Britain, April. A game called "ping-pong", or table tennis, is growing rapidly in popularity.

London, 1 May. The miners' conference recommends a strike unless there is a cut in the coal export tax (→ 4/9).

South Africa, 9 May. Lord Kitchener introduces new tactics enabling the fast call-up of reinforcements by telegraph (→ 16/6).

Cowes, Isle of Wight, 22 May. The king has a narrow escape when the America's Cup yacht *Shamrock II* is damaged in a squall (→ 4/10).

Atlantic Ocean, 16 June. The liner *Lucania* is used for trials of wireless telegraphy at sea (→ 11/12).

Westminster, 17 June. The Liberal MP David Lloyd George attacks the government over the alarming death rate in South African "concentration camps" (→ 15/11).

Humberside, 18 September. Fifty-nine people die as the torpedo boat *Cobra* is wrecked off Grimsby.

New York, 4 October. The US yacht *Columbia* beats Britain's *Shamrock II* in the America's Cup.

South Africa, 15 November. Reports speak of goats' dung tea being served up in the "concentration camps" (→ 19/12).

Birmingham, 19 December. Lloyd George is forced to flee from a pro-Boer meeting as riots break out (→ 13/2/02).

Edward inherits a crown and empire

Windsor, Berkshire, 4 February

The queen who gave her name to an era was buried today as she had wished – "next to my dearly loved husband in the mausoleum". The mourners were led by her eldest son and successor, King Edward VII. He has inherited not only the crown but also the greatest empire that the world has ever seen.

Nearly one person in four lives under British rule in one form or another in an empire that now covers one-fifth of the world's surface. Edward is emperor of India as well as king of Great Britain, the symbol of a mother country to diverse peoples in every continent. Many of these peoples were represented at today's funeral. So, too, were the many royal families of Europe to which Britain's new king is related; among those attending is Edward's nephew, Kaiser William of Germany.

If today was an occasion to pay homage to the past, there are already signs that the new king intends to put his own distinctive stamp on the monarchy. For a start he chose the name of Edward VII, rather than Albert I as his mother had wanted. Later this month he plans to open the new session of parliament himself; the late queen had not done this since 1886. The new king intends to restore much of the pageantry which was abandoned during Queen Victoria's long years of mourning for Prince Albert. Edward also hopes to use his contacts in Europe to help the government to improve relations with Britain's continental neighbours. Already 59, the king will waste no time in making the most of his inheritance (→ 24/6/02).

A portrait of Queen Victoria on her deathbed in Osborne House.

King Edward VII leads the mourners at Queen Victoria's state funeral.

Curzon creates a new frontier for India

Calcutta, India, 12 February

The Indian empire is to be extended by the creation of a new frontier province in the north of the Punjab, bordering Afghanistan. The viceroy, Lord Curzon, said today in a communiqué that there had been so much fighting in the tribal areas of Peshawar, Khyber and Waziristan that they needed to come under the control of the central government. The proposed frontier will cover a tenth of the area of the Punjab and a twentieth of the people in a mountainous region where the warring tribes have been a constant source of difficulty for the imperial authorities. The northern frontier has always assumed great importance for the British because of the perceived need to keep the Russians from invading across Afghanistan into the jewel in Britain's imperial crown (→ 20/8/05).

Census reveals a population boom

London, 9 May

The population of Britain has reached a new peak of 41.5 million, according to this year's census. The total has now overtaken that of France. Ireland's total has fallen by 300,000 to 4.4 million, but elsewhere in the United Kingdom emigration and a lower birth rate were offset by a fall in the death rate.

Anger over British-run Boer prison camps

London, 14 June
The British policy of herding Boers into "concentration camps" came under fierce attack today by Sir Henry Campbell-Bannerman, the Liberal leader, who denounced "methods of barbarism in South Africa". His speech intensifies the pressure on the government, and parliament has been told that Sir Alfred Milner, the high commissioner for South Africa, is attending personally to improving conditions.

There is justice in the criticism, but the irony of the affair is that the camps were originally set up for humanitarian reasons – to feed and protect refugees whose farms had been destroyed in the war. Four months ago, however, General Kitchener decided to intern all families whose men were still fighting for the Boers in order to "limit the endurance of the guerrillas".

Since then the army has swept some 75,000 people, mostly women and children, into the camps, which cannot cope with such large numbers. The camp sites have been badly chosen, with little regard for hygiene or the need to supply food. The result is hunger and pestilence, with inmates dying of typhoid and measles. This is through inefficiency, but the charge of cruelty is ringing round the world (→ 17).

British brutality to Boer women – as seen by a German newspaper artist.

Unions hit by ruling on strike damages

Westminster, 4 September
Trade union leaders were outraged by today's decision in the House of Lords that employers can sue unions for damages arising from strike action. As a result the Amalgamated Society of Railway Servants will have to pay £32,000 in costs and damages to the Taff Vale Railway Company.

Today's decision confirms the ruling of Mr Justice Farwell in the high court, which was later overturned in the court of appeal. The Trades Union Congress promised that it would fight today's ruling, which provides a golden campaigning issue for the newly formed Labour Representation Committee, which aims to win Labour seats in the House of Commons (→ 8/9/05).

Temperance linked to Irish freedom

Dublin, 6 October
Father James Cullen, famous for his missionary zeal in promoting the virtues of temperance, has held the first annual general meeting of the Pioneer Association in Dublin, attended by 900 people.

Father Cullen is a staunch nationalist and believes that he has detected a deliberate attempt on the part of the English to keep Ireland submissive through drink. He is confident that the growth of national self-esteem will go hand in hand with the temperance movement and has adopted the motto "Ireland sober, Ireland free". He sees priests and children as being of major importance, with children raised on abstinence leading to the triumph of the movement (→ 10/1/02).

Above and below the waves, scientists transform the world of communications

On the sea: the newest craft for the fleet, the Holland nine-man submarine.

Cornwall, 11 December
At six o'clock this evening the three dots for the letter "S" in morse code were tapped on a machine here in Cornwall. The signals were heard, faintly but clearly, over 2,000 miles away in Newfoundland, opening a new era in global communications.

The transmission across the Atlantic Ocean was a triumph for Guglielmo Marconi, the Italian pioneer of wireless. In transport, too, there have been scientific breakthroughs this year, yet none was as dramatic as today's wireless transmission.

Marconi had begun his experiments in Italy, but lack of interest at home brought him to Britain where organizations as diverse as the Post Office and the Royal Navy soon took a keen interest in his work. Today, from an aerial 49 metres (164 feet) above the Lizard peninsula in southern Cornwall to an aerial on a kite above St John's, Newfoundland, they demonstrated that sound could be transmitted through the air.

The first British submarine, the *Holland I*, is a more local triumph, since the Americans have already tested vessels which go beneath the waves. Its nine-man crew breathe compressed air while it stays submerged for up to four hours. Another nautical first was the world's first steam-turbine powered passenger ship, the *King Edward*, launched at Dumbarton this year, while on land the king inaugurated London's first electric tramcar service.

Science has also been boosted by prizes to be awarded annually for achievements in various disciplines, funded from money left by the Swedish manufacturer Alfred Nobel. The first were presented in Oslo yesterday (→ 29/3/03).

Marconi, the pioneer of wireless telegraphy across the Atlantic Ocean.

Westminster, 10 January. Irish MPs protest about interference at meetings and suppression of free speech (→ 10/7).

London, 14 January. Universal state pensions are supported by over 300 trade unions (→ 29/11/4).

London, 28 January. The population is 6,581,372, according to last year's census.

Australia, 4 February. England score 769 runs in a single test innings.

Westminster, 13 February. A German Boer relief committee wishing to visit "concentration camps" in South Africa is refused permission by the government (→ 1/6).

Westminster, 18 February. A petition demanding votes for women is presented to parliament by over 37,000 women textile workers (→ 22/4).

Dublin, 2 April. The first performance of W B Yeats's *Cathleen ni Houlihan* takes place.

Glasgow, 22 April. Magistrates require barmaids to be replaced by men (→ 12/5).

London, 29 May. The London School of Political and Economic Science opens.

London, 24 June. King Edward VII is operated on successfully for the appendicitis which has delayed his coronation (→ 9/8).

Westminster, 3 July. A ruling by the Lords restricts betting to the sites of sporting events.

Westminster, 10 July. Charges of jury packing are renewed by Irish Nationalists (→ 14/9).

Westminster, 9 August. Edward VII is crowned.→

Isle of Wight, 11 August. The king gives Osborne House, where Queen Victoria died, to the nation (→ 1/1/03).

London, 18 August. The shah of Persia begins a state visit.

Westminster, 10 September. A royal commission is to investigate British preparedness for the Boer War (→ 23/4/03).

Dublin, 14 September. An estimated 20,000 people demonstrate against strict law and order measures imposed by the government under a state of emergency (→ 14/8/03).

London, 8 November. In the hope of improving Anglo-German relations Kaiser William begins a 12-day visit (→ 8/4/04).

British Boer War victory

London, 1 June
The news that Britain has been waiting for with such expectancy broke tonight when a banner strung between the pillars of London's Mansion House announced "Peace Is Proclaimed". Nearly two years and eight months after the first shots were fired the Boer War is over.

The treaty was signed at Pretoria just before the midnight deadline yesterday after the Boer delegation reluctantly recognized that it could not continue the fight. After nine days of negotiation the Boers spent another two days arguing over whether to accept the British terms. Yesterday morning it seemed impossible that they could agree, but the respected General Christian de Wet suddenly changed his mind and voted for peace.

Jan Smuts and Judge Hertzog then drew up a statement agreeing to the terms, and the Boer leaders voted 54 to six to end the war. Lord

Peace comes – with a bitter taste.

Kitchener, who did so much to bring about the Boers' defeat, went among them, shaking their hands and saying: "We are all friends now." There is, however, bitterness among the Boers (→ 10/9).

Rosebery's return divides the Liberals

London, 26 February
Lord Rosebery, the former Liberal prime minister, re-entered the political arena today after an absence of five years to announce his break with the Liberal Party leadership and to trigger a battle between the party's imperialist and radical wings. He plans to head a new organization, to be called the Liberal League, to revitalize Liberal principles after years of internal squabbling over Irish home rule and foreign policy.

Rosebery is a supporter of the war in South Africa. He has the backing of Herbert Asquith and Sir Edward Grey but is opposed by more radical Liberals, such as David Lloyd George, who back the present party leader, Sir Henry Campbell-Bannerman (→ 12/7).

Twenty die at international soccer match

Glasgow, 5 April
Twenty people died and at least 200 were injured today when terracing collapsed at the Ibrox Park stadium during a match between Scotland and England. More than 70,000 spectators were at the game when part of the wooden north-western terrace gave way. Some people plunged 15 metres (50 feet) to their deaths, but others died by being crushed as panicking fans sought safety on the pitch; their screams were lost in the cheers. The scale of the disaster was not at first apparent: play continued while mounted police rode into the area thinking that a disturbance had broken out.

Ibrox disaster: 20 fans are dead.

Schools to be taken over by councils

Westminster, 23 March
Major reforms of schools in England and Wales were outlined in an education bill today. County councils and the larger urban authorities are to take over responsibility for all secondary, elementary and technical schools in their areas, sweeping away the powers of several thousand school boards and the managers of voluntary schools.

For the first time public money will be made available for the education of children in all schools in an area. However, this reform, championed by the government as a means to improve educational standards, has encountered strong criticism from the nonconformist churches. They resent the use of taxes and rates to finance Anglican and Catholic schools, particularly when these schools will retain considerable autonomy from local authority control (→ 7/4/03).

Colonies resist calls for imperial unity

London, July
The fourth colonial conference has met in London to discuss greater unity, only to find that the self-governing colonies – Australia, Canada, Cape Colony, Natal, New Zealand and Newfoundland – are increasingly asserting their own independence. The conference passed resolutions in favour of imperial preference to boost trade within the empire but made little progress in developing closer links over defence. This disappointed Britain's colonial secretary, Joseph Chamberlain, who wants a council of the empire to be created (→ 8/3/06).

Major wins award

Stockholm, 10 December
A British Army major is one of the prize-winners in the second of the awards established under the will of a Swedish chemist, Alfred Nobel, for achievements in science. Major Ronald Ross is this year's laureate for medicine because of his work relating the causes of malaria to the bites of mosquitoes.

Balfour follows his uncle to be premier

London, 12 July
Arthur James Balfour, a Tory MP for almost 30 years, today succeeded his uncle, Lord Salisbury, as prime minister. He was leader of the outgoing government in the Commons as first lord of the treasury where he has been piloting the Education Bill through parliament. Another government change is the appointment of C T Ritchie, formerly the home secretary, as chancellor to replace Sir Michael Hicks-Beach, who goes to the Lords. The populist Joseph Chamberlain stays as colonial secretary (→ 22/8/03).

Balfour: 30 years an MP.

Crucial alliance for Britain and Japan

London, 30 January
Britain and Japan today concluded a treaty of great mutual benefit which also ends an era of what has been called "splendid isolation" in British foreign policy. It aims to protect their parallel interests in China and Korea. Both countries guarantee not to make treaties with other nations without consultation. Each needs an ally in the area: following the Boxer rebellion, Britain considers its interests in China endangered by other European countries, notably Germany, while Japan is alarmed by Russian advances in Manchuria.

Edward VII crowned after postponement

A coronation feast for the poor.

Regal robes for a king: Edward VII.

London, 9 August
Edward VII was crowned today in Westminster Abbey. In his 61st year he has finally assumed the mantle of monarchy to which he was born, after spending a mainly hedonistic life waiting in the wings.

It was the first coronation in Britain in most people's lifetimes – 64 years – and the thousands lining a route bedecked with flags to the abbey were eager to cheer their new sovereign and his wife, Queen Alexandra, particularly as the king was still recuperating from an operation for near-fatal appendicitis which had delayed the ceremony by two months. In deference to the king's health the service was shortened, and Edward was spared the burden of carrying the heavy sword of state to the high altar. The king appeared, however, to be full of vigour.

The only hitch occurred when the king himself had to raise the frail archbishop of Canterbury, Frederick Temple, from his knees after he had sworn allegiance to his new sovereign on behalf of the church. Absent from the abbey were a number of the foreign heads of state who had returned home after coming to London in June when the coronation was originally to have been held (→ 11).

Barmaids win sex battle in Glasgow

Glasgow, 12 May
An appeal court ruled today that women can, if they so choose, be exposed to bad language, lewd suggestions and crude jests. These, it was said, were the hazards of working as a barmaid in a Glasgow pub. Last month magistrates here were sufficiently concerned by the threat to morality and public order that in effect they barred women from working in bars. Pubs employing women would not have their licences renewed. But today the appeal court reversed the decision, following protests by publicans, barmaids and public (→ 10/10/03).

Venezuela bombed by British gunboats

Caracas, 31 December
The British and German fleets have seized the Venezuelan navy and shelled a fort in Caracas this month to enforce demands for payment for property seized without compensation during the 1899 revolution. Venezuela, which denies all liability, has agreed to submit the dispute to the Hague tribunal. The two powers will continue to blockade Venezuela until their claims are met. The United States, invoking the Monroe Doctrine, has put pressure on them to end the blockade and refer the matter to the international court at the Hague.

Unions back call to elect Labour MPs

London, 3 September
The Trades Union Congress voted in London today to back independent Labour candidates to win power at Westminster rather than to rely on local alliances with Liberals. The TUC plans to set up a central organization which will boost the Labour Representation Committee which it set up two years ago. Where possible, Labour candidates will fight constituencies independently.

One Liberal was given a hearing by the TUC, however. David Lloyd George, the Liberal MP for Carmarthen, urged support for quarrymen at Penrhyn who have been fighting for union recognition in a dispute lasting two years.

Automobiles tested

Folkestone, Kent, 1 September
Horse-drawn transport still rules the road, but not for long if the Automobile Club has its way. Today the club organized trials of motor cars designed to show the reliability of the internal combustion engine. The tests involved 63 cars, which were required to travel from the Crystal Palace in south London to Folkestone and back again. Most completed the 139-mile route without mishap, with club officials logging the performance of each car (→ 14/7/03).

A tiny book for children, "The Tale of Peter Rabbit", by Beatrix Potter – who also illustrates the text – is a popular bestseller.

Delhi, 1 January. King Edward VII is proclaimed emperor of India (1/5).

East Africa, 4 January. British troops under General Manning land at Obbia to attack the forces of the "Mad Mullah", Mohammed bin Abdullah.

London, 27 January. Fifty-one people die in a fire at the Colney Hatch mental hospital.

London, 10 February. Two new streets are named Kingsway (after the king) and Aldwych.

Atlantic Ocean, 22 February. The first ship's newspaper is published on the liner *Etruria*.

Westminster, 26 February. A Commons debate calls for immigration restrictions.

Fife, 6 March. As the German navy grows, a huge new Royal Navy base is to be built in the Firth of Forth at Rosyth.

Dublin, 27 March. By the Bank Holiday (Ireland) Act, St Patrick's day (17 March) is to be a public holiday.

London/New York, 29 March. A regular news service using the Marconi wireless system begins (→ 28/12/04).

Westminster, 23 April. The government admits that the Boer and Boxer Wars cost a third of the national budget (→ 12/1903).

Paris, 1 May. Edward VII starts a goodwill visit (→ 1/8).

Belfast, 11 June. An independent Orange Order, more militantly Protestant than the main Orange organization, is formed.

Cork, 11 July. The Royal Cork Yacht Club stages the world's first power-boat race.

Westminster, 14 July. The government is to reject calls for penalties for drunken drivers, driving tests and vehicle inspection (→ 4/5/04).

Ireland, 1 August. At the end of a tour, the king expresses his hope that "a brighter day is dawning upon Ireland" (27/2/07).

Southern England, 10 Sept. A great storm causes widespread damage and deaths (→ 3/2/04).

London, 6 October. The duke of Devonshire resigns from the government.

London, 15 December. The Australian chamber of commerce here approves a UK preference in international trade.

Chamberlain quits over empire trade row

Westminster, 17 September
The House of Commons was rife today with speculation about the resignations of four of the most powerful members of the cabinet, including the colonial secretary, Joseph Chamberlain. For some months the cabinet and the party have been split over the issue of free trade versus imperial preference.

Chamberlain, the most passionate advocate of empire unity, has been arguing for preferential tariffs to foster empire trade. The duke of Devonshire, C T Ritchie, Lord Balfour of Burleigh and Lord George Hamilton have been pressing equally fervently for maintaining total commitment to free trade.

Whitehall insiders were saying today that the steely hand of the prime minister, Arthur Balfour, was behind the so-called resignations. According to them Chamberlain offered to resign over a week ago. Three days ago Balfour sacked Ritchie and Balfour without telling them about Chamberlain's offer. Both the duke of Devonshire and Lord George Hamilton resigned in protest. Balfour then accepted Chamberlain's resignation but managed to persuade the duke to stay before today's announcement of the four "resignations". Balfour is de-

Joseph Chamberlain, the apostle of empire trade, juggles with bread.

termined to find a compromise to heal the party split, but it seems unlikely that he will be able to retain Devonshire for long.

For Chamberlain it is a bitter disappointment. Ever since the fourth colonial conference last summer he has been convinced that imperial preference is the only tangible policy upon which the new self-governing colonies can all agree. But he has failed to persuade his own prime minister and colleagues to give up free trade (→ 6/10).

Army criticized in Boer post-mortem

Whitehall, London, December
Wide-ranging reforms in the army and navy are likely to follow the reorganization this year of the committee of imperial defence. The committee had existed before the South African war, but it had been little more than a group of ministers: now it is to bring together the professional chiefs of the services with the most senior ministers under the chairmanship of the prime minister. There will also be a permanent secretariat, including army and navy officers.

The revamped committee is now considering the report of the royal commission into the Boer War. This has highlighted weaknesses in the army's organization and chain of command. The army never had a proper plan of campaign, regarding the war as a minor colonial skirmish, not a major affair against a well-organized enemy equipped with artillery, fighting in a style well suited to the terrain. The army's training and intelligene gathering were also criticized. One option is to abolish the post of commander-in-chief and create an army council similar to the admiralty board (→ 7/12/09).

Official inquiry is launched into London's traffic problem

A traffic jam at the Bank of England: can "twopenny tubes" be the answer?

London, 6 February
A new network of roads extending from the centre of London to the suburbs is among schemes to be considered by a royal commission set up today to examine the capital's rail and tramway systems. Street congestion has increased dramatically in recent years.

Proposals for electric-powered trams in the City and west end, such as those already working in cities such as Bristol and Manchester, would add to the pressure on the capital's roads. However, these would be quicker and cleaner than the horse-drawn vehicles which form the biggest part of the traffic on London roads. The commission will also look at plans for new underground railways, following the success of the "twopenny tube" Central Line which opened from Shepherd's Bush to the Bank three years ago (→ 12/3/04).

Irish tenants can now own freeholds

Women suffragists prepare for action

Ireland, 14 August
Irish tenant-farmers will be helped to purchase the freeholds of their lands under a land act which has now been approved by parliament in Westminster. George Wyndham, the Irish secretary, backed reform to try to remove some of the economic grievances which have fed past nationalist agitation. The new act will use public funds to help bridge the gap between what tenants can pay and what landlords are willing to accept.

These developments reflect increased prosperity. Cooperative creameries are being encouraged, agricultural wages are rising, and industry is benefiting from exports of linen-weaving and spinning, brewing and distilling (→ 2/1/04).

Rural economy: Irish tenant-farmers at the Carndonagh sheep fair.

Manchester, 10 October
A more militant campaign for women's suffrage was signalled tonight with the formation here of a new group under the leadership of Mrs Emmeline Pankhurst, the widow of a leading Manchester member of the Independent Labour Party. "Deeds, not words" is to be the motto of the Women's Social and Political Union. Until now women have sought to win the vote by trying to persuade sympathetic MPs to back electoral reform, but this has made no progress. Mrs Pankhurst favours a more active campaign. The new society, which met in her house, is to be confined to women and independent of all party affiliations (→ 12/5/05).

Company plans to build first 'garden city'

Hertfordshire, December
A company has been formed this year to turn the dream of "garden cities" into reality. Just under 1,600 hectares (4,000 acres) of land have been acquired by the company in Letchworth, north of London, and it is here that building will begin next year. The vision of creating a new environment, blending town and country, was first put forward by Ebenezer Howard in 1898. Re-published last year as *Garden Cities for Tomorrow*, his work has been widely translated and inspired architects all over the country. The idea is to create new communities where industry and shopping zones will be separated from housing by open spaces. A belt of countryside will stop the city sprawling endlessly. Leafy streets, houses with gardens and open spaces will all contribute to the "garden" image.

Liberals in secret pact with Labour group

London, December
A secret electoral pact has been agreed by the Liberal chief whip in the Commons, Herbert Gladstone, and the secretary of the fledgeling Labour Representation Committee, James Ramsay MacDonald. They expect the Tories, deeply split by the tariff reform issue, to fall, and in the ensuing general election the Liberals will give Labour candidates a clear run in certain constituencies. Several branches of the socialist Independent Labour Party will be angered if told not to oppose Liberal candidates, but the pact offers the trade unions the prospect of quick results for their decision in 1900 to set up the Labour Representation Committee. Gladstone's enthusiasm for the pact stems from his concern at the growing strength of what is seen as an embryonic Labour Party (→ 5/12/05).

British explorers get closer to South Pole

Antarctica, March
Three British explorers, Lieutenant Ernest Shackleton, Captain Robert Scott and Dr Edward Wilson, have crossed the 80th parallel and have thereby travelled further towards the South Pole than any previous expedition. The epic journey began two years ago when the National Antarctic Expedition, led by Captain Scott, left McMurdo Bay in Victoria Land and headed south.

Since then the expedition's members have battled the elements and overcome a number of setbacks – notably the death of their dog-teams, after which they had to pull the sledges themselves – to achieve their goal. On the way they have discovered several new mountain ranges and gathered much valuable scientific information (→ 9/1/09).

One of Scott's team is rescued.

Four times prime minister Salisbury dies

London, 22 August
Robert Arthur Talbot Gascoyne Cecil, the third marquis of Salisbury, four times Tory prime minister, died today aged 73. He is best known for his determination to preserve the union with Ireland, and for his mastery of foreign affairs amid growing imperial rivalries.

Lord Salisbury had suffered from a heart condition for some years; it was the deciding factor in his resignation from the premiership last year. His nephew and successor as prime minister, Arthur Balfour, was at his bedside when he passed away on the 50th anniversary of his first election to parliament. King Edward VII and other members of the royal family have expressed "profound sorrow" at Salisbury's death (→ 17/9).

Lord Salisbury: four-time premier.

Dublin, 2 January. Arthur Griffith proposes that Ireland should separate from England but keep the same king (→ 3/2).

Somalia, 11 January. British troops kill 1,000 rebels under the command of the Islamic leader known as "the Mad Mullah".

Westminster, 3 February. The Irish Nationalist John Redmond renews the call for home rule (→ 12/1905).

Southern England, 3 February. A tidal wave devastates the Channel coast (→ 15/3/05).

Merseyside, 12 March. The first electric main-line train in the British Isles runs from Liverpool to Southport (→ 9/4).

Plymouth, Devon, 9 April. A train runs non-stop from here to London in less than four and a half hours – a record (→ 22/1/06).

Westminster, 22 April. The Commons approve a bill allowing "peaceful picketing".

London, 26 April. Tobacconists protest at a threepenny increase on the tobacco tax.

Co Cork, 4 July. The first summer school for training teachers of Irish opens at Ballingeary.

London, 5 July. Edward Elgar is knighted following the March festival of his music at Covent Garden (→ 12/1908).

London, 12 July. A five-year treaty between Britain and Germany, to resolve disputes through arbitration, is signed (24/7/05).

Liverpool, 17 July. A foundation stone is laid for a new Anglican cathedral.

British Isles, 17 August. Postcards increased in popularity by 25 per cent last year, according to a report by the postmaster-general.

Lhasa, 7 September. An Anglo-Tibetan treaty gives Britain trading posts in Tibet and a promise that the Dalai Lama will not cede territory to a foreign power such as Russia.

London, 1 November. George Bernard Shaw's play *John Bull's Other Island* has its première (→ 1/1/05).

London, 27 December. James Barrie's *Peter Pan* has its first performance.

London, 28 December. The first weather forecasts by radio telegraphy are published.

'Entente Cordiale' signed with France

London, 8 April

Britain has abandoned its "splendid isolation" in Europe to form an *Entente Cordiale* with France. This does not mean that Britain is allied with France against Germany, but the Germans will see it as a step in that direction.

France and Britain have signed agreements settling all their disputes. The most important concerns Morocco: Britain recognizes French primacy there. If the sultan's government collapses, France will take over. This means that Britain prefers France to Germany, which also covets Morocco. In exchange, France has at last accepted Britain's occupation of Egypt.

Another agreement settles a dispute over fishing rights off Newfoundland that goes back two centuries. France renounces some of its rights in exchange for minor colonial concessions in West Africa. A third agreement covers cooperation in the New Hebrides.

Britain's isolation was demonstrated during the Boer War, when it discovered just how unpopular it was everywhere. Relations with France had been strained since the Fashoda incident in 1898 when the countries had clashed over territorial rights in the Nile valley. But

Hand in hand: London celebrates.

Germany's naval armaments programme is a greater menace, and the government was ready to listen when the French foreign minister, Théophile Delcasse, proposed a general settlement.

The improvement in relations was helped by both King Edward VII's visit to Paris last year and President Loubet's return visit. Edward charmed the French. He speaks the language well and signed himself "Edouard". The *entente* permits the Royal Navy to concentrate on the North Sea, leaving the Mediterranean to France (→ 12/7).

Dalai Lama flees as British seize Lhasa and war continues

Lhasa, Tibet, 3 August

Tibet's religious ruler, the Dalai Lama, has fled from Lhasa at the approach of the British mission led by Colonel Francis Younghusband. Lord Curzon, the viceroy in India, dispatched the mission in a bid to counter growing Russian influence over the rulers of Tibet on India's northern frontiers.

No real opposition has been offered to the British forces since a sharp engagement in the Karo Pass in May when 3,000 armed Tibetans positioned behind a wall connecting two stone forts poured a hail of fire on the advancing British, Sikh and Gurkha soldiers. The day was saved by the Gurkhas, who climbed a precipice to fire down on the Tibetans while the Sikhs outflanked the forts. The Tibetans fled, losing 400 dead, while the mission continued its arduous trek to the rooftop of the world. Colonel Younghusband is now camped outside the "forbidden city" of Lhasa. He has assured Tibetan officials that the mission will leave as soon as a treaty is signed between Britain and Tibet (→ 7/9).

Record-breaking Rolls signs agreement to make cars with Royce

Manchester, 4 May

One of the pioneers of motoring has signed an agreement with a leading Manchester engineer who has just produced his first automobile. The Hon Charles Rolls, who set a world land-speed record of 93mph last year at Phoenix Park, in Dublin, today agreed to sell cars produced by Henry Royce under their joint names – "Rolls-Royce".

Rolls was the overall winner of the Thousand-Mile Trial of 1900 which first popularized motoring in the British Isles. He runs a London company which sells and repairs cars. Royce is a self-made engineer who set up his electrical engineering company in Manchester. Last year Royce turned his attention to cars with his first model, a ten-horse-power vehicle being praised for its "excellent running". The two men's companies will not, as yet, merge completely (→ 29/6/05).

Mr Rolls (left) and Mr Royce: quality motor cars for people of quality.

Poverty is getting worse, says survey

Dinner time in a London workhouse.

Westminster, 29 November
Clear evidence of the extent of poverty was provided by new poor relief figures published today. Over 520,000 people in England and Wales are now on poor relief – more than at any time since 1888. A further 250,000 are in workhouses, 11 per cent up on last year. Low wages put a third of the total population near or below the poverty line. Half the population of Scotland and one-sixth of that of London live with more than two people per room. One result is poor health: two in five men who applied to enlist during the Boer War were rejected as medically unfit. The proportion was even higher from industrial areas (→14/3/06).

Hull trawlers are sunk by Russian ships

Hull, Humberside, 22 October
The Russian Baltic fleet, on the first stage of a voyage half-way round the world to give battle to the Japanese, opened fire on Britain's North Sea fishing fleet last night, sending its big shells crashing into the frail trawlers peacefully fishing the Dogger Bank. One of them was sunk, two of the Hull skippers were killed, and several fishermen were wounded.

It appears that the Russian commander, Admiral Rozhdestvensky, believed that the Japanese would attempt to repeat their devastating torpedo-boat attack on Russian warships at Port Arthur by sending ships under false colours to ambush him in European waters. As soon as he sailed from St Petersburg he posted extra lookouts and ordered his captains to be watchful for a surprise attack. It was in this trigger-happy atmosphere that the Russian ships suddenly found themselves surrounded by a flotilla of small ships in the dark of the night.

Without waiting to identify the "enemy" they opened fire. It was only after the first salvoes had fallen among the astonished trawlermen that the Russians realized what they done. Even then the admiral, still nervous at the possibility of a torpedo attack, did not stop to help but steamed off into the night.

The people of Hull were furious when the battle-scarred fishing fleet returned, and pressure is growing for the government to send the Royal Navy after the Russians to "teach them a lesson" (→9/3/05).

Dogger Bank aftermath: fishermen and their families survey the damage.

The Abbey is set to be national theatre

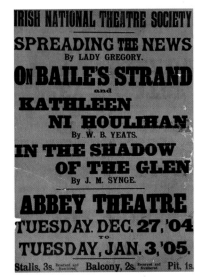

Curtain up at the Abbey theatre.

Dublin, 27 December
The Abbey theatre, Ireland's first national theatre, opened tonight in the former Mechanics' Institute in Abbey Street, Dublin. The lease was bought by an Englishwoman, Annie Horniman, the patron and friend of the poet W B Yeats.

Yeats, together with Lady Gregory and Edward Martyn, has been the guiding force behind the idea for a national theatre. It was appropriate, therefore that his play *On Baile's Strand* was chosen to inaugurate the theatre.

The Abbey, it is hoped, will become a focus for the national movement which incorporates literature and drama and also has a political dimension.

Eleven die as sub sinks in the Solent

Hampshire, 18 March
Eleven men died today when their submarine was hit by a liner in the Solent off Portsmouth. The submarine was one of six undergoing trials, and the accident happened just days after the Royal Navy had shown its confidence in the vessels by taking the prince of Wales – a former naval officer – on an underwater trip around Portsmouth harbour. All the men aboard the submarine today died in the accident which occured when she was manoeuvring in busy shipping lanes.

Fingerprints boost fight against crime

London, 23 September
The potency of a new weapon in the war against crime was shown again today when a fingerprint left by an alleged burglar was sufficient to commit the man for trial. The court at the Mansion House was told that Scotland Yard's fingerprint "bank" now exceeded more than 70,000 – and no two prints were identical. Magistrates have sent a 20-year-old clerk for trial after being told by police that his fingerprints had been found at the scene of a burglary in the Ludgate Circus area of London.

Wishing you were here: postcards are selling in their thousands as the new Edwardians travel further in search of sunshine and sandy beaches.

Women step up campaign for votes

MPs 'talk out' bill for suffrage reform

Westminster, 12 May

Moves to give women the vote were "talked out" in the House of Commons today. Under the rules of parliament a bill is automatically lost if MPs are still talking when the house is due to adjourn, as was the case today. Women have lobbied MPs to back their campaign for an extension to the franchise, but their parliamentary allies found too few friends in the house today. The debate was interrupted by constant laughter from MPs and one noisy interlude from the gallery. It is unlikely that today's setback will deter the women's suffrage movement.

For over 40 years women have been fighting for the right to vote. Nearly 100 different societies have been formed. One of these, the Women's Social and Political Union (WSPU) founded by Mrs Emmeline Pankhurst two years ago, has emerged as the champion of a more militant approach which can only be strengthened by the failure to persuade MPs by normal lobbying. Mrs Pankhurst rallied sympathetic MPs to plead the

Irony: words – and chains – are the suffragettes' principal weapons.

WPSU's cause, but the society has often been frustrated by parliament's refusal to debate the subject. Now, when a suffrage bill was finally proposed, it never even came to a vote.

This seems certain to plead the WSPU's cause who argue that women must fight to win the vote by adopting a more radical strategy, even breaking the law if necessary to shock the all-male parliament into action (→ 4/10).

Suffragettes choose jail instead of fines

Manchester, 4 October

The women's suffrage movement has revealed a new militancy today when, for the first time, two of its members elected to go to prison rather than pay fines. Christabel Pankhurst and her colleague Annie Kenney were arrested for assaulting police at the Free Trade Hall where a leading Liberal politician, Sir Edward Grey, was addressing a meeting. They were sentenced for up to seven days in prison.

It is two years since Mrs Emmeline Pankhurst, the mother of Christabel, founded the Women's Social and Political Union (WSPU) at her home in Manchester. She said then that its aims were to "secure for women the parliamentary vote as it is or may be granted to men; to use the power thus obtained to establish equality of rights and opportunities between the sexes and to promote the social and industrial well-being of the community".

"Deeds, not words" is the motto of the organization. Now the founder's daughter has shown that this is no empty slogan (→ 17/4/06).

Curzon quits over Indian Army changes

London, 20 August

Lord Curzon has resigned as viceroy of India in a dispute with Lord Kitchener, the army commander-in-chief, and the government. He will be succeeded by Lord Minto.

Lord Curzon has been viceroy since 1898 and has defended India's interests vigorously, claiming that it should be the key to imperial policy. He even had his own foreign policy, sending an army into Tibet last year. He also tried to control the army in India directly, against the wishes of the home government.

Lord Kitchener, the commander-in-chief in India, thought that he, not the viceroy, should exercise that control. The final, trivial dispute concerned the appointment of a military member of the viceroy's council. Kitchener and ministers in London opposed Curzon's nominee, so the viceroy resigned.

Lord Curzon: a viceroy steps down.

Motorists found a 'protection society'

London, 29 June

Fifty pioneer motorists met in London's Trocadero restaurant today to form an "Automobile Association" to counter what they see as popular prejudices and police hostility towards the motor car. The new association's objectives were defined at the meeting as "the protection and advancement of the legitimate interests of motorists and opposition to restriction on the use of the roads". Motorists complain particularly of speed-traps set by the police for anyone driving faster than 20mph, claiming that the stop-watches often used by policemen are inaccurate. For two guineas [£2.10] a year motorists now have an association to champion their cause in the country, if not in the courts (→ 19/12).

Liberal is new premier

London, 5 December

After 37 years as an MP Sir Henry Campbell-Bannerman, the Liberal leader, is to take over as prime minister at the age of 69 following the resignation yesterday of Arthur Balfour, whose Tory Party is in disarray over tariff reform. During his audience with the king Sir Henry said that it would take several days for him to form his cabinet, and Balfour is hoping that it might split before the next general election.

Indeed, the new premier's first task is to frustrate moves by more conservative Liberals to capture the top posts in his cabinet. He made many enemies in the party during the Boer War by his criticisms of British policy, and the conservative imperialist wing would have much preferred to see Herbert Asquith become prime minister. However, Campbell-Bannerman, for all his amiable easy-going ways, intends to ask the king to dissolve parliament for a snap general election which, if the Liberals won, would enhance his own authority.

Two powerful Liberal imperialists will need to be placated, though. Asquith is to become chancellor, and Richard Haldane will go to the war office with the task of reorganizing the army after the dis-

The new premier: history is made.

asters in South Africa. He plans to set up an imperial general staff on the lines of the German army.

The new prime minister has already secured his place in constitutional history: he will be the first to hold the post as an office of state. In the past, the head of the British government has been obliged to take a post formally recognized by the constitution, usually that of first lord of the treasury, a sinecure. Now the king has promised a royal warrant creating the post of prime minister (→ 13/1/06).

New nationalist party, 'Sinn Féin', formed

Ireland, December

A new political party, Sinn Féin [We Ourselves], has been formed by a Dublin printer, Arthur Griffith, the founder of a weekly paper, the *United Irishman*, in which he preaches the doctrine which has now formed the basis of Sinn Féin. Griffith believes that Ireland must be politically free before it can be economically prosperous. In 1900 he organised a movement against the Boer War. Known as *Cumann na nGaedheal*, it has been seen as a broad front for cultural and economic nationalism.

With the formation of his new party he is urging a policy of non-cooperation. The Irish members would withdraw from the Westminster parliament and set up an Irish government which would be followed by the peaceful withdrawal of the British (→ 12/2/07).

Arthur Griffith, the mouthpiece for a new mood of Irish nationalism.

Dr Barnardo, champion of children, dies

Surbiton, Surrey, 19 September

A doctor who gave his name to homes for deprived children has died aged 60. Dr Thomas John Barnardo had meant to become a missionary after finishing his medical studies, but he was so shocked by the plight of homeless children in London's east end where he was studying that he found his vocation within the British Isles. He set up his first "home" in 1870 – a simple shelter and school in a former stable – and by the time his death was announced today there were 112 Barnardo homes.

No child was ever turned away, it was claimed, and many found new lives overseas. Some 17,000 children emigrated to Canada through the organization created by the Irish-born doctor.

Actors banned for indecency in Shaw play

A poster for "Man and Superman": provocative philosophical comedy.

New York, 1 November

A controversial play by the Irish writer George Bernard Shaw about prostitution, *Mrs Warren's Profession*, got a brief showing here this week after being banned in London. But the play was promptly closed by the police who arrested the theatre manager, Arnold Daly, and his actors for offences against public decency. Chief Commissioner McAdoo testified that the play was "nauseating where it is not boring". Shaw spoke of his "pity for all those foolish people".

Shaw has other hits in London, too. *John Bull's Other Island* was seen by the king, who broke his chair laughing. *Man and Superman* followed, in which the superman was played by Harley Granville-Barker made up to look like Shaw. A third play, *Major Barbara*, opens later this month (→ 10/12/25).

Queen Alexandra visits the East End: loyalty is shown to royalty in the new Edwardian era, despite reports that millions live "in chronic poverty".

Liberals sweep to landslide victory

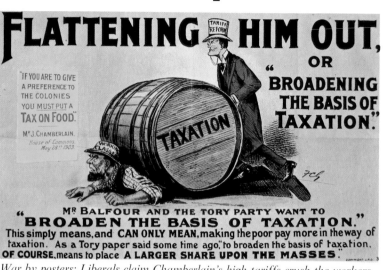

"IF YOU ARE TO GIVE A PREFERENCE TO THE COLONIES YOU MUST PUT A **TAX ON FOOD**." Mr J. CHAMBERLAIN, House of Commons, May 28th 1903.

"MR BALFOUR AND THE TORY PARTY WANT TO **BROADEN THE BASIS OF TAXATION.**" This simply means, and **CAN ONLY MEAN**, making the poor pay more in the way of taxation. As a Tory paper said some time ago, to broaden the basis of taxation, **OF COURSE**, means to place **A LARGER SHARE UPON THE MASSES**.

War by posters: Liberals claim Chamberlain's high tariffs crush the workers.

Government to enforce new welfare plans

Westminster, 7 February
Pressure for radical social changes has been intensified within the Liberal government by the success of Labour candidates in the general election. David Lloyd George, the 43-year-old president of the board of trade, is telling his cabinet colleagues that they must commit the government to a wide-ranging reform programme if they wish to stem the tide of socialism.

Lloyd George, a fiery champion of the radical Liberal wing, says that the traditional Liberal preoccupation with such nonconformist issues as education and teetotalism must give way to the notion of "positive liberty". This means a willingness to use the power of the state to give the "labouring classes" some form of help in time of need.

Sir Henry Campbell-Bannerman has dashed Tory hopes of a Liberal split first by succeeding in forming a government and now by winning a stunning election victory. However, he must keep his party together. The Liberal benches in the Commons are still largely occupied by men from the trading and manufacturing classes who have long been opposed to state intervention. Even more hostile to radicalism is the House of Lords, where the Conservative majority remains intact. →

Unions win battle over Taff Vale case

Westminster, December
A five-year campaign by trade unions to reverse a court ruling that gave strike damages to employers from union funds has ended in total victory. The Trades Disputes Bill was one of the first to be produced by the new Liberal government – and it has been approved untouched by the Tory-dominated House of Lords. The bill restores the protection to union funds which was generally thought to have existed before a 1901 case involving the Taff Vale Railway came before the law lords (→ 13/8/07).

Labour grows, but Tories flop at poll

London, 7 February
Sir Henry Campbell-Bannerman has led his Liberal Party to a landslide victory in the snap general election he called within weeks of becoming prime minister when the Conservative government resigned. There are now 400 Liberal MPs against 184 elected in 1900, with a majority of 130 over other parties.

The poll has been a disaster for the Tories, who held only 157 of their 402 seats – and even these are split between supporters of Balfour and of Chamberlain. The 83 Irish Nationalists appear to be a more cohesive group than has sometimes been the case in the past, but the most significant portent may be the success of the Labour candidates.

A secret pact with the Liberals gave Labour a free run against the Tories in key constituencies, and 29 of 50 candidates from the trade-union-backed Labour Representation Committee (LRC) have been elected. Another 24 MPs are Labour under various names, but not linked as yet to those from the LRC who intend to operate as an independent party. Labour's share of the total vote is still small at 4.8 per cent, but it has trebled since the 1900 election and threatens the two-party dominance of the Liberals and their Tory rivals (→ 12).

Jewel of the principality: the newly completed Cardiff city hall wins near-universal admiration as a triumph of Victorian-style architecture.

Britannia rules the waves with the launch of the world's most imposing battleship

HMS "Dreadnought": the supership will outgun and outpace any others.

England, 10 February
HMS *Dreadnought* was launched by King Edward VII today and immediately made every other battleship in the world obsolescent. The brainchild of the first sea lord, Admiral Sir "Jackie" Fisher, this revolutionary ship will mount ten 12-inch guns in five turrets. Eight of the guns will be able to fire salvoes of armour-piercing shells on either side of the ship, compared with the four guns of the present generation of battleships.

The *Dreadnought* is being equipped with steam turbines fuelled by oil, a system never tried before in a battleship. Much faster than previous ships, she will also be able to attack her enemy from a greater distance. Despite these overwhelming technical improvements, the *Dreadnought* programme aroused opposition within the admiralty. Some senior officers argued that making Britain's battlefleet obsolete destroyed the Royal Navy's numerical advantage over its rivals. But the blow to Germany will be even greater: the Kiel canal will have to be rebuilt if ships of this size are to pass through to the North Sea.

The need for such a warship was demonstrated, however, during the Russo-Japanese War when naval engagements were fought at long range. Naval strategists learnt that torpedo boats would have to be destroyed before they could get close enough to launch their deadly missiles, which have increased greatly in range and accuracy (→ 28/2/07).

Eleven suffragettes jailed for their cause

London, 24 October
Women brought their campaign for the vote to Westminster yesterday in a rowdy demonstration at the Commons which saw several leading suffragettes arrested. Eleven of them – all members of the Women's Social and Political Union (WSPU) – were jailed today after refusing to pay fines of £10. Most of those arrested refused to acknowledge the court.

Among those beginning their sentences in Holloway prison tonight are Sylvia Pankhurst, a daughter of the WSPU's leader, and Emmeline Pethick Lawrence, the organization's treasurer. Mrs Pethick Lawrence said: "Women of England, we are going to prison for you and therefore we do it gladly. We call upon you to take up the standard and bear it on to victory."

This autumn has brought a new, violent chapter in the fight for women's suffrage. The WSPU take its task very seriously and uses its

Sylvia Pankhurst: chose Holloway.

headquarters in Clement's Inn as a "battle headquarters". It favours a far more militant approach than the longer-established suffrage societies which generally prefer persuasion to protest (→ 25/12).

British Empire spans one-fifth of the globe

London, 8 March
It is official: Britain's empire now occupies one-fifth of the world's land surface. This and many other facts are published today in a 300-page government "blue book" drawing on data from the English local government board. The survey reveals that 400 million people now live under the British Empire. Its borders extend over 11.5 million square miles (29.79 million sq km), a third of which have been acquired in the last 25 years alone.

Just over a century ago Britain was still smarting at the loss of its American colonies. Now, by contrast, it has an empire on which the sun will never set – if only because, as someone has quipped, God would not trust an Englishman in the dark (→ 22/5).

More Londoners go down the 'tube'

London, 15 December
Another underground railway was inaugurated in London today, the second this year, running from Hammersmith to Finsbury Park. In March services began between Baker Street and Waterloo on what has been nicknamed the "Bakerloo" line. Both new lines, like the Central Line opened in 1900, run through circular tunnels (or tubes) at far greater depth than the older "cut and cover" Metropolitan and District Lines. A third new "tube", from Charing Cross to Golders Green, opens next year (→ 22/5/15).

'Man of Property': new style of novel

London, 31 December
John Galsworthy has come up with a new kind of novel this year which reflects changing society in succeeding generations of a single family. *The Man of Property*, its title, refers to Soames Forsyte, an Edwardian solicitor who values his houses, art collection and even his wife Irene as part of his social position. He is not a sympathetic character but is portrayed as typical of the upper-middle classes. Soames has doubts about the future, however, which would never have occurred to the Victorian ruling classes (→ 12/1913).

Cornish tin miners make the most of "croust time", a break for pasties. Many children start working in the mines as early as the age of 12.

Suffragettes shout down cabinet minister

Warwickshire, 16 November
Militant suffragettes shouted down Herbert Asquith, the chancellor of the exchequer, at a meeting here today as part of their campaign to harass the government into support for a suffrage bill giving women the vote. The government has yet to throw its weight behind reform, and private bills have foundered, as did one introduced in March by James Keir Hardie, the Labour leader, for instance.

An act was passed this year to extend the right of women to sit as councillors, but they still lack a parliamentary vote. The failure to make progress has contributed to tensions within the suffrage movement. Some women are contemplating the formation of a new group, the Women's Freedom League, in protest against what they see as the domineering leadership of Mrs Emmeline Pankhurst, who heads the Women's Social and Political Union (WSPU). Yet internal divi-

Suffragettes: now the fight hots up.

sions have not staunched the increasing militancy. Ministers are shouted down; women opt to be jailed rather than pay fines after being arrested; protests are staged in parliament (→ 30/1/08).

Riots in Dublin theatre over new play

Dublin, 28 January
Rioting in the Abbey theatre has broken up the first performances of *The Playboy of the Western World*, a new play by J M Synge set in the west of Ireland. The audience accused the author of misrepresenting peasant life in Ireland.

There was silence at the première until the third act, when fighting broke out. One of the theatre's founders, the writer W B Yeats,

was sent a telegram in Scotland after the second act: "Play a great success." This was followed by a second telegram: "Audience broke up in disorder at the word shift [a woman's under-garment]." Police attended the second performance, but there was still uproar. The play focuses on a youth, Christy, who boasts that he has killed his father. Yeats plans to return from Scotland to defend the play.

Yeats defends "The Playboy of the Western World" from the Abbey stage.

Concern grows over children's smoking

Exeter, Devon, 2 August
The king does it. Gentlemen and even some ladies do it. But doctors think too many children do it. Smoking amongst young people is increasing rapidly, and today at a meeting here of the British Medical Association doctors voiced their concern at this trend. Dr Herbert Tidswell, a Devon GP, attacked the habit as evil and claimed that it was damaging the health of the nation, causing, amongst other ailments, forms of cancer. He urged a campaign to stop children starting to smoke, although some other doctors said that the risks of moderate smoking had not been proved.

Starting young on a royal habit.

War office unveils army reform plans

Whitehall, London, 13 January
Richard Haldane, the secretary of state for war, today announced far-reaching reforms in the administration and organization of the army. A general staff will head an army with an "expeditionary force" of six infantry divisions supported by a cavalry division plus artillery and logistical support to enable rapid mobilization. Support will also be provided by reorganizing the volunteer and militia detachments into a new "territorial force" organization of 14 divisions.

Two die as troops fire on strikers

Belfast, 13 August
A crippling three-month-old strike by dockers and unskilled workers in Belfast claimed its first victims when two civilians were shot dead yesterday by British soldiers protecting people still working in the Catholic Falls Road area of the city. One was a woman of 23, looking for her child, and the other was a man returning from his work.

A magistrate, Major Martin Thackeray, attempted to read the Riot Act to a crowd of 500 stone-throwers after four soldiers were injured but admitted that he was inaudible. James Larkin, the dockers' union leader, had urged mill workers to join the strike against low pay – often under 10 shillings [50p] a week – and the army decided to extend its protection to the Falls. By then both Protestant and Catholic workers were involved. Riots followed, becoming more serious until on 11 August a police van was ambushed on Grosvenor Road. The crowd grew to 2,000, and when a barracks was attacked

Belfast docks: bayonets are out as the Royal Irish Constabulary mobilizes.

the authorities sent in 2,600 soldiers, 80 cavalry and 500 police.

Soldiers admitted to smashing windows and doors on the pretext of bayonet and cavalry charges. After the deaths yesterday the lord mayor responded to pleas by Catholic clergy and laity to withdraw the soldiers, who were originally deployed because some policemen were also on strike. Many Catholics feared attacks from neighbouring loyalist areas, but so far these have not materialized (→ 5/6/08).

English ship rules transatlantic waves

The SS "Lusitania": £2.6m to snatch the blue riband back from Germany.

New York, 11 October
Sirens resounded across New York harbour today to mark the arrival of the English ship *Lusitania* after a record-breaking crossing of the Atlantic. She had made the trip in just four days 19 hours and 52 minutes to beat the previous record by 11 hours and 46 minutes – at an average speed of just over 24 knots. This regains the "blue riband" for

the fastest Atlantic crossing for Britain from Germany. The loss of the record had stung British pride and persuaded the government to give Cunard a loan of £2.6 million to build two new turbine vessels. Now the first, the *Lusitania*, has set a record without even trying, with the second, the *Mauretania*, due to make her maiden crossing next month (→ 13/5/15).

Stars go on strike in the music halls

London, 15 March
The show goes on again tonight as music halls reopen their doors after a pay dispute. Performers had gone on strike last month to back up their demand for more money, forcing several theatres to close or to use amateurs to provide entertainment for their customers. The strikes were by no means total, but no business was bad business for show business; after mediation the hall owners offered a deal which was accepted today.

Music halls draw far larger audiences than any other form of entertainment, with stars such as Marie Lloyd, Harry Lauder and George Robey known throughout the land. Most towns of any size have their own variety or music halls. So far music halls have not suffered unduly from the challenge of a new form of entertainment – cinema. However, the attraction of moving pictures is growing, which was another reason why the hall-owners wanted to end the pay dispute.

United Methodist Church holds first annual conference

London, 18 September
Nearly one thousand people were crammed into the City Road chapel of John Wesley in Islington today for the first conference of the United Methodist Church. It represents a three-way merger of the United Methodist Free Churches, the Methodist Connexion and the Bible Christians.

After the merger resolution was formally adopted the delegates rose and let themselves go in true Methodist fashion. The chapel rang to the sound of "Praise God, from whom all blessings flow". The newly elected president, the Rev Edward Boaden of Leamington, aged 80, then addressed the assembly. He said that the three groups "had met, not only because they thought union a good thing, but because they could not keep apart".

The new church has 184,000 members and 908 ministers. Other Methodist churches sent messages of support to the new church, and delegates were hopeful that it will lead to the union of all British Methodists. The strength of the movement as a whole can be gauged from the annual report of the Wesleyan Methodist Sunday School Union, which is just about to be issued. It will state that there are just over a million pupils in the 7,566 Methodist Sunday schools.

The "Nulli Secundus", Britain's first airship, rounds St Paul's after a flight from Farnborough. Strong winds later forced it to land at the Crystal Palace.

London, 30 January. Nine suffragettes are arrested after incidents at the homes of cabinet ministers (→ 24/10).

Westminster, 27 February. A Licensing Bill which would cut drinking licences by a third is introduced (→ 26/9).

London, February. Lord Northcliffe, formerly Alfred Harmsworth, buys The Times.

Isle of Wight, 2 April. The destroyer HMS Tiger collides with the cruiser HMS Berwick; 35 sailors die.

Westminster, 7 May. The government proposes a weekly old age pension of 5/- [25p] for single people over 70, 7s 6d [37.5p] for a married couple (→ 24/9).

London, 19 May. A meeting calls for the establishment of a "national theatre".

Britain, 5 June. The Miners' Federation decides to affiliate to the Labour Representation Committee (→ 6/11).

Reval, Estonia, 9 June. King Edward VII meets the czar during the first visit by a reigning British monarch to Russia (→ 7/5/10).

London, 13 July. Controversy grows over why the Labour leader James Keir Hardie is not invited to the royal garden party for MPs.

Westminster, 1 August. The Irish Universities Act provides for two new universities in Ireland: one for Ulster, the other for the three southern provinces.

London, 15 August. Winston Churchill, the president of the board of trade, announces his engagement to Clementine Hosier (→ 23/10/11).

London, 26 September. An estimated 500,000 people demonstrate against the Licensing Bill in Hyde Park.

Britain, 31 October. Kaiser William of Germany causes an uproar by his anti-British remarks in an interview with the Daily Telegraph (→ 21/3/09).

Lancashire, 6 November. A cotton strike ends after seven weeks as workers agree to a wage cut (→ 28).

London, 28 November. The court of appeal rules that trade unions cannot use funds for political purposes (→ 2/9/10).

Stockholm, 10 December. Ernest Rutherford wins the Nobel prize for chemistry for his work on atoms.

Asquith steps up to be prime minister

Asquith: fondness for good life.

Churchill: expecting promotion.

Biarritz, France, 12 April
Herbert Asquith today became the first British prime minister to be appointed by kissing hands with his sovereign at a foreign hotel. He had travelled to Biarritz where King Edward VII is holidaying, following the resignation through ill health of Sir Henry Campbell-Bannerman. In fact Asquith has been acting premier for some time as Sir Henry's illness worsened.

There will be no dispute among Liberals about Asquith's right to succeed. He and Sir Henry had been rivals once, but he served loyally as chancellor of the exchequer and developed a high reputation as both a parliamentary performer and an administrator. He is a Yorkshireman, now aged 55, with a fondness for good living and, by his own admission, "clever and attractive women". He is not associated closely with the cause of social reform espoused by some of his more radical colleagues, but he is expected to promote the foremost of these, David Lloyd George, to be his own successor at the treasury. Two able junior ministers, Walter Runciman and Winston Churchill, can expect elevation to cabinet posts for trade and education (→ 24/4/09).

'White City' marks Anglo-French entente

London, 14 May
Even a downpour could not dim the splendour of the Franco-British exhibition which was opened today by the Prince of Wales. More than 80 hectares (200 acres) of west London have been transformed by 25 palaces and halls, gardens and lakes to be a showcase for the two countries. The gleaming stone of many buildings has earned the exhibition the popular name of "White City". Also part of the site at Shepherd's Bush is a large sports stadium which will be used for the Olympic Games later this summer. As a symbol of Anglo-French accord four years after the Entente Cordiale, the White City seems certain to be a hugely popular success. Already a "tube" line has been extended to bring the crowds.

The "flip-flap" exhibition ride.

'Boy scouts' set up camp for first time

London, 16 January
The first edition of a new magazine, Scouting for Boys, is published today to encourage the growth of a new movement which is headed by Sir Robert Baden-Powell, the hero of Mafeking. He wrote a book on the idea in 1906 and last year took 20 boys from widely different backgrounds on an experimental camping holiday to Brownsea Island in Poole harbour. There they were introduced to what Sir Robert sees as the character-forming activities of army scouts living in the open, such as fire-making, woodcraft and life-saving. The first scout "troops" were formed last year (→ 4/9/09).

Baden-Powell: scouting hero.

Cricket shocked by life without Grace

Gloucestershire, September
The most famous cricketer in the world has played his last first-class match. At the age of 60 Dr William Gilbert Grace (but better known by his initials "W G") played for the Gentlemen of England against Surrey this season but has said he will not play again. Thus ends a career which began in 1870 with Gloucestershire and included 22 caps for England. He was the first man to score a century for his country, the first to score 1,000 runs in May, the first to score 100 centuries and the first to perform the "double" of 1,000 runs and 100 wickets in a season. In all he scored 54,211 runs and took 2,808 wickets in first-class cricket (→ 8/5/23).

Court sends the Pankhursts to prison

London, 24 October
The leader of the most militant suffragette group, Mrs Emmeline Pankhurst, and one of her daughters, Christabel, were jailed today at the end of a sensational trial which saw two cabinet ministers summoned to appear as witnesses for their defence. The two women were found guilty of conduct likely to cause a breach of the peace by inciting members of the public to "rush" the House of Commons nine days ago.

Mrs Pankhurst, who heads the Women's Social and Political Union, startled the court by calling Herbert Gladstone, the home secretary, and David Lloyd George, the chancellor of the exchequer, as witnesses for her defence. The

ministers had been reluctant to attend, but compelled to do so they attested to the orderliness of the demonstration on 13 October. So did other witnesses; one woman said that she had been jostled more at society weddings.

However, Mr Gladstone rejected Mrs Pankhurst's claim that she and her supporters should be treated as political prisoners. And the magistrates were equally unmoved by both the ministerial evidence and the spell-binding oratory of Mrs Pankhurst's tearful closing address. Five thousand police had been needed to keep order, and if the Pankhursts would not be bound over to keep the peace, or be willing to pay any fines levied by the court, they must go to jail (→ 12/10/09).

Solidarity: the Pankhursts in jail.

Old people sign up for first pensions

British Isles, 24 September
Old people queued today to register for the first pensions, payable in the New Year. The principle of old age pensions was announced in the budget last May. They were proclaimed by Herbert Asquith, the prime minister, as non-contributory pensions for everybody, but they only begin at the age of 70 and the money on offer is relatively modest: five shillings [25p] for an individual and – as though to penalize marriage vows – seven shillings and sixpence [37.5p] for a married couple. Those earning ten shillings [50p] or more a week are disqualified from the scheme. Payments will be made at post offices, with the first payday set for 1 January 1909 (→ 1/1/09).

Britain is the proud host to Olympics Games

Marathon man: Dorando is helped at the tape but later wins a gold cup.

London, July
An Italian runner who lost won the hearts of London at the Olympic Games this month. It was the first time that the Olympics have been staged in Britain, with no fewer than 21 different sports in what was the greatest sporting festival ever seen in this country. The centrepiece was the new stadium at White City in west London, and it was here that Dorando Pietri had his moments of glory – and agony. He had entered the stadium with a commanding lead in the 26-mile

(42-km) marathon, only to stumble and stagger towards the finishing line. Well-meaning stewards picked him up so that, although he crossed the line first, he was later disqualified. The crowd's admiration for his courage was so great, however, that he later received a gold cup from Queen Alexandra.

Competitors from Britain offered the greatest challenge to the United States in the athletics events and dominated the rowing (staged at Henley), boxing, yachting, archery and cycling events.

Elgar's reputation soars to new heights

Manchester, December
It was here in the Free Trade Hall that the year's most notable musical première took place. Sir Edward Elgar's first symphony was an immediate popular success, so much so that it has already been performed nearly 100 times. But it has also confirmed Elgar's status as England's leading composer. The sym-

phony, like his oratorio *The Dream of Gerontius* in 1900, is a work on the grand scale yet full of the melodies which appeal to the Edwardian public. The trio from the first of his four *Pomp and Circumstance Marches* was set to words in coronation year by A C Benson to become a rival national anthem as *Land of Hope and Glory* (→ 4/5/24).

Cowboy makes first flight in British Isles

Hampshire, 16 October
A former American cowboy in a French-engined aeroplane today became the first man to make a powered flight in the British Isles. He also became the first to crash. Samuel Cody was flying a plane financed by the war office at Farnborough in Hampshire. Helped by a strong tailwind the plane, *British Army Aeroplane No 1*, rose to 30

feet and continued for just over a quarter of a mile (400m) before Cody took too sharp a turn and crashed. Bleeding but undaunted, Cody emerged from the crash still wearing his Texas hat and apologized for the accident. He said, however, that he had "constructed a machine which flies". Britain has so far lagged behind the French and Americans in aviation (→ 19/3/09).

"British Army Aeroplane No 1" is wheeled out for trials at Farnborough.

1909

Fears grow as arms race gathers speed

A new arm of the Royal Navy: submarines gather in Dover harbour.

Westminster, 21 March

There was dismay in the House of Commons today when Reginald McKenna, the first lord of the admiralty, told the house that the government had underestimated Admiral von Tirpitz's programme to rebuild the German navy.

Von Tirpitz intends to dispute Britain's naval supremacy and, according to Mr McKenna, may soon have more of the new Dreadnought-class battleships than the Royal Navy. The admiralty has been aware of this danger for some months and wanted to build six new Dreadnoughts. Some cabinet ministers feared that the cost of these more powerful and faster capital ships would torpedo the government's social reforms and so proposed a compromise: four ships this year and four more in the future. This has not appeased critics of the government. "We want eight and we won't wait" has become a popular slogan as pressure mounts on Asquith's government (→ 7/9).

Commission condemns workhouse laws

No more workhouses for children.

London, 17 February

No more children should live in workhouses, says a royal commission on Britain's poor laws. The commission split over the scale and speed of changes, but both majority and minority reports call for the boards of guardians who control poor law relief to be scrapped in favour of local government control.

Up to a third of people living in Britain's major cities and towns end their days in poor law institutions. These include children's homes, infirmaries and lunatic asylums as well as the workhouses themselves which have come to symbolize the poor law system. Old age pensions introduced this year are a modest attempt to ease poverty in the wider community as an alternative to institutional help. The commission backs this approach and wants children in particular to be helped outside the workhouse (→ 4/5/11).

White South Africa forms a new Union

London, 7 December

The Union of South Africa was proclaimed today, uniting the British Cape Colony and Natal with the Boer Transvaal and Orange River colonies. The act marks the fulfilment of a promise made at the end of the Boer War. All the white colonies in the British Empire are now self-governing.

The Afrikaners, having lost the war, have won the peace, although English settlers remain strong politically, economically and socially. Apart from the Coloureds in the Cape, the native people (plus Asiatics and people of mixed descent) have no vote.

General Botha, the Boer leader who has emerged as the most prominent advocate of reconciliation with the British, will be prime minister of the new dominion.

Hunger strike ends in 'force feeding'

Birmingham, 12 October

The high court today ordered an inquiry to be held at Winson Green prison in Birmingham after allegations by a suffragette that she was repeatedly force fed. Mrs Laura Ainsworth was imprisoned for obstructing the police and in jail adopted the new suffragette tactic of going on hunger strike. In an affidavit Mrs Ainsworth, who is now recovering in a nursing home, claims that after three days she was pinioned by wardresses while a prison doctor tried to force a cup through her teeth and a tube 60cm (2 feet) in length up her nostrils. Medical evidence to the court said that this entailed grave risks and should be investigated (→ 26/1/10).

Advertising a new detergent.

Budget stuns the Tories

Lloyd George raises taxes for pensions

Westminster, 24 April

David Lloyd George, the Liberals' radical chancellor of the exchequer, today stunned the Tory opposition with a "supertax" of sixpence [2.5p] in the pound on people earning over £5,000 a year. For people earning £2,000 a year the standard rate goes up to 1s 2d [6p].

There were other taxes, too, in his budget – new ones on petrol, car licences and land value, plus higher ones on tobacco and alcoholic drinks. These have all been imposed to pay for welfare schemes such as old age pensions and labour exchanges plus a major rearmament programme provoked by Germany's rapidly growing naval power. Money raised by taxes on motorists will also go into a special road fund to build new roads to accommodate the increasing number of motor cars. Altogether the new taxes make the budget the biggest in the nation's history.

One after another, Tory MPs denounced the budget as an attack on the propertied classes, who were described as the foundation of the nation's prosperity. The doubling of death duties, it was claimed, would lead to penny-pinching on large estates and harm local tradesmen and the labouring classes.

To the Tory-controlled House of Lords, the most provocative aspect

Lloyd George: new taxes anger rich.

of Lloyd George's budget is a scheme to be implemented later. All the land in the country is to be valued and a 20 per cent tax levied on "unearned increment". Yet Lloyd George has fashioned a politically astute package of measures, with many widely popular social reforms that have already led to the nickname "the people's budget".

Lloyd George is unruffled by the Tory uproar; there is nothing he enjoys more than "dishing the dukes". Labour MPs view the budget with mixed feelings. They agree with many of its proposals, but are irritated that it has enabled the Liberals to seize the initiative on social reform (→ 30/11).

'People's budget' thrown out by Lords

Westminster, 30 November

In the House of Lords tonight, with bejewelled peeresses looking on from the public galleries, the Tory-dominated peers overwhelmingly rejected Lloyd George's "people's budget", a controversial package of higher taxes and social reforms. The stage is now set for a major constitutional crisis which has been building up since the Liberals were returned to power in 1906 after years in the political wilderness.

Tory peers soon began rejecting bills sent up by the new government. A licensing bill to cut down the number of public houses was

thrown out, as were other bills on education and Scotland. The Liberals did not react at the time, but it was a different matter when the Finance Bill implementing this year's budget proposals was attacked by the Lords.

For half a century it has been accepted that the non-elected Lords cannot reject a money bill from the Commons. But the Tories argued that the budget had too many non-money measures to be accepted as a finance bill. Faced with the peers' intransigence, the prime minister, Herbert Asquith, will call an election (→14/2/10).

Mackintosh is the toast of Glasgow in a resurgence of British architectural style

Glasgow, December

Glasgow School of Art, a revolutionary building designed by a local architect, Charles Rennie Mackintosh, has been completed this year with the addition of its library wing. It is perhaps the highlight of a resurgent confidence among British architects.

Mackintosh won the competition to build the school of art when he was only 26. His style is spare and simple in outline, with tall projecting glass casements and light airy balustrades of ironwork for its only decoration. The interiors, also by him, have exposed structural beams of steel or timber. The overall plainness is relieved by the angular, yet subtly geometrical shapes of his tables and chairs. He is much admired abroad.

The competition to design Liverpool's Anglican cathedral was won in 1903 by Giles Gilbert Scott, who was then 22 and had built nothing. Work began in 1904, but Scott has changed his Gothic design to one with a huge central tower, baroque in spirit with Gothic details. Baroque is the fashion for public building, as in Aston Webb's work (the Victoria and Albert museum) and, also in London, the new county hall (Ralph Knott, 1907) and the Old Bailey (E W Mountford, 1907).

The solidity and pomp of the baroque style appeal to the

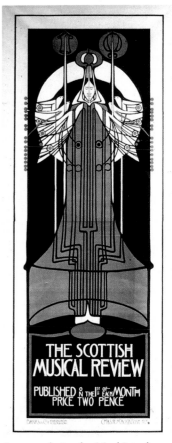

A poster design by Mackintosh.

Edwardian mind. A more individual style is being developed by Edwin Lutyens. So far this has been confined to country houses, such as Castle Drogo now being built in Devon, but it seems only a matter of time before he finds a more public stage.

Heathcote, a house at Ilkley designed by Edwin Lutyens in 1906.

Britain, 8 January. Germany's military build-up becomes an election issue (→ 2/2).

London, 26 January. Police rescue the prime minister, Herbert Asquith, when he is mobbed by furious suffragettes (→ 17/6/11).

Britain, 1 February. The new labour exchanges are besieged by job-hunters.

Britain, 2 February. A report says that the country could face a serious shortage of horses should war break out (→ 22/7/12).

Westminster, 21 February. Sir Edward Carson is elected as leader of the Irish Unionist MPs (→ 23/9/11).

London, 22 February. Thomas Beecham conducts the first performance of Frederick Delius's opera *A Village Romeo and Juliet*.

London, 8 March. A royal commission is told that the cost of an undefended divorce is £81 and that of a defended one £121.

Wales, 11 March. In a dam-burst in the Rhondda valley 500 children are swept away; 494 are rescued (→ 26/8/11).

Westminster, 14 April. Asquith tells MPs that he has discussed with the king creating 300 new peers to approve the new Parliament Bill curbing the Lords (→ 16/6).

London, 6 May. Edward VII dies (→ 20).

Britain, 31 May. A sister organization to the Boy Scouts is formed, to be known as the Girl Guides.

London, 1 June. Captain Robert Scott sets out on a new attempt to reach the South Pole (→ 14/12/11).

London, 23 June. The king's eldest son, David, is created prince of Wales.

Bournemouth, 12 July. Charles Rolls, co-founder of the Rolls-Royce car company, dies in a flying accident (→ 13/4/12).

Britain, 2 September. Shipbuilders give 24 hours' notice of a lockout of 40,000 boilermakers (→ 9/11).

London, 23 November. Dr Crippen is hanged for his wife's murder.

Ireland, November. The first issue of *Irish Freedom*, the monthly publication of the Irish Republican Brotherhood, appears (→ 23/9/11).

Edward VII mourned by the nation

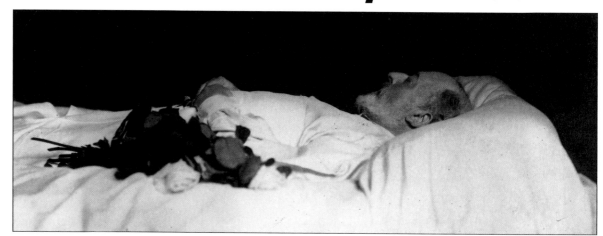

Edward VII lies in state: a beloved king who waited long in the wings. He shed his playboy image to work for peace.

Windsor, Berkshire, 20 May
The people of Britain were in deep mourning today for their beloved King Edward VII. The sovereign who had shed his playboy image to become a peacemaker was buried in the family vault in St George's chapel, Windsor Castle. He had died of bronchitis on 6 May barely a week after returning from what was intended to be partly a convalescent holiday in Biarritz. On 29 April he attended the opera at Covent Garden before spending the weekend at Sandringham. He returned to London with a chill but continued to work despite increasing difficulty breathing. The queen was in Corfu when he was taken ill and was only able to get home the day before the king died.

Edward was 59 when he finally came to the throne after a lifetime as prince of Wales which saw him embroiled more than once in scandal. He at once brought a sense of fun to court life, after the dour Victorian years; but he revealed a capacity for hard work and diplomacy that surprised many. Visits to France paved the way for the *Entente Cordiale* of 1904, and he was close to the rulers of other European countries, notably Germany and Russia. He is succeeded by his son, George (→ 1/2/11).

Radio link catches alleged killer at sea

Canada, 31 July
Transatlantic radio was used to arrest a suspected murderer today when Dr Hawley Harvey Crippen was taken into custody by police in Quebec. Police have been looking for Crippen and his mistress, Ethel le Neve, since they found the mutilated and dismembered body of his wife beneath the floorboards of his London house. Crippen and le Neve had posed as "Mr Robinson and son" on the SS *Montrose* from Antwerp to Canada, but the captain became suspicious. He radioed British police, who caught a faster ship to arrest the couple on their arrival in Canada (→ 23/11).

Crippen and le Neve are arrested.

Pit disaster kills 'up to 350 men'

Bolton, 22 December
The pit village of Westhoughton near Bolton is in mourning tonight after an explosion at the colliery which threatens to be Britain's second worst mining disaster. Up to 350 men are missing, and hope is fading. So far only one 16-year-old miner has been brought out alive, although rescue attempts continue. The cause of the blast, at a mine previously regarded as one of the safest and best-equipped in the county, is not yet known. If no more survivors are found, some 1,000 children will be orphans.

Nation pays tribute to Florence Nightingale, pioneer of nursing

London, 20 August
St Paul's Cathedral was packed today for a memorial service to Florence Nightingale, the great pioneer of nursing, who died last week at the age of 90. Later her coffin was drawn by two horses through the streets of London on its way to Waterloo and a family funeral in Hampshire. The coffin was covered by floral tributes – from Queen Alexandra, from London hospitals and from veterans of the Crimea. One of the wreathes was shaped like the army lantern she carried on her rounds in Scutari hospital during the Crimean War. She first made her name there, but she also left a lasting impression on the organization of nursing in hospitals at home.

King, peers and MPs split over who rules Britain

Labour props up Liberals after election

An election poster shows how strongly Tories feel about "the people's budget".

Westminster, 14 February
The general election has failed to give Herbert Asquith's government a "people's mandate" to push through last year's supertax budget against the opposition of the Lords. The chastened Liberals now have 273 MPs against 397 in the last parliament. The Tories also now have 273 MPs, Labour 42 and the Irish Nationalists 82. Asquith has returned to London from Cannes to find that his survival as prime minister depends on the support of Labour and the Nationalists. The Tories are being attacked because their defeat of the Finance Bill in the House of Lords has landed the treasury with a £10 million debt.

It is now expected that the combined Liberal-Labour-Nationalist majority in the Commons will resubmit the Finance Bill, and that the Lords will accept it. Then the real struggle will begin – to curb the powers of the peers. It is a battle which could embroil the crown in the party political fight (→ 14/4).

Commons backs moves to curb the Lords

London, 16 June
Leaders of the main parties met at Downing Street today for a constitutional conference first suggested by the new king, George V. He had come to the throne after the Commons had passed the Parliament Bill which enables measures passed by the Commons in three separate sessions to be given the royal assent without the consent of the Lords. A money bill would become law one month after passing the Commons.

If the Lords put up a fight, the prime minister, Herbert Asquith, intends to ask the king to create upwards of 300 new peers to swamp the hereditary Tory majority there. George hopes that talks will avoid this, but most politicians believe that a second election over "who rules Britain" is inevitable (→ 20/12).

The new king: seeking a truce between the Commons and the Lords.

Reluctant king backs plan to beat Lords

Westminster, 20 December
The second general election in 12 months over the constitutional clash with the has left the strength of the parties virtually unchanged. The Tories have 273 MPs, the Liberals 271, Labour 42 and the Irish Nationalists 84. But with Labour and Nationalist support the Liberal government can now push through the House of Commons its bill to curb the powers of the Lords. Herbert Asquith, the prime minister, will do so armed with the pledge given – albeit reluctantly – by King George V that he will create several hundred new peers to overwhelm any resistance by diehard peers. Even so some Tories plan to continue the fight which began when the Lords rejected the 1909 "people's budget" (→ 10/8/11).

Troops patrol Welsh streets after strikers clash with the police

Mid-Glamorgan, 9 November
A squadron of the 18th Hussars appeared on the streets of Tonypandy in south Wales today following clashes yesterday between strikers from the Cambrian collieries and police "specials" sent from London. The troops had been summoned after the strikers had stoned the police. Winston Churchill, the home secretary, ordered them to wait at Cardiff overnight, but the failure of a second police force to restore order brought the soldiers under General Macready. They found the strikers silent but orderly. "We might fight the police, but not regular soldiers with rifles," said one miner (→ 26/8/11).

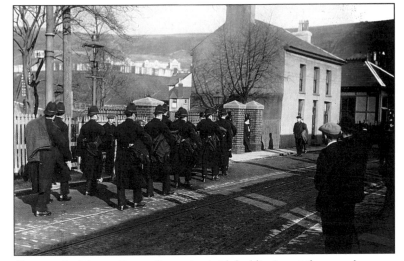

Tonypandy: Metropolitan police arrive (with bedding) as strike spreads.

Nationalism stirs Scots and Welsh

Westminster, November
The confrontation between the Commons and the Lords has effectively sidelined discussion of greater independence from Westminster for Scotland and Wales. Until recently talk of "home rule" has focused solely on Ireland, but the model of a federation in Canada was raised at the constitutional conference set up at the behest of the king which ended without success this month. Home rule for Scotland is Liberal policy, but the government does not want to embark on another constitutional clash with the Tories, who oppose the idea.

Two die as blaze ends 'anarchist' siege

Sidney Street: The home secretary, Winston Churchill, watches and waits.

London, 3 January

The siege of Sidney Street in the east end of London has ended with at least two members of an alleged "anarchist" gang being burnt to death in the house where they had been cornered by 1,000 soldiers and armed police. The gang's leader, known as "Peter the Painter", may have escaped. An unprecedented operation, personally supervised by Winston Churchill, the home secretary, was set in motion after three policemen had been murdered by the gang. Armed detectives arrived at 4am at 100 Sidney Street, just off the Mile End Road, to be met by a volley of pistol fire. One policeman was wounded.

Reinforcements included Scots Guards from the Tower of London, with a Maxim gun, and soldiers of the Royal Artillery with two 13-pounders. Pistol- and rifle-fire was poured into the house, while the anarchists replied with automatic weapons. Ten people were injured.

Smoke came from the chimney at 12.50pm, but Churchill forbade firemen to intervene. Within an hour the house was ablaze. Later two charred bodies were found (→ 18).

Tory peers bow to power of Commons

Westminster, 10 August

In the last hour before midnight, Tory peers shrank back from a last-ditch fight and, with most of them abstaining, allowed the controversial Parliament Bill to be passed by 131 votes to 114. The bill decrees that the Lords will have no legal power over money bills and will be able to hold up other measures passed by the Commons by no more than two years.

With the supremacy of the elected Commons now beyond question, MPs have agreed to reduce the maximum interval between elections from seven years to five. The Commons can thus effectively override the Lords only in the first years of a government's life, when it can claim a popular mandate.

The Tories were decisively influenced by the knowledge that, if they continued to fight, King George V would accept the list prepared by Herbert Asquith, the prime minister, and create upwards of 300 new peers who would vote for the bill.

Though much has been made of the fact that the Commons are an elected body, they are less than fully representative. There are around eight million voters in a population of over 42 million. Only six out of ten adult males have the vote, and women are still excluded from the franchise (→ 13/11).

Father and son crowned king and prince in year of pageantry

Royal occasions: King George V is crowned head of the world's greatest empire on 23 June. The following month his son, Edward Albert (known to the family as David), is invested as prince of Wales at Caernarfon Castle.

Troops and unions clash

Liverpool: 50,000 armed soldiers prepare to break riots in the north.

Liverpool, 31 August
A long hot summer of riots and strikes is ending, but only after bloody clashes between troops and trade unionists in what has been the hottest summer since 1868. Action by seamen in June sparked the wave of unrest. They won concessions which encouraged others, notably dockers who struck in several major ports. A settlement was reached in London, but the Liverpool dispute flared into serious rioting. Troops were sent, and on 15 August two men were shot dead in clashes. Two men were also killed

by troops in Llanelli, where shops and a train were looted; five more died there in an explosion.

Industrial relations were equally explosive; the railway unions rejected the prime minister's plea and called their first national strike. With the country almost at a standstill David Lloyd George took over for the government and with Labour's James Ramsay MacDonald had talks with the railmen, reaching agreement on 19 August. Deals with the dockers followed and, as temperatures fell below 32C [90F], an uneasy peace ensued (→27/12).

Sickness insurance scheme is planned

Westminster, 4 May
A national insurance scheme to protect workers against sickness and unemployment was unveiled today by David Lloyd George, the chancellor of the exchequer, as the latest chapter of the Liberal government's social reforms. Old age pensions, labour exchanges and trade boards are now to be followed by a scheme in which employers, employees and the state all pay weekly premiums into a fund for sickness and unemployment benefits. The sickness scheme will cover 15 million workers with wages below £3 a week, but the unemployment insurance will cover only 2.25 million out of 19 million workers. Both schemes are intended to be self-financing (→13/1/13).

King is crowned emperor of India

Delhi, 10 December
King George was today enthroned as emperor of India in a ceremony of great pageantry and splendour. The cabinet was unenthusiastic about the king's determination to attend today's *durbar*, but the monarch wanted to demonstrate the importance he accorded to his Indian empire. He also used the occasion to announce that the capital is to be transferred from Calcutta to Delhi, where the architect Sir Edwin Lutyens is to design imposing new buildings as symbols of British rule in what is by far the largest and most populous country in the empire (→30/3/15).

New leaders named

Westminster, 13 November
The Conservative Party today became the second party to change its leader this year. Andrew Bonar Law, aged 53, succeeds Arthur Balfour, who has resigned for health reasons. In February, James Ramsay Macdonald took over from James Keir Hardie as Labour leader. Both of the new leaders are Scots, although Bonar Law was born in Canada before being brought up in Glasgow (→25/5/15).

Carson addresses anti-home rule rally

Edward Carson: "Prepare to govern!"

Belfast, 23 September
The prospect of an Ulster Unionist backlash against home rule for Ireland came closer today with a defiant warning by Sir Edward Carson, the leader of the Irish Unionist MPs at Westminster. At a rally attended by 50,000 Ulster loyalists Sir Edward denounced home rule as "a tyranny to which we cannot submit". The Dublin-born lawyer, a former Irish solicitor-general, solemnly called on loyalists to defeat "the most nefarious conspiracy that has ever been hatched against a free people". He added: "We must be prepared ... ourselves to become responsible for the government of the Protestant province of Ulster." To cheers he said that Irish loyalists "should undertake the administration of the districts they are entitled to control" (→9/5/12).

Art without taste finds champions in Camden Town

London, December
The newly formed "Camden Town Group" of 16 painters is holding an exhibition as a breakaway from the new English Art Club. Founded by Walter Sickert, a pupil of Whistler and an admirer of Degas, the group was much influenced by the Post-Impressionist exhibition of the works of Gauguin, van Gogh and Cézanne put on in London last year by the critic Roger Fry, which was met with a furore of incomprehension.

Sickert named the group after the working-class area of north London where he set up a studio to paint what are thought "sordid" subjects – prostitutes' bedrooms, music-hall galleries and cloth-capped passers-by "going to the pub". Taste, Sickert declares, is the death of a painter; he says: "The more our art is serious, the more it will tend to avoid the drawing room and stick to the kitchen." His associates, Harold Gimna, Spencer Gore, Charles Ginner and Robert Bevan, find their subjects in cheap eating-houses, railway stations and industrial landscape. In contrast the portrait work of Augustus John is firmly traditional, although his bohemian life-style is notorious. His sister Gwen's portraits of women are ultra-restrained.

"The Café Royal" by Charles Ginner, a member of the group.

The 'unsinkable' sinks

The "unsinkable": last moments.

Newspapers report the tragedy.

North Atlantic, 15 April

The pride of British shipping, the SS *Titanic*, sank in the early hours of this morning after hitting an iceberg on her maiden voyage. More than 1,500 of the 2,340 passengers and crew aboard a liner proclaimed as "unsinkable" are feared to have drowned. If so, it would be the highest-ever death toll in a shipping disaster.

The *Titanic* was regarded as unsinkable because of her 16 watertight compartments. But as the ship sped through the icy ocean in pursuit of the fastest-ever Atlantic crossing she hit an iceberg and sank within hours. The wireless operator, Harold Bride, was one of the survivors. He described the scene as he swam for his life: "The ship was tilting gradually onto her nose, like a duck going for a dive. The band was still playing. I guess all of them went down."

Several millionaires and the managing director of the White Star line got away in the first lifeboat. Others told of swimmers being pushed away from the lifeboats as the panic mounted, and passengers who sacrificed their lives helping women and children to safety. One question for an inquiry will be why there were so few lifeboats. Another will be whether any warnings about icebergs were ignored (→18).

Welsh Church Bill gets second chance

Westminster, 16 May

Despite protests by church leaders MPs have backed a bill that would disestablish the Church of England in Wales. Herbert Asquith, the prime minister, argued that the "clear and firm" precedent of Irish disestablishment gave parliament the right to legislate in this area. He said that the bill would remove the greatest obstacle to cooperation among Christians in Wales where nonconformist chapel membership is strong. If the Lords object, as is widely expected, the new powers of the Parliament Act could enable the bill to become law in three years if it is supported each year by the Commons.

Attempts to spread the dock strike flop

London, 15 June

Attempts to turn the London dock strike which began last month into a national dispute have collapsed. The fledgeling National Transport Workers' Federation today admitted that the national strike called five days ago had failed to win support outside the capital. The Sailors' Union, the biggest union in the new group, had withheld support as signs grew that even in London there was opposition to the strike. It began over one foreman working without a union card. Over 100,000 men went on strike, but the employers took a tough stand, refusing mediation and insisting on surrender (→26/8/13).

Shops are attacked as suffragettes try more violent style

London, 1 March

Suffragettes deployed new militant tactics today as they stepped up their campaign for the vote. More than 120 women were arrested, including the suffragette leader Mrs Emmeline Pankhurst, after a series of attacks on shops in London's west end. Women, many with stones and hammers hidden in their muffs, caused thousands of pounds' worth of damage by smashing windows as they rampaged through the streets. Two women also hurled stones at No 10 Downing Street.

The attacks appear to have been well-planned, as groups of women struck almost simultaneously. Within 20 minutes a trail of devastation stretched from Oxford Street to the Strand. Swan & Edgar's store at

Suffragettes: a smashing day out.

Piccadilly Circus was one of several famous shops to be attacked. Most of the women made no attempt to elude arrest after the attacks, which signal a new phase in the suffragette campaign reflecting the increasing influence of Christabel Pankhurst. Militancy has grown as suffragettes have seen the government grant concessions to railwaymen and miners after strikes had escalated into serious public disorder. By no means all suffragette leaders agree, but the militant wing of the movement hopes that it, too, can achieve its aims through disorder (→4).

Tensions rise over Irish home rule

Ireland is promised its freedom by 1914

Westminster, 9 May

The Liberal government's attempt to meet Irish demands for home rule took a decisive step forward tonight when the Commons gave a second reading to the Home Rule Bill by 360 votes to 266. Tory MPs remained firmly opposed, and the government depended on Irish Nationalist and Labour MPs for its majority. If Tories in the Lords continue to oppose the bill, last year's Parliament Act ensures that it will still become law, and Ireland could have home rule in 1914.

The real threat to home rule lies elsewhere. The enmity between the Catholic majority in Ireland and the Protestants in Ulster has been sharpened by the prospect of home rule. In Belfast a flourishing ship-building industry has grown up in the past 50 years. It is now the biggest city in Ireland, and the merchants are at one with the workers in rejecting rule by Dublin.

Sir Edward Carson, a Dublin-born Protestant and former solicitor-general for Ireland, is planning to recruit some 80,000 armed volunteers who, he says, are ready to fight for Ulster's right to remain a province of the United Kingdom. But Herbert Asquith, the prime minister, says: "The British people, just and generous by nature, are not going to be frightened out of doing a just thing by the language of intimidation" (→ 12/7).

Ulster Day, Belfast. The signed covenant aims to stop the Home Rule Bill.

'Covenant' signed by Protestant loyalists

Belfast, 28 September

A ten-day speaking tour by Sir Edward Carson, the leader of the Ulster Unionists, reached its climax today when huge crowds queued for hours in Belfast to sign a "solemn covenant", swearing defiance against Irish home rule. In all, 471,414 signatures were collected as Ulster's self-styled "loyalists" declared their determination to stay part of the United Kingdom – some signing in their own blood.

In the words of the covenant, signatories declared that "being convinced in our consciences that home rule would be disastrous to the material well-being of Ulster, as well as the whole of Ireland" they pledged themselves as loyal subjects of the king to stand by one another in defending their equal citizenship in the United Kingdom.

The covenant threatens to use "all means which may be found necessary" to defeat home rule and, if a parliament is forced on Ulster, "to refuse to recognize its authority". Desks stretched for over 580 yards along the city hall corridors, allowing 540 people to sign simultaneously (→ 31/1/13).

Labour enters the newspaper battle

London, 15 April

First-day sales in excess of 200,000 copies were claimed in London alone today for a new national, socialist newspaper, the *Daily Herald*. Printed in London, Manchester and Glasgow, on cooperatively owned printing presses, the newspaper is edited by Charles Lapworth, who said: "We know there is a real need for a first-class socialist newspaper."

The *Herald* has a fight on its hands, however. The last 16 years have seen a revolution in popular journalism, spearheaded by Lord Northcliffe, who as Alfred Harmsworth in 1896 introduced the *Daily Mail* as the first halfpenny daily and then turned an ailing *Daily Mirror* (first published in 1903) into the first picture paper. He also bought *The Times* in 1908.

"Daily Herald": Labour's voice.

Report calls for sexual equality in divorce

London, 11 November

A royal commission today offers some encouragement to women campaigning for greater rights. It says that men and women should be treated equally by divorce laws. At present, for instance, a husband can seek a divorce on the grounds of his wife's adultery, but the wife cannot petition on the grounds of a faithless husband; she must prove additional grounds for divorce if her petition is to be granted.

The 200-page report by the royal also urges that grounds for divorce be widened to include desertion for three years, cruelty, habitual drunkenness and insanity. The report, which says that divorce should no longer be the preserve of the rich, has been welcomed by women's groups, but there is some scepticism over whether the all-male Commons will back the proposed reforms. So far they have failed to pass suffrage bills even when those have been backed by the government, the most recent defeat being by 14 votes of a "Conciliation Bill" last March (→ 5/2/13).

London's central telephone exchange: now to be run by the Post Office.

Police play 'cat and mouse' with women

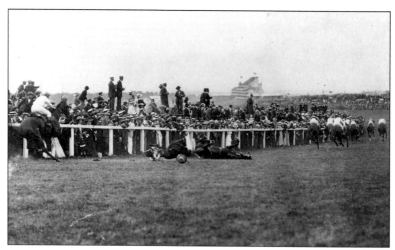

A martyr's death: Emily Davison is trampled by the king's horse, Anmer.

Plymouth, Devon, 4 December

Emmeline Pankhurst, the leader of the most militant suffragette group, was arrested here today on her return from the United States after a year of unprecedented violence by women campaigning for the vote. The last 12 months have seen:

* the death of a suffragette, Emily Davison, after she threw herself under the king's horse in the Derby at Epsom in June;

* physical attacks on the prime minister, Herbert Asquith, as he visited Scotland in August and November;

* widespread arson ranging from setting alight letters in pillar-boxes to fires at buildings including a railway station and Kew Gardens;

* the trial of Mrs Pankhurst after a bomb attack on the Surrey home of David Lloyd George, the chancellor, in February.

This new militancy followed another parliamentary rebuff when, in January, the speaker ruled a franchise bill out of order. But the recourse to more violent tactics had begun before then, largely orches-trated by one of Mrs Pankhurst's daughters, Christabel. The authorities hit back with a "Cat and Mouse" Act enabling the release of hunger-strikers so that they did not die in prison but leaving them liable to be rearrested (→ 3/1/14).

THE CAT AND MOUSE ACT
PASSED BY THE LIBERAL GOVERNMENT

THE LIBERAL CAT
ELECTORS VOTE AGAINST HIM!
KEEP THE LIBERAL OUT!

BUY AND READ 'THE SUFFRAGETTE' PRICE 1D

Poster: women's fury mounts.

Ministers exonerated in share scandal

London, 13 June

Two leading government ministers who were involved in the so-called "Marconi scandal" have today been cleared of wrongdoing, but they have emerged with their reputations badly shaken.

Last year David Lloyd George, the chancellor of the exchequer, was persuaded by his friend Sir Rufus Isaacs, the attorney-general, to buy £1,000 worth of shares in the American Marconi radio corporation.

Shortly afterwards it became known that the British Post Office was negotiating a lucrative contract with the British Marconi company. The two companies are quite separate, and the ministers have been shown to have been unaware of the British negotiations.

The 'modern' novel adds class to the literary ingredients

Britain, December

The appearance of *Sons and Lovers* has thrust the name of David Herbert Lawrence to the front in a period already rich in literary brilliance. Lawrence is the son of a Nottinghamshire miner and a middle-class mother to whom he was abnormally close. Ill-assorted parents and mother/son conflicts are at the heart of this probing of painful adolescence.

The last decade has seen the birth of the "modern" novel. Henry James, a long-established master, achieved new psychological sophistication in *The Ambassadors* (1903) and *The Golden Bowl* (1904). The sea-faring Joseph Conrad, a man's writer with none of James's feminine intuition, wrote superb studies of male strength and moral weakness in *Lord Jim* (1900), *The Secret Agent* (1907) and this year's *Chance*. He is most blackly pessimistic in *Heart of Darkness* (1902).

The new realists deliberately went down the social scale for their characters. Arnold Bennett finds his among the lower middle class of his native Potteries, as in *The Old Wives' Tale* (1908) and *The Card*, a picaresque comic novel (1911). H G Wells, the son of a housekeeper and himself a draper's apprentice, put his good-humoured observation into *Kipps* (1905) and *The History of Mr Polly* (1910).

John Galsworthy is a chronicler of the moneyed and complacent middle class with the Forsyte family of *The Man of Property* (1906). E M Forster goes more subtly into their inhibitions in *A Room With A View* (1908) and *Howards End* (1910).

Welsh pit disaster

Wales, 14 October

More than 400 miners are missing tonight after an explosion and fire ripped through a pit at Sengenhydd in the Aber valley. The blast was heard 11 miles away in Cardiff. Some 500 men escaped, but 21 bodies have been brought to the surface and a further 418 men are missing. Rescuers said tonight that there was no hope for them.

Scott of the Antarctic is found dead

Antarctica, 10 February

Captain Robert Falcon Scott and four companions have been been found dead, frozen to death just 11 miles from the safety of their camp. The five men had reached the South Pole on 17 January 1912.

Reaching the Pole was the climax of Scott's expedition, which had set off in October 1911, but even this triumph was marred when, after overcoming many difficulties, the team found that it had been beaten to its goal. A Norwegian expedition, under Roald Amundsen, had arrived one month earlier, and the Britons were greeted by evidence of their camp.

If the journey out had been hard, the return, with worsening weather, dwindling supplies, and the knowledge of being beaten, was worse. One by one Scott's men died: Petty Officer Evans on 17 February, Captain Oates a month later. Scott, Dr Wilson and Lt Bowers seem to have

The "Daily Mirror" breaks the news.

died together, around 29 March, when Scott wrote in his journal: "The end cannot be far. It seems a pity, but I do not think I can write any more."

Rioting flares in Dublin after lock-out

Dublin, 26 August

A major industrial dispute has resulted in serious rioting. Earlier this year James Larkin of the Irish Transport Workers' Union had organised the Dublin tramwaymen and other poorly paid workers in the city to demand more wages. Strikes were followed by a lock-out by the employers, resulting in violent demonstrations and clashes with the police. The strikers and their supporters have claimed that

the police acted in an aggressively brutal manner and have retaliated by forming the Irish Citizen Army for their own defence.

The army is led by J R White, an Ulster Protestant nationalist, and James Connolly who had been trying to convert the Belfast workers to socialism before being called to assist Larkin in Dublin. The spirit of the Citizen Army is seen as being close to that of revolutionary socialism (→ 30/8/18).

Ulster plots its defiance

Belfast, 23 September

The constitution of a provisional government for Ulster – to be implemented as soon as Irish home rule becomes law – was agreed today at a meeting of the Ulster Unionist Council. The standing committee of the council is to be the central authority, with Sir Edward Carson as its chairman. "We will scientifically, deliberately and carefully work out a plan which will make it impossible for a parliament in Dublin to govern this province," said Sir Edward.

The full panoply of an alternative government is being planned. In addition to a military council there will be committees for areas such as finance, education, agriculture and

the law. Sir Edward, the parliamentary leader of the Unionists, dismissed claims that the action being taken was seditious. Unionists had exhausted every means to bring the government to a real sense of the problems, he claimed, and if surrender was out of the question, what else could they do?

The council decided to raise a £1,000,000 indemnity guarantee fund for the Ulster Volunteer Force, the loyalist militia, to insure its members against loss or injury when acting on behalf of the provisional government. Ulster's resistance is alarming Irish Nationalists who fear that the province may be excluded from home rule legislation (→ 25/11).

Edward Carson: statesman or rabble rouser? It depends where you live.

Emigration soars to reach new records

British Isles, December

Emigration has now reached record levels, with over half the people seeking a new life overseas now choosing the dominions of the empire. The average total of emigrants for the last three years has been 464,000, compared with an average of 284,000 in the first decade of the century.

Although the birth-rate is also falling it is sufficient, with some immigration from Europe, to ensure that the overall population is still growing, albeit more

slowly. But the surge in emigration is having a marked effect on the average age of the people left behind. Most emigrants tend to be young, so that the boom of the last three years has exacerbated a trend towards an ageing society highlighted in the 1911 census report. This warned of the military and economic dangers of a falling proportion of "workers at the most economically efficient ages". In 1841 just under half the population was under 20; by 1911, less than a third was in this group (→ 8/4/25).

Liverpool: emigrants head for Canada on the "Empress of Britain". More and more Britons are leaving for a new life in the dominions.

Parties deadlocked over future of Ulster

London, 24 July

Leading British and Irish politicians have failed to agree on the future of Ireland at a conference held at Buckingham Palace with King George V in the chair. He has been criticised for intervening by Irish Nationalists but did so with the government's support. He told the party leaders: "For months we have watched with deep misgivings the course of events in Ireland. Today the cry of civil war is on the lips of my most responsible and sober-minded citizens."

However, the royal plea for "generous compromise" has failed to end the crisis. A home rule bill now before parliament would allow counties to vote on staying out of home rule for six years, until there had been two British general elections. Yet this has proved un-popular with both "loyalists" (who oppose the time limit) and national-ists (who oppose any exemptions).

The crisis has intensified over the last year as first Andrew Bonar Law, the Tory leader, threw his weight behind a plan to exempt Ulster from home rule, and then British Army officers had resisted moves to make them use force against Ulster. On 20 March, 57 out of 70 officers of the 3rd Cavalry Brigade based at the Curragh said that they would "prefer to accept dismissal if ordered north". Talks in London appeased them but in-furiated supporters of home rule in Britain as well as Ireland. Then in April the Larne gun-running epi-sode [*see below*] equipped the Ulster Volunteers as a fully armed force. With nationalists also arming, the stage was set for civil war (→18/9).

'Loyalists' unload gun cargo in Ulster

Larne, Co Antrim, 25 April

About 25,000 rifles and three million rounds of ammunition bound for the Ulster Volunteer Force (UVF) have been landed in at Larne to boost the campaign headed by Sir Edward Carson to keep Ulster free of Irish home rule.

The UVF took over the town for the night, severing communications and distributing the arms in 700 lorries and cars while the authorit-ies looked on helplessly. The *Clyde-valley*, a collier, also landed guns at Bangor and other Ulster ports. The gun-running coup was organized by a Boer War veteran, Col Fred Crawford. The guns, bought in Hamburg, were loaded on the 480-ton *Fanny* (described as "zinc plates") before being moved to the *Clydevalley* at sea (→24/7).

Sir Edward Carson presents colours to Unionist volunteers.

Women take their protests to palace

Palace arrest: Mrs Pankhurst held.

London, 22 May

Emmeline Pankhurst was among 57 women who were arrested today after clashing with police guarding Buckingham Palace. They were attempting to present a petition to the king in support of their cam-paign for the vote. Another fran-chise bill was defeated earlier this month as the protests by suffra-gettes continued unabated.

Some of this year's actions have alienated their own supporters, however. There have been attacks on paintings in the National Gal-lery and Royal Academy, bombs hurled at a London church and the pier at Great Yarmouth, arson at-tacks on private houses as well as public buildings. These tactics have been opposed by Emmeline Pethick Lawrence, one of the early leaders of the Women's Social and Political Union which was founded by Mrs Pankhurst (→24/2/15).

One Dubliner in five lives in tenements 'as squalid as Calcutta'

Dublin, 7 February

A major report on working-class housing in Dublin has revealed that 22 per cent of the population live in one-room tenement buildings in conditions of horrific squalor.

The Dublin housing inquiry be-gan last year in the hope of improv-ing the living conditions of the working class, and, later in the year, Dublin corporation set up a housing committee. The report has found that many houses are served by merely one tap in the yard. The basement rooms have little light or ventilation, and inspectors have found human excreta scattered about the yards and in the passages of houses. Some 118,000 people live in the Dublin tenements, and their conditions have been compared to those in Calcutta. The report ac-knowledges that the high Dublin mortality rate is a direct result of poor housing, and death from tu-berculosis is the highest of any city in the United Kingdom. It is noted that when working-class girls are live-in servants their life expect-ancy improves considerably. Spas-modic attempts have been made to improve housing conditions in the city, but without success.

Britons go to war as Europe becomes a battlefield

Bloodshed at Mons dims the euphoria

France, 31 August
Cheering crowds greeted the declaration of war against Germany on 4 August, but the reality of war became apparent last week when the British Expeditionary Force (BEF) met the Germans at the Belgian town of Mons. The military skill of the British regulars held the Germans at first, but the weight of the German offensive drove back the French, leaving the British flank exposed. The BEF, forced to abandon its positions, is now retreating with the French to the Somme, where the allies plan to halt the German rush on Paris.

It was the German advance on France through Belgium that brought Britain into a war barely a month after the heir to the Austro-Hungarian empire was assassinated by a Serbian nationalist at Sarajevo. Austria delivered a tough ultimatum to Serbia, bringing in Russia as Serbia's ally. Germany backed Austria, France backed Russia, and Britain declared war on Germany for failing to respect the neutrality of the Belgians (→ 9/9).

British troops help to rebuff Germans

France, 30 September
Paris can breathe again: the Germans have been stopped at the Marne and are retreating. It was a close-run thing, however. At one stage 600 Paris taxis were commandeered to rush troops to the front. One French general, Ferdinand Foch, under severe pressure, reported: "My centre is yielding, my right wing is giving way. An excellent situation. I attack tomorrow."

The BEF played a vital part in the battle, crossing the river into a gap between two German armies, threatening to outflank them and forcing them to abandon the battlefield. British losses have been heavy. Posters saying "Lord Kitchener wants you" posters are aimed at recruiting the 500,000 volunteers wanted by the war minister (→ 4/10).

Faces of war: British "Tommies" prepare for trench warfare in Flanders.

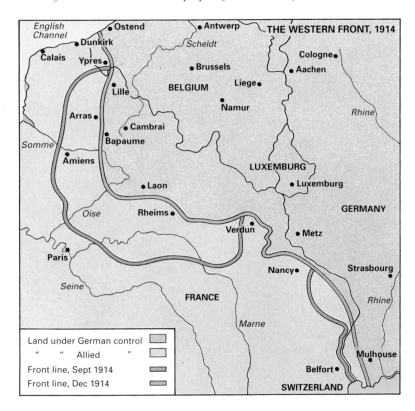

THE WESTERN FRONT, 1914

English Channel · Ostend · Antwerp · Dunkirk · Scheldt · Calais · Ypres · Cologne · Aachen · Brussels · BELGIUM · Liege · Lille · Namur · Arras · Cambrai · Bapaume · Somme · Amiens · LUXEMBURG · Laon · Luxemburg · Oise · Rheims · GERMANY · Verdun · Metz · Paris · Nancy · Strasbourg · Seine · FRANCE · Rhine · Marne · Mulhouse · Belfort · SWITZERLAND · Rhine

Land under German control
"   "   Allied   "
Front line, Sept 1914
Front line, Dec 1914

Front-line trenches dug across Europe

France, 31 October
The swirling battles of the rivers in northern France have given way to a new type of warfare, with lines of opposing trenches stretching from the sea to the Swiss border. Fierce struggles are going on for strong points along this line, with the BEF holding on to the Flanders town of Ypres. Aircraft, Zeppelins and submarines are also playing important roles. Paris has been bombed, and a U-boat has sunk three British cruisers. British airplanes have raided the Zeppelin sheds (→ 31/12).

Europe's war goes round the world

France, 30 November
While stalemate settles over the mud and barbed wire of the trenches in France the war is spreading to every part of the world. An Anglo-French fleet has bombarded the Dardanelles. The *Sydney*, an Australian cruiser, has sunk the German raider *Emden* off Sumatra. Britain has annexed Cyprus, and Russia has invaded Armenia. There is fighting also in Europe's empires. In East and West Africa British and German-led native troops have clashed, while loyal South Africans are moving against the German colony of South-west Africa (→ 31/12).

A Christmas truce, but no homecoming

France, 31 December
Soldiers who had expected to be "home for Christmas" have shocked their generals by holding a spontaneous truce in the front line, exchanging jam for cigars and playing football with the Germans before returning to their trenches. At sea the Royal Navy has won a great victory off the Falkland Islands, sinking Admiral von Spee's fleet. The German navy retaliated by shelling towns in eastern England, killing 100 people (→ 19/1/15).

Berkshire, 7 January. Severe floods hit the Thames valley and turn Windsor Castle into an island.

Norfolk, 19 January. A Zeppelin bombs Great Yarmouth and King's Lynn (→ 22/4).

France, 24 February. One thousand British suffragettes arrive for war work (→ 10/11).

London, 30 March. King George V offers to give up alcohol as example to munitions workers (→ 28/10).

Western front, 22 April. Germany introduces a new weapon – poison gas (→ 8/5).

Turkey, 26 April. On the day that Britain, France and Italy sign a secret war treaty, Allied troops land at Gallipoli (→ 20/12).

London, 13 May. Kaiser William is stripped of the Order of the Garter by his cousin, the king.

Britain, 13 May. Street violence against "suspect" aliens follows the sinking of the Lusitania.

Ghent, 8 June. Flight Sub-Lieutenant Reginald Warneford wins a Victoria Cross for bringing down a Zeppelin with bombs (→ 15/12).

London, 1 July. The "brides-in-the-bath" killer George Smith is to be hanged for the murders of three bigamous wives.

Wiltshire, 21 September. Prehistoric Stonehenge is auctioned for the knockdown price of £6,600.

Britain, 13 October. "Treating" – buying drinks for others – is banned to try to deter excessive drinking by industrial workers.

France, 28 October. King George is badly bruised by falling from his horse while inspecting troops,

London, 6 November. Police raid offices of The Globe newspaper after its false reports on Lord Kitchener, claiming he had resigned.

Britain, 10 November. A survey shows that women war workers have enabled factories to increase production by up to two and a half times (→ 31/12).

France, 15 December. Sir Douglas Haig replaces Sir John French as commander of British forces in Europe in a shake-up of Allied commands (→ 31/12).

War changes life on the home front

Women fill men's roles in the factories

Britain, 31 December
Women are playing an increasingly important part in the war effort, filling the gap left by the men at the front. As clerks, bus conductors, farm hands or industrial workers, over a million more women are now working full-time. Not only are women doing work they have never done before – most visibly in transport, most significantly in engineering factories – but they may be doing it better than men: a survey indicates that some munitions factories are now two-and-a-half times more productive with women workers. And they have been backed by the suffragettes. Christabel Pankhurst led a Whitehall march in July demanding women's "right to serve" and, for possibly the first time in her life, the authorities welcomed her presence (→ 1/1/16).

Home front: women take over.

Political parties in wartime coalition

Westminster, 25 May
The scandal of the shell shortage on the western front has today forced Herbert Asquith, the Liberal prime minister, to agree to a coalition cabinet in which 13 Liberals are joined by eight Tories and one Labour minister.

The grave situation facing British troops in France because of the lack of high-explosive shells was exposed by the Daily Mail. Copies of the paper were burned by scandalised stockbrokers in the City. But a shaken government has had to respond, and Lloyd George has been appointed to a new ministry of munitions. Lord Northcliffe, the Mail's owner, is being attacked by the Liberal press but says he welcomes the advertising (→ 7/12/16).

Germany threatens an unlimited naval blockade of Britain

"Lusitania" propaganda starts.

Queenstown, Co Cork, 8 May
The giant luxury liner Lusitania had just sighted land when two torpedoes struck. Twenty-one minutes later she reared up and slid under the waves, taking 1,200 passengers and crew, including women and children, with her. This was the latest move by Germany in its submarine blockade of Britain after Britain's unsuccessful attempt at a naval blockade of Germany.

The casualties included 128 Americans, among them the multi-millionaire Alfred Vanderbilt and several close friends of President Woodrow Wilson. Most of the survivors brought ashore at Kinsale were too exhausted to talk, although one Canadian journalist said that he had seen the U-boat's

conning tower and a torpedo heading for the ship.

The savagery of this latest attack has brought universal condemnation of Germany in Britain and the United States. In Washington – where the German ambassador took newspaper space to warn Americans not to sail on the Lusitania last week – the former president Theodore Roosevelt condemned the sinking as an "act of piracy". The Wilson government's neutrality policy is certain to be reviewed.

In Liverpool, the ship's home port, serious rioting has broken out and no German shop is safe. Within hours of the news reaching London, well-dressed people crowded Cunard's offices in Cockspur Street for news of relatives (→ 8/6).

More than 200 soldiers die in Britain's worst-ever train crash

Dumfries and Galloway, 22 May
Over 200 officers and men of the 7th Royal Scots were killed today when a crowded troop train was one of five involved in a multiple collision at Quintinshill, near Gretna, ten miles (16km) north of Carlisle. Errors by signalmen are

thought to have been responsible for the highest death toll in British railway history.

The southbound troop train crashed into a local train standing at Quintinshill shortly before 7am today. Its coaches were crushed, and as survivors struggled to escape

it was hit by an express travelling north. Two other trains also waiting at Quintinshill were now entangled in the wreckage, which was swept by fire as the cylinders of the gas-lit troop train ignited. The final death toll is not known, but is feared to be 225 or more (→ 1/1/23).

Death and destruction as war encircles the globe

The beaches at Gallipoli: high hopes and then disaster for the Allies.

France: makeshift gas masks for French troops as a new weapon is born.

Gallipoli: Allies retreat from disaster

Gallipoli, 20 December

The Allies stole away from Suvla Bay and Anzac Cove on Gallipoli last night without losing a single man. The evacuation was carried out with great ingenuity. During the day the Turks could see reinforcements and stores being unloaded, but when darkness fell thousands of men, mules and guns were lifted off the beaches. They left behind rifles set to fire at intervals. At the last moment a destroyer trained its searchlight on the trenches, the Turks opened fire on the ship and, under the cover of their barrage, the allied rearguard finally slipped away.

It only remains for the men at Cape Helles to be evacuated for this whole sorry Gallipoli adventure to be ended. It is a story of bad luck, muddle, indecision – and the outstanding heroism of the soldiers on all sides of whom, for the Allies, a high proportion were Australians and New Zealanders.

The expedition was born out of a wish to circumvent the deadlock on the western front and to assist Russia by knocking Turkey out of the war and opening up a supply route across the Black Sea. At first it was thought that seapower alone could force the Dardanelles, but the loss of three battleships sunk and three crippled in the Turkish minefields ended that hope.

The expeditionary force landed on 25 April. On some beaches the men came ashore virtually unopposed, but at Sedd-el-Bahr the British soldiers walked into a wall of fire and died in their thousands. They hung on, their bravery matched only by the blunders of their commanders. Some generals have been sacked, and it seems impossible that Winston Churchill, judged responsible for the débâcle, can keep his post at the admiralty.

Europe: stalemate brings army changes

France, 31 December

Stalemate has settled over the frozen mud of the trenches which run from Ostend to the Swiss frontier. Their line has hardly changed despite the bloody fighting and appalling casualties which have marked this year.

The great offensives of September, with the British attacking at Loos in support of the French assault in Artois, which were brought to an end by bad weather in mid-October achieved little on the ground. The fighting cost the British 60,000 casualties to the Germans' 20,000, while the French lost 100,000 to 120,000.

Nowhere have the Allies made progress. The Gallipoli expedition has been abandoned [*see report left*]. General Townshend has been beaten back from Baghdad and shut up in Kut. The Italians, who entered the war on 24 May, failed in their offensives against the Austrians. The Russians have suffered a terrible defeat at the hands of General Falkenhayn at Gorlice. Serbia has been overrun.

The sense of failure at the lack of progress after 16 months of war is reflected in changes at the top of the Allied command. General Joffre was made commander-in-chief of the French army at the beginning of December, and Sir Douglas Haig replaced the ineffectual Sir John French as commander of the British forces on the western front. At the same time Haig's chief of staff and friend, Sir William Robertson, who rose from the ranks to become a general, has been made Chief of the Imperial General Staff.

These appointments reflect the disappointment felt in Whitehall at Lord Kitchener's conduct of the war, and his position as war secretary is at risk. More is expected of the new team (→ 6/1/16).

Victims of the war fought to end all wars

The British nurse Edith Cavell (l), accused of spying, died "bravely" in front of a German firing squad; the poet Rupert Brooke (r), the romantic symbol of his age, died of an infection while travelling to the Dardanelles.

Nationalists stage an 'Easter Rising'

Hundreds die after republic is declared

Dublin, 29 April

An insurrection led by the Irish Republican Brotherhood has taken place in Dublin, leaving 450 dead and nearly 3,000 wounded. The main instigators of the rising five days ago on Easter Monday were Arthur Griffith, the founder of Sinn Féin; Thomas James Clarke, a leader of the Irish Republican Brotherhood; James Connolly, the founder of the Irish Citizen Army; and Patrick Pearse, a schoolmaster from the Gaelic League. Pearse has been influenced by the cult of violence which has spread through Europe in the past 20 years.

The insurgents were forced to use their meagre resources to the best effect, and plans were laid to get arms and ammunition from Germany, with the help of Sir Roger Casement, the Irish-born British diplomat. Although the British authorities suspected that a rebellion was imminent, the events of this Easter Rising seem to have taken them completely by surprise.

Unfortunately for the insurgents the ship bringing arms was captured and Casement taken prisoner on 21 April. Despite this setback, the Rising went ahead. The holiday crowds paid little attention to the

British troops man a barricade in Talbot Street during the rebellion.

columns of soldiers marching down O'Connell Street on Easter Monday morning. Without opposition they took possession of the General Post Office where they set up their headquarters.

From the steps in front of the building Pearse read a proclamation declaring the establishment of a republic and the constitution of a provisional government.

Many British officers had been given leave to attend a race meeting, and there were only 1,200 troops in the city. By the time that the authorities realized what was

happening, the insurgents had captured almost the whole of the centre of Dublin and established a cordon of fortified posts in the suburbs. But as soon as reinforcements began to arrive, armed with heavy artillery, the hopelessness of the insurgents' position became apparent. The General Post Office caught fire and was evacuated, leaving many dead. After five days of bloodshed the rebellion effectively ended today when Pearse and Connolly offered their unconditional surrender. But harsh reprisals now seem certain to begin (→1/5).

Roger Casement is hanged for treason

London, 3 August

Roger Casement, the Irish-born former British diplomat, was received into the Roman Catholic Church and hanged today in Pentonville prison. Regarded in Ireland as a patriot and humanitarian, he had sought aid for the Irish cause in Germany but had returned, disillusioned, in April to try to stop what he saw as a futile insurrection. However, he was arrested, found guilty of treason and sentenced to death. Intense efforts were made for his reprieve, but circulation of his "black diaries" by the prosecution (with the tacit approval of the cabinet) revealing his homosexuality damaged him further and made his reprieve impossible (→23/12).

Casement: guns for Sinn Féin.

Leaders of 'Easter Rising' executed

Dublin, 12 May

The British military authorities said today that James Connolly had been executed. This means that all seven men who signed the proclamation of an Irish republic are now dead. They were tried by courts martial set up by the military forces now running Ireland under martial law. Augustine Birrell, the chief secretary for Ireland, has resigned. Fifteen of the captured leaders of the insurgence have been shot by firing squads. Feelings against Britain are running high, even among many out of sympathy with the revolt, with the insurgents widely regarded as martyrs (→29/6).

Victory remains elusive as the bloodshed worsens

Single men will be conscripted for war

Westminster, 6 January

The Commons today gave their backing to the controversial Conscription Bill making armed service compulsory for single men between the age of 18 and 41, by 403 votes to 103. The Liberal Party was not as divided as Herbert Asquith, the prime minister, had feared, although Sir John Simon is resigning as home secretary.

Until now volunteers have been relied on to fill the ranks. In the early months of the war there was a fervent response to the recruiting posters of Kitchener's pointing finger and the appeal of the slogan "Your King and Country Need You!" Other registration and recruitment schemes followed, leading some 2.3 million men to enlist by the beginning of this year.

But there are still more men of military age outside the services, and numbers entering the army have fallen. Many civilians have failed medical tests, and some have been granted exemptions because of important war work at home. However, this has not necessarily spared them from abuse from the self-appointed "Order of the White Feather". Provision is to be made under the new bill for conscientious objectors to do noncombatant work such as driving ambulances (→ 5/3).

The great battle of the Dreadnoughts: HMS "Warspite" at Jutland.

Rival navies each claim victory at Jutland

North Sea, 31 May

A huge area of the North Sea was awash with hundreds of bodies of young British and German sailors tonight after what has been described as the "greatest sea battle in history". Both sides claim victory in the battle at Jutland: the Germans speak of the "destruction of the British Fleet", while the Royal Navy insists that it has routed the imperial German fleet.

The German commander, Grand Admiral Scheer, was determined to destroy at least part of the British fleet which was successfully blockading German ports. The British had the advantage of knowing the German codes, and Vice-Admiral David Beatty succeeded in luring the enemy into the gunsights of the rest of the British fleet commanded by Admiral Sir John Jellicoe.

German ships suffered more hits than the British – the guns of HMS *Queen Mary* and *Invincible* were still shooting with "commendable accuracy" when the ships blew up. Poor design and lack of magazine protection are blamed for the British losses. Britain is reported to have lost one battleship, one battle cruiser, five destroyers and 6,907 men. German losses include a battleship, a cruiser and a destroyer plus 2,545 men (→ 6/6).

War raises price of bread – and of sex

London, 3 November

Britain's bakers faced allegations of profiteering today after raising the price of bread to tenpence [4p] a loaf. The country's poorest families are complaining that the new price will deprive them of their staple diet at a time of particular hardship, and the government is also concerned about bakers increasing profits – knowing that prices are likely to be frozen by law following a report by a commission on wheat imports. Trade unionists have protested in their thousands in London's Hyde Park about increased food prices, and the government is proposing a meatless day once a week in the hope of reducing them.

While the price of food is arousing concern on the home front, the price of sexual promiscuity is alarming doctors after an apparent increase in syphilis, with over 50,000 cases reported among servicemen. Doctors are to help to provide diagnostic tests and drugs in the hope of combating disease, and a royal commission has been set up to examine the problem. Prostitutes "who haunt the camps of the men in training" are blamed by Dr Mary Scharlieb, a specialist in sexual diseases. Young men "overflowing with animal strengths and spirits" are easy prey, she adds (→ 2/5/17).

YOUR KING & COUNTRY NEED YOU

A WEE 'SCRAP O' PAPER' IS BRITAIN'S BOND.

TO MAINTAIN THE HONOUR AND GLORY OF THE BRITISH EMPIRE

Sign up: a new recruiting poster.

'Tank' powers to success in its first foray on the battlefield

France, 15 September

A new weapon which could break open the deadlock of trench warfare was used today with startling results. Codenamed "the tank", this armoured monster rolled over the muddy battlefield of the Somme on its tracks, spitting bullets and spreading panic through the German lines. Some German soldiers fled shouting: "The Devil is coming." Within two hours the attacking British and Canadian troops had gained all their objectives and taken more than 2,000 prisoners. Open country was reached, but the reserves could not get up in time to exploit the tank's success (31/10).

British and German tanks clash in one of the first battles of machines.

Slaughter at the Somme: the army's worst days

By the end of day one, 19,000 were dead; four months later, 420,000 men were lost – and two miles were gained

The Somme, 15 November

The slaughter on the Somme is subsiding in the mud which drowns the wounded, makes attack impossible and has brought the exhausted soldiers to the very limit of endurance. The casualties are beyond belief. The British Army's dead and injured total 420,000 men; the French have lost 200,000, the Germans 450,000. At Verdun, where the French have withstood ten months of German attacks, both sides have lost some 400,000 men.

The German onslaught at Verdun drew French strength away from the Somme offensive, and, far from being the battering ram which would break through the German fortifications and bring victory to the Allies, it became a long-drawn-out battle of attrition.

The Germans were well aware that the "Big Push" was coming. They gathered huge stocks of ammunition and sat in their comfortable deep bunkers waiting for the storm to break over them. It came in the form of an artillery barrage which lasted for five days, thus destroying the last vestiges of surprise but not the German bunkers.

When the barrage lifted at breakfast time on 1 July, the Germans raced up ladders to their machine

The devastated Somme landscape: a muddy, bloody battlefield, and burial ground, in a war that seems endless.

guns to greet the men of Haig's new army advancing in extended lines, their bayonets fixed, each man carrying his personal kit and weapons along with grenades and mortar bombs. The minimum load carried by any man that hot summer morning was 30 kilograms (66 pounds).

Thirteen divisions went "over the top". It is said that some men kicked footballs as they advanced. They were scythed down by the German machine guns playing along the lines as the Allies advanced. At the

end of that first day 19,000 men lay dead and 57,000 were wounded – the greatest loss in a single day ever suffered by a British army.

The few gains that were made were mostly lost by bad communications and slowness in exploiting the success. On 3 July Haig reopened the attack, but the guns had little ammunition, the losses had weakened the attackers, and that night rain turned the battlefield into a quagmire, making advance impossible.

On 17 July General Rawlinson

tried a new tactic, a night attack, and succeeded in punching a gap in the German line; but once again the success was not followed up. The same thing happened when tanks were introduced. Their breakthrough was not exploited.

So this bloody slogging match continued into the autumn. The British sacrifice saved the French at Verdun, but Haig's new army died on the Somme, and with it died the idealism of men who had marched so eagerly to war (→ 31/12).

Lloyd George to be new prime minister

Westminster, 7 December

After months of relentless criticism in the press and in parliament, and much behind-the-scenes intrigue, Herbert Asquith has resigned as prime minister and has been replaced tonight by David Lloyd George, the war secretary, with a commitment to wage all-out war against Germany. He takes over with strong support from hawks on

the Tory back benches. Some Liberal colleagues of Lloyd George are persuaded that he has been conspiring with the Tories to oust Asquith. The new premier intends to replace the committee of 20 ministers which has been overseeing the war with a small action group of four or five ministers. He will work closely with the Tory leader, Andrew Bonar Law (→ 7/8/17).

Deadlock in west, Russia split in east

France, 31 December

The third Christmas of the war has passed without optimism. Nothing seems able to break the deadlock on the western front, where the slaughter continues, with both sides committed to a process of attrition.

The Russian army is riddled with revolutionaries. The czar's confidant, Rasputin, has been murdered, and there is fear that the army will

collapse, freeing Germany's eastern army for service on the western front.

There is, however, a prospect of change. Three weeks ago the silver-tongued David Lloyd George was appointed, after much high-level intrigue, to succeed Herbert Asquith as prime minister. He has promised a more vigorous prosecution of the war (→ 4/1/17).

1917

U-boat attacks push America into war

Washington, DC, 6 April
The United States entered the war today as President Wilson signed the war resolution passed by large majorities in congress. He told them that this was a war "to make the world safe for democracy".

Ironically, Wilson was re-elected last year as the "man who kept us out of the war". It all changed on 1 February when Germany began unrestricted submarine warfare, causing heavy losses to US ships. A German telegram was also decoded revealing an attempt to persuade Mexico to attack the US to recover lost territory. America has already made a huge contribution by financing the Allies and manufacturing armaments, but its army will not be ready for months. Germany hopes to win the war first (→ 16).

August: newly arrived US troops dip their flags to the king and queen.

Air 'aces' give new dimension to warfare

France, 31 December
The war now being fought in the air has developed more rapidly than any previous form of warfare. Three years ago flimsy unarmed planes were used only for reconnaissance. Today daring aviators known as "aces", flying fighters equipped with twin machine guns, are popular heroes. Various types of aircraft spot for artillery, take photographs, bomb and "strafe" the trenches, take off from ships and drop torpedoes. Long-range bombers drop their deadly loads on munitions factories and marshalling yards. The air has become increasingly important for fighting wars. Bombing has also become a means of terrorizing nations, bringing the horror of war into the homes of civilians (→ 1/4/18).

War in the air: a German fighter finally downs Captain Albert Ball VC.

Convoys tackle the U-boat challenge

Western Approaches, 1 June
A large convoy of merchant ships protected by Royal Navy warships sailed into British waters today after an incident-free voyage from Gibraltar. Another convoy is due shortly from the United States. Naval experts believe that the convoy system is the answer to German submarines which have claimed thousands of tons of Allied shipping since the Battle of Jutland last year when Germany began trying to blockade Britain and France.

U-boats sank more than a hundred ships last month. Bitter rows have taken place in the war cabinet and the admiralty on how best to protect British ships. Royal Navy personnel wearing civilian clothing are taking a toll of U-boats as crews of "Q-ships" – merchantmen which lure U-boats to the surface before opening their gun-ports at the last possible moment (→ 14/6).

Irish hunger striker dies in Dublin jail

Dublin, 30 September
Around 40,000 Dubliners today defied the British government by turning out on the streets of the city to attend the funeral of Thomas Ashe, one of the leaders of the Irish Republican Brotherhood. He died five days ago in Mountjoy prison while on hunger strike, following an attempt by the prison authorities to feed him forcibly.

Many of the mourners followed the hearse to Glasnevin cemetery. They included a large contingent of Volunteers and members of the Irish Citizen Army led by Countess Markievicz, a member of a Protestant family, who had fought in the Rising. A volley of shots was fired over the grave, and Michael Collins, a militant leader of Sinn Féin, delivered an oration.

Ashe's arrest was one of a number carried out in an attempt to curb the increasing membership of Sinn Féin and the Volunteers. He led a campaign for prisoner-of-war status, and when this was refused he and 29 others went on hunger strike. The forcible feeding caused widespread revulsion (→ 27/10).

British troops stuck in Flanders mud

Flanders, 20 August

Field Marshal Haig's great offensive, designed to break out of the Ypres salient, drive to the Belgian coast and then roll up the entire German front, is foundering in the mud of Flanders.

Haig's enthusiasm for this offensive, which he is convinced will win the war, wore down the doubters in the war cabinet, but when he launched the assault on 31 July it was proved once again that the essential initial breakthrough could not be made against German machine gunners in well-protected bunkers by the old way of bombardment followed by "over the top" attacks.

Rain lashed the battlefield, and the bombardment of over four million shells from 3,000 guns broke up the network of streams and dykes on which the Flanders drainage system depends.

The attackers struggled forward up to their waists in mud; men who fell off the duckboards which were laid across the morass drowned under the weight of their equipment. Guns and horses sank irretrievably; tanks could not be used.

At the British HQ Haig remains calmly optimistic and speaks of "successful operations by our troops" and "the capture of a series

British troops struggle knee-deep in Flanders mud to save a comrade.

of strong points and fortified farms" but then concedes that the actual ground gained can be measured in "a few hundred yards".

The French, operating on the flank of the British offensive, are having far more success. They have learnt new methods of trench warfare and are moving forward in loose storming parties, taking advantage of the ground and shell-holes, unlike the British attempts at parade-ground precision. The soldiers also have a new enemy as well as the mud and machine guns –

aeroplanes, having been used for reconnaissance, are now being used for the first time as flying artillery, swooping over the battlefield to bomb and machine-gun the enemy. Dogfights rise over the lines watched by soldiers envious of the pilots who, if they survive, fly back to good meals and clean sheets.

Down below, as the fighting builds towards a bloody climax in the morass around the Belgian village of Passchendaele, Haig is confident that the enemy may collapse "at any moment" (→ 13/4/18).

British troops capture Jerusalem as Ottoman Empire crumbles

London, 9 December

Jerusalem was captured today by the British Army under the command of General Edmund Allenby. It was the climax of an offensive begun on 31 October with an attack on Gaza and Beersheba, and it reverses the defeat which Britain suffered at Gaza last spring.

The Turks have now withdrawn northwards. General Allenby expects to resume the attack in the spring, together with the Arab armies moving up to the east. Baghdad was captured last March, and the 600-year-old Ottoman Empire – from Turkey to Mesopotamia – is clearly on its last legs.

The British and French governments proposed a "national home for the Jews" in Palestine last month, and the capture of Jerusalem was a necessary first step in that direction (→ 25/4/20).

Men of the Hampshire Regiment march into Baghdad in triumph.

Government wields draconian powers

Britain, 31 December

The year is coming to a gloomy end tonight, with the war seemingly no closer to an end. Despite the success of the convoy system, food remains in short supply and strict rationing is in force. Never has a democratic British government taken such draconian powers. Individuals can be interned without trial; and now manpower is being conscripted – except, as yet, from Ireland – equally for war work at home or for fighting on the western front (→ 22/1/18).

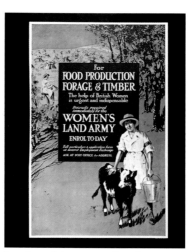
Land work is war work today.

Lords debate the 'sale of honours'

Westminster, 7 August

A controversial king's birthday honours list, drawn up by the prime minister, David Lloyd George, provoked an indignant debate in the House of Lords today, with peers complaining that the many honours acquired simply by making donations to party funds had become a national scandal.

Lloyd George was not mentioned by name, though it is widely accepted that he is building up a secret fund in readiness for the general election after the war. The Earl of Selbourne, however, insisted that Tories as well as Liberals "are tarred with the same brush". He said that every recommendation for an honour should be accompanied by a declaration that no money or favour was involved (→ 28/12/18).

Germans launch strong spring offensive

One last effort: the Germans launch a surprise spring offensive at Villers.

Lille, France, 13 April
Field Marshal Sir Douglas Haig has issued a personal call to all ranks of the British Army in the face of General von Ludendorff's offensive. It says: "Every position must be held to the last man: there must be no retirement. With our backs to the wall and believing in the justice of our cause, each one of us must fight on to the end."

The German commander, bolstered by 70 divisions released by the withdrawal of Russia from the war, launched his offensive against the junction of the British and French armies on the Somme on 21 March. His plan is to drive the Allies out of the war before the fresher American armies arrive.

Ludendorff used new tactics: there was a short "hurricane" bombardment, then small parties of shock troops probed the line for weak spots. Advancing under cover of fog, they left strong points to be dealt with later. The British line was deeply penetrated, and the Germans quickly advanced 40 miles (64km). Now his attack has been switched to Flanders; the Allies have their backs to the wall (→ 8/8).

Flying aces win an independent air force

Britain, 1 April
A third arm of the British armed forces was born today with the creation of the Royal Air Force. It has been formed by merging the Royal Flying Corps and the Royal Naval Air Service into a new body independent of both the army and the navy. An air ministry in London will be the equivalent of the war office and the admiralty, with Lord Rothermere, the newspaper tycoon, as its first head and Major-General Hugh Trenchard as the first RAF chief of staff.

Aviation has been transformed by the war. Initially used for reconnaissance, planes are now deployed to attack troops, supply lines and towns. In 1914 Britain had barely 100 planes; by the end of this year it will have more than 22,000. German raids on Britain aroused vociferous calls for revenge attacks. Last year this popular cry received high-powered backing in a report by Jan Smuts, the South African defence minister who joined the British war cabinet in June 1917. He argued that given enough aeroplanes air power alone could win the war. As the toll of casualties in the ground war mounted endlessly, the Smuts report was seized upon by politicians and paved the way for the birth of the RAF (→ 9/12/19).

Sinn Féin banned and leaders seized

Ireland, 18 May
In an attempt to curb the growing power of the Irish revolutionary movement, the British government has proclaimed Sinn Féin and the Volunteers to be illegal organizations and arrested many of their leaders, including Eamon de Valera and Arthur Griffith. All public meetings are also to be banned.

During the past year Sinn Féin, the political wing of the revolutionary movement, has been strengthened by many new members, mostly the internees and prisoners who had taken part in the 1916 Rising and who were released as a gesture of goodwill by Lloyd George. Sinn

De Valera at a Sinn Féin rally.

Féin candidates have been successful in two recent by-elections.

The intention of the government to extend military conscription to Ireland has encountered fierce opposition across the political spectrum, but it is Sinn Féin, as the diehard opponent of British rule, which is benefiting most from the furore. De Valera is the best-known of the leaders arrested today. He fought in the Rising and was sentenced to death but later reprieved. As a Sinn Féin candidate he was returned for East Clare with a huge majority and later replaced Griffith as leader of Sinn Féin. He was also elected president of the Irish Volunteers and thus exercises authority over the movement's military and political wings (→ 20/6).

Allied counter-attack cuts deep into German lines

France, 8 August

The Allies today launched a great offensive against Ludendorff's army south-east of Amiens. Led by 420 fighting tanks and 120 supply tanks, and covered by swarms of RAF aircraft, British, Canadian, Australian, French and fresh US troops have inflicted a stunning defeat on the German army.

At last the lessons have been learnt. Surprise and secrecy were the watchwords. Low-flying aircraft drowned the noise of the tanks moving forward, and at first light they carried out pre-emptive attacks on German airfields.

The movement of the Canadians into the battle area was concealed by fake wireless traffic. A few tanks drove backwards and forwards to draw attention to the wrong area. Ammunition dumps were camouflaged, and the guns were registered without being fired.

The attack opened before dawn with 1,000 guns laying down a creeping barrage. Just 182 metres (200 yards) behind the shells came the tanks in groups of three, followed by small columns of infantry. The tanks crushed the wire; the infantry dealt with the pillboxes.

The Germans, worn out by the failure of their own spring offensive and demoralized by news of hunger, rioting and strikes at home, collapsed under the surprise and ferocity of the attack.

By midday, when the morning mist had burnt off, the battlefield had become a highway, with infantry, cavalry and field artillery going east and parties of prisoners moving west. The heavy guns have ceased firing because their targets have retreated out of range.

One Whippet tank wiped out a German battery and then caught a party of soldiers packing their kit. It then shot up many columns of retreating Germans before it was put out of action. The Canadians have destroyed two divisions; the Australians have virtually wiped out another. Tonight the Allies are in open country, eight miles in front of their start line. It remains to be seen if the breakthrough will be exploited, but there is no doubt that, in Ludendorff's words, this has been "a black day for the German army" (→ 11/11).

Disarmed German prisoners.

Lawrence leads the Arabs into Damascus

Lawrence: inspired the Arab revolt.

Cairo, 1 October

The Arab forces of Emir Feisal have entered Damascus. On horse and camel they poured into the city, like their ancestors in the days of the *caliphs*. Major T E Lawrence, who inspired and guided the Arab revolt, arrived in an armoured car.

They had fought their way up from Medina, where Shereef Hussein, Feisal's father, had proclaimed the revolt in June 1916. General Allenby won a crushing victory over the Turks in Palestine last month and is driving them in rout to Anatolia. They abandoned Damascus, and General Allenby allowed the Arabs the honour of liberating it. The British will now take over the city. The French, who have been promised a post-war mandate over Syria, were not consulted.

Ireland reprieved from conscription

Dublin, 20 June

The government has bowed to widespread protests against plans to extend conscription to Ireland, but it also anounced today the postponement of home rule. Nationalist opinion in Ireland has swung towards the militant Sinn Féin, with the British relying increasingly on military force (→ 21/1/19).

U-boat sinks Irish mailboat: 587 die

Irish Sea, 10 October

The war ended early and horrifically for 587 passengers on the Irish mailboat *Leinster* today when she sank after being torpedoed by a U-boat off the Irish coast. Only four days ago two liners, one of them a US troopship, collided off the Scottish coast, killing 430 people, most of them servicemen.

Guns fall silent on Armistice day

Compiègne, France, 11 November

After four years and three months, and upwards of ten million dead, the guns have fallen silent. Two German generals and a Catholic politician put their signatures to an armistice document shortly before dawn today in a railway carriage in the forest of Compiègne. Six hours later, at 11am on the eleventh day of the eleventh month, all fighting ceased on the battlefields.

The end came more swiftly than the Allies had expected. As late as the end of September the British, the French and the newly arrived Americans were planning a campaign in 1919. But General Erich von Ludendorff panicked when an Allied offensive, spearheaded by British troops, drove into the German lines. He collapsed foaming at the mouth and then begged Kaiser William to seek an armistice immediately.

Germany must hand over 5,000 heavy guns, 30,000 machine guns, 2,000 warplanes and all U-boats. The Germans must pay for Allied occupation of the Rhineland (→ 19).

Peace at last: members of the 6th Infantry celebrate the Armistice.

How the Great War transformed Britain

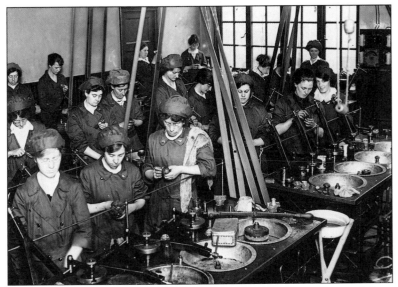

British women were fully employed backing the war effort. Many of them worked in factories, such as those seen here working in a lens factory.

Britain, 11 November
Church bells rang out at 11am today as war-weary Britain celebrated peace. The "Great War" was over, at last. Three-quarters of a million men from Britain – plus a further 200,000 from the empire – have been killed and 1.5 million seriously injured. The conflict has also transformed Britain, forging a sense of national identity out of adversity which is today erupting in a tidal wave of joy.

The authority of the state is now greater than ever, with emergency powers, state intervention in industry and controls over food and pub licensing hours. Trade unions and women's groups gained ground by backing the war effort. Labour politicians served in the coalition government and trade unions have joined "Whitley councils" to plan post-war industries. Women have worked in their millions and won the vote, at least for those over 30.

Rising prices and food shortages eroded some gains of higher wages ("meat every day" was one recruiting slogan), but overall it was a time of full employment and overtime bonuses. Gambling, smoking and movies boomed, with Charlie Chaplin the undisputed star.

Lloyd George wins the 'coupon election'

Westminster, 28 December
David Lloyd George has won his first general election as prime minister and the first in which women could vote after their years of often violent campaigning.

Lloyd George, the wartime coalition premier, has been returned in power with an overwhelming Commons majority. Within days, almost, of the war ending he called the election and asked the people to vote for those Liberal and Conservative candidates who received his letter – or "coupon" as Herbert Asquith, the former prime minister, called it – of endorsement.

It soon became known as the "coupon election", and now Lloyd George has the support of 478 MPs.

The opposition has 229 MPs, of whom 63 are Labour. Asquith has lost his seat, as have two leading Labour figures, Arthur Henderson and James Ramsay MacDonald.

The first general election for eight years was also the first in which any women could vote. Years of war work by women finally won the vote where pre-war suffragette protests had failed. In addition to women over 30, all men over 21 were given the vote, almost trebling the size of the electorate. One women was elected: Countess Markievicz for a Dublin constituency. But as a Sinn Féin Nationalist she refuses to take the oath of allegiance to the king and will not take her seat in the house (→ 21/3/21).

Children to stay at school till 14

Westminster, December
A higher school-leaving age and new responsibilities for local authorities in child welfare are the first fruits of legislation designed to introduce social reforms after the war. The Education Act makes school compulsory under the age of 14 (compared with 13) and encourages local authorities to develop a system stretching from nursery schools to evening classes.

A further boost to the powers of local authorities, as long as they have the money, came with a Maternity and Child Welfare Act, also passed this year. This enables councils to expand provision of school meals, welfare clinics and ante-natal services. A ministry of health is likely to be formed next year.

Spanish flu takes its toll of Britons

Nov 20. Preparing to disinfect London's buses in the Spanish flu epidemic which has killed thousands – even returning troops.

London bobbies down their truncheons

August 30. London policemen went on strike for the first time today. Some prisoners were taken to court in taxis rather than Black Marias, but fears of a widespread crime wave have not yet materialized. Bus drivers helped to keep the traffic moving by doing point duty at busy junctions. More than 2,000 police officers marched to Tower Hill where a rally backed their claims for more money and the reinstatement of a man dismissed for his allegedly political activities. Underlying the dispute, though, is a demand for union recognition. Trade unions have grown significantly during the war – from 4,145,000 members in 1914 to 6,533,000 in 1918 – but this is the first time that working-class solidarity has shown itself in forces previously used to keep union disputes in order (→ 28/1/19).

Women vote at last – at least some do

The clerks seem more interested in the camera than the nurses at the ballot box as women over 30 are allowed to vote in an election for the first time.

Co Sligo, 15 January. The municipal elections are the first in Britain or Ireland to use proportional representation.

Britain, 28 January. Over 200,000 workers are on strike in many industries, including coal-mining (→ 31).

Glasgow, 31 January. A sheriff is hit by a bottle as he reads the Riot Act during clashes between demonstrators and police; 40 people are seriously injured (→ 11/2).

London, 9 February. The first air service to Paris is inaugurated (→ 15/6).

Glasgow, 11 February. Strikers postpone their fight for a 40-hour week and return to work (→ 5/10).

Archangel, Russia, 1 April. British troops supporting the White Russians beat off a Bolshevik offensive (→ 22/11/21).

Dublin, 4 April. Dáil Eireann authorizes the issue of "republican bonds" (→ 5).

Dublin, 5 April. Sinn Féin elects Eamon de Valera as its president (→ 12/9).

Norwich, 15 May. The body of Nurse Edith Cavell, shot in Belgium as a spy, is reinterred.

Scapa Flow, Orkney, 21 June. German sailors scuttle 70 ships held captive by Britain.

Britain, 23 June. Nationalization of the mines is recommended by a government commission.

Co Galway, 15 June. A Vickers Vimy bomber piloted by Captain Alcock and Lt Brown lands near Clifden after the first non-stop flight across the Atlantic (→ 24/5/30).

London, 6 July. A service of thanksgiving for the Versailles Peace Treaty signed on 28 June is held in St Paul's Cathedral.

London, 3 November. In the capital's municipal elections Labour wins control of 14 out of 28 boroughs.

Ireland, 25 November. A proclamation is issued suppressing Sinn Féin, the Irish Volunteers, the Gaelic League and kindred bodies throughout Ireland (→ 19/12).

Dublin, 19 December. The Irish Republican Army (formerly the Irish Volunteers) makes an unsuccessful attempt on the life of Lord French, the lord lieutenant of Ireland (→ 2/1/20).

Divided Ireland moves closer to war

Sinn Féin rebels meet at the unofficial "Irish" parliament in Dublin.

Rebel parliament declares independence

Dublin, 21 January
Sinn Féin members who won seats in last month's British general election have ignored Westminster and met today in Dublin to proclaim themselves as the parliament of the Irish republic – Dáil Eireann. They reaffirmed the 1916 declaration of independence and adopted a provisional constitution. Delegates were chosen to attend the post-war peace conference in France.

Of the 69 members elected as MPs, only 25 were present at the rebel parliament in the Mansion House. Two are ill, seven absent on Sinn Féin business, one has been deported and 34 are in prison. Among the latter is Eamon de Valera, and in his absence Cathal Brugha, who also fought in the 1916 Rising, was elected as acting president. Despite efforts by the British authorities to quell the popularity of Sinn Féin, its success at the polls is enabling the party to claim that it now represents a majority of the Irish people.→

Dáil is banned, but Collins has escaped

Dublin, 12 September
Michael Collins, one of Ireland's most charismatic leaders, escaped through a skylight yesterday when police and troops surrounded the Mansion House where the Irish parliament was meeting. The parliament, or Dáil Eireann, was banned today, but the escape of Collins will only enhance his growing reputation within Ireland. Still only 28, he mobilizes irregular forces of around 30 men to carry out raids while also acting as finance minister. His aim is to create a state of disorder which will force Britain to withdraw. His intelligence network and military skill have put the British on the defensive; they now plan to bring in ex-soldiers to reinforce the police (→ 24/11).

Ministers hear plan to partition Ireland

Westminster, 24 November
Proposals to split Ireland in two were submitted to the British cabinet today. The Irish committee of the government is recommending that two parliaments, one for the Ulster counties and one for the rest of Ireland, be set up in Ireland, linked by a Council of Ireland. Both would remain subservient to the Westminster parliament in areas like foreign policy and defence. Each of the Irelands would continue to be represented at Westminster, should the committee's proposals be accepted. The concept of a partitioned Ireland will not be welcomed by Irish Nationalists. They oppose any dilution of "home rule", leading to a single independent parliament for Ireland (→ 25).

Republicans set to fight for freedom

Co Tipperary, 21 January
Irish Volunteers today ambushed a cart carrying gelignite at Soloheadbeg. The theft – on the very day that the rebel Irish parliament was proclaimed – symbolizes the readiness of a growing body in the Irish republican movement to use violence in the campaign to win freedom from British rule.

The more extremist Volunteers have formed themselves into a unit known as the Irish Republican Army, and they are increasing pressure on Sinn Féin to support their more confrontational tactics. These amount, essentially, to shooting policemen, on or off duty, on the grounds that the Royal Irish Constabulary represents an alien oppression. Some republicans hope that American influence may yet persuade Britain to give Ireland its freedom, but with British policy veering between ineffective repression and hopes of reconciliation Ireland appears to be perilously close to war.

Sinn Féin's political success has polarized the divisions within Ireland. The parliament set up today is expected to hold effective control over at least half the country. Many local authorities are also dominated by republicans, and arbitration courts have virtually superseded the courts of the crown. With two governments in existence, clashes seem inevitable (→ 4/4).

An Irish policeman at pistol practice.

Scientist shows how to 'split' the atom

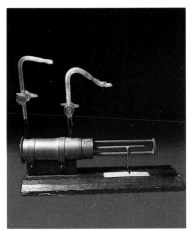

Apparatus for "splitting" the atom.

Manchester, 3 January
Atoms, the smallest particles of matter, are not indivisible, as was previously supposed for Professor Ernest Rutherford of Manchester university has succeeded in "splitting" the atom. And in doing so he transmuted atoms of one element, nitrogen, into those of oxygen.

What this first-ever artificial transmutation from one element to another – part of the alchemist's dream of old – portends is difficult to say, but scientists regard Professor Rutherford's achievement as a major breakthrough. As long ago as 1911 he outlined a theoretical model of atoms. Now he has demonstrated that atoms are not indivisible by using the alpha particles which are transmitted by some radioactive materials to bombard nitrogen atoms (→ 12/1932).

Rail strike settled as civil unrest grows

Britain, 5 October
A week-long rail strike was settled tonight, with victory for the unions, in a year marked by an explosion of civil unrest – a year when policemen went on strike and servicemen mutinied over their slow demobilization. Race riots in several ports led to three deaths in Cardiff and one in Liverpool, while another man was killed in Liverpool when troops opened fire to control looting during the police strike in August.

Over 30 million days have so far been lost through strikes this year compared with 5.8 million last year. Soaring prices, as wartime controls ended, were a principal cause of discontent, but many MPs believe that the militancy is fanned by Bolshevik agitators inspired by the 1917 Russian Revolution.

In Glasgow, the red flag was indeed hoisted over the city as workers struck in January for a 40-hour week to provide jobs for all workers. A sheriff read the Riot Act as police broke up a demonstration. Troops were also sent to "Red Clydeside", and, with some key unions refusing support, the strike failed. None the less it alarmed the government, as has the decision by railwaymen, miners and transport workers to reform their pre-war "triple alliance". Lloyd George was anxious to settle the rail dispute before it spread to other workers.

Forces of law and order close in on a union demonstrator in Glasgow.

Versailles treaty is approved by MPs

Westminster, 22 July
Lloyd George was praised for his role as a peacemaker when MPs today debated the treaty signed at Versailles last month. Only four MPs opposed the terms of the treaty – three of them Irish members objecting to the failure to grant home rule. The British prime minister has spent much of the last five months in Paris at the peace talks where he sought to counter French demands for punitive measures against Germany. More extreme proposals for partitioning Germany have been rejected, but some territory is to be yielded, the Rhineland demilitarized and high compensation payments, or "reparations", imposed. A league of nations, first proposed by the US president, Woodrow Wilson, is to be created to monitor the peace (→ 8/3/21).

Jazz is new sound down at the palais

London, December
A new type of music is being heard in Britain. It is known as "jazz" and was first brought here by American troops during the Great War. Although jazz music is associated with the black people of America, it was the all-white Original Dixieland Jazz Band which was the first to tour this year, playing at venues such as London's newly-opened Hammersmith Palais de Danse.

British massacre protesters at Amritsar

India, 13 April
British troops opened fire today on demonstrators in Amritsar, the Sikh holy city in the Punjab. There had been a series of riots following a call for a business strike by the radical Congress leader Mohandas Gandhi who advocates a policy of non-cooperation with the authorities. When a large crowd gathered on wasteland at Amritsar the local army commander, Brigadier Dyer, ordered his troops to fire without warning, killing 379 people and wounding 1,200. Many women and children are believed to be among the dead (→ 28/7/21).

A flogging during the Amritsar riots.

Influenza epidemic has killed 150,000

Britain, 18 March
The outbreak of influenza known as "Spanish flu" has returned to strike again in the first three months of this year. Figures released today show that for the first time deaths exceeded births in the last quarter of 1918, largely as a result of the flu epidemic. Now, with the virus striking again, the death toll in England and Wales alone is forecast to be 150,000 since the first outbreak last year. The flu has spread around the world, causing more deaths than those in the Great War.

Dec 1. Nancy Astor becomes the first woman MP to take her seat.

1920

Striking miners defy state of emergency

A poster justifies the British government's stance against the miners.

London, 18 October

Once again the miners are locked in a full-blooded confrontation with the government. Not a single mine is expected to open this morning. Over the weekend the government has declared a state of emergency to preserve coal stocks. Train services will be cut and all advertisement and display lighting is forbidden. The people are even being urged to economize on water consumption to save the fuel needed to operate pumps.

The miners are striking for more money, but underlying their action are political concerns. At present the mines are still under government control as they were during the war. But the owners want them to be returned to private enterprise. The miners, for their part, are using their new clout to call for nationalization.

They have formed an alliance with the transport workers and the railwaymen to get support. With trade union membership at a new peak of eight million and the recent by-election successes of Labour candidates, they think the time is ripe to press their claims (→ 15/4/21).

'Wee drams' cheer prohibition defeat

Edinburgh, 5 December

Thousands of Scots have enjoyed their amber-coloured fluid with extra relish tonight as they celebrated victory after a hard-fought campaign against prohibition. It was a battle between the "wee dram" supporters, backed by the distillery lobby, against the churches, particularly the strict Sabbatarian "wee frees".

The "wee frees" fought on economic grounds with the church, from the pulpit, stressing the high level of alcoholism in Scotland, particularly in city slums. The whisky lobby used more secular methods – like dropping "No Change" leaflets from aircraft.

British mandate in Palestine endorsed

San Remo, Italy, 25 April

The British mandate to control Palestine and Mesopotamia was confirmed here today by the League of Nations. There was hardly any discussion: Britain was given a new, Middle Eastern, domain from the debris of the Turkish empire in just three hours.

The mandate has delighted the Zionist movement because it incorporates the 1917 Balfour Declaration which promises the Jews a national home in Palestine. "Here we are, here we remain," said Dr Max Nordeau. The Arabs, however, are bitterly opposed and the Holy Land seems destined again to be the cockpit of intense rivalries (→ 25/8/29).

Dame Nellie loses Marconi its licence

Chelmsford, November

The Marconi company, which has transmitted experimental broadcasts by wireless from its factory at Writtle near Chelmsford, Essex, has had its licence withdrawn by the Post Office under pressure of people who disapprove of wireless telegraphy being used for mere entertainment. On 16 June the *Daily Mail* sponsored a Marconi broadcast by Dame Nellie Melba, the opera singer, which was picked up by listeners all over Europe, and even in faraway Newfoundland. Other radio manufacturers are now seeking air time. The armed services believe that broadcasting will interfere with aircraft signals. Commercial exploitation of the airwaves is rife in the US (→ 15/11/22).

Insurance extended

Westminster, December

Unemployment insurance is to be available to an additional nine million workers. The system of contributions and benefits introduced in 1911 was confined to building, engineering and shipbuilding. It was extended to munitions during the war and to ex-servicemen on a temporary basis after the war. Now it will cover virtually all people earning less than £5 a week.

Supporters chair a jubilant Albert Hill after his victory in the 1500 metres, his second gold medal of the Olympic Games at Antwerp.

Bloody war of independence ravages Ireland

Three Sinn Féiners lie dead as Black and Tans round up possible suspects.

'Bloody Sunday' reprisals leave 23 dead

Dublin, 21 November

In what is being regarded as a horrific climax to the reprisal killings which are prevalent throughout the country, the new police reinforcements, nicknamed the "Black and Tans" [*see below*] have fired into a football crowd causing 12 deaths, many people being crushed to death in the ensuing stampede.

Earlier in the day the IRA had shot and killed 11 unarmed British officers in Dublin on suspicion of their being intelligence operatives.

The possibility of martial law is being considered, and it is felt that Sinn Féin will now be seen as waging a war against Britain, instead of merely targeting local policemen. Britain's refusal to recognize this "war" has meant reliance on the police and not the army.

As a result the army has been a less popular target for the IRA. To date, only 160 soldiers have been killed, compared with 400 policemen. Police resignations have now reached a critical level (→ 10/12).

Cork set ablaze in wake of martial law

Ireland, 12 December

The end of a year of terror and counter-terror in Ireland has been marked by the introduction of martial law in the south-west and the destruction of parts of Cork city by the Black and Tans and the "Auxies", an auxiliary division of the Royal Irish Constabulary. The City Hall and much of St Patrick Street in Cork were gutted yesterday in retaliation for the losses inflicted on police and soldiers by IRA flying columns in Co Cork.

In Ireland generally the combined force of police and military numbers around 40,000 at the moment. They face an estimated IRA force of 15,000 although only 3,000 can fight effectively. The IRA's greatest strength lies in the loyalty of the local people. When that fails, spies and informers are shot, and their bodies are left in the open.

The IRA has also resorted to use of the hunger-strike weapon. Back in October world attention was focused on the young lord mayor of Cork, Terence MacSwiney, who died in Brixton prison after 73 days on hunger strike. The British public, and some members of the government, are beginning to be disturbed by the savagery of the war being waged in Ireland (→ 23).

Cork: a city sacked and in ruins.

Belfast backlash over police murder

Belfast, 24 July

The murder by the IRA of Colonel Smyth, a Royal Irish Constabulary divisional commissioner, in Cork a week ago has created a violent backlash here. Thirteen people have so far died – seven Catholics and six Protestants – in three days of intensive rioting in east Belfast.

Trams carrying shipyard men home from work were attacked in the Catholic Short Strand area while Catholic workers came under attack at the Harland and Wolff shipyard. Some even jumped into the river Lagan and swam to safety. Loyalist groups are demanding that the government drive out Catholics and socialists from the yard (→ 27).

How 'Black and Tans' enforce British law

Dublin, 10 December

Martial law was declared today in south-west Ireland as the British authorities step up what has become an all-out war against Irish nationalists. At the forefront of this struggle has been a group of auxiliaries who have become hated by the Irish people. The "Black and Tans", as they have become known from their uniform, are theoretically linked to the Royal Irish Constabulary; but they are in reality an anti-terrorist cadre · operating a shoot-to-kill policy that is alarming politicians in Westminster as well as in Dublin. Many Black and Tans are jobless war veterans who were enlisted through advertisements last year seeking men for "a rough and dangerous task" (→ 12).

Black and Tans present arms.

Westminster backs Ireland's partition

London, 23 December

King George today signed the act of parliament which partitions Ireland into two. The proposal, first floated a year ago, creates two Irish parliaments - one for 26 counties of Ireland in Dublin and the other for six counties of Ulster in Belfast. The Government of Ireland Act also envisages both parts of Ireland sending MPs to Westminster and creates an all-Ireland council to discuss unity. A year of bloodshed since partition was first mooted has all but destroyed its chances of success. Sinn Féin refuses to recognize the southern parliament while the Ulster Unionists reject the Council of Ireland (→ 4/1/21).

1921

First birth control clinic opens in London

London, 17 March
Britain's first birth control clinic has opened today in the Holloway Road in north London. The clinic is the result of work by Dr Marie Stopes, a pioneer of birth control information, whose controversial best-selling books *Married Love* and *Wise Parenthood* appeared three years ago.

Dr Stopes, a fossil botanist rather than a physician, has long been established as a passionate advocate of a more open attitude to sexual matters in general, and of a commonsense discussion of birth control in particular. Above all she believes that family planning, for many people a taboo subject, is the basis of a truly fulfilled marriage.

Marie Stopes: women's best friend?

Women jurors begin to hear divorce cases

London, 25 January
In a move that is guaranteed to shock legal traditionalists, six women were sworn in as jurors in the divorce court today – the first of their sex ever to serve in a case concerning marital breakdown.

The move is an example of the greater role women are playing in public life since the war and the logical extension of the 1919 Sex Disqualification (Removal) Act, giving women access to the professions. Although some feared that the details of cases might shock the ladies, none chose to stand down, although the possibility of exemption does exist.

Nonetheless, proprieties were scrupulously observed. When what were described as "abominable and beastly" letters were produced in evidence, it was agreed that their content would offend, even terrify, the female jurors. Accordingly the letters were read only by the six males; the ladies simply chose not to look.

Allied troops to occupy Rhineland

Düsseldorf, Germany, 8 March
British, French and Belgian troops crossed the Rhine early this morning and are now on the streets here and in many other towns of the Ruhr. So far it has been a peaceful invasion. The Allies are hoping that the threat will be enough to impel Germany to pay war reparations.

Local opinion does not agree. Most Germans seem to think that the £6.5 million demanded is far beyond the country's ability to pay. Neither military threats nor taxes on German goods seems likely to work. The burden is just too heavy for an economy still ravaged by the war (→ 8/8/24).

Land sales boom

England, December
A quarter of England has changed hands since the end of the war, claims a report in the *Estates Times*. Land sales have boomed with between six and eight million acres changing hands since the beginning of 1918. This represents the most dramatic change since the dissolution of the monasteries in the 16th century. The agricultural depression, higher wartime taxes and death duties have led many landed families to sell their estates.

National strike called off as miners lose allies on 'Black Friday'

Wigan miners are urged to stand their ground despite dwindling support.

London, 15 April
The national strike called for ten o'clock tonight by the railway and transport workers in support of the miners, their allies in the "triple alliance" of key unions, has been called off. The miners have been locked out by the pit owners since 1 April in a pay dispute. The owners wanted lower wages and greater regional variations; the miners sought a "national pool" to equalize wages; the government urged both sides to talk. The pit owners suggested a pay standstill while there were negotiations over a national pool, but the miners' executive today rejected this by a majority of one. Its allies in the triple alliance backed off from a strike – on a day miners are calling a "Black Friday" of betrayal (→ 24/3/26).

Surprise peace treaty creates Irish Free State

London, 6 December
Following protracted negotiations between the British prime minister and a delegation from the self-styled Irish Republic an historic treaty was signed tonight in London. It confers dominion status (equivalent to that of Canada) on an Irish Free State, which will be made up of 26 southern counties – six of the nine counties in Ulster will remain part of the United Kingdom. The treaty concedes certain naval facilities to Britain. Members of the Free State parliament must take an oath of allegience to the king, but they will be allowed first to proclaim allegiance to the constitution of the Irish Free State.

A torrent of recrimination seems likely to engulf the signatories. But much criticism is also reserved for Eamon de Valera, the president of the Irish parliament or Dàil. Pre-occupied with his wish for unity which he hoped to achieve through a subtle plan of "external association", he stayed at home and sent the finance minister and IRA military strategist Michael Collins as part of the negotiating team.

It can never be known whether de Valera could have gained time had he been in London by resisting Lloyd George's threat to end the summer truce. As it was, there was little consultation between the London delegation and the cabinet members who stayed at home. Four cabinet members are thought to be against the treaty (including de Valera) and three are for it on the grounds that it was the best available short of all-out war (→ 7/1/22).

Cease-fire declared after a year of terror in the Irish 'troubles'

Ireland, 22 July
A truce has been declared in the Anglo-Irish war which has continued now for two years. Known in Ireland euphemistically as the "troubles" it has seriously embittered Anglo-Irish relations. The truce has been brought about by strong public opinion in Britain following King George's dramatic appeal for conciliation at the opening of the Northern Irish parliament last month. The United States, too, has urged Britain to seek a solution. Eamon de Valera, the Irish leader, has made a financially successful, if politically controversial, tour of America.

The struggle has been characterized by guerrilla warfare, ambushes, raids on police barracks and planned assassinations on the one side, with reprisals, shootings and burning of towns on the other. During the past year the crown for-

Burning buildings have become a familiar sight to the people of Dublin.

ces have lost 525 men with 1,000 wounded. At least 700 civilians have died already this year.

Greatly disturbed by what he found on his return from the United States, de Valera quickly realized that negotiations towards peace must get under way. It was a relief, therefore, when the British prime minister, David Lloyd George, followed the king's appeal by proposing a truce.

Poplar councillors jailed in rates row

London, 6 September
Five women councillors are facing prison sentences tonight after being arrested for their part in the refusal by Poplar borough council to levy a rate. A crowd of 3,000 people gathered outside Poplar town hall in the East End to protest, but one of the councillors, Susan Lawrence, said she and her colleagues were determined to go to prison like 25 male councillors who were jailed last week.

The dispute has arisen over protests by Labour-controlled Poplar council over a central rate equalization scheme which, it argues, means poor areas like Poplar paying more than richer areas. Poplar, led by George Lansbury, refused to set a rate with the result that councillors have been imprisoned for defying the law (→ 11/10).

Charlie Chaplin mobbed by fans as 'the Tramp' returns home

A hero's welcome: Chaplin reads in the "Daily Mail" of his triumphant return.

London, 9 September
Charlie Chaplin returned to Britain today and disappeared into the mob of thousands who waited at Waterloo to welcome him from the boat train. More surrounded the Ritz hotel in Piccadilly where he is staying – a long way socially from his native Lambeth. London cinemas are showing his classic films *Easy Street*, *The Immigrant* and his latest, *The Kid*. He explained how he chose his famous costume as the Tramp: "I wanted to create a satire on man – the cane for his dignity, the moustache for his vanity, the boots for the cares that weigh him down. That's how my character came about" (→ 26/3/27).

Women outnumber men by two million

Britain, 23 August
First results of this year's national census show an increase of almost two million in the total population of Britain since 1911 – despite the losses of the Great War. The preliminary total is put at 42,767,530 of whom some 7.4 million live in London. Wartime losses obviously affected the totals, but not so dramatically as might be imagined: more people emigrated in the pre-war years than died annually during the war. There are now two million more women than men, but the ratio is much the same as it was before 1914.

Tory rebels oust PM

Westminster, 19 October

Lloyd George has fallen. The man who "won the war" and promised to win the peace resigned as prime minister this afternoon after Conservative MPs meeting at the Carlton Club deserted him and voted to fight the forthcoming general election as an independent party.

Lloyd George believed he could carry the wartime coalition into the peace. But first the newly confident Labour Party pulled out and then the Liberals' Asquith wing rejected his overtures. Since the 1918 election, Lloyd George has been sustained by the votes of 339 Tory MPs with only 134 Liberals remaining loyal to him.

The Tories, who have not formed a government since 1906, have been increasingly restless in the coalition harness; now power is within their grasp. At the Carlton Club meeting, Lloyd George, "the Welsh Wizard", was attacked as "a dynamic force ... a terrible thing" by Stanley Baldwin, a wealthy ironmaster who gave a fifth of his fortune to help reduce the national

The new PM: Bonar Law.

debt. As president of the board of trade, Baldwin has been only a minor political figure, but his words reflected the opinion of another political ironmaster, the Canadian-born Scot Andrew Bonar Law.

After the meeting voted 185 to 88 to quit the coalition, Bonar Law became Tory leader; despite his poor health he expects to be prime minister next month (→ 23).

Sale of honours scandal causes a storm

Westminster, 30 June

The prime minister, David Lloyd George, has been forced by the House of Commons to hold an inquiry into the abuse of the honours system. For some time there has been disquiet at his wholesale handing out of titles and honours to many rich "profiteers" who qualified by making contributions to his personal political fund. The Lloyd

George fund is rumoured to stand at over £3,000,000. Evidence was cited of people being approached by intermediaries such as the notorious Arthur Maundy Gregory and invited to contribute £80,000 to be a baron, £40-50,000 for lesser titles and around £12,000 for a knighthood. In the last 18 months 74 baronetcies and 294 knighthoods have been granted.

When the sun is out, the roof folds down: Austin's convertible Seven.

Daily broadcasting plans for wireless

London, 15 November

The British Broadcasting Company formed last month took over 2LO, Marconi's London station, yesterday and today opened stations in Birmingham and Manchester in a national service. The BBC is a consortium of radio manufacturers. Its general manager is John Reith, an engineer from Aberdeen. Since February the Marconi company has been transmitting weekly half-hour broadcasts from Chelmsford, and daily from 2LO, on top of Marconi House in the Strand. Most listeners with crystal sets are members of wireless societies (→ 1/5/23).

'Obscene' novel is published at last

Dublin-born James Joyce.

Paris, 2 February

James Joyce's eagerly awaited novel *Ulysses* has been published here in a limited edition of 1,000 copies. The book has already been the subject of legal action against its serial publication in the *Little Review* in New York, because of its alleged obscenity, and is considered too pornographic to be published in London. The author was born in Dublin but has lived abroad since 1904. He began writing *Ulysses* in 1914; it was championed by the international literary establishment and achieved notoriety well before its publication this week.

Twelve months in the bloody birth of free Ireland

MPs approve a Bill for Irish Free State

Ireland, 17 February
The terms of the historic treaty signed last December have been hotly discussed during parliament's Christmas recess. Since parliament reassembled, both sides have argued their case with conviction. Arthur Griffith and Michael Collins (both signatories of the treaty) saw it as a stepping stone on the way to full independence and a considerable achievement. Others, like Liam Mellows and Cathal Brugha, rejected the treaty, stating that "the honour of Ireland is too sacred a thing to make a bargain over".

Eamon de Valera, the president of the Irish Republic, believes his alternative to the treaty – "external association", a loose association between an independent Ireland and Britain – has been misrepresented and never discussed in the parliament as an alternative. This has led to de Valera's resignation as president, followed by the election of Griffith and the formation of a provisional government (→ 15).

Spiral of violence spreads to Ulster

Belfast, 15 February
Loyalists today hurled a bomb into a group of Catholic children in the north of the city, killing six, in revenge for the murder of four policemen in Clones, Co Monaghan. Winston Churchill, the colonial secretary, said it was "the worst thing that has happened in Ireland in the last three years". In all 31 people have died in four days of violence which the London *Star* called "a sort of Protestant pogrom against the Catholic minority".

The IRA launched a major offensive in January, but the spark for loyalist violence was an attack on a platoon of 16 policemen at Clones. The police shot dead the local IRA commandant, but an IRA guard killed four, wounded eight and took four prisoners. In Belfast, Catholics hit back by bombing trams bound for the shipyard (→ 30/3).

A ruined building provides Free State riflemen with a hidden gun post.

Civil war breaks out over peace treaty

Dublin, 28 June
Violent repercussions have followed the signing of the treaty setting up the Irish Free State. Six days ago Field Marshal Sir Henry Wilson was gunned down in London. Now civil war is breaking out in Ireland itself over the peace treaty. The provisional government under its president, Arthur Griffith, is trying to take control but the anti-treaty faction within the IRA is defying the Free State army by occupying buildings here, notably the Four Courts, and by turning much of the city into a battlefield (→ 22/8).

Michael Collins is killed in ambush

Cork, 22 August
Michael Collins, one of the most admired and charismatic leaders in the fight for Irish independence, has been killed during an ambush at Bealnablath in his native Co Cork. Collins was one of the team which negotiated the Anglo-Irish Treaty in 1921. He is already recognized as having established new criteria for both urban and rural guerrilla warfare. He had also been the finance minister and at the time of his death was chairman of the provisional government and commander-in-chief of the army (→ 25).

Royalty proclaims Ireland's freedom

Ireland, 6 December
The Free State Constitution Act and the consequential Provisions Act have received the royal assent, and the Irish Free State today comes officially into existence. The king has also approved the appointment of veteran parliamentarian Timothy Healy as the Free State's first governor-general. He is to live in the former vice-regal lodge in Phoenix Park, Dublin, which Dubliners have already nicknamed "Uncle Tim's Cabin" (→ 17).

Wilson: assassinated in London.

Collins: the warrior politician.

Ireland, 23 January. A United Council of Christian Churches in Ireland meets for the first time, but the Catholic church is not represented.

London, 7 March. Neville Chamberlain becomes minister of health in succession to Sir Arthur Boscawen, who lost his seat two days ago (→ 27/8).

British Isles, 31 March. Customs barriers between the United Kingdom and the Irish Free State become effective (→ 10/4).

Waterford, 10 April. Liam Lynch, head of the anti-treaty IRA "Irregulars", dies in police custody after being wounded in fighting with Free State troops (→ 27).

London, 26 April. The duke of York marries Lady Elizabeth Bowes-Lyon in Westminster Abbey (→ 12/12/36).

London, 1 May. The BBC opens central London wireless studios at Savoy Hill; a new programme, "Woman's Hour", will be launched tomorrow (→ 23/4/24).

Bath, 8 May. The Surrey and England opening batsman Jack Hobbs scores 116 against Somerset to become only the third cricketer to achieve 100 centuries, after Dr W G Grace and Tom Hayward (→ 18/2/25).

London, 21 May. Stanley Baldwin becomes prime minister on the resignation of Andrew Bonar Law, who has incurable throat cancer; Baldwin remains chancellor of the exchequer for the time being (→ 21/11).

London, 13 July. Lady Astor's Liquor Bill, prohibiting the sale of alcohol to people under 18, is passed by the Commons.

London, 21 August. A seven-week-long dock strike ends.

London, 27 August. Neville Chamberlain succeeds Baldwin as chancellor of the exchequer; Sir William Joynson-Hicks takes over as minister of health.

Geneva, 10 September. The Irish Free State is admitted to the League of Nations (→ 10/5/24).

Africa, 1 October. Britain agrees to establish an autonomous government for Southern Rhodesia, which was ceded to direct crown control by the British South Africa Company on 12 September (→ 30/5/24).

De Valera calls off anti-treaty struggle

Ireland, 27 April
Peace of a sort has come to Ireland after its terrible civil war. Following the death this month of the IRA chief-of-staff, Liam Lynch, Eamon de Valera has called off his struggle against the treaty. He has sent a message to his republican followers ("Irregulars" and rebels in the eyes of the Free State's government) saying: "Further sacrifice of life would now be in vain. Military victory must be allowed to rest for the moment with those who have destroyed the republic."

Nearly 4,000 people have died, and the damage to property is estimated at £30 million. The bitter legacy of the past year will divide families for generations to come. The resistance of the anti-treaty minority has been broken by the determination and ruthlessness of the Free State government, together with lack of support from ordinary people. Over 12,000 people (amongst them 400 women) have been imprisoned under emergency powers, and a man can now be executed for having in his possession any plan or document prejudicial to the safety of the state.

The republican tactic has been to provoke destabilization by declaring the Free State government, courts and police illegal, and therefore legitimate targets. The policy of assassinating Dáil members and judges has produced strong reac-

President of the Irish Free State, William Cosgrave speaks his mind.

tion from the provisional government. During the blackest weeks of the civil war 77 executions without trial were carried out. De Valera, a former president of the Dáil, led the political opposition to the treaty.

The conflict will leave deep scars for years, if not decades, to come. A deep divide has been established between revolutionary republicanism, which believes passionately in the unfinished business of uniting Ireland, north and south, and a strongly law-and-order administration which, under its president, William Cosgrave, has set a stamp of stern justice and inflexible authority on the running of the fledgling state (→ 10/9).

Sexual equality is reflected in divorce

London, 2 March
Until today a man could divorce a woman for adultery but a woman had to prove cruelty or desertion as well – and all but the fiercest backwoodsmen had come to recognize this as intolerable. Hence the cheers that greeted the passing of the Matrimonial Causes Bill, by 231 votes to 27, that evened matters up.

There have been numerous other victories for equality since Mrs Pankhurst raised the standard for women's suffrage 20 years ago. Besides the winning of the vote itself in 1918, triumphs include Nancy Astor as the first female MP to take her seat in 1919, Mrs Ada Summers the first JP in 1920, and Dr Ivy Williams, first woman to be called to the English bar in 1922. An estimated 4,000 women are now magistrates, mayors and councillors.

Much more noticeable is the contrast between Mrs Pankhurst's stiff Edwardian dresses and today's rising hemlines, short hair and lighter clothes; even she might have been shocked by the advertisements for "lingerie" and "undies" now seen in the newspapers. All are signs of the new freedom that allows a girl to go to the cinema with her boyfriend – unthinkable even ten years ago – and the numbers of divorces to rise from 823 per year in 1911 to 3,619 last year.

Mass disaster narrowly avoided at first Wembley football final

Astride a white horse, PC George Storey helps to clear the crowds at Wembley.

Wembley, 28 April
Mounted on a white horse, a lone policeman played a major part in averting disaster at the vast new Wembley Stadium today. The stadium, which will house much of next year's Empire Exhibition, is designed to hold a crowd of 100,000. But today's attendance was swollen to nearly double that by chaos at the turnstiles and by fans who climbed boundary walls to watch the FA Cup Final.

Fans spilled onto the pitch and organizers were about to cancel the match between Bolton Wanderers and West Ham – with the chance of a riot – when Constable George Storey quietly persuaded the invaders back on to the stands. Bolton won the cup 2-1.

Baldwin is rebuffed at snap election

Guests at the Savoy Hotel are kept informed of the latest election results.

Facing defeat: Stanley Baldwin.

Westminster, 21 November
Stanley Baldwin's decision to call a snap election only six months after becoming Conservative prime minister is being described today as a colossal misjudgement or, alternatively, a clever political tactic to dish the Liberals.

When Andrew Bonar Law resigned last May after doctors told him he was suffering from incurable throat cancer, King George sent for Baldwin rather than Lord Curzon, then foreign secretary, believing the premier should be in the

Commons. Tory MPs duly made Baldwin their leader, though one speaker described him as "a person of the utmost insignificance". Baldwin likes to present himself as a simple country gentleman; in fact, in Lloyd George's words, he is "a formidable political antagonist".

The new prime minister revived an old controversy – tariff reform. Rising unemployment, he declared, could only be tackled by imposing tariffs on imports to protect the home market. He asked for a mandate from the voters. What he has

received is a smart rebuff. In the new parliament Conservatives have 258 MPs, Labour 191 and the Liberals 159. It is the second time Labour has overtaken the Liberals.

Baldwin is certain to be defeated when the new House of Commons meets. Ramsay MacDonald, the Labour leader, will then expect to be asked to form a government, with the half-hearted support of the Liberals. Baldwin expects Labour and Liberals between them to make a mess of things and the voters to turn to him (→ 22/1/24).

Land Act holds out hope of new deal for Irish tenants

Dublin, 9 August
Under the 1923 Land Law Act introduced in the Irish parliament by Patrick Hogan, the agriculture minister, a land commission has been reconstituted to replace the Congested Districts Board and the Estates Commission.

The Hogan Act has made compulsory the sale to tenants of all land not yet dealt with. Rents fixed before 1911 have been reduced by 35 per cent, and those fixed later by 30 per cent. All rent arrears due up to 1920 have been forgiven and arrears after 1920 have been reduced by 25 per cent. Illegal sub-tenants are now recognized as tenants and sub-letting or sub-division of land is prohibited.

Given the importance attached to land legislation in Ireland, the Hogan Act is seen as a significant conclusion to a process which had begun in the last century when in 1870 the then British prime minister, William Gladstone, introduced the first major legislation.

From then on the landlord and tenant relationship began to change in favour of the tenant. Gladstone's legislation allowed tenants to be advanced two-thirds of the price of their farms to be repaid with interest over a 35-year period.

Reorganization of railway companies

Britain, 1 January
Britain's railways steamed into a new chapter of their history today when services began under the four new companies created by the Railway Act of 1921. The railways had been taken over by the government during the war, but the ambitious schemes for redevelopment and electrification were jettisoned two years ago in favour of a return to private ownership. But the pre-war companies have been reorganized into four regional groups, of which only the Great Western is similar to its predecessor. The others are the London and North Western, London and North Eastern, and the Southern Railway (→ 30/4/28).

Poetic voice of new Ireland wins prize

Dublin, 14 November
Ireland's most famous poet, William Butler Yeats, has been awarded the Nobel prize for literature. The award has created immediate controversy, coming as it does so soon after the creation of the Irish Free State.

Throughout the poet's career, in spite of his involvement in the Irish literary revival, he has been a member of the British literary establishment. But later he supported the 1916 Rising and wrote movingly about the relationship between literature and the acts of the rebels. This identified him clearly as the poetic voice of the new Ireland.

Puzzling those who were present, Edith Sitwell's latest poetic offering, "Façade", was delivered by the author via a megaphone behind a curtain.

Labour comes to power for first time

Westminster, 22 January

The illegitimate son of a Scottish serving girl was today asked by the king to become prime minister of Britain's first Labour government. James Ramsay MacDonald hired court dress from Moss Bros for his visit to Buckingham Palace, where George V urged him to exercise prudence and sagacity.

The advice was hardly necessary. MacDonald's cabinet of 20 includes 11 with solid working-class backgrounds, two are Tories, one a Liberal and only one is left-wing. He is John Wheatley from Red Clydeside, a Roman Catholic born in poverty who became a successful businessman – but he, too, hired court dress and returned from the palace having charmed the king. MacDonald had decided to form a minority government before meeting his parliamentary party. He ridiculed leftwingers who wanted him to deliver a ringing socialist speech and then quit. That, he said, would be a betrayal of those who had voted for the party. Admitting that Labour was "in office but not in power", he said it had to show that the party was fit to govern.

In spite of MacDonald's resolute moderation, a Labour government represents a social revolution; for the first time the ruling elite of public school and Oxbridge are out.

Two ministers in particular will be worth watching: Wheatley at health plans a big public housing programme and Charles Trevelyan at education intends to provide working-class children with more than the three Rs (→ 1/2).

Ramsay MacDonald: Labour PM.

Wireless puts its stamp on empire show

Wembley, London, 23 April

Royalty became a little less remote today when millions of Britons, owners of the new wireless sets, heard their king's voice for the first time. The occasion was the opening of the British Empire Exhibition at the stadium here with hidden microphones on the royal dais carrying the king's message to listeners as far away as northern Scotland.

New technology was a feature of today's ceremony. The king sent a telegram to himself – routed via Canada, New Zealand, Australia, South Africa, India, Aden, Egypt and Gibraltar, and finally brought back to the king by a telegram boy, immaculate in blue suit and pillbox hat, a telegram pouch on his belt.

The exhibits here include a coal mine with real pit ponies, a Maori village, an effigy in butter of the prince of Wales and a working replica of Niagara Falls. There are vast exhibition halls and lakes, but with its fine scaled-down Chippendale and Queen Anne furniture and miniature watercolours by top artists, it was Queen Mary's dolls' house, designed by Sir Edwin Lutyens, that drew the largest crowds (→ 15/9).

Visitors flock to the British Empire Exhibition at Wembley, west London.

Storm looms over borders for Ulster

Ireland, 10 May

The government of Northern Ireland has refused a formal request from the British government to appoint a member to the proposed boundary commission. There are fears in Dublin and London that the governments there may fall on the issue.

The 1921 Anglo-Irish treaty allowed Northern Ireland to opt out of the Free State and remain part of the United Kingdom, in which case a boundary commission was to determine the boundaries of Northern Ireland. The Irish negotiators believed that the commission would give them at least three of the North's six counties and that an uneconomically viable Ulster would then be forced to join the Free State, thus ensuring longed-for unity. This swayed them to sign the treaty. Lloyd George, on the other hand, called the commission project "a slight readjustment".

Last July, the Free State government, which had been strongly criticized for inaction by the republican opposition, put the onus of responsibility on Britain by appointing its commissioner, Eoin MacNeill. The refusal of the Northern Ireland government to make its nomination is a serious complication (→ 5/6).

'Red Letter' scare topples Labour

Minority rule ends over sedition row

Westminster, 9 October

The life of the Labour government is in jeopardy tonight after Ramsay MacDonald lost a vote of confidence in the House of Commons by 364 votes to 198. The prime minister will advise the king to call a general election.

MacDonald took power as head of a minority government and was at pains to demonstrate its constitutional rather than revolutionary credentials. The Housing Act was probably its greatest domestic success, but it was over relations with communism that Labour came to grief.

Attempts to improve relations with the Bolsheviks had aroused vocal opposition even before the event which led to the government's downfall. This involved J R Campbell, editor of *The Worker's Weekly*, a communist magazine. Campbell, decorated in the war for bravery, had urged servicemen not to break strikes.

He was charged with incitement to mutiny, which outraged Labour MPs. The attorney-general then dropped the prosecution, outraging opposition MPs who claimed that improper political pressures had been exerted. It seems that it was more a muddle than anything, but the opposition scented blood – and the government fell (→ 26).

Zinoviev: was his letter forged?

Winston Churchill: Tory recruit?

Tories romp home; Liberals shattered

Westminster, 31 October

The Conservatives have romped to a general election victory in a campaign dominated by a "Red Letter" scare. Four days before the poll a letter, purportedly from a Soviet leader called Zinoviev to the tiny British Communist Party, was published by the *Daily Mail*. It gave instructions from the Soviet Union on how to start a revolution and was hailed by Tories and their supporters in the press as evidence that Labour was soft on communism.

Soviet diplomats claimed that the letter was a forgery, but the damage was fatal to a Labour Party already on the defensive over its handling of the Campbell affair [*see report left*]. The Conservatives won 419 seats compared to 258 in the last parliament while Labour has slumped from 191 to 151. The biggest losers, though, are the Liberals: the party of government less than a decade ago, they now have only 40 MPs as against 159 in the last parliament. Labour, in fact, gained one million more votes than a year ago. Among the Liberal casualties was Herbert Asquith, the former premier.

Stanley Baldwin will now return to Downing Street one year after he gambled on – and lost – a snap election. Winston Churchill is tipped to return to Tory ranks after 20 years as a Liberal (→ 21/11).

Two climbers lost within 1,000 feet of Everest summit

Mallory: presumed dead.

Khatmandu, June

With just a thousand feet between them and the elusive 29,028-foot summit of Mount Everest, British climbers George Leigh Mallory and Andrew Irvine were "going strong" in their latest attempt on the world's highest mountain. It was then that the support party below lost sight of the British climbers as a sudden snowstorm overwhelmed them. No trace has been found of the two men, who set off with high hopes that supplies of bottled oxygen would help them win. Asked on a US lecture tour last year why he was so obsessed with Everest, Mallory replied: "Because it is there."

Imperial Airways takes to the skies

Croydon, 1 April

Britain now has a national airline – Imperial Airways, an amalgamation of four of Britain's pioneering airlines: Handley Page Transport, Daimler Airway, Instone Airline and British Marine Air Navigation. Each of these private companies has had great problems in making profits. Just as their European rivals get strong financial support from their governments, so state ownership is seen as the only viable future for air travel on this side of the English Channel (→ 24/5/30).

De Valera ends 11 months in prison

Ireland, 16 July

The republican activist Eamon de Valera has been released after 11 months in prison, during which time he received a huge vote for Sinn Féin in the general election. Hundreds of men and some women continue to be detained, untried, and 146 men went on hunger strike for almost 40 days in Kilmainham gaol. Despite the ending of the civil war, Free State troops have continued to carry out raids and arrests amid an atmosphere of disunity and bitterness (→ 1/11).

Refusing to run in heats on Sunday, Scotland's Eric Liddell withdrew from the 100 metres, but snatched Olympic gold and a record in the 400 metres.

Twickenham, 3 January. In a match against England Cyril Brownlie of New Zealand becomes the first rugby union player to be sent off for foul play in an international.

London, 17 February. Herbert Asquith, the former Liberal prime minister, takes his seat in the House of Lords as earl of Oxford and Asquith (→ 18/5).

Melbourne, 18 February. England win the fourth test by an innings and 29 runs – their first win against Australia since August 1913 (→ 18/8).

London, 13 March. MPs approve the Summer Time Bill, making annual daylight saving permanent.

Asia, 19 March. Plans are announced for a major Royal Navy base at Singapore.

London, 9 April. The government accepts guidelines on teachers' pay recommended in a report by Lord Burnham.

Cyprus, 1 May. The island, under British administration since 1878 and annexed from Turkey in 1914, becomes a crown colony.

Britain, 18 May. A report by the Trades Union Congress dismisses the "Zinoviev Letter" as a forgery (→ 14/10/26).

London, 30 May. King George opens the rebuilt Great West Road, hailed as a model for post-war development.

London, 24 July. Patricia Cheeseman, a patient at Guy's Hospital, is the first person to be successfully treated for diabetes with insulin (→ 24/1/27).

Britain, 19 August. Miners agree to cooperate in a government enquiry into their pay.

Shanghai, 7 September. Around 20,000 mainly student demonstrators stone British constables during protests against the British and other Western concessions (→ 31/1/27).

Britain, 29 September. White lines are to be painted on roads in a bid to reduce traffic accidents (→ 20/11).

Westminster, 20 November. MPs approve a £50 fine and four months in prison for people convicted of drunken driving (→ 29/3/27).

London, 25 November. Twelve leading communists arrested last month are jailed for sedition.

Britain returns to the gold standard

Westminster, 28 April
Britain has returned to the gold standard. The chancellor of the exchequer, Winston Churchill, made this announcement in his budget today. He told the Commons that he did not intend to renew the act of 1919 which suspended the standard.

Churchill hopes that this great symbolic act will boost the morale of his party and the confidence of the country. It suggests a return to prewar normality. It harks back to the Victorian age when the City of London was pre-eminent. The gold standard is the hallmark of stable money and a stable political society. A return will please businessmen and most academic economists.

There is only one major dissenting voice – that of the Cambridge economist John Maynard Keynes. Two years ago he published a devastating critique called *A Tract on Monetary Reform*. In it, he demonstrated that the United States was only pretending to maintain the gold standard.

According to Keynes the US does not ensure that the dollar matches the value of gold; it manipulates the price of gold at great expense to ensure that it stays level with the dollar. "This is the way by which a rich country is able to combine new wisdom with old prejudice," wrote Keynes. Britain by implementing the change makes itself the victim of a policy dictated by US power.

The Churchill budget also takes sixpence off income tax and brings in a new national pension scheme.

Hobbs's hundreds outscore W G Grace

Schoolboys surround their hero Hobbs, hoping for an autograph.

Taunton, 18 August
Cricket history was made today before a modest weekday crowd here at Somerset's county ground. Jack Hobbs scored his second hundred in two days for Surrey: his first equalled the record total of 126 first-class centuries set by W G Grace, the second surpassed that total. Today's effort was also the 14th century scored this season by the Surrey and England opening batsman – another record.

Hobbs is 42, but seems to be at the height of his powers, with no thought of retirement. He played his first match for Surrey in 1905 and within two years was capped by his country. He has taken wickets as a medium-pace bowler, but it is as a batsman that he has been acclaimed as one of the great players of all time. His elegance and his skill – especially on difficult wickets – have earned him worldwide recognition as "the Master". He has achieved particular success against England's greatest rivals, Australia. Last year Hobbs began a promising partnership with Yorkshire's 30-year-old opener, Herbert Sutcliffe (→ 18/8/26).

Cheap loans lure people to emigrate

Touting the delights of Canada.

London, 8 April
Plans were announced today to encourage 450,000 Britons to emigrate to Australia over the next ten years. Low-interest loans will be made available to the prospective settlers by a scheme to be funded jointly by the British and Australian governments. Although the figure seems high, it is in fact no more than the total average emigration from Britain in a single year during 1911-13. In the first decade of the century emigration averaged 284,000 a year, mostly to the United States and the dominions.

Legion is formed to tackle immorality

Ireland, 15 November
A new organization, the Legion of Mary, has been formed in Dublin to tackle what it says are widespread problems of drunkenness, prostitution, crime and disease. Its founder, Frank Duff, is a civil servant and a former active member of the Society of St Vincent de Paul.

In a city where open brothels operate on a scale scarcely paralleled in Europe and where drink always seems to be available, the Legion has taken the unprecedented step of opening a hostel for prostitutes willing to make a fresh start. Members go into the roughest parts of Dublin to offer help and advice to women living in conditions of poverty and degradation.

New party to back Welsh nationalism

Pwllheli, 5 August

When the first official meeting of the two clandestine Welsh nationalist groups, represented by Saunders Lewis and H R Jones, took place at the Maesgwyn temperance hotel, Pwllheli today, the event was hailed by the chairman as the first public meeting of Plaid Cymru, a "new" Welsh nationalist party. Dismissing supporters of Welsh home rule within the Labour Party, Saunders Lewis declared: "One cannot serve England and Wales." He stressed the need for unity and argued that persuasion by physical force should not now be necessary. His plan for a wholly Welsh-speaking summer school at Machynlleth in August 1926 was rapturously received.

A Nobel for Shaw

Stockholm, 10 December

George Bernard Shaw, regarded by many as the world's best-known living playwright, was awarded the Nobel Prize for Literature today. A non-believer in prizes, he declined to attend the award ceremony, however, and intends to use the prize money to create an Anglo-Swedish Literary Foundation. His plays include *Arms and the Man*, *Major Barbara* and the highly successful *St Joan* (→ 2/11/50).

Irish commissioner resigns in border row

NEW BOUNDARY DEFINES NORTHERN IRELAND

Dublin, 20 November

Eoin MacNeill has resigned from the boundary commission, set up under the Anglo-Irish Treaty of 1921 to determine the Irish border. This followed a crisis debate in the Dáil, after a leaked report, with map, in the *Morning Post* on 7 November predicted that there would be only minor adjustments.

The Free State was to gain parts of south Armagh, south-west Fermanagh and west Tyrone, while Northern Ireland was to acquire small portions of Donegal and Monaghan. It would have reduced the north's population by 1.8 per cent and its area by 3.7 per cent. Fearing defeat in the Dáil, Irish leaders sought a meeting in London to suppress the report. In debates on the treaty, members of the Dáil had assumed that the commission would bring major territorial gains, forcing the collapse of the Northern Ireland economy (→ 16/5/26).

Wireless broadcasts reach ten million people, claims the BBC

The magic of wireless is demonstrated in the Harrod's department store.

London, 3 December

The British Broadcasting Company can now reach 40 million people with its broadcasts and John Reith, its general manager, claimed today that it has an audience of over ten million listeners. The number of ten-shilling wireless licences issued is 1,654,000, so it is assumed that many listeners have not yet got round to buying the licence.

There has been a boom in sales of wireless sets – the BBC supplies crystal sets for £2 to £4 – but many people make their own. The BBC puts out 10,000 talks a year, classical concerts and live dance music from the Savoy hotel. Reith's plan is to lead public taste, not to follow it (→ 1/1/27).

Charleston gives a new kick to the Roaring Twenties

Britain, 31 December

This was the year the Charleston arrived from the US and carried away society high and low. Once the prince of Wales had done it, everybody was doing it. Dancing is the craze of Bright Young Things and the hit tune "I Want To Be Happy" is their guide. The foxtrot, tango, the Black Bottom and many more are performed nightly in smart hotels, known for their bands: Carroll Gibbons at the Savoy, Jack Hylton at the Piccadilly, Teddy Brown at the Café de Paris, Bert Ambrose at the Embassy Club.

The "flappers" are still waiting for the vote but not to shock their elders by smoking and applying lipstick in public, sipping cocktails, swearing, making life one long fancy dress party where morals are emancipated. Busts were banished in 1923; skirts grow shorter every year like hairstyles – from the bob to the shingle and this year's ultimate "Eton Crop".

Men have followed the prince into flapping Oxford bags, Fair Isle sweaters and caps. Their other model, Nöel Coward, who has three plays running in London at the age of 24, wrote for C B Cochran's new revue *On With the Dance* a song that asks "Cocktails and Laughter – but what comes after?"

Everybody's doing it.

TUC calls its first-ever general strike

Violence is avoided as class war erupts

Britain, 10 May

The first week of the first general strike in British history has accentuated class divisions but has not so far led to the violence which many feared. The strike began on 3 May after the TUC decided to back the miners in their strike against pay cuts and longer working hours.

Talks at Downing Street failed to avert the stoppage and broke down over a refusal by the TUC to repudiate action by printers at the *Daily Mail* who refused to print an anti-union editorial. A state of emergency has been declared and troops were deployed in south Wales, Yorkshire and Scotland.

The TUC stressed that foodstuffs would be exempt from the strike, which in heavy industry, building, railways, transport, gas, electricity and printing has been virtually 100 per cent effective. But the middle classes have been equally eager to offer their services free to stave off what they see as a threat. Students, ex-officers, retired managers and others have come forward in droves to drive lorries and buses or to act as special constables.

Winston Churchill is editing the *British Gazette* on behalf of the government, denouncing the working man as the enemy, but many others are trying to keep the temperature down. Apart from isolated incidents in Glasgow and Northumberland there has been little violence. In many areas police and strikers are combating the tedium by playing each other at football (→ 12).

Steel-helmeted troops man tanks leaving Wellington barracks in London.

A woman's work is never done: female volunteers assist at a post office.

Miners, bitter at desertion by TUC, continue the struggle

London, 20 May

Delegates at the miners' conference today showed their determination to fight on. They are still extremely bitter at the TUC's decision to call off the general strike a week ago, but they are in no mood to accept the latest terms of the prime minister, Stanley Baldwin, for settling the coal dispute. They intend to fight on alone. The TUC has opted for a compromise plan for a national wages board for coal. This would cut miners' wages, but only when the owners have agreed to adopt the Samuel commission proposals for the reorganization of the industry.

TUC leaders hoped that by calling off the strike public opinion would force the owners to a more moderate approach. The miners are sceptical. TUC leaders clearly have no stomach for the kind of revolutionary attempt to bring down the government of which their enemies accuse them. The emergency plans of the government also worked well. Essential supplies were getting through with the help of eager voluntary labour. As soon as workers saw this there was a gradual drift back to work on the railways and in other industries. With a choice between escalation into a constitutional crisis or surrender, the TUC chose surrender (→ 12/11).

Old empire to be new commonwealth

London, 20 November

The changing nature of the British Empire was acknowledged today when the Imperial conference here announced that Canada, Australia, New Zealand and South Africa will be self-governing dominions within the British Commonwealth. The declaration recognizes the independence of the dominions which will be equal in status to that of Britain "united by a common allegiance to the crown". Yet even the king's title is changed, for the Irish Free State, although also a dominion, does not recognize the monarch of Great Britain and Northern Ireland as its sovereign. But the king remains emperor of India, whose non-independent status is unchanged by the conference (→ 12/3/28).

De Valera to head 'soldiers of destiny'

Dublin, 16 May

Eamon de Valera, former president of Sinn Féin, has held an inaugural meeting in the La Scala theatre in Dublin to launch Fianna Fail (Soldiers of Destiny) as his new political party. In a rousing speech he told members that the main challenge facing them was the reunification of Ireland. No true republican, said de Valera, could accept the present division of the country, which stood in the way of the nation's advancement (→ 10/7/27).

National electricity grid planned for UK

Britain, 31 December

Millions will soon have electricity on tap to their homes thanks to the Electricity Supply Act. With many small competing power companies, progress has been slow and only about one in ten homes can run the new vacuum cleaners.

Now there is to be a Central Electricity Board which will enforce a uniform system and set up a National Grid. It will take some seven years to complete. By then about half the homes in the country will be wired up for electricity.

Britain, 1 January. The BBC (formerly British Broadcasting Company, now Corporation) makes its first broadcasts as a company incorporated under royal charter (→ 15/3/32).

London, 24 January. The British Medical Association warns that deaths from cancer, particularly of the chest and tongue, have risen sharply in the past 20 years (→ 30/9/28).

Britain, 31 January. A 12,000-strong British Army division is ordered to China to defend British nationals in Shanghai, where the Chinese civil war is posing a threat to the Western enclaves.

Glamorgan, Wales, 1 March. Over 50 miners are feared dead in a firedamp explosion at Ebbw Vale; 150 are trapped.

London, 30 March. The Convocation of the Church of England approves changes to the Book of Common Prayer, including equal marriage vows for men and women (→ 15/12).

USA, 30 June. American golfers beat a team from Britain and Ireland to win a new trophy awarded by Samuel Ryder.

Dublin, 20 July. The Free State government introduces the Public Safety Bill giving it powers to deal more effectively with disorder (→ 11/8).

Dublin, 16 August. William Cosgrave, president of the Free State executive council, is opposed in a no confidence vote in the Dail by Eamon de Valera's new Fianna Fail party and wins only on the casting vote of the speaker (→ 20/9).

Edinburgh, 8 September. The TUC votes to cut ties with Soviet trade unions.

Irish Free State, 20 September. A general election gives Cosgrave 61 seats to Fianna Fail's 57; the government has an overall majority of six (→ 8/2/29).

Lancashire, 28 October. A great storm leaves a reported 50 dead and 400 homeless.

Westminster, 25 November. MPs approve the establishment of a commission to study the government of India, headed by Sir John Simon (→ 3/2/28).

London, 10 December. As greyhound racing booms, London's third track opens at Wembley, to join those at Harringay and White City; Britain's first track opened at Manchester last year.

Speed battle pushes record over 200mph

Malcolm Campbell prepares for a land speed record with BP's assistance.

Florida, 29 March

The rivalry between two Britons has taken the world land speed record to beyond 320 kilometres per hour (200mph) for the first time. The new record-holder is Major Henry Segrave who at the Daytona Beach racetrack in Florida today smashed the speed set only last month by Malcolm Campbell. In his *Mystery* car, Segrave reached 203.841mph – 30mph faster than the record set by Campbell along the Pendine Sands in South Wales on 4 February.

Campbell, a three-time record holder, had reached 174.224 mph in Wales and he was among the first to congratulate Major Segrave. He said it was an "excellent feat", but said that he was already practising in a faster car with which he was confident of regaining the record.

At a time when the motor car is growing dramatically in popularity, there is great enthusiasm for the efforts of pioneers like Campbell and Segrave. But there is also concern for their safety.

During a pit-stop to change the tyres on his 1,000hp car, Major Segrave said the wind pressure at such high speed had made steering virtually impossible. And when Campbell set his record, the wind blew off his goggles, temporarily blinding him. "It was most terrifying," Campbell said (→ 19/2/28).

Labour MPs livid at anti-union bill

Westminster, 16 May

Labour MPs lost their battle to talk out the Trade Disputes Bill today when the government used the guillotine. The bill makes any strike illegal that is "designed or calculated to coerce the government". It rules out actions like last year's general strike when other unions came out in sympathy with the miners.

The new bill also forbids civil service unions to affiliate to the TUC and hits at Labour Party finances by forbidding political levies unless members contract in.

De Valera to take his seat in the Dáil

De Valera: in the Dáil at last.

Dublin, 11 August
Eamon de Valera has finally taken his seat in the Dáil. His Fianna Fáil party won 44 seats in the June general election, but were locked out of the Dáil chamber when they refused to take the oath of allegiance to the British crown which de Valera described as an acquiescence to a foreign power that made a nonsense of democracy. His attempt to have the matter resolved by a referendum was defeated.

Recognizing that his position was untenable, de Valera has satisfied his conscience by agreeing to take the oath having first removed the Bible which lay beside it, and then covering the oath with some papers before signing it (→ 16).

Support grows for British-made films

London, 26 March
Britain is to make serious efforts to make its own films, despite the lead that the war gave to Hollywood. Today saw the founding of the Gaumont-British Film Corporation, hot on the heels of British Incorporated Pictures. A new Cinematograph Films Act will oblige exhibitors to show a minimum quota of British films, beginning at 7.5 per cent and rising to 25 per cent. Last year only 5 per cent of the films shown in Britain were British-made and many talented actors, such as Charlie Chaplin, have gone to America (→ 17/3/30).

IRA assassinates Irish Free State minister

Dublin, 10 July
The Irish Minister for Justice, Kevin O'Higgins, has been assassinated by what is believed to be a dissident faction of the IRA as he walked home after Mass.

An able, energetic and fearless individual, O'Higgins was seen as the strong, if unpopular, arm of the government. His recent attempts to introduce an Intoxicating Liquor Bill were defeated by an outcry from 15,000 publicans. He was dedicated to rooting out militarism and stamping a civilian imprint on Irish government, and had actively pursued a policy (despite criticism) of replacing the 7,000 armed RIC men with 5,250 unarmed police. His death will be seen as a long-term loss for his party and for the country (→ 20).

O'Higgins: murdered after Mass.

Government expels all Soviet diplomats

London, 24 May
A series of espionage scandals led today to the severing of relations between Britain and the Soviet Union. Ordering all Russian diplomats and the Soviet trade mission to leave within ten days, Sir Austen Chamberlain, the foreign secretary, accused the USSR of spying and subversion throughout the British empire and said: "The limits to our patience are now reached."

The break followed a police raid on the Soviet trade organization, Arcos, in London. The security service had been tipped off that Arcos had acquired a document containing the RAF's plans for strategic bombing and recommended that it should be raided. The prime minister, Stanley Baldwin, gave permission and the raid was mounted at dawn 12 days ago.

When the police burst through a basement door they discovered two men and a women burning papers. The stolen document was not found but there was much evidence proving Arcos was a front for a campaign of espionage (→ 29/7/29).

Baldwin refuses to meet Welsh miners

London, 22 November
Two hundred unemployed miners were snubbed by the prime minister today at the end of a 180-mile march from south Wales. They had walked from the Rhondda valley to draw attention to high levels of unemployment in mining areas following the failure of the pit strike last year. But Stanley Baldwin, the prime minister, refused to see a delegation of the miners. His decision angered the miners' leader, Arthur Cook, who told a rally that in the interests of the nation "the government will be compelled to take over the mining industry".

New prayer book is called too 'popish'

Westminster, 15 December
The ability of the internal affairs of the Church of England to cause uproar in British political life was proved again today when the House of Commons rejected a revised prayer book which had been prepared by the Church Assembly and passed by the House of Lords. When the vote was read out hats and order papers were thrown into the air and wild cheering mingled with shouts of "No popery".

The revised book is anathema to low churchmen and their fears were voiced by Sir Thomas Inskip, the solicitor-general, who claimed the book goes too far towards Rome in its provisions for Anglo-Catholic practices such as those for the sacrament of Communion. Another major objection by the Commons, a bastion of male chauvinism, was to changes in the marriage service freeing brides from the obligation to "obey" their husbands.

The rejection of the revised book has, therefore, infuriated not only the bishops but also the feminists, a powerful combination. It has, moreover, raised the question of disestablishmentarianism, for the state is seen as preventing the church from conducting its domestic affairs as it wishes. A compromise is in the making, however, with bishops authorizing the use of certain sections of the revised book by their vicars (→ 27/7/28).

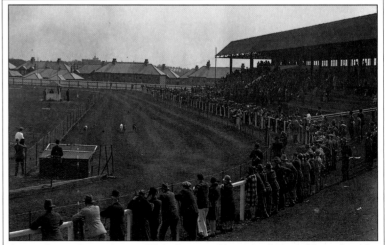

As an alternative to the established sport of horse racing, greyhound tracks are fast becoming popular, providing the punter with an opportunity to have a flutter as the dogs chase a hare around the track. Here at Dumpton Park in Kent, they are up and running, watched by a cheering crowd.

1928

London, 16 January. The novelist and poet Thomas Hardy, who died two days ago at the age of 87, is buried in Westminster Abbey.

Britain, 19 January. Figures show the birth rate last year was the lowest on record.

India, 3 February. Riots mark the arrival from Britain of the Simon Commission to report on the future government of India (→ 2/1/30).

Britain, 12 February. Eleven die as gales sweep the country (→ 5/12/29).

Oxford, 15 February. The Oxford English Dictionary is completed after 70 years' work.

Daytona, USA, 19 February. Malcolm Campbell's *Bluebird* reaches 332kmph [206.35mph], a new land speed record (→ 1/8).

London, 20 February. Britain, which has a League of Nations mandate for Palestine, recognizes the independence of Transjordan.

Malta, 12 March. The British colony becomes a dominion (→ 12/1931).

Britain, 30 April. The *Flying Scotsman* non-stop rail service is launched between London and Edinburgh; speeds of over 112 kmph (70mph) are reached during the 392-mile journey (→ 27/6).

London, 14 June. Veteran women's suffrage campaigner Mrs Emmeline Pankhurst dies at the age of 69 (→ 31/5/29).

Darlington, 27 June. A rail crash leaves 23 dead (→ 5/7/32).

Oxford, 1 August. The Morris Minor car is launched (→ 29/11).

Glasgow, 16 September. The P & O *Viceroy of India* is launched; it is the first liner to have oil-fired electric turbines.

Newcastle-upon-Tyne, 10 October. King George opens a new Tyne Bridge; it has Britain's biggest steel arch.

Britain, 22 November. The first £1 and ten shilling [50p] notes enter circulation.

London, 12 December. King George V, who fell dangerously ill with a chest infection on November 23, is reported much improved after a lung operation (→ 2/7/29).

London. Two sculptors, Henry Moore and Barbara Hepworth, each stage their first London exhibitions this year.

Private motoring booms, but so does the number of traffic accidents on the roads

Lane discipline is not apparent at Hyde Park Corner, where traffic is heavy.

Britain, 29 November
Figures released today show that traffic accidents have continued to soar this year. Last year's totals of 133,943 accidents and 5,329 deaths prompted demands for new laws to control the boom in private motoring. The number of private cars registered – just 200,000 in 1920 – is forecast to top a million by the end of the decade. Yet controls are few. Anyone over 17 can drive, subject only to an unsupported declaration of physical fitness. There is no driving test, although moves are beginning in parliament to press for one. Changes to the widely ignored 20 mph (32 kmph) speed limit have also been suggested. Motoring remains the preserve of the wealthy, but the Austin Seven car, introduced in 1921 at a price of £225, brought cars within reach of far more people (→ 16/6/29).

Fourteen killed as Thames bursts banks

London, 7 January
The calamity that many have been predicting for years finally happened this month when the Thames burst its banks, flooding low-lying districts of London, drowning 14 people and causing millions of pounds worth of damage. Telephone lines were cut off as floodwaters rose and hundreds of people have been left with their homes uninhabitable.

A sudden thaw and strong winds combined with a high tide to wreak havoc along substantial tracts of the swollen river. Four young sisters – drowned in their basement home – were among the casualties. Twelve Landseer paintings were badly damaged at the Tate gallery, although the priceless Turner collection there was saved.

The pub will not be dry inside or out.

Floods engulfed the vaults of the palace of Westminster and water (and swans) returned to the moat of the Tower of London for the first time in many years (→ 12/2/28).

Germ-killing mould found by chance

London, 30 September
The blue mould spots that appear on stale bread may be able to cure disease. That anyway is the hope of Professor Alexander Fleming of St Mary's Hospital in London, who discovered that when the mould, *penicillium notatum* as it is known, comes into contact with the bacterium staphylococcus, which is responsible for many human infections, the bacterium is killed off.

He made the discovery when a dish of the bacteria was left out by mistake and became contaminated. *Penicillium* does not harm human white blood cells so it may be safe to use on humans. However extracting the active chemical is likely to be difficult (→ 3/2/41).

Flappers win vote

Britain, 7 May
Five million more women will be able to vote in the next general election thanks to an act of parliament which puts them on the electoral roll on an equal footing with men – the age comes down from 30 to 21. The act was introduced by the Tory government without any particular pressure, but many believe that the "flapper" vote will benefit Labour (→ 14/6).

Dixie Dean scores a record 60 goals

Liverpool, 1 May
There is a double celebration in Liverpool tonight: Everton are the champions of the Football League and Dixie Dean, their centre forward, has hit a record 60 league goals in a season. He scored today in the final match of the season to help Everton clinch the title by two points from runners-up Huddersfield Town. Dean has achieved his record total from only 39 of his team's 42 league games. Not surprisingly Everton scored more than 100 goals this season, one of seven English and two Scottish sides to hit a century of goals. In Scotland's less competitive second division, Jimmy Smith of Ayr United even beat Dean's total with 66 goals.

Archbishop resigns over new prayer book

London, 27 July
Randall Davidson, the archbishop of Canterbury, is to retire in November after 25 years as head of the Church of England. He is bitterly disappointed that the revised *Book of Common Prayer* was rejected for the second time by the House of Commons last month.

Yet his departure will not end the controversy as he is to be succeeded by Cosmo Lang, the chief advocate of the revised book and a powerful figure in the House of Lords. Sir William Joynson-Hicks, the home secretary and a leading opponent of the revisions, today called for Lang to "devote himself to the real call of the church – the evangelization of the people".

Dr Davidson and his wife.

Theatre in Galway aids Gaelic revival

Galway, 27 August
The Galway Gaelic theatre has opened with a production of *Diarmuid agus Grainne*, written and produced by Micheál MacLiammóir. The theatre has caused great excitement amongst Irish language enthusiasts as it represents another aspect of the Gaelic revival which began with the Gaelic League founded by Douglas Hyde 35 years ago. Its aims have been to renew interest in Irish culture, art and, most important of all, the Irish or Gaelic language.

Britain signs treaty to 'renounce war'

Paris, 27 August
Nearly ten years after the Armistice which ended the Great War, representatives of 15 countries today signed a pact here today renouncing war. Britain was among the signatories and the German foreign minister, Gustav Stresemann, was loudly cheered when he produced a large gold pen with which to add his name. The pact follows intense lobbying by the US secretary of state Frank Kellogg and Aristide Briand, his French counterpart. The pact bears both their names.

Britons are greatest cigarette smokers

Smoking: a burning desire.

Britain, 10 August
Britons are world leaders – in cigarette smoking. In 1924 we puffed our way through an astonishing 77,458,000 pounds of tobacco, up from 23,766,000 pounds in 1907, according to a report of the Imperial Economical Committee. Last year we burnt up an average of 3.4 pounds of tobacco per head.

All the increase has come from sales of cigarette, boosted by gimmicks such as give-away cards; cigar and pipe smoking have actually declined. The cigarette held between slim fingers has become one of the symbols of female emancipation, while lighting a girl's cigarette is fast becoming a romantic cliché.

London, 4 February. Britain's first "green belt", a five-mile-long stretch of countryside near Hendon to be protected from development, is approved.

France, 12 February. Lillie Langtry, an actress who became a mistress of King Edward VII when he was prince of Wales, dies.

London, 15 April. The 325-year-old tea duty is abolished in Chancellor Winston Churchill's budget, knocking fourpence [2p] off the price of a pound of tea.

Karachi, India, 26 April. Twelve days after the first airmail flight from India to Britain, an RAF Fairey monoplane completes the first non-stop flight from Britain to India in 50 hours and 37 minutes (→ 24/5/30).

Britain, 31 May. The general election, in which six million more women voted, returns 13 women to the Commons, including Lloyd George's daughter Megan.

France, 16 June. Britain's Bentley team takes the first four places at this year's Le Mans 24-hour endurance race (→ 3/4/30).

London, 2 July. King George opens Parliament, delivering the first King's Speech for a Labour government (→ 25/12/32).

Dublin, 16 July. The Censorship of Publications Act comes into force; it provides for a board to censor or ban publications for obscenity or other reasons.

London, 29 July. The foreign secretary, Arthur Henderson, has talks with a Soviet representative on the restoration of Anglo-Soviet relations (→ 18/4/33).

London, 6 August. Britain agrees a draft treaty under which it will withdraw troops from the whole of Egypt except the Suez Canal.

Jerusalem, 25 August. The British declare martial law in a bid to quell clashes between Arabs and Jews which have left 60 dead (→ 19/10/38).

New York, 24 October. Shares crash on Wall Street.

Britain, 2 December. The first 22 public telephone boxes become operational.

Britain, 5 December. A 151 kmph [94mph] hurricane sweeps the country, causing 26 deaths.

'Chain stores' boom in the High Street

Britain, January
"Chain stores" have begun to change the British way of shopping during the present decade and none more so than those of the American-owned Woolworth's company. Its high street shops offer a wider range of mass-produced goods at lower prices than is available at traditional corner shops or individual department stores. A British company founded in Leeds called Marks and Spencer is also expanding around the country.

Woolworth's: a shopper's delight.

The river Shannon goes hydro-electric

Ireland, 21 October
A major initiative by the Irish government, the Shannon hydro-electric scheme, has begun commercial operations. Electricity is now to be generated by damming the river Shannon. The scheme is seen as a radical departure from the conservative policies of the prime minister, William Cosgrave. Until now all of the country's electricity has been provided by private generating operations, but only one-third of Dublin and a quarter of Cork has electrical power. The new scheme will dramatically increase the supply of electricity at a cost of around £5 million.

Labour returns to power

Labour's first cabinet, led by the prime minister, Ramsay MacDonald.

Westminster, 7 June
Ramsay MacDonald returned to No 10 Downing Street today with a pledge that his new Labour government will tackle the problem of unemployment, now passing the one million mark, almost 10 per cent of the workforce. Jimmy Thomas, the railwaymen's leader, is lord privy seal with the task of cutting the dole queues.

Any idea of giving socialism a trial is ruled out by the fact that once again Labour is without an overall Commons majority; last month's election gave Labour 288 seats, Tories 260 and Liberals 59. But the leadership anyway has little taste for left-wing nostrums.

The cabinet is resolutely respectable, with Philip Snowden as chancellor of the exchequer to keep firm control of public spending. The token left-winger is George Lansbury, the one-time East End councillor who scandalized Tories by paying high rates of poor relief not approved by government. One innovation is the appointment of Margaret Bondfield as minister of labour – the first woman cabinet minister (→ 20/5/30).

September 7. Britain wins the Schneider Cup and sets a new air speed record using this Supermarine S6, here being refuelled at Calshot, Hants.

Cinema blaze kills 69 Scottish children

Paisley, 31 December
Tragedy cast a terrible pall over the great Scottish festival of Hogmanay tonight as 69 children were found dead after a fire in a cinema here. Most of the dead, aged between 5 and 14, were crushed or suffocated as they fled in panic to escape the fumes, caused by a burning reel of film. A further 37 are badly injured, and the death toll may rise.

A special children's show had attracted an audience of 2,000 at the Glen cinema. Soon after the alarm sounded, there was a rush for the exits. Firemen who broke in found a pile of dead and dying children just ten steps from safety on a stairway. An 18-month-old child was on top of the pile.

Elsewhere, the corpses of children were found huddled together in the orchestra pit, beneath the seats, and beside the screen, which they had tried to climb to safety. Gas lights were broken in the chaos and some of the victims may have been asphyxiated. Fire doors had been ignored in the panic. This was the worst cinema fire in Britain, and might well have been avoided. The burning reel which started the fire was thrown out of a window before the panic started.

De Valera is arrested in Northern Ireland

De Valera: a month in jail.

Belfast, 8 February
Eamon de Valera has been arrested at the Northern Ireland border on his way to attend a function in Belfast hosted by the Gaelic League and the Gaelic Athletic Association. He was arrested on a previous occasion five years ago, ignoring warnings forbidding him to enter the six counties – despite the fact that he was an elected representative for Down, though he never attended the Belfast parliament.

This time he was taken from the train by the Royal Ulster Constabulary, brought to Belfast, where he was tried for contravening the exclusion order which had been issued against him five years ago, and sentenced to one month's imprisonment (→ 5/9/31).

Poor Law guardians to be swept away

Britain, December
The Poor Law guardians will soon be no more. Since 1834 they have administered the Poor Law, under which the starving and destitute could receive at least a bare minimum of subsistence help, but they are to be abolished next year. The move, embodied in this year's Local Government Act, is the culmination of a series of moves designed to reorganize the way the nation's poor are treated. Up to one and a half million people will be affected.

The 19th-century Poor Law has been seen as increasingly ineffective since 1909, when a royal commission suggested many of the changes which have now been achieved. The Poor Law unions and the guardians themselves have been swept away. Poor Law Hospitals have been turned over to local authorities as have the hated old workhouses (since 1913 known as Poor Law institutions). But the buildings will still be used to house the impoverished aged and infirm.

It is hoped that the new system will improve treatment for such unfortunates, up to a third of whom have still been dying in the workhouse, whatever its name, but some fear that a new authority will not mean the end to the old Victorian rigour (→ 12/2/32).

Arts and entertainment in the 'roaring twenties'

Everybody's going to 'the pictures'

The great new place to go for entertainment in the 1920s has been "the pictures". Every week people of all classes and ages go to sit before the silent screen accompanied by a pit pianist. The coming of "talkies" in 1927 increased the audiences, although many people predicted that sound was merely a passing fad, as Charlie Chaplin had declared it was. At least half the population are weekly cinemagoers. Glasgow had 96 cinemas by 1928.

Although our screens are totally dominated by Hollywood stars, such as Douglas Fairbanks and Mary Pickford, Chaplin and Buster Keaton, and now Mickey Mouse in place of Felix the Cat, the number

Anny Ondra in "Blackmail".

of British films made jumped from a mere 34 in 1926 to 128 in 1927. The "quota" imposed by the Cinematograph Act will rise annually towards 20 per cent made in Britain.

The two leading production companies are Gaumont-British and Gainsborough, with the Elstree studios of British International Pictures (BIP) described as Britain's Hollywood. Michael Balcon at Gainsborough has lost his tyro director, Alfred Hitchcock, to BIP where he directed *Blackmail*, the first British thriller talkie about a girl who stabs a man and is blackmailed. Her voice was "dubbed" by an actress standing just out of shot.

Singer Monti Ryan with Percival Mackey's dance band on the Savoy roof.

Jazz music puts its stamp on the decade

The American novelist Scott Fitzgerald dubbed the decade "the Jazz Age", and jazz bands were spearheads of the American invasion of British life. But "jazz" is a term for all kinds of sound – even Al Jolson counts as a "jazz singer".

The real thing was first heard in the Original Dixie Jazz Band's visits to London in 1919 and 1920, which brought audiences to their feet with *Tiger Rag*. They were followed by Paul Whiteman and his "jazz orchestra" which had given the première of George Gershwin's

Rhapsody in Blue. Records of the jazz greats playing in Harlem or Chicago, of King Oliver, Louis Armstrong, Duke Ellington or Fats Waller, can only be obtained with difficulty in Britain.

British bands exist primarily for dancing. The BBC relays the Savoy Orpheans under Carroll Gibbons, Bert Ambrose from the Mayfair hotel and Jack Payne's BBC Dance Orchestra. They play *Yes, Sir, That's My Baby* or *I Can't Give You Anything But Love, Baby* – and that, baby, is "jazz".

Dance craze attracts millions to the Palais

The alternative to going to the pictures for a cheap night out has turned out to be going to the Palais. The craze for dancing – the foxtrot, the tango, the Black Bottom and of course, the Charleston – began as the war ended. The first "Palais de Danse", at Hammersmith in London, opened in 1919, and it has been copied in most other cities. Admission costs only a shilling [5p]. London hotels offer teadances and restaurants boast of their bands – one in the West End has them on all four floors. After hours there are the night clubs: the Embassy, with Ambrose's band and the prince of Wales's table always reserved, is the smartest.

Charleston: dance of the decade.

Literature explores modern wasteland

"Modernism" characterizes those writing in the Twenties. There has seldom been such a break with the past, led by two poets, Irish and American by birth. W B Yeats, the father of the Celtic twilight, has transformed his romantic style into a harsher one for brutal times in *Easter, 1916* and *Byzantium*, while T S Eliot, from Harvard, baffled but fascinated readers in 1922 with *The Waste Land*, which was ruthlessly edited by his fellow American Ezra Pound. Its bleak notes of despair and disgust echoed the traumatized post-war feelings of his young contemporaries.

In the same year James Joyce's epic *Ulysses* appeared, making

Wells: obsolete novelist?

Edwardian novelists such as Wells, Bennett and Galsworthy look obsolete, though they continued to write. Galsworthy completed his saga of the Forsytes in five sequels to *The Man of Property*. Like Joyce, D H Lawrence was banned and chose voluntary exile from Britain. *Women in Love*, a sequel to *The Rainbow*, did not find a publisher till 1921, and *Lady Chatterley's Lover*, published abroad, was accused of obscenity. Virginia Woolf experimented on Joycean lines with the "stream of consciousness" in *Mrs Dalloway* and *To The Lighthouse*, while E M Forster cut free from Edwardian domesticity in *A Passage to India*.

Elgar falls silent so Holst picks up the musical mantle

After his 1919 cello concerto Sir Edward Elgar fell virtually silent, and British music was without its leading composer. The mantle fell first on Gustav Holst, whose suite *The Planets*, written during the Great War, was first performed in 1920, immediately becoming one of the most popular works in the repertoire. He followed it with a comic opera, *The Perfect Fool*.

New operas were not plentiful. One by Rutland Boughton, *The Immortal Hour*, with its well-known *Fairy Song*, ran for over 200 performances. Ralph Vaughan Williams's *Pastoral Symphony* was first performed in 1922. Then came his ballad opera *Hugh the Drover*, a ballet score, *Job*, and an opera based on Shakespeare's Falstaff, *Sir John in Love*. Frederick Delius provided the haunting score for the exotic play *Hassan* by James Elroy Flecker, a popular triumph in 1923. That was the year of the first public performance of poems by Edith Sitwell, *Façade*, declaimed through a megaphone to witty music by William Walton, a youth of 21 who was a protégé of the Sitwells. After showing his facility at parody of popular dance styles in *Façade*, he went on to produce an effective viola concerto in 1929, the year his friend Constant Lambert wrote the jazzy tone poem *The Rio Grande*.

Noël Coward is theatre's new shining star

Noël Coward (centre) stars in a scene from his own play "The Vortex".

The theatre has had two great playwrights and one entertainer of genius this decade, which is more than most decades can muster. The playwrights are George Bernard Shaw and Sean O'Casey, the entertainer is Noël Coward.

Shaw's decade got off to a slow start with *Heartbreak House*, produced in 1921. It was too long and too slow, and its run was short. One critic unkindly called it "Jawbreak House", but Shaw restored his reputation with *St Joan* in 1924. In it he created a heroine he was perfectly serious about and Sybil Thorndike was his perfect Joan. Sean O'Casey worked as a labourer in Dublin before writing three tragi-comedies about the troubles, which were mounted by the Abbey theatre. *The Shadow of a Gunman, Juno and the Paycock* and *The Plough and the Stars* (which was greeted by riots) won him a place beside Synge in the Irish pantheon.

Noël Coward's year of brilliance was 1925 when he was appearing as a drug addict in his play *The Vortex*, which scandalized, wrote a drunken scene for two ladies in *Fallen Angels* (more scandal) and then in three days turned out *Hay Fever*, in which actors humiliate weekend guests. And he was co-author of a revue still running in London.

How taboo topic of war has been ended in the arts

In 1920 the poems of Wilfred Owen appeared, made even more poignant by the fact that he was killed only a week before the Armistice. Poems such as his *Anthem for Doomed Youth* sounded a bitterly different note from the glory in war suggested by Rupert Brooke before he had seen any fighting. Owen's work was edited by his friend Siegfried Sassoon, whose own poems are full of scorching sarcasm at commanders' incompetence.

For nearly a decade of peace the subject of the war was taboo, but since 1928 the books have poured forth. First, from the German side, came *Im Westen Nichts Neues* – the ironic news bulletin tag, *All Quiet On The*

A scene from "Journey's End", one of this year's stage hits.

Western Front, from Erich Maria Remarque. The English poet Edmund Blunden published *Undertones of War*, and this year brought the memoirs of Robert Graves, another war poet, *Goodbye to All That*, and Richard Aldington's *Death of a Hero*. All these are anti-war books attacking the false values put forward to justify it. Even more powerful is *Journey's End*, a play by R C Sherriff that tells the truth about trench warfare, which opened to critical acclaim this year. The only "clean" war that arouses enthusiasm is the *Revolt in the Desert* of T E Lawrence.

Abstract sculpture and bleak landscape set style in visual arts

The war artists who saw such destruction in Flanders found themselves without a war to portray. Paul Nash somehow makes his landscapes of England as bleakly empty as the western front; Stanley Spencer paints his memories of the ranks on the walls of Burghclere chapel, a private memorial, and sets his visions of the crucifixion and resurrection in the churchyard of his native Cookham. Elemental carving by Epstein now adorns the headquarters of London Underground. Similar massive simplicity is found in Henry Moore's carving of *Mother and Child* and *Reclining Figure*, and Barbara Hepworth's birds show a matching abstraction.

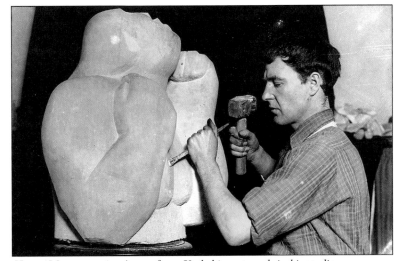
Henry Moore, a miner's son from Yorkshire, at work in his studio.

Novice is first to fly solo to Australia

Darwin, Australia, 24 May

Amy Johnson, a 26-year-old Englishwoman who won her pilot's licence just last year, has landed here at the end of an epic flight. Huge crowds turned out to welcome Johnson, the first woman to fly solo across the world.

Johnson – or "Johnnie" to her friends – took off on 6 May from Croydon in a second-hand de Havilland Gipsy Moth called *Jason*. It was a gruelling journey from the start. She nearly crashed into a mountain in Turkey and had to make an emergency landing in the Iraqi desert because of a sandstorm. Johnson sat the storm out in her cockpit, pistol at the ready in case of attack by wild dogs.

Johnson's arrival in Karachi on 10 May cut two days off the London-to-India record set by Bert Hinkler. The fact that she failed, however, to beat his record for the whole route has done nothing to dampen today's ecstatic welcome at Fanny Bay. She can now look forward to a well-earned rest before the return flight – courtesy of Imperial Airways (→ 5/10).

Airborne adventurer Amy Johnson.

Commission calls for Indian federation

Westminster, 23 June 1930

After three years of deliberations, a statutory commission on the future of India has rejected nationalist demands for independence. The commission, chaired by former Liberal minister Sir John Simon, proposes self-government at provincial level in a federation with the princely states, under a British viceroy at the head of the central government.

The commission's findings are presented against a background of widespread civil disobedience instigated by nationalists led by a lawyer Mohandas Gandhi, who combines a saintly bearing with wily political skills. He embarrasses the authorities with calls for nonviolent protests – which often lead to rioting.

When the commission visited India to gather evidence, it was greeted by noisy crowds waving "Simon Go Home" banners. In its report the commission highlights the bewildering diversity of the subcontinent's 319 million people, divided by race, religion, language and caste, and implies that British rule holds the country together.

Ramsay MacDonald, the prime minister, is planning a round-table conference in London to consider the proposals of the Simon commission. Gandhi, who has been in detention since May, is calling for a boycott.

Gandhi, a peaceful protester.

Slum clearance is boosted by new act

Westminster, 21 April

A new Housing Act becomes law today, providing subsidies for slum clearance. Arthur Greenwood, the housing minister, believes the act will complete the postwar transformation of Britain's housing. Since Lloyd George launched the "homes fit for heroes" scheme in 1918, more than one million homes have been built. These dwellings are a mixture of council homes with controlled rents, and modest, often semi-detached private homes that cost about twice the annual salary of the average professional man. New building is concentrating on large estates on the fringes of the big cities.

Charities to profit in hospital lottery

Ireland, 4 June

Faced with the possible closure of hospitals owing to lack of finance, the government has reluctantly agreed to setting up the Irish Hospital Sweepstakes. The organizers are basing the gamble on English races such as the Grand National and the Derby, thus ensuring large fields and maximum publicity. As well as helping the hospitals, the "Sweep" is expected to employ large numbers of women, and to boost the economy.

Portmeirion: an Italianate model village in Wales designed by Clough Williams-Ellis.

Two million out of work

Unemployed march along the Embankment to County Hall in Lambeth.

London, 7 August
Unemployment figures released today show that over two million are now out of work, the biggest number since 1921. The economic recovery of the last half of the 1920s was stopped in its tracks by last year's Wall Street crash. The collapse in US confidence has hit world trade generally and British exports and shipping.

So far the crisis has hit the older industrial areas, with coal, iron and steel, shipbuilding and textiles being the most severely affected. The Midlands, thanks to the motor car firms, and the south, which is more concerned with supplying domestic consumers, are more buoyant.

The financial crisis this year has added to the downward spiral. Falling food prices have hit developing countries which can no longer afford to buy British capital goods and shipping is facing its worst-ever slump. Even many of those not registered as unemployed are only working part of the year (→ 4/7/31).

R101 airship crashes over French fields

Beauvais, France, 5 October
Britain's secretary of state for air, Lord Thomson, and Major General Sir Sefton Brancker are among the 48 people who died when the R101 airship crashed in the early hours of this morning. There are only six survivors from what is believed to be British aviation's worst disaster.

The R101 took off yesterday from Cardington, Bedfordshire, on its way to India via Egypt but soon ran into trouble. Rain and a faulty engine forced it to fly low over the Channel and to keep low when it reached France. By that time the airship was also seen to be pitching and rolling.

Shortly before 2am over fields near the village of Beauvais the R101 suddenly dived. In a desperate attempt to gain height, water ballast was poured from the airship but it sank to the ground and burst into flames.

One witness said it looked "as if the whole world had exploded". Within seconds all that remained of the 237-metre (777-foot) R101 airship was a charred wreck (→ 5/3/36).

The burnt out skeleton of the R101 airship lies where it crashed near Beauvais.

Tory defeated by Beaverbrook's United Empire Party candidate

London, 31 October
A retired vice-admiral standing as an Empire Free Trade candidate in the South Paddington by-election has defeated the official Conservative candidate. Lord Beaverbrook, the press tycoon and strident advocate of the Empire policy, is exultant. "What a life!" he says. "A day to remember." The Tory leader, Stanley Baldwin, who regards Beaverbrook's free trade ideas as impractical, reacted to calls for his resignation by seeking a vote of confidence from Tory peers and MPs; the resolution was passed by 462 votes to 116. Beaverbrook said the 116 represent "the real spirit of the party". But critics say he is using his United Empire Party to increase the circulation of his Express newspapers (→ 17/3/31).

Lord Beaverbrook (third from right) rallies the United Empire Party's faithful.

Youth hostels give value to travellers

London, December
A new organization was formed this year to meet the growing demand for cheap accommodation in the countryside. Cycling and hiking are both increasing in popularity and a number of groups have provided cheap and basic accommodation in areas such as the Lake District and the Pennines. Now a new organization called the Youth Hostel Association (YHA) is being created along lines pioneered in Germany in 1914. The first permanent YHA hostel will be in Winchester with hundreds more planned throughout England and Wales. Separate YHA organizations are likely to be formed in Scotland, Ulster and Ireland.

Britain, 1 January. The Road Traffic Act comes into force, making third party insurance compulsory (→ 12).

Westminster, 26 January. Winston Churchill quits the Tory shadow cabinet in protest over moves to give India greater freedom (→ 28/11/34).

Florida, 5 February. Malcolm Campbell sets a new world land speed record of 394kpmh [245mph].

London, 27 March. Lord Beaverbrook ends his empire crusade movement after his candidate lost to a Tory at a by-election this month.

Westminster, 20 April. A bill to allow cinemas to open on Sundays is given a second reading.

Britain, 4 June. Cuts in unemployment pay are urged by a royal commission as a means to avert an economic crisis (→ 31/7).

London, 1 July. Trolley buses begin regular services in the capital, 20 years after their introduction in Yorkshire.

Britain, 6 July. Census returns reveal a drift of population to the southern half of the country; London's population tops eight million, a growth of almost ten per cent since 1921.

Westminster, 31 July. Salary cuts and lower unemployment benefit are recommended in a report which threatens to split the Labour cabinet (→ 24/8).

Westminster, 28 August. Ramsay MacDonald is ousted as Labour leader to be replaced by Arthur Henderson (→ 20/9).

Ireland, 5 September. The first issue of *Irish Press*, the journal of Fianna Fail, is published (→ 20/10).

Britain, 7 September. The king decides to take a pay cut because of the economic crisis.

Dublin, 20 October. The IRA is among 12 groups banned as a tribunal is set up to punish "treasonable activities".

Westminster, 4 November. Herbert Samuel succeeds David Lloyd George as Liberal leader (→ 28/9/32).

London, 1 December. A round-table conference on India fails to reach agreement.

Britain, 15 December. Traffic lights are to be introduced throughout Britain, following their success in London (→ 8/1932).

Mosley breaks away from Labour Party

Mosley addresses a gathering in the hope of gaining support for his new party.

London, 28 February 1931
Sir Oswald Mosley, the wealthy Sandhurst-trained Tory who became a Labour MP in 1924, has stormed out of the party after having his radical plans for tackling unemployment decisively rejected. Since the minority Labour government took office in 1929, pledged to reduce unemployment, the dole queue has more than doubled to over two million. The prime minister, Ramsay MacDonald, seems resigned to impotence; capitalism is collapsing, he says.

Mosley's plans call for state direction of industry, a big increase in public spending and controls on imports. When the cabinet rejected his proposals, Mosley took them to the parliamentary party. His speech was loudly cheered by MPs, who then turned him down by 202 votes to 29. He appealed to the party conference and was again defeated.

So now he is launching his own movement, the New Party, which, he says, will be "a party of action" resolved to transform parliament "from a talk-shop to a workshop".

Mosley is promising "a mobilization of energy, vitality and manhood to save the nation". Four Labour MPs have followed him into his New Party; one of them is his wife Cynthia (→ 31/7).

Press lords likened to harlots by PM

Westminster, 17 March
Stanley Baldwin, the Conservative leader, has tonight rounded on the newspaper proprietors Lord Beaverbrook and Lord Rothermere. They have backed an Empire Free Trade candidate in a London by-election and are confident of beating the Tory candidate, as they did at another by-election last October. Baldwin tonight sought to rally anti-press opinion by denouncing the two lords for wanting power without responsibility. This, he said, was "the prerogative of the harlot throughout the ages" (→ 27).

The empire evolves – except in India

London, December
The great changes taking place in the British empire have been formally recognized. The Statute of Westminster over which Lord Balfour's committee has laboured for five years defines Great Britain and the dominions as "autonomous communities within the British empire, equal in status, in no way subordinate one to another in any aspect of their domestic or internal affairs, though united by a common allegiance to the Crown, and freely associated as members of the British Commonwealth of Nations".

The independence which the dominions enjoy in practice has thus been constitutionally confirmed. Only in India does the Raj continue unchanged.

Ford factory opens

Essex, December
The giant Ford Motor Company of America this year opened its biggest European plant on the banks of the Thames at Dagenham, east of London. Henry Ford set up his first European plant at Trafford Park in Manchester as long ago as 1910, but the Dagenham factory is much larger and it epitomizes the trend away from coach-building to production-line car manufacture. The new factory expects to be employing more than 7,000 men by the end of next year (→ 15).

Three Port of London Authority policemen put their trust in their new kapok-filled lifejackets as they take the plunge into the river Thames.

Economic crisis brings down Labour government

Ministers are split over economic cuts

Westminster, 24 August

The Labour government today fell after days of impassioned debate about how to tackle the economic crisis. Ramsay MacDonald, the Labour premier, will now head an all-party "National" government and has been denounced as a traitor by most Labour ministers and MPs.

MacDonald himself twice went to Buckingham Palace to resign, but was persuaded by King George to head a coalition government. The king also won backing for a National government from Stanley Baldwin and Sir Herbert Samuel, the Tory and Liberal leaders.

It was the run on the pound that brought the crisis to a head this month. The Labour cabinet had been rocked by a report in July calling for swingeing cuts in public spending to pull the country back from economic disaster. The report came from a committee of businessmen and trade unionists set up by the government in February and chaired by Sir George May, a former Prudential Assurance executive.

The report called for tax rises, pay cuts for police, teachers, civil servants and the armed forces, and a 20 per cent cut in the dole. Ministers were deeply divided, with a large minority threatening to resign over the dole cuts. The May report was taken by bankers as confirmation of their worst fears, intensifying withdrawals of funds from London and causing gold reserves to plummet. The Bank of England warned that national bankruptcy was near (→ 28).

Scuffles break out as police attempt to seize a red banner from protesters.

Ramsay MacDonald prepares to make a broadcast from the cabinet room.

Pay cuts provoke anger and a mutiny

London, 30 September

Philip Snowden's emergency budget of higher taxes and pay cuts has been followed by a month of demonstrations, clashes with the police and even a brief naval mutiny. In the House of Commons, Labour MPs have bitterly accused Ramsay MacDonald and Snowden, only last month comrades in the socialist cause, of betrayal and surrender to a "bankers' ramp".

But Snowden, the chancellor, stood firm and balanced his budget. Everybody paid by the state, from cabinet ministers and judges to the unemployed, has had to make sacrifices. Income tax has been raised to 5s [25p] in the pound.

The dole has been cut by 10 per cent, half the figure proposed in the controversial May report, but still enough to provoke cries of hardship. Outside Battersea town hall tonight some 5,000 unemployed staged a demonstration and in the West End postal workers brought traffic to a halt. Civil servants, too, have joined in protest marches.

The mutiny, by ratings at Invergordon, on Cromarty Firth, broke out on 15 September when word went round that their pay was to be cut by 25 per cent. The men defied their officers, held mass meetings and refused to take the fleet to sea. Discipline was restored after two days when the Admiralty promised a cut of only 10 per cent.

The mutiny has helped others. The teachers' 15 per cent cut has been reduced to 10 per cent. The police have done best with a cut of just five per cent (→ 28/10).

Run on the pound leads to devaluation

London, 20 September

Legislation is to be rushed through parliament tomorrow to do the very thing the Labour government was told only a month ago was impossible. The gold standard is being abandoned and sterling will be allowed to float. The National government acted under pressure from Sir Montagu Norman, governor of the Bank of England, who reported that reserves had been exhausted by speculation against the pound. This had intensified after the Invergordon mutiny five days ago. The pound's value against the dollar is expected to fall by a quarter to $3.40. Imports will be more expensive, but exports will be more competitive (→ 30).

Labour routed as coalition wins election

Westminster, 28 October

The Labour Party has been overwhelmed at the polls after an election campaign led by the man who was, until this summer, its admired leader, but is now seen as a traitor. Ramsay MacDonald is prime minister of a National government with the support of 554 MPs, 473 of them Tories, 68 Liberal and just 13 self-styled National Labour. MacDonald accused his old colleagues in the Labour cabinet of running away from the economic crisis and he appealed to voters to give his all-party government a doctor's mandate to restore foreign confidence in Britain. Voters have responded by returning just 52 regular Labour MPs (→ 4/11).

De Valera topples Cosgrave to form a new government

Ireland, 9 March

Fianna Fáil today formed a new government with the support of the Labour Party. This follows the defeat in last month's election of William Cosgrave's party, Cumann na nGaedheal. The new prime minister, Eamon de Valera, has already given assurances that there will be no victimization of those who supported the 1921 treaty. As proof of this, his justice minister is a former Cumann na nGaedheal supporter. De Valera is taking the external affairs portfolio himself and Sean Lemass has been appointed minister for industry and commerce.

De Valera is widely seen as the embodiment of Irish national aspirations and inspires devotion in his followers. His party fought a well-organized campaign in which its leader appeared at many meetings throughout the country wearing a black cloak and riding a white horse. The new government is expected to introduce tough social and economic measures, as well as removing the oath of allegiance to the British king (→ 16).

Dartmoor governor is saved by inmate

Princetown, Devon, 25 January

Troops with machine guns are ringing the bleak walls of Dartmoor prison tonight following a riot in which 70 inmates and six warders were injured. Police were rushed from Plymouth and other centres to join prison warders in a series of charges with truncheons on rampaging convicts armed with homemade spears.

The prison governor and a Home Office Commissioner owe their lives to George Donovan, serving a life sentence for murder, who put himself between them and ringleaders of the mutiny. Donovan was reprieved an hour before he was due to hang.

Prisoners were complaining of poor and inadequate food, damp cells and the difficulties faced by relatives in reaching the remote granite prison on the moors.

Peak District hikers risk imprisonment

Ramblers gather in support of public rights of way across the countryside.

Edale, Derbyshire, 24 April

Five men were arrested today after a "mass trespass" involving thousands of hikers on the grouse moors of Kinder Scout above Edale. The men, who could face jail sentences, were arrested after clashes with gamekeepers who were seeking to keep the ramblers off private land.

Public access to the countryside has become increasingly contentious as cars, motor-cycles and bikes have brought once remote areas within reach of millions of town-dwellers. Hiking is booming as a recreation combining aesthetic appreciation of the countryside with the vogue for healthy outdoor fitness. The Peak District, close to Manchester, Sheffield and Derby, is in the forefront of the campaign for greater access: only 1,212 acres out of 150,000 acres of moorland are open to the public.

Norfolk rector in sex case is defrocked

Norfolk, 21 October

The parish of Stiffkey is to have a new clergyman. A consistory court has today defrocked the Reverend Harold Francis Davidson after he had been found guilty earlier this year of behaviour causing "grave scandal to the Church".

Mr Davidson, which is how the former rector of Stiffkey must now be called, was brought before the consistory court last March. The rector's frequent visits to London and his alleged association with young girls kept the press happy, although he denied the charges.

The prosecution alleged that Davidson, aged 60, spent Sundays in his parish but weekdays in a bed-sitter in Shepherd's Bush, London. Waitresses from Lyons's and ABC tearooms complained that he had pestered them and a model told the court that he had set her up in lodgings. While the court deliberated, Davidson caused a scene in

The guilty rector leaves court.

June by attempting to grab the bible of a clergyman deputizing for him at Stiffkey. But he was found guilty of associating with women of loose character and of accosting young women for immoral purposes.

Ramsay MacDonald isolated in cabinet as Liberal ministers quit government

Westminster, 28 September

Ramsay MacDonald's government is looking less and less National and more and more Tory since the abrupt resignation of four prominent cabinet ministers, three of them Liberals, the fourth, Philip, Viscount Snowden, the Labour veteran who became the "Iron Chancellor" in the first weeks of the National government. The resignations were provoked by agreements limiting tariffs on trade with the dominions and raising them on trade with foreign countries. Thirty back-bench Liberals have gone over to the opposition in protest at the government's repudiation of free trade principles (→ 3/1933).

Ramsay MacDonald: out of step.

Three Methodist churches agree to unite

Britain, 20 September

The Methodist churches will speak with one voice from today. After lengthy negotiations, the Primitive Methodists, the United Methodists and the Wesleyan Methodists have all agreed to transcend their differences and unite.

The Methodists are only the latest of the "low church" denominations to attempt to deal with the falling attendances and declining faith that some have attributed to the horrors of the Great War, by sinking their differences. In 1929 the United Free Church in Scotland, itself formed in 1900 from a union of the United Presbyterians and most of the Free Church, rejoined the Church of Scotland.

Certainly, in the face of competition on Sundays from motor cars and railway trips, the churches can no longer afford the attitude of one 19th-century Methodist preacher who said of another: "They say this dog barks well but he comes from a dirty kennel."

Land row starts Anglo-Irish trade war

Dublin, 15 July

True to its electoral pledge, Fianna Fáil has refused to pay land annuities to the British government. The annuities amount to around £5 million a year and Fianna Fáil believes there are economic, moral and legal reasons why they should no longer be paid. The British government, already smarting over Fianna Fáil's plan to drop the oath of allegiance to the crown, has responded to the challenge by imposing a 20 per cent duty on Irish agricultural exports. Eamon de Valera, the Irish premier, in turn is imposing duties on British coal.

De Valera does not intend to abolish the annuities but to halve them and retain the money for his government. But this would deprive farmers of 10 per cent of their net income, so feelings are running high. Cattle prices have dropped to 1914 levels, and farmers, recalling speeches by Fianna Fáil candidates, are refusing to pay their share of the annuities (→ 28/1/33).

Unemployment hits an all-time record

Britain, 30 September

Nearly three million workers are now out of work – one in four of the total British labour force. Yet the real situation is thought to be even worse. The official statistics exclude many agricultural workers, the self-employed and married women, who do not usually sign on the dole.

Many people have been driven below the poverty line. In Stockton-on-Tees, for instance, the average income for unemployed families is 20s [£1] a week against 51s 6d for those in work. However, those able to get unemployment relief are in some cases better off than workers in the lowest-paid jobs (→ 13/10).

King 'speaks from heart' at Christmas

Sandringham, 25 December

In a room under the stairs once used by his father's secretary, King George V today made his first Christmas broadcast to the nation and the empire. "I speak now from my home and from my heart to you all," the king said. His voice was first broadcast in 1924, when he opened the Empire Exhibition at Wembley. John Reith, general manager of the BBC, urged him to use the wireless again to speak directly to his subjects, but until today he has resisted. George was nervous – the broadcast was "live" – but it is thought likely that the royal message will become a Christmas tradition (→ 18/7/34).

Oswald Mosley to head new fascist movement in Britain

London, December

Sir Oswald Mosley, who left the Labour government two years ago over his radical solutions to unemployment, has formed a new party this year. Members of the British Union of Fascists will wear black shirts, like their Italian counterparts. Sir Oswald is apparently undaunted by the failure of the party he formed last year – the New Party, dedicated to mobilizing "energy vitality and manhood" – in the 1931 general election.

He advocates control of industry and massive state borrowing at a time when the new National government is cutting public spending. Many Conservatives, and newspaper tycoon Lord Rothermere, are said to support him (→ 22/8/33).

Mosley's new fascist party holds its first meeting in Trafalgar Square.

Atoms smashed in 'Brave New World'

Cambridge, December

Science made important strides this year at the Cavendish Laboratory in Cambridge. John Cockcroft and Ernest Walton, under the leadership of the Nobel prizewinner, Sir Ernest Rutherford, split the atom, as Rutherford had foreseen in 1919 could be done. Their atom smashing machine also transmuted lithium atoms into those of helium – the first artificial transformation. Also at Cambridge, James Chadwick discovered a new sub-atomic particle: the neutron. Not everyone is thrilled by science. Aldous Huxley, in *Brave New World* published this year, offers a bleak vision of people bred by test-tube.

'Bodyline' rumpus threatens cricket tour

Woodfull is forced to take evasive action as Larwood delivers a thunderbolt.

Adelaide, Australia, 23 January
Cricket authorities in England and Australia have clashed bitterly off the field as their players fought out a bitter confrontation in the third test here at Adelaide. The dispute centres on what the Australians call "bodyline" and what the English captain, Douglas Jardine, calls "leg theory". By the time the test ended the Australian authorities had sent a telegram to the MCC in London protesting that the tactics, whatever they were called, were "unsportsmanlike" and should cease.

Jardine developed his controversial tactics as a ploy to counter the brilliance of Australia's batting hero, Don Bradman. It involves bowling fast deliveries on the line of the leg stump and batsman's body with a cordon of close fielders on the leg side. If bowlers are accurate, batsmen are forced to play, with any mishit likely to offer a catch.

Tempers flared when Australia's wicketkeeper Bert Oldfield was hit on the head by a ball from Larwood. After he was helped from the pitch, the home team's captain Bill Woodfull (who had been hit twice by bouncers) protested that there were two sides playing but "one was not playing cricket". The Australians fired off their telegram but, with a diplomatic row brewing, the MCC has declared its confidence in the English captain and deplored the accusation of "unsportsmanlike" behaviour (→ 16/2).

British engineers are tried as spies

Moscow, 18 April
In one of Stalin's "show-trials" in which nothing is what it seems, two British engineers working for Metropolitan-Vickers have been imprisoned for "spying, wrecking and bribery". Three other Britons are to be deported and a sixth was acquitted. After being held for a month in the Lubyanka prison one of the defendants "confessed" but another protested that the case was "a frame-up, staged on the evidence of terrorized Russians". The Foreign Office deplored the sentences and Britain is expected to impose sanctions on Russia.

Fascist 'Blueshirts' banned in Ireland after IRA clashes

Dublin, 22 August
The Army Comrades Association, led by Eoin O'Duffy, a former chief of police, has turned itself into the "National Guard" aimed at the overthrow of communism. Known as the "Blueshirts", the Guard has clashed so frequently with the IRA that the Irish government led by Eamon de Valera has now banned the movement.

Fascism has grown on fertile ground in Ireland. Hardship and unemployment are everywhere and Irish exports dropped by half last year as a result of de Valera's trade war against Britain. The Army Comrades Association was established last year, declaring its aim to guarantee free speech by creating a "volunteer force". By the end of 1932 it claimed 30,000 active members. They wore blue shirts, drilling and saluting in the fascist manner – their leader admires Benito Mussolini, the Italian dictator, and wishes to see an end to parliamentary democracy.

Eamon de Valera's government has made several attempts to suppress the Blueshirts but to no avail. Their stern authoritarianism, seductive in these troubled times, has attracted public figures as diverse as the poet W B Yeats and the prominent Catholic churchman, John Charles McQuaid (→ 21/1/34).

'Corner House' offers a food revolution

Tea for two, or three or four...

London, 23 October
Over 1,000 staff are poised to serve 2,000 customers in a huge new Lyons "Corner House" which is to open today claiming to offer a revolution in mass catering.

The revolution lies behind the kitchen doors. While the customers listen to background music, the waitresses will hurry down a "one-way" production-line system, passing over their orders at points signposted with notices like "fried fish" and "soups". The idea is that service should be as quick as possible.

Last year Lyons's smaller tea-shops won notoriety as places frequented by the defrocked rector of Stiffkey

De Valera cuts links with British crown

Dublin, 9 October

The Irish parliament has jettisoned the oath of allegience to Britain by passing the Removal of the Oath Act, thus ending a long-standing Irish grievance. Together with the partition of the country and the continued British military control of the treaty ports, the oath has always been particularly objectionable to anti-treaty republicans since it appeared to affirm Britain's right to rule Ireland, and was in direct contrast to the long separatist tradition going back to Wolfe Tone and the 1798 rebellion.

Meanwhile the other major issue – the payment of land annuities to the British exchequer – remains unresolved. Eamon de Valera, the Irish prime minister, has been holding talks with members of the British cabinet and arbitration was being considered when, last July, the House of Commons passed a resolution to enable the British government to make good money lost by means of customs duties on imports from Ireland.

De Valera has sought further to reduce British influence with his request that the representative of the crown in Ireland – the governor-general – be removed from office. This was accepted and James McNeill, the present incumbent, was replaced by de Valera with Domhnall O Buachalla, a Fianna Fáil grocer from Co Kildare who has kept firmly out of the public eye ever since, thus dealing the office a death blow (→ 11/12/36).

Eamon de Valera, the Irish premier, presides over his Fianna Fáil cabinet.

New map launches reorganized 'Tube'

London, 1 July

Londoners travelled to work or pleasure today as customers of the world's largest transport organization. The new London Passenger Transport Board combines all the bus, tram, trolley and underground services that serve not only the capital but an area of some 2,000 square miles within a 20-30 mile radius of Charing Cross. Only the mainline railway companies are excluded from this new publicly owned organization which has been formed to coordinate services and promote expansion of the network. Symbolically, there is also a new diagrammatic map for the "Tube" designed by Harry Beck.

Britain reluctantly boosts its defences

Westminster, 29 November

Britain is to strengthen its armed forces to match those nations which refused to follow Britain's example of unilateral disarmament. Lord Londonderry, the air minister, told the Lords: "We cannot continue in our present inferiority. Our air force must be as strong as that of any other nation." In the Commons, the lord president, Stanley Baldwin, announcing measures to meet potential dangers, said that Britain could not continue to stand alone, half disarmed. He hoped, however, for international controls on arms spending and warned that increases in air force budgets would worsen relations with Germany (→ 25/6/34).

Economic improvement offers no cheer to industrial regions living on the 'dole'

Britain, December

Nearly three million people were registered as unemployed last winter – one in four of the insured working population. It now appears that this winter's figure will be lower, raising hopes that the worst of the depression is over. But more than two million people remain unemployed and this total excludes farm labourers, self-employed workers and married women. National figures also mask the continuing severity of the slump in some areas.

Although the depression hit all industries, its effects have been at their most savage and have lasted longer in regions dependent upon heavy industry. Unemployment in mining, shipbuilding and steel has been twice as high as the average for all industries; in cotton it has also been significantly higher. Last year, for instance, three in five shipbuilding workers were unemployed and two in five miners.

In many cases these industries were in decline even before the present slump, so the extent of long-term unemployment has been greater in the areas where these industries are concentrated – in particular, north-eastern England, south Wales, Northern

Ex-soldiers sing for their supper.

Ireland and central parts of Scotland. With few alternative jobs men have often been out of work for years (some school leavers have never worked). With unemployment insurance benefits limited to 26 weeks, they have to apply for "transitional payments" which are subject to a much-hated means test. Life on the "dole", as the benefits are known, is hard and often humiliating. A glimpse into proletarian realities was movingly provided this year by *Love on the Dole*, a stage hit based on the novel by Walter Greenwood.

On the march: women join unemployed men from London to Brighton.

Mosley calls for fascist dictatorship

In characteristic black, Mosley outlines his plans for a government of action.

Birmingham, 21 January
A slim, upright figure in black shirt and slacks held by a wide leather belt, he raises his voice in well-rehearsed cadences as he calls on his audience of 10,000 to support his aim of a "modern dictatorship" to solve Britain's social and economic problems. This is Sir Oswald Mosley, whose chequered political career has taken him from the Tory Party into a Labour government and on to the British Union of Fascists, which he founded less than two years ago and modelled on the fascist and Nazi movements of Italy and Germany. Though Mosley is a wealthy man there is speculation that secret sympathizers are funding his movement.

In Birmingham tonight arms are upraised in the fascist salute as he steps forward to address his biggest ever rally. He promises that his fascist government, which he counts on coming to power after next year's election, will arm itself with emergency powers to "overcome the problems the people want to overcome".

Much of his speech articulates the impatience many people feel at the apparent impotence of democratic politicians faced with economic collapse and widespread unemployment. His mix of nationalism and socialist rhetoric goes down well. But there is a more sinister thread running through his strident denunciations of the old politicians at Westminster. There are sudden references to the malign influence of Jewish intrigues and Jewish money, which are enthusiastically applauded by at least a section of the audience, doubtless Mosley's own recruits. Anyone in the audience who tries to heckle or ask an awkward question is likely to be pounced upon by black-shirted stewards and roughed up before being thrown out of the hall.

This, by now, familiar feature of Mosley's meetings has lost him the support of right-wing Tories and of the press, though Lord Rothermere's *Daily Mail* continues to provide a platform for him (→ 8/6).

Suburbs boom as city houses sprawl

Britain, 6 April
Figures released today show that in the last ten years 1,900,000 houses have been built in Britain. State subsidies for slum clearances and for rented housing have helped local authorities build more houses; and mortgages averaging around 4.5 per cent interest rates have fuelled a boom in private housing. "Speculative" estates are creating new suburbs on the fringes of cities, offering semi-detached houses for prices as low as £450.

As many as 350,000 private houses are expected to be completed next year. With bathrooms, gardens and in some cases garages, these are a far cry from the overcrowded conditions still prevalent in major cities. But calls are growing for planning controls as suburbs spread into the countryside.

Double sporting win for British hosts

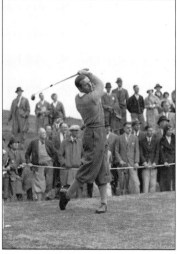

July. Britain has played host to two great sporting events and ended up winning both of them. Henry Cotton (left) drives off from the fourth tee on his way to victory at the Open Golf Championship at Sandwich, Kent, bringing the title back to Britain after 11 years abroad. Meanwhile at Wimbledon Fred Perry (right) strokes his way to victory in the men's final; Dorothy Round won the women's singles and the mixed doubles.

Tributes flow in to Sir Edward Elgar

Elgar: an unpompous man.

Worcester, 23 February

Sir Edward Elgar died at his home overlooking the Malvern Hills today and tributes came from the leaders of the musical world, Richard Strauss and Sibelius among them, to "the greatest English composer since Purcell".

One of his *Pomp and Circumstance* marches was given the words *Land of Hope and Glory*, but his genius was first shown in the *Enigma Variations* of 1899. His First Symphony (1908) was performed over 100 times within a year, but after the Great War he wrote only one major work, the cello concerto, first performed in 1919.

Novice motorists to face stiff driving test

London, 28 March

For the first time since men with red flags had to walk in front of motorized vehicles, new drivers will have to prove their ability in a test. Until today, the only requirement for drivers has been an unsupported declaration of physical fitness by anyone over the age of 17. A speed limit of 30mph (48kmph) will be imposed in built-up areas – defined by the number of street lights – and experiments with pedestrian crossings are to be made in London.

Although private cars have increased ninefold since 1918, the number of drivers charged with offences under the traffic acts has only doubled, with pedestrians being blamed for many accidents.

Under the Government's Road Traffic Bill published today, pedestrians, too, face fines for walking dangerously, and the use of horns by drivers will be subject to official scrutiny (→ 12/6).

Pedestrian crossings halt traffic.

Hope fades for 262 men after pit blast

Wrexham, 21 September

An explosion today at the Gresford colliery near here has resulted in one of the worst mining disasters of all time. The death toll now stands at 262 with hope abandoned of finding anyone alive. Three of those who have died were among the rescue teams which battled against flames and poisonous fumes. All day relatives waited in silence at the pit-head. As night fell, only 16 bodies had been brought to the surface leaving 243 entombed in the pit below ground. Few escaped the ferocity of the blast, although one man did inch to safety up a 200-feet vertical shaft just two feet wide. The chief inspector of mines, Sir Henry Walker, said the mine might have to be sealed and closed with the loss of 2,000 jobs.

Churchill warns of weak UK defences

Westminster, 28 November

Winston Churchill today continued his campaign for Britain to rearm in order to counter increased German strength. The former Tory and Liberal cabinet minister, now a backbencher, moved a Commons amendment declaring that "the strength of our national defences, and especially of our air defences, is no longer adequate to secure ... peace, safety and freedom".

He told a packed, attentive House that Germany's munitions factories were already working "under practically war conditions" and that even if there is "no acceleration on the part of Germany, and no slowing down on our part" the German military air force will have nearly double the strength of the RAF by 1937.

He warned that Britain's weak defences could lead to the nation being "tortured into absolute subjection", with no chance of ever recovering, in a war with Germany. Churchill said that while there was no reason to think Germany would attack, it was not pleasant to think that it could: "The time has come when the mists surrounding German armaments should be stripped away." His argument was rejected by fellow-Tory Stanley Baldwin, speaking for the government, who argued that Britain would retain a 50 per cent superiority over Germany (→ 4/3/35).

Telephones ring the exchanges in Britain

MAKE LIFE EASIER

TAKE THE TELEPHONE INTO YOUR HOME
Enquire at any Post Office

Every home should have one.

London, 1 January

There are now over two million telephone subscribers in Britain. The number of new installations has jumped to average 275,000 a year. Last year exchanges in London handled almost 800 million calls, the Post Office announced today. More than half of them were dialled through automatic exchanges and 637,000 were to countries overseas.

The roadside telephone kiosk, which first appeared in 1926 in a great variety of shapes and colours, has been redesigned by Sir Giles Gilbert Scott, architect of Liverpool Cathedral. His design, in prefabricated concrete painted red, won a Fine Arts Commission prize.

September 26. People hurry across fields at Glasgow to gain a riverside view and watch Queen Mary launch her namesake built by Cunard.

'Lawrence of Arabia' dies after accident

Dorset, 19 May

One of the most romantic heroes of the Great War died today after five days in a coma, his skull fractured in a motorcycle accident.

Colonel T E Lawrence, or "Lawrence of Arabia", captured the imagination of Britain when, after years of desert warfare riding alongside his Arab allies, he helped to take Baghdad in 1918. His account of those times was told in his best-seller *Revolt in the Desert*. But the full story, including his capture and assault by the Turks, is contained in *The Seven Pillars of Wisdom* which he refused to publish in his lifetime.

He leaves behind two mysteries: the identity of "S A", to whom the book is dedicated, and the reason he joined the RAF to become Aircraftsman Shaw for 14 years. He left the RAF only two months ago and died when, riding his motorcycle from Bovington camp to his home, he swerved to avoid two boy cyclists.

The secretive Lawrence of Arabia.

Thousands protest over 'means test'

South Wales, 18 March

Nearly 300,000 people took to the streets today in the biggest protest yet against the hated means test and regulations laid down by the new Unemployment Assistance Board (UAB). There were similar protests in Sheffield. Although these demonstrations were organized by the Communist-led National Unemployed Workers' Movement, they symbolize grievances that have festered for several years.

The spread of unemployment has made more and more families face the humiliation of being visited by their local public assistance committee, now replaced by the UAB. They have been obliged to reveal their personal lives, have their furniture valued and, in many cases, have their benefit reduced because of contributions from children or parents living with them.

The Unemployment Insurance Acts, introduced last year, were supposed to relieve hardship. But when details were published recently, relief scales in some areas were lower than those paid by the local authorities.

Defence spending is set to increase

Westminster, 4 March

The government today produced a White Paper on defence which contains plans for a significant increase in the strength of all three services. The emphasis of the paper is largely on defence against attack from the air with more fighters for the RAF, new anti-aircraft defences and increased protection for ships against bombers.

Presenting the paper, which represents a considerable shift in the government's position, Stanley Baldwin said: "Our attempt to lead the world towards disarmament by unilateral example has failed." The fault, he argued, lay with Germany whose rearmament threatened to put peace at peril. The government hopes that Britain's determination will be made plain to the German chancellor, Adolf Hitler, through a meeting which is shortly to take place in Berlin (→ 22/5).

Use all your vigour to keep your figure

London, 8 October

Britain is fast becoming a nation of keep-fit fanatics. At least, that is what officials of the newly established Central Council of Recreative Physical Training are telling us. Women, young and old, are especially enthusiastic, flocking to the council's gymnasia with their slogan "Use your vigour to keep your figure", but men, boys and girls are not missing out. A spokesman declared: "A survey we have just completed shows that there are thousands of men, women and adolescents anxious to form keep-fit classes." Indeed, new gyms cannot open fast enough, and many classes are over-subscribed.

So widespread is the new fitness craze that no fewer than 130 organizations, each devoted to a form of physical activity, have set up a special conference in London.

Lunch-hour exercise classes keep office workers full of vim and vitality.

Tories surge to victory

Stanley Baldwin leads the Tories back into power with an increased majority.

Westminster, 16 November
Only a few National Liberal and National Labour remnants have survived the election to sit with the massed ranks of Tories to give the prime minister and Tory leader, Stanley Baldwin, the backing of 432 MPs. Ramsay MacDonald, who formed the National government in 1931 and retired as premier last June, was crushingly defeated in the Seaham mining constituency, picking up fewer than 18,000 votes against the 38,000-plus cast for his

Labour opponent, the fiery Clydesider Emmanuel Shinwell. Labour has trebled its strength to 154 MPs; Liberals are down to 20.

Firmly on the election agenda were housing and unemployment, but the issue of rearmament was fudged. Baldwin, believing that the country has become pacifist, insisted in his speeches that "there will be no great armaments". But the election victory now gives him a solid parliamentary majority for rearmament (→ 28/5/37).

Allen Lane launches paperback books

London, July
The first ten paperback books, known as "Penguins" and selling at sixpence, have been published by Allen Lane to a chorus of disapproval. Lane had the idea on a station platform where there was nothing to buy for the journey but expensive novels or garish reprints. His aim is to sell well-produced reprints of top quality books. Woolworth's has ordered 10,000 copies of each title; these include Ernest Hemingway's *A Farewell to Arms* and two detective novels by Agatha Christie and Dorothy L Sayers.

A formal portrait to mark the occasion of the Silver Jubilee of King George V and Queen Mary.

Hoare quits over Abyssinian deal

Westminster, 18 December
Sir Samuel Hoare has been forced to resign as foreign secretary following his deal with France's premier, Pierre Laval, appeasing Mussolini over Abyssinia. The deal, which involved the recognition of Italy's right to keep the fertile areas she has occupied in her invasion of Abyssinia, has raised a storm of protest throughout Britain.

It brought the threat of resignation from Anthony Eden, minister for League of Nations affairs, unless Baldwin disowned the deal and Sir Samuel. With a Commons debate looming the prime minister gave his foreign secretary a choice: apologize or resign.

Sir Samuel has chosen to resign and the Hoare-Laval pact is dead but the world is faced with the danger that the League of Nations is impotent unless its members stand up to dictators.

Radio waves used to detect aircraft

Britain, December
Scientists under the direction of Robert Watson-Watt have this year patented a way of detecting aircraft by bouncing radio waves off them. The time that the waves take to return is also used to calculate the aircraft's distance from the transmitter.

In July researchers used the new method, called "radio direction finding", to track a Hawker Hart aeroplane as it flew to a distance of 34 miles (54.4km) over Suffolk. A formation of other aircraft was also successfully located and counted as blips on a cathode ray tube.

The new technology would enable Britain's air defences to detect aircraft over the horizon, and so has great military potential. Given the possible threat from Germany, it is ironic that it was a German scientist, Heinrich Hertz, who first discovered radio waves (→ 22).

Campbell breaks own land speed record

Sir Malcolm Campbell poses for photographers in front of his new "Bluebird".

Utah, 3 September
Speed hero Sir Malcolm Campbell narrowly escaped death today as he slowed down after beating his own world speed record on the Bonneville Salt Flats. Campbell, who has devoted much of his life to gaining records on land and sea, achieved an average speed of 485kmph (301mph) in his streamlined car

Bluebird – even though he was temporarily blinded by a stream of salt whipped up by wind. Fifty-year-old Campbell's previous best speed was 442 kmph (276mph) set at Daytona beach last March. His sponsor, Esso, is making great play of the fact that the ethyl fluid used in *Bluebird* is also used in petrol sold from its pumps (→ 19/11/37).

Sandringham, 20 January. King George V dies.→

Cheltenham, 12 March. Golden Miller wins the Gold Cup for the fifth successive year.

Dublin, 27 May. Aer Lingus makes its first commercial flight from here to Bristol.

Southampton, 27 May. The liner *Queen Mary* leaves on her maiden voyage to New York.

Britain, May. The Left Book Club is formed this month.

London, 3 June. Haile Selassie, emperor of Abyssinia, arrives in exile after defeat by Italy.

Wimbledon, 3 July. Fred Perry wins the singles title for the third successive year.

Yugoslavia, 10 August. King Edward VIII begins a cruise on the yacht *Nahlin* with Mrs Wallis Simpson (→ 27/10).

London, 21 August. The BBC makes its first television broadcast from Alexandra Palace (→ 2/11).

London, 26 August. A treaty gives Britain use of the Suez Canal for 20 years.

Buckinghamshire, September. New film studios are opened at Pinewood (→ 31/12/37).

London, 11 October. An estimated 100,000 people try to prevent fascist supporters of Sir Oswald Mosley marching through the East End (→ 10/11).

Ipswich, 27 October. Mrs Wallis Simpson wins a decree nisi from her second husband, Ernest (→ 16/11).

London, 16 November. The king tells the prime minister and his family that he intends to marry Mrs Simpson (→ 3/12).

Wales, 19 November. The king completes a tour of Wales in which he said "something must be done" about unemployment.

London, 30 November. Crystal Palace, designed for the 1851 Great Exhibition, burns down.

Britain, 3 December. British newspapers end their silence on the crisis over the king and Mrs Simpson (→ 10).

Windsor, 10 December. King Edward VIII signs the "instrument of abdication"; he is to be known as the duke of Windsor (→ 12).

Britain. John Maynard Keynes, a leading British economist, publishes a theory on how to combat (and prevent) recessions.

New powers to aid police against fascists

Police arrest a woman demonstrator during Mosley's East End march.

London, 10 November
Sir Oswald Mosley, the fascist leader, will need to rid himself of his black shirt and riding breeches if he wishes to lead political demonstrations in future. The thuggery which has become a familiar element in meetings organized by Mosley's British Union of Fascists finally persuaded the cabinet to take action.

A Public Order Bill, published today, will be rushed onto the statute book, banning the wearing of political uniforms and giving the police power to ban political demonstrations likely to cause disorder. Mosley's use of violence during meetings and marches is deliberately provocative; he then blames the subsequent disorder on Jews and communists – "Red agitators from the ghettos," he cries.

Three months ago, when he led 7,000 blackshirts into the Jewish neighbourhood of London's East End, 80 people, including 15 police, were injured. He hoped he could repeat the street battles between Nazis and communists that helped Hitler's rise to power (→ 1/1/37).

'Spitfire' prototype takes to the skies

Southampton, 5 March
The first flight took place today of the prototype of the Supermarine company's latest fighter – the Spitfire. "Don't touch anything," said an enthusiastic test pilot, "Mutt" Summers, after landing the plane at the Eastleigh aerodrome near here. The aircraft has striking, clean lines, but its future RAF pilots will probably be more impressed by its battery of eight machine guns mounted under the wings and the power of its Rolls-Royce PV-12 "Merlin" engine.

This engine is streamlined, with a small frontal area which offers less air resistance than similar engines and therefore greater speed and manoeuvrability (→ 27/5/36).

King George V dies

Sandringham, 20 January
King George V, monarch of Britain and her empire for the past 26 years, died today at the royal residence at Sandringham. He was 70. He is succeeded by his son, formerly the highly popular prince of Wales, now King Edward VIII. Thanks to the newly invented radio and the broadcasts he started making, King George was perhaps the best-known monarch in history.

Jarrow's crusade of unemployed workers fails to move Baldwin

Jarrow marchers leave a Bedfordshire village on their way to London.

Westminster, 11 November
The Jarrow crusade has failed to move the prime minister. Today Stanley Baldwin told the Commons that he would not meet the marchers: "This is the way that civil strife begins, and civil strife may not end until it is civil war."

It is a brutal snub for what has been one of the most peaceful of all the protest marches. Organized by the local council in a town where two-thirds are unemployed, it was supported by Labour and Conservatives and blessed by a bishop.

The 200 marchers bore a casket containing a petition with 11,572 signatures. On their walk south they gained favourable press comment, much public sympathy and the attention of the new cinema newsreels.

Edward VIII abdicates throne for love

Portsmouth, 12 December
The former king Edward is sailing for France and exile late tonight and for eventual reunion with Wallis Simpson, the American divorcee for whom he gave up his throne. Tonight he broadcast his decision to abdicate the throne – an act unprecedented in more than 1,000 years of British monarchy.

He said he found it impossible to carry the burden of kingship and discharge his duties "without the help and support of the woman I love". He said that the decision was his alone: "the other person most concerned has tried to persuade me to take a different course." King Edward VIII has reigned for only 11 months. He succeeded his father George V on 21 January.

It was soon apparent that he was bored by the duties of dealing with state papers and court functions; but he retained an ability to strike a chord with the public – which knew nothing of his romance with Mrs Simpson [*see below*] – as when he visited unemployed miners in South Wales last month, declaring "something must be done". But by then he had told the prime minister Stanley Baldwin and his family that he would renounce the throne rather than give up his plan to marry Mrs Simpson (→ 3/6/37).

Edward VIII: the final broadcast.

Secret royal romance rocked the world

Wallis (second left) alongside the future king with friends on holiday.

London, December
The infatuation of the future King Edward with Mrs Wallis Simpson from Baltimore had begun in 1933, when he started going to dinner with her and her second husband, Englishman Ernest Simpson, who soon resented the prince's attentions to his wife. In 1934 Wallis alone joined his summer party at Biarritz and they took a cruise together. Thelma, Lady Furness, his long-standing mistress, was summarily dismissed. His complete subjugation to the striking American woman was the talk of high society. She had clearly captivated him.

On becoming king, Edward invited Mrs Simpson to see him proclaimed at St James's and in August the couple openly cruised the Adriatic and Aegean in the steam yacht *Nahlin*. Their relationship was plain to the watching crowds and widely reported in the press everywhere but in Britain. Even Simpson's arranged divorce by his wife (her second divorce) was reported merely routinely, at the king's request, through a sympathetic newspaper baron, Lord Beaverbrook.

It could not last – and when the bishop of Bradford said in a sermon the king should show more awareness of his Christian duty, the publicity broke and Mrs Simpson fled to France. From there she said she was willing to withdraw from an "unhappy and untenable" situation, but to the dismay of his family Edward was adamant he could not reign without her.

Shy Bertie becomes king as George VI

London, 12 December
Edward's younger brother Bertie, the duke of York, has been proclaimed king with the title of George VI and a natural reluctance to take on the burdens of the crown. His first act was to create the ex-king HRH the Duke of Windsor – but the courtesy title of "royal highness" is not to be extended to his brother's future wife.

The new king, who is 41, suffers from nerves and a stammer, which he has taken lessons to improve. During the crisis doubts were raised about whether he is competent to reign. His most popular act as duke of York was to marry a Scot, Elizabeth Bowes-Lyon, an extrovert wife. The couple have two daughters (→ 12/5/37).

George VI (l) at his father's funeral.

Sound and pictures broadcast by BBC

London, 2 November
The first public television service in the world was inaugurated by the BBC today from Alexandra Palace, north London. Transmissions were first made in August to the Radio Olympia exhibition, where sets costing about £110 were on view. Only 280 homes have sets. The Baird system with 240 lines on the screen is being used alternately with that of his rival, Isaac Shoenberg, for Marconi-EMI, which has 405 lines. The BBC has recruited two women announcers from 1,100 applicants, and one man, Leslie Mitchell.

Irish bill removes deference to crown

Ireland, 11 December
With masterly timing, the Irish prime minister, Eamon de Valera, has taken advantage of the British government's preoccupation with the abdication crisis to launch his External Relations Bill. Instead of waiting for the completion of the new constitution, the new bill will remove all the references to the British crown and the governor-general. While the king no longer has any say in the internal affairs of the Free State, he will retain certain ceremonial functions in external affairs (→ 30/4/37).

Spending can cure crisis, says Keynes

London, December
One of the most talked-about books of the year has one of the dullest titles – *The General Theory of Employment, Interest and Money* – but it seems set to be highly influential. John Maynard Keynes, a former Treasury official and British economist, offers a way to combat (and prevent) economic depressions. These are caused, he says, by insufficient demand in the economy. Investment should be stimulated by spending on public works and by lowering interest rates, even if it unbalances the budget, in order to boost consumer demand.

Chamberlain succeeds Baldwin as PM

Westminster, 28 May

The man Lloyd George dismissed as "a pinhead" has taken over from Baldwin as prime minister: Neville Chamberlain, now aged 68, was a dismal failure as director of national service in 1917, but went on to initiate major reforms in local government, housing and public assistance before becoming chancellor of the exchequer. Now, however, he will be obliged to turn from domestic questions to foreign policy and the increasingly bellicose dictators in Europe.

Chamberlain is said to have little time for Sir Robert Vansittart, the foreign office permanent undersecretary, and his dire warnings about Nazi Germany echoed in the Commons by Winston Churchill.

Chamberlain, the new premier.

'Green belts' may check London sprawl

London, 1 April

A "green belt" around London was proposed today in a bid to stop the capital's sprawl into the surrounding countryside. London County Council, which plans to spend up to £2 million buying land in the home counties, also sees "green belts" as offering recreation opportunities for its growing population.

Over eight million people now live in London, but the conurbation is much larger as suburbs have been spawned by new tube lines or as "ribbon developments" along new arterial roads. There has been a similar suburban sprawl around other major cities and it has been estimated that by the mid-1930s some 60,000 acres were being lost to agriculture each year. Some curbs were imposed on ribbon development in 1935, but groups such as the Council for the Preservation of Rural England want even greater controls and more "green belts".

Conference urged on piracy in Med

London, 2 September

Foreign secretary Anthony Eden today demanded the setting up of an international conference to discuss "submarine piracy" in the Mediterranean following the sinking of merchant ships carrying supplies to the republican side in the civil war being waged in Spain. The submarines are said to belong to Spain's nationalist leader, General Franco, but there is little doubt that they belong to the Italian navy.

Eden, encouraged by Winston Churchill, intends to demand the establishment of patrols by French and British warships under orders to attack any "submarine pirates" they encounter.

Millionaires are growing in number

Britain, 3 March

Britons are getting wealthier and the taxman is reaping the benefit. An additional 50,000 people earned enough last year to pay income tax, according to figures released today. That makes 3,350,000 income tax payers, although new rules freed 250,000 from tax. There are now 824 millionaires and 85,449 people earning more than £2,000 a week.

Audiences flock to luxurious shrines of the cinema boom

London, 31 December

Cinemas and film audiences are booming in Britain, where 40 per cent of the adult population "go to the pictures" at least once a week. Cinema circuits began building in 1933 with the Odeons. Gaumonts, Granadas, Regals and Roxys now rise in Babylonian splendour, combining *art deco* style with rich trimmings of chrome and glazed, coloured tiles. Many seat 4,000 in escapist luxury. A ticket from as little as sixpence offers two features, a cartoon, a newsreel and serenading by a mighty Wurlitzer organ. Most films are also escapist. This year's British hits are Anna Neagle as *Victoria the Great* and Flora Robson as Queen Elizabeth in *Fire Over England* while *Oh! Mr Porter!* introduces Will Hay (→ 1/3/40).

In order to meet the increasing popularity of moving pictures, architects are designing ever more luxurious cinemas, monuments of the silver screen.

Crash in a Scottish snowstorm kills 35

Glasgow, 10 December

Thirty-five passengers were killed and 179 injured tonight when the Edinburgh to Glasgow express, hurtling through a snowstorm at 70mph, ploughed into a train standing at the small station of Castlecary near Glasgow.

The disaster followed a string of misunderstandings between signalmen. Despite the wintry weather the Pacific *Grand Parade* was almost at full speed when she hit the express from Dundee to Glasgow pulled by *Dandy Dinmont*.

Steel-built rolling stock saved many lives in the crash; and many passengers in the Edinburgh express stepped onto the platform unaware that a collision had taken place. Modern steel-built coaches are thought to have saved many lives in three serious train crashes in the past three years.

New constitution for Eire takes effect

De Valera (l) with Irish colleagues.

Dublin, 29 December

Eamon de Valera, leader of the ruling Fianna Fáil party, has introduced a new constitution for the Irish Free State which is now to be called Eire. It lays down a system of government which places author-ity in the prime minister, now to be known as the Taoiseach. The Senate has been restored and proportional representation is retained for election to the Dáil.

But this democratic approach is combined with an assumption that the Irish identity is Catholic, reflected in five articles defining "rights". Divorce is prohibited, the idea of working mothers is denounced and the Catholic Church is granted a special position "as the guardian of the faith professed by the great majority of citizens".

Despite this, the first articles of the constitution claim that Eire includes all 32 counties of Ireland and that subsequent provisions apply to the six of these counties in Northern Ireland pending "reintegration of the national territory". This may satisfy republicans, but it also confirms fears of Ulster Protestants that a united Ireland would be totally Catholic (→ 19/1/38).

Triumphant London debut for Fonteyn

Fonteyn in her debut as Giselle.

London, 19 January

The stage has a new ballerina who made a triumphant debut in the testing title role of *Giselle* last night at Sadler's Wells. She is only 17 and her stage name is Margot Fonteyn. She was trained at the Sadler's Wells school, founded by Ninette de Valois along with the ballet company in 1931.

After Alicia Markova left in 1935, Fonteyn was gradually given her roles and last year she helped to create a new ballet, *Apparitions* by Frederick Ashton, with her partner Robert Helpmann. He partnered her again in *Giselle* and they are to dance the Swan queen and prince in *Lac des Cygnes*. Fonteyn's real name is Peggy Hookham.

Orwell travels the 'Road to Wigan Pier'

London, March

Subscribers to the Left Book Club received a shock with this month's title, *The Road to Wigan Pier* by George Orwell. After passages of brilliant reportage of the poverty, squalor and hopelessness that the depression caused in the north, Orwell tackles the evils of snobbery – he himself went to Eton – and declares that "the lower classes smell. That was what we were taught. We were brought up to believe they were dirty ..." He claims that that is how the middle classes do feel. Repelled by the socialism advocated by vegetarian, sandal-wearing, bearded Marxist cranks whom he detests, he fears that the middle class will embrace fascism rather than abolish class distinction. The book's publisher Victor Gollancz writes a foreword apologizing to readers whom the book may offend. Its author is in Spain fighting for the republicans.

MPs back shelters as war fears grow

Westminster, 16 November

Plans to build air-raid shelters in Britain's towns and cities were backed by the House of Commons today as fears grow about the possibility of another war in Europe. This year has already seen increases in the defence budget which take spending on the Royal Navy, for instance, to the highest levels since the Great War. With war raging in Spain, piracy in the Mediterranean and bellicose noises from the fascist leaders of Italy and Germany, the international scene is more threatening than for many years.

Winston Churchill, the most vocal proponent of rearmament in the Commons, welcomed today's vote in favour of shelters, saying that they were "indispensable". He wants the RAF to be boosted, too, but said that well-organized precautions would mean that air attacks on Britain would not be worthwhile. Fears of air attacks have grown since the bombing of Guernica in Spain last April. This has given new menace to the warning of Stanley Baldwin, the former premier, that "the bomber will always get through" (→3/1/38).

The duke and duchess of Windsor alongside the German chancellor, Adolf Hitler, during the couple's controversial visit to Germany in October. →

The defrocked rector of Stiffkey met his maker after performing in the lion's den at Skegness.

Britain, 3 January. All schoolchildren are to be issued with gas masks, the government says (→ 24/3).

London, 3 January. The BBC begins its first foreign language service – in Arabic.

London, 19 January. Eamon de Valera ends two days of talks with British leaders with prospects growing of a new Anglo-Irish agreement (→ 25/4).

Westminster, 21 February. Anthony Eden resigns as foreign secretary in protest over policies of appeasement towards Italy over its annexation of Abyssinia.

Westminster, 24 March. Neville Chamberlain pledges Britain to defend France and Belgium against attack in a statement ten days after German troops had occupied Austria (→ 29/4).

London, 31 March. Plans are unveiled for a national theatre to be designed by Sir Edwin Lutyens and to be built in South Kensington.

Britain, 7 April. All bicycles should be fitted with rear lights, the police say.

London, 29 April. Talks between the British and French governments end with a vague promise to defend Czechoslovakia against attack (→ 15/7).

Dublin, 25 June. Douglas Hyde is inaugurated as president of Eire after Fianna Fáil retains power in this month's general election (→ 11/7).

Britain, 15 July. The government orders 1,000 Spitfire fighters for the RAF as part of a general increase in strength of the armed forces (→ 30/9).

Paris, 19 July. King George and Queen Elizabeth receive an enthusiastic welcome at the start of a state visit (→ 8/6/39).

Glasgow, 27 September. The world's largest liner, the *Queen Elizabeth*, is launched.

Westminster, 19 October. The cabinet abandons plans to partition the mandated territory of Palestine.

Britain, 21 December. Plans are announced to spend £200,000 on air-raid shelters.

Britain. New publications this year include an illustrated weekly, *Picture Post*, and a comic, *Beano*.

Britain. The US-owned Gallup Opinion Polls forms a company in the United Kingdom.

Britain returns navy bases in Irish treaty

Dublin, 25 April
Eamon de Valera has scored the greatest political achievement of his career. The Irish prime minister has persuaded Britain to return the Irish ports which they had retained under the 1921 Treaty at Berehaven, Cobh, Lough Swilly, Haulbowline and Rathmullen.

Neville Chamberlain, the British premier, sees it as a gesture of appeasement – apparently believing that the ports could be made available again in time of war – but his backbench Tory critic Winston Churchill is said to be infuriated by the decision. De Valera believes that the return of the ports will make Eire's neutrality all the easier in the European war which he feels is imminent. Important trade concessions have also been agreed. The land annuities, so long a bone of contention between Britain and Ireland, have been cancelled in favour of a lump sum; trade duties and restrictions have been reduced on many items; and preference is allowed for some British goods.

Given that 96 per cent of all Irish exports go to British markets, the trade war between the two countries has affected all sections of the economy, and the balance of payments deficit has eaten into the government's reserves. De Valera has used the economic war to brilliant political effect on the home front, enhancing his reputation, and ensuring electoral support (→ 25/6).

Football pools are 'menace to society'

London 25 April
Postal workers, tradesmen and Baptists have joined forces against the "menace" of football pools. As greyhound racing and other forms of gambling enjoy continuing popularity, ten million people are now thought to be filling in their pools coupons every week. While Baptists disapprove on moral grounds, sub-postmasters want extra cash for handling pools mail, which has grown enormously since the 1920s. And a Worthing butcher claims his customers are buying cheap foreign meat to save up for the pools.

Education reforms planned in Britain

London, 30 December
Free secondary education and raising of the school leaving age to 16 are advocated in a report sent to the Board of Education today by the Spens Committee. In the wake of the reorganization of most elementary schools, the report suggests expanding technical high schools, keeping "grammar" and "modern" schools. It favours progressive methods that encourage curiosity and do not allow examinations to dominate. It has been welcomed by teachers, but the government may not be so keen.

King George opens Empire Exhibition

The king tours the exhibition.

Glasgow, 3 May
Mary Morrison flew from the island of Barra – "riding all the way in an aeroplane" – to meet the king and queen today at the opening here of the Empire Exhibition. The royal couple met Mary spinning wool and singing "Leaving Barra" outside a mock thatched cottage in a replica highland village.

This was the final stop in a five-hour royal tour of the huge exhibition, during which King George and Queen Elizabeth ascended the Tower of Empire in a lift travelling at 500 feet a minute. They were equally fascinated by the "Fitter Britain" display in the United Kingdom pavilion that used ping-pong balls to illustrate blood circulation in the human body (→ 19/7).

Workers go off to holiday camps with their first 'holiday pay'

Billy Butlin's camp at Clacton in Essex is full of happy holidaymakers.

Blackpool, 1 August
Bank Holiday crowds thronging the country's most popular holiday resort have more than usual to celebrate this summer. The Holidays with Pay Act passed this year will increase the number of people entitled to a paid holiday from the present three million to 11 million. In most cases, the holiday will be for a week. Resorts such as Blackpool have boomed in recent years anyway, with motor coaches (or "charabancs") and trains bringing in visitors. And last year a "holiday camp" was opened by Billy Butlin at Skegness, Lincolnshire, which proved an instant success.

Chamberlain bows to Hitler in Munich

Czechoslovak deal averts war threat

Munich, 30 September
Flying from London yesterday, the British prime minister Neville Chamberlain refused to discuss policy and tactics with his French counterpart, Edouard Daladier, but at once opened negotiations with the German leader, Adolf Hitler. At 1.45 this morning, after 12 hours of talks, Chamberlain and Hitler signed a paper which sets out the terms for settling the Czechoslovak question without a war. The Italian dictator, Mussolini, and Daladier also signed, but they had been onlookers. This is essentially a deal between Britain and Germany.

Chamberlain has accepted the demands he rejected in meetings with Hitler earlier this month. All Czechoslovak territory identified as being occupied by ethnic Germans is to be handed over to Germany. This territory, Sudetenland, strips Czechoslovakia of her frontier defences. In return, the truncated Czechoslovakia is given a four-power guarantee of its security.

It was Chamberlain's idea that Hitler should join him in putting his signature to a promise that Britain and Germany will "never go to war with one another again". In future, consultation not conflict will be the rule. The British prime minister is delighted (→6/10).

Chamberlain holds aloft the Anglo-German agreement he signed with Hitler.

MPs protest over appeasement of Hitler

Westminster, 6 October
After a three-day debate MPs have approved Chamberlain's agreement with Hitler at Munich, but the growing unease was reflected in the abstention of 30 Tories. The first lord of the admiralty, Alfred Duff Cooper, has resigned, saying that Britain should have gone to war, not to save Czechoslovakia, but to prevent one country (Germany) imposing its will "by brute force". He said the difference between himself and the prime minister was that Chamberlain believed in approaching Hitler with "sweet reasonable-ness", whereas "I have believed that he was more open to the language of the mailed fist."

Churchill was greeted with roars of protest when he said: "We have sustained a total and unmitigated defeat." He said Munich was only the beginning of a bitter reckoning.

Divisions are beginning to appear in the cabinet. Chamberlain returned from Munich saying: "I believe it is peace for our time." But most of his colleagues are saying that "our time" is merely a breathing space and that Britain should rearm fast (→9/2/39).

Hutton hits record test score of 364

London, August
A 22-year-old Yorkshireman set a new cricket record this month with a score of 364 in the final test against the Australians. It was the highest individual score in test history, eclipsing the 334 set by Don Bradman at Headingley in 1930. Hutton batted for 13 hours and 17 minutes to help his team towards other landmarks: their first innings total of 903 for seven wickets and their winning margin of an innings and 579 runs were also records. Len Hutton's triumph comes barely a year after an inauspicious test debut: 0 and 1. But a century followed in the next match to reward the selectors' faith in their new young opening batsman.

Last British troops withdraw from Eire

Cork, 11 July
The last British troops have handed over Spike Island to the Irish Army before finally leaving the country. It was a ceremony of military respect and political friendship between Britain's most fractious dominion and Ireland's oldest foe unparalleled in Anglo-Irish history. The Union flag was lowered and the green, white and orange tricolour of Eire was raised, as an Irish private, speaking the Irish language, took over the guard (→17/1/39).

The steam train now arriving is the record-breaking 'Mallard'

Leaving Kings Cross Station, "Mallard" heads for the record books.

Peterborough, 3 July
Mallard, a British locomotive of the Gresley A4 Pacific class, set a new world record speed for steam engines when, between London and Newcastle, it touched 126 mph (203 kmph). Driver Duddington and Fireman Bray were joined on the footplate by Nigel Gresley, designer of the engine, as it attempted its record run. The locomotive, using the tracks of the London and North Eastern Railway, maintained a speed of over 120 mph for more than five miles, easily surpassing the previous record, 114 mph (183 kmph), achieved by *Coronation Scot* last year.

"The Beano", a companion to "The Dandy", makes its debut.

Fears of war intensify

London, 31 March
The clouds of war gathering over Europe grew more ominous today when the prime minister, Neville Chamberlain, informed a crowded, cheering House of Commons that, if any action threatened Polish independence and the Poles felt it vital to resist, Britain and France would come to their aid. Chamberlain has written to Colonel Beck, the Polish foreign minister, making this offer, and it is reported that Beck accepted "between two flicks of the ash off his cigarette".

This hardening of the British and French position towards any further Nazi encroachments comes at the end of a tumultuous month. On 15 March Hitler made a triumphal entry into Prague and slept in Hradcany Castle, the former palace of the Bohemian kings. On 23 March he forced Lithuania, under threat of air attack, to surrender Memel. Now he is demanding Danzig from Poland, and tonight there are rumours that German troops are moving towards the Polish border.

It is apparent that, despite all the attempts to appease Hitler, he remains determined to plant his jackboots all over Europe. War seems inevitable. There is a scramble to re-arm. Plans have been made to evacuate children from cities vulnerable to air attack. Even Neville Chamberlain, who declared "peace for our time" after Munich, seems determined to fight (→ 31/8).

Bomb kills five in Coventry: IRA blamed

A man receives first aid amid the debris caused by the explosion.

Coventry, 25 August
Five people were killed today and nearly 50 injured when a bomb exploded without warning in the main street of Coventry. Police believe that the bomb was planted by the Irish Republican Army. If that theory is confirmed, this would be the most deadly episode yet in the campaign of violence launched by the IRA on the British mainland last January.

A series of blasts in London, Manchester and Birmingham signalled the start of the campaign by Irish republicans dissatisfied with last year's Anglo-Irish agreement. The IRA wants a united Ireland with no British presence. So does Eamon de Valera, the Eire leader, but two months ago he banned the IRA after bombs had exploded at London tube stations and in letter boxes around Britain; hundreds of suspected IRA sympathizers were rounded up by the police.

Today's bomb appears to have been left in a tradesman's bicycle. Exploding at 2.30pm, it shattered shopfronts, overturned cars and left Broadgate, the main street of this Midlands city, resembling a bloody battlefield. Coming at a time when war seems imminent in Europe, the outrage seems sure to foster anti-Irish opinion (→ 17/9).

Mighty 'voice of Ireland' is silenced

Yeats: a Nobel laureate.

France, 28 January
William Butler Yeats, Ireland's most famous poet and playwright, has died in France, aged 74. Born in Dublin of Irish Protestant stock, he was educated in London, and he later settled there, moving in aesthetic, literary and spiritualistic circles. Later, with the help and encouragement of his patron, Lady Gregory, he established the Abbey theatre in Dublin and was very much part of the revival of Irish literature this century.

He was awarded the Nobel prize for literature in 1923 and was an Irish Free State senator from 1922 to 1928. Together with George Bernard Shaw and George Russell he founded the Irish Academy of Letters in 1932. He reached the peak of poetic achievement with *The Tower* and *The Winding Stair*.

Seventy die in sub

Liverpool, 4 June
More than 70 men have died in the submarine *Thetis* after three days of rescue attempts failed. The new submarine sank just off Liverpool, but her stern was visible above the surface. Crewmen were heard tapping morse messages. Four escaped through a hatch, but it could not be closed and seeping water caused the sub to sink. Salvage vessels brought it to the surface. Six more men emerged, but the cables snapped sending the vessel back below the waves too late for further rescue.

PM: 'This country is now at war with Germany'

London, 3 September
At 11.15 this morning, 15 minutes after the deadline for Germany to stop all aggressive action against Poland and begin to withdraw from Polish territory, the prime minister, Neville Chamberlain, declared that "no such undertaking has been received and consequently this country is at war with Germany".

The country fell silent as families gathered round their wireless sets this sunny Sunday to hear the sombre voice of Chamberlain taking Britain into war with Germany for the second time in 25 years. Almost immediately their worst fears of a devastating aerial bombardment appeared about to be realized as air-raid sirens wailed over London, sending people scurrying to the shelters. It was a false alarm, but a fearful indication of destruction which might yet come.

The French ultimatum to Germany expired at five this evening, and despite the last-minute hopes of Georges Bonnet, France's foreign minister, that Mussolini might be able to avert war by persuading Hitler to attend a "big powers" conference, the French too are at war with their old enemies.

The British armed forces have already mobilized, and parliament today passed the National Service (Armed Forces) Act making all men aged between 18 and 41, other than those in reserved occupations, liable to be called to the colours. One old warrior who has joined the fray is Winston Churchill, who has been appointed first lord of the admiralty in the new war cabinet. While the Allies prepare to take the field, the news from Poland is grim. Hitler's tanks, supported by dive-bombers used as flying artillery, are carving their way through the Polish army which has been fatally concentrated along the border.

Polish lancers are bravely, but futilely, charging the panzer tanks, and the Luftwaffe's modern Messerschmitt fighters are hacking the obsolete Polish aircraft out of the sky. Warsaw has been heavily bombed, and the roads are now clogged with refugees who are being mercilessly attacked from the air (→ 11).

Children evacuated from major cities

London, 30 September
All this month parties of schoolchildren with labels on their coats and homemade knapsacks on their backs have been gathering at railway stations to be evacuated from cities believed to be in danger from German bombers. Leaving weeping mothers, they have steamed away, often for unknown destinations.

In the first three days of this mass movement nearly 1,500,000 "evacuees" were carried to safety; 827,000 were schoolchildren and 535,000 were women who are pregnant or have children under school age. Some made long journeys from London to small villages in Devon and Cornwall. One party of children from Dagenham went by pleasure steamer to Yarmouth.

On arrival the children have been taken to reception centres to be allocated to "billeters" who are being paid 10/6 [52.5 pence] a week to feed and look after one child and 8/6 a week for each extra child. The money will no doubt be welcome in many homes, but both evacuees and billeters are having to make considerable adjustments.

Some of the youngsters, especially those from London's East End, have never seen the countryside before. Some are also finding it hard to cope with an unusual, though healthy, diet. Their billeters are similarly finding it a challenge to cope with city habits and language. Evacuation may save many lives; it may also have profound sociological effects (→ 16/8/40).

Tearful farewells as helpers check labels of children awaiting evacuation.

Anxious crowds read newspapers while they wait in Downing Street.

First British troops set out for France

Western front, 30 September
The British Expeditionary Force (BEF) has crossed safely to France and taken up position alongside the French army. The movement of four divisions – 158,000 men with 25,000 vehicles – along with their weapons, ammunition, fuel and supplies took place under conditions of great secrecy.

Regiments from all parts of Britain were carried by troop trains and lorries to ports in the south of England where ferries and transports escorted by destroyers took them across the Channel. There was no interference from U-boats or the German air force.

The men passed through towns their fathers knew well in the Great War as they moved up to the Belgian border. They are billeted in barns and stables and are living rough but like true Tommies are keeping their sense of humour. General Lord Gort, VC, a fighting soldier from the Great War who was previously chief of the imperial general staff, leads the BEF, but he comes under the overall command of General Gamelin, the French supreme commander.

There are no doubts about the fighting qualities of the regular British soldiers, but there remain serious deficiencies in their equipment. Of the 352 anti-aircraft guns assigned to the BEF only 152 have been delivered. There are also misgivings about the quantity and quality of the equipment of the RAF squadrons in France (→ 31/12).

Nations take sides as first shots of war are fired

Eire stays neutral, but empire rallies

London, 17 September
Eamon de Valera, the Irish prime minister, has made it plain that Eire, although still a member of the broader commonwealth, will not join the war against Hitler. If he maintains this policy it could cause problems for Britain because the navy would be unable to use Irish ports against a U-boat campaign.

Other members of the British Empire have come to Britain's aid without hesitation. The Australian prime minister, Robert Menzies, committed his country to the war only an hour after Neville Chamberlain. "There can be no doubt," he said, "that where Britain stands, there stand the people of the entire British world."

New Zealand's prime minister, Michael Savage, agreed: "Where Britain goes, we go; where she stands, we stand." The Canadian parliament debated the issue for three days before agreeing, with one vote against, to join the war. In South Africa the prime minister, General Hertzog, who wanted to stay out of the war, was forced to resign and was replaced by the pro-British General Smuts who immediately declared war (→ 3/1/40).

The final moments of the "Graf Spee" before she sinks below the waves.

'Graf Spee' scuttled as sea war hots up

Uruguay, 17 December
The war at sea, being fought in fierce contrast to the inactivity in western Europe (see report right), reached a blazing climax today when the German pocket battleship *Graf Spee* was scuttled at the mouth of the river Plate in the mistaken belief that an overwhelming force of British ships was waiting for her to put to sea. The *Graf Spee* had sunk ten merchant ships totalling 50,000 tons in the South Atlantic and Indian oceans.

Found by the cruisers *Exeter*, *Ajax* and *Achilles*, Captain Hans Langsdorff severely damaged the *Exeter*, but he was also hard hit and took refuge in Montevideo. Hitler told him: fight or scuttle. Explosions which ripped through the ship gave his answer: Langsdorff chose to scuttle rather than take his crew to their deaths (→ 8/4/40).

'Phoney war' drags on, except at sea

France, 31 December 1939
The year's end has brought no change to the "phoney war" or "sitskrieg" in France. Apart from a few patrols between the opposing Maginot and Siegfried line fortifications, there has been little activity and the cold, bored troops dig trenches and wait for a war which shows little signs of arriving.

After the brutal, lightning occupation of Poland, it had been expected that fighting would swiftly open on the western front but neither the Allies, unprepared for war, nor Hitler, quarrelling with his generals about the best route for attack, have made a decisive move before the onset of winter.

There is a similar lack of activity in the air. After a flurry of daylight raids on German shipping in which RAF bombers suffered heavy casualties, most of their work is restricted to night-time leaflet raids and chasing the occasional German on reconnaissance over Britain.

The "phoney war" mentality has led to many evacuees returning to the cities and schools have reopened. Only at sea, where the Germans are using U-boats and magnetic mines to challenge the Royal Navy's supremacy and harass merchant shipping, has the real battle begun (→ 3/5/40).

Belts tighten on home front as petrol and food rationing loom

A woman hands over her ration coupons at a petrol station in London.

Britain, 25 December
Most Britons were able to enjoy their traditional Christmas dinners today despite shortages of luxuries such as sweets and sugar, and also inadequacies in the food distribution system which have produced gluts and shortages of the same foodstuffs in different districts. Some shopkeepers will only serve their regular customers.

These anomalies are expected to disappear when food rationing is introduced. Preparation for the fair distribution of food to everyone has been under way for several months, with the ministry of food drawing on the experience of the last war. Petrol rationing has already been introduced with heavy penalties for "black marketeers" (→ 8/1/40).

Commando training in Scotland.

Winston Churchill is new war premier

Allies are forced to pull out of Norway

Trondheim, Norway, 3 May
The Allied attempt to force the German invaders out of Norway is going badly. The 13,000 British, French and Polish troops who were landed in Norway to take Trondheim have been defeated by 2,000 Germans and have been evacuated from Namsos and Andalsnes. The Allied forces were ill equipped for fighting in Arctic conditions and found themselves up against highly trained mountain troops.

They were also inadequately supported from the air and suffered constant attack from Ju87 Stuka dive-bombers operating from captured Norwegian airfields. After Major-General Sir Adrian Carton de Wiart, one of the British commanders, had asked for permission to evacuate, the rearguard got away from Namsos early this morning.

One allied force remains in Norway. Assigned to take the northern town of Narvik, it failed to attack when the Germans were vulnerable and now faces a hard slog. The only aspect of this campaign which provides any satisfaction is that the Norwegian coastal batteries and the Royal Navy have inflicted crippling losses on the German fleet (→ 10).

The man of the hour: Winston Churchill becomes prime minister.

All-party coalition to rule the country

London, 10 May 1940
Winston Churchill is to be Britain's new prime minister at the head of a coalition government. Summoned to Buckingham Palace tonight, he told King George VI that he would build an all-party team to achieve victory against Hitler.

Two senior members of the new government will be Clement Attlee, the Labour leader, and his deputy, Arthur Greenwood; they effectively put Churchill in power by making it clear that they would join a coalition only if it was led by Churchill rather than Lord Halifax, the foreign secretary, who critics say has a record of appeasement.

Churchill's appointment follows two of the most turbulent days in the history of Britain's parliament. When the Commons met after the defeat in Norway, Leo Amery, a senior Tory, flung Oliver Cromwell's words at Neville Chamberlain: "You have sat too long for any good you have been doing. Depart, I say, and let us have done with you. In the name of God, go!"

Chamberlain, who sought peace, has gone. In his place is the pugnacious Churchill. He has no intention of seeking peace, only victory.

Mosley is detained as the government takes emergency powers

London, 31 May
Sir Oswald Mosley, his wife and 32 other leading British fascists including Captain A M Ramsay, the Tory MP for Peebles, were arrested tonight under Defence Regulation 18B which gives the home secretary the power to detain members of organizations which may be used for "purposes prejudicial to national security". The move has been greeted with much satisfaction.

All German subjects in Britain are also being interned despite the fact that nearly all of them are Jews who have fled from Hitler's terror squads and most of the remainder were political opponents of the Nazi regime. As such, they are unlikely to perform actions "prejudicial to national security", and many are distinguished scientists working on defence projects; however, the fear of a "fifth column" of traitors is so great they have all been rounded up. Posters urge people to beware of gossip.

These dictatorial measures have been adopted by the government in order to fight the war. On 22 May parliament took under three hours to pass the Emergency Powers Act – arguably the most drastic legislation in British history. It gives the government almost unlimited power over the life, liberty and property of every person in the land. The most sweeping powers have been granted to Ernest Bevin, the former trade union leader who is now minister of labour in the coalition government (→ 1/12/43).

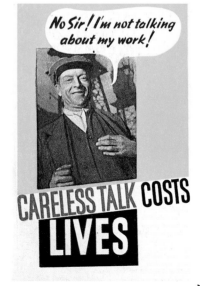

No Sir! I'm not talking about my work!

CARELESS TALK COSTS LIVES

Posters warn against gossip.

Luftwaffe attacks to prepare for German invasion

London, 16 August
The fierceness of the aerial battles over southern England increases daily as the Luftwaffe tries to win air superiority so that Hitler can launch an invasion across the English Channel. The young Spitfire and Hurricane pilots have no intention of being swept aside, however, and they are battling Goering's fighters and bombers in the skies.

The battle raged all along the east coast from Tyneside to Kent and then west along the Channel to Devon yesterday as German planes took off from airfields ranging from Norway to Brittany. The day belonged to the RAF, which shot down 90 planes for the loss of 42.

The Germans returned today, flying 1,700 sorties, and received the same medicine, losing 44 to the RAF's 24. But they concentrated their efforts on the defenders' airfields and Radio Direction Finding [radar] stations and caused great damage. According to the invasion timetable these attacks ought to have brought the Luftwaffe within sight of victory, but it has still not won air superiority.

Winston Churchill followed the progress of the battle from the "ops room" of No. 11 Group at Uxbridge, west of London. As he was driven home, the prime minister said: "Don't speak to me. I have never been so moved" (→20).

Scramble: RAF fighter pilots race to their planes after another alert.

Allies escape from Dunkirk bombardment

A wounded soldier limps home.

Dunkirk, 4 June
Operation Dynamo, the evacuation of British and other Allied forces from Dunkirk, was completed today in spite of intense aerial bombardment and shellfire. In all, some 338,226 men of the army which had been forced to retreat to this Channel port have been transported to safety. Around 800 civilian "little ships" and 222 naval vessels took part in an operation which Winston Churchill describes as "a miracle of deliverance".

Perversely, the British are defiantly looking on the evacuation as a victory rather than a defeat, even though most of its army's heavy equipment has been lost (→10).

Channel Islands fall to invading Germans

Guernsey, 13 June
The Channel Islands have fallen to the Germans without a shot being fired. The government decided earlier this month that they could not be defended without a huge loss of civilian lives. British nationals drew their money from the banks, shot their cats and dogs and crowded onto the evacuation boats.

The Germans gave their orders for the surrender of the islands in canvas bags dropped from aircraft. Today every house displays a white sheet, and the Germans are landing in force. The only incident so far has been a pub fight between an Irish worker and a German soldier. The Irishman won (→27/4/41).

German guns at Guernsey harbour.

Veterans are 'proud to do their bit' and enrol in Home Guard

London, 23 July
Britain's Local Defence Volunteer force, now over a million strong, was officially renamed the Home Guard today. Veterans of the Great War, anxious to "do their bit", are flocking to join this nationwide force. Generals and admirals with several rows of medals are serving in the ranks. The veterans are short of weapons and uniforms; many of them are drilling with broom handles, while farmers with shotguns patrol their land on horseback, prepared to fight the invaders. So far they have only had to cope with shot-down enemy pilots.

A Home Guard unit drills in a high street "somewhere in England".

'Lord Haw-Haw' is new voice of Berlin

London, 1 March
William Joyce, a Briton who now lives in Hamburg, has become the voice of German propaganda. Research just completed for the BBC shows that two-thirds of the adult population in Britain have listened to his propaganda talks, with one in six apparently being regular members of his audience. Joyce's drawling nasal voice has earned him the nickname of "Lord Haw-Haw" as he sneers at claims made by British politicians and newspapers about the war (→26/6/45).

RAF claims victory after the 'battle of Britain'

London, 15 September

RAF Fighter Command withstood everything the Luftwaffe could throw at it today and chased the Germans back across the English Channel, leaving southern England littered with the burning wrecks of enemy aircraft. This was probably the most crucial day of the "battle of Britain", the day on which the German air minister, Goering, had planned finally to sweep aside what he told his pilots were Britain's few remaining Hurricanes and Spitfires and so clear the path for Hitler's "Operation Sealion" – Germany's invasion of Britain.

It did not happen like that. As the blips of the attacking force showed on the RDF [radar] sets this fine, sunny morning, Air Vice Marshal Keith Park, commanding 11 Group, sent up 11 squadrons, about a hundred fighters, to harry the German formations as they headed for London. Over the capital they were met by Douglas Bader, the "legless ace", at the head of his "big wing" of five squadrons.

Four Hurricane squadrons met the German bombers head-on, breaking up their formation so that their bombs were scattered over a wide area. The fight raged all the way from the coast and back again with British fighters chasing crippled bombers and fuel-short Messerschmitt 109 fighters at wave-top height. The Germans came back in the afternoon, with 150 bombers preceded by fighters. This tactic did not work either.

Air Chief Marshal Sir Hugh Dowding, who has been conducting the RAF's battle with a fine economy, was warned of their impending arrival by decoded German signals and his young pilots were ready to pounce on the Germans as they crossed the coast. Those who did get through were once again met over London by the daunting sight of Bader's 60 machines tearing in at them.

The RAF's victory today was brought about not only by the courage and skill of the pilots and the careful husbanding of men and machines but also by a Luftwaffe error in switching its attacks from airfields and radar stations to London in retaliation for an RAF raid on Berlin on 25 August. If Goering had maintained the assault on the airfields, he might still have won, but by striking at London he gave the fighter pilots some rest.

Even so there were anxious moments today. Winston Churchill, visiting an RAF operations HQ at Uxbridge, watched the commander feeding squadrons into the fray. As the battle reached a ferocious climax Churchill asked: "What other reserves have we?" He was told: "There are none" (→15/11).

British cities 'blitzed' by German air war

What was once a street in Bristol lies devastated after a November raid.

London, 30 December

The City of London is still smouldering this morning after a series of fire raids in which over 22,000 incendiary bombs and 127 tons of high explosive were dropped by 136 bombers. Many of the City's finest buildings were destroyed, among them the Guildhall, eight Wren churches and three hospitals. St Paul's Cathedral, although damaged, stands proudly among the gutted shells of its neighbours.

These raids were among the most ferocious and damaging inflicted on the capital by the almost continuous bombardment which has been maintained since that first terrible afternoon of 7 September when the Luftwaffe switched its attacks from the RAF's airfields to the streets and houses of Britain's cities.

Since then thousands of civilians have died, 3,700 this month alone, in what has come to be known as "the Blitz". Coventry has had its heart ripped out, and many of Britain's major cities have been severely damaged. For the moment there seems little that the RAF can do to counter the night bombers, which are directed to their targets by beams. Scientists are working on airborne RDF [radar], but until it is ready the nightfighters are blind and bombs rain down (→2/1/41).

U-boats step up attacks to block Atlantic

A U-boat on patrol: hunting in "wolf packs" in the Atlantic war.

London, 26 October

Germany's U-boats are waging a ferocious war to sever Britain's Atlantic lifeline. Despite the British system of sending boats in convoys, the U-boats, using new tactics devised by their commander, Admiral Karl Dönitz, are sinking ship after ship. Allied shipping losses this week total 88,000 tons, more than eight times greater than the average losses at the beginning of the year.

The U-boats operate in "wolf packs", forming a patrol line and then gathering when one of the boats spots a convoy and signals its position and course. When gathered they often outnumber the convoy's armed escorts and steam into the convoy, picking off their targets with the escorts unable to protect the vulnerable merchant ships.

One of the problems is that the escort's detection equipment can only spot the U-boats when they are submerged, so the Germans attack on the surface at night, virtually invisible with their low silhouettes. The defenders are also hampered by a lack of long-range aircraft, while the Germans fly from French airfields to lead the wolf packs to their prey. So effective is this that 30 ships from two convoys were sunk in just two days earlier this month (→27/5/41).

Civilians learn to cope on front line

January: a bomb near the Bank of England rips London's streets apart.

March: school lessons continue in an air raid shelter in Bermondsey.

April: rescue workers salvage belongings after raids on Belfast.

How blitzed cities struggle through

London, 16 April

German bombers have renewed the Blitz on the cities of the United Kingdom after the bad weather of the winter. Early this morning it was the turn of Belfast, where more than 700 people are feared to have died in what was one of the most concentrated raids of the war to date. Fire brigades were sent from Eire as well as Northern Ireland.

Major industrial centres and ports have been the principal targets of the Luftwaffe, but the bombs are hitting all classes and all regions. Buckingham Palace was hit on the night of 8/9 March, and the Café de Paris nightclub was destroyed in the same attack. Terrible damage was inflicted on Clydeside on 13 March – with only seven houses left undamaged in the shipbuilding town of Clydebank. The raid left 1,100 dead in Scotland's worst raid so far. Bristol, Cardiff, Plymouth, Birmingham, Merseyside and Portsmouth figure in the long list of places battered.

There have been instances of panic, but people are learning to "live with the bomb". In London thousands take shelter in the Underground. The government, which originally tried to prevent the use of the Underground system as shelters, is now fitting bunks and sanitary facilities. Regulars are given tickets for specific bunks. In Portsmouth many shelter in the tunnels of Portsdown Hill, and there is an exodus from Plymouth every night as people head for the safety of the countryside pushing treasured possessions in carts and prams.

Yet, despite the death and destruction, the Blitz appears to be bolstering the nation's resolve. Even in Coventry, where the damage was so great that the army wanted to impose martial law, people soon returned to the factories, and production actually rose. The RAF is also gaining the upper hand in its struggle with the German bombers. New nightfighters equipped with RDF [radar] are, as Churchill says, "clawing the Hun out of the sky" (→ 11/5).

Nazi troops tighten grip on Europe

Crete is abandoned by the Allied forces

Crete, 1 June
After a week of some of the fiercest fighting yet seen in this war the Allied forces on Crete have been defeated, and the Royal Navy, under incessant attack from the air, is endeavouring to evacuate as many as possible. It is almost exactly a year since it performed the same task at Dunkirk.

The battle started following the fall of Greece when Germany's General Kurt Student's paratroopers established a bridgehead on the island and flocks of JU52 transports laden with airborne troops were sent in. Many were shot out of the sky, and Student's élite force has suffered appalling casualties.

It was touch and go despite the Germans' total air supremacy – the few RAF planes on the island were withdrawn rather than suffer annihilation – but "Creforce" was disposed to face an attack from the sea rather than the air and the Germans were able to take Malame airfield and pour in reinforcements.

So far the Royal Navy has taken off 18,000 men – but at great cost, losing three cruisers and nine destroyers, with 17 other ships crippled and 2,011 men dead (→ 14/11).

A British merchant ship under attack by a German commerce raider.

Air cover goes as 'Ark Royal' capsizes

Gibraltar, 14 November
Constant German claims to have sunk the aircraft carrier *Ark Royal* became reality when the ship capsized and sank at 6.13 am today. She was torpedoed by a U-boat yesterday, but it was hoped that she could be saved. However, as she was towed towards Gibraltar, 25 miles away, fire broke out, her list increased, and she was abandoned.

With the *Illustrious* and the *Formidable* under repair in the US, the Mediterranean Fleet is left without air cover at a time when Hitler is transferring bombers from the USSR to Sicily to step up the attack on Malta. It is not all bad news from the Mediterranean, however: the cruisers *Aurora* and *Penelope* have sunk two Italian destroyers and ten merchant ships.

There is also good news for Britain in the battle of the Atlantic to follow the success in May when the much feared battleship *Bismarck* sank. The United States has now decided that it will escort convoys carrying lend-lease materials as far east as Iceland (→ 19/8/42).

Churchill and US sign 'Atlantic Charter'

Washington, 14 August
President Roosevelt and Winston Churchill have signed an "Atlantic Charter", an historic declaration of Anglo-American aims and principles. It declares that neither country seeks territorial gains from the war and that both look forward to a lasting peace and the end of the use of force. It also says that it hopes all nations will cooperate economically after the war.

The charter, stemming from the US president's wish that the Western democracies should make their aims clear to the Soviet Union, was signed during a series of meetings over the past five days on the US cruiser *Augusta* and the British battleship *Prince of Wales* at Placenta Bay off Newfoundland (→ 26/12).

Churchill: the voice of Britain.

Desert armies face winter campaigns

Western Desert, 13 November
The North African armies fighting under the leadership of Generals Erwin Rommel and Claude Auchinleck are both preparing decisive winter campaigns. The Germans are planning to take Tobruk, cut off for nine months, and then crash into Egypt. However, Auchinleck knows of Rommel's plans through intercepted German signals and intends to forestall him.

The Allies outnumber the Germans two to one in tanks and aircraft, but no Eighth Army tanks can withstand the German 88mm gun. The British also have to face the superb generalship of Rommel, "the Desert Fox" (→ 21/6/42).

Women called up to meet wartime labour shortages

Westminster, 4 December
Unmarried women in their 20s now face the call-up. Female conscription was announced today by Winston Churchill as one of a series of moves to combat a critical labour shortage. The government is also requiring married women up to the age of 40 and single women in their 30s to register as labour which can be directed to industries.

Men are not forgotten in this new extension of conscription – the call-up comes down to 18 years and six months, with men in their 40s also now liable for military service – but it is the powers over women which are unprecedented. Single women in their 20s will be sent to join the police, fire service or to non-combat roles in the forces.

Since last April they have had to register for war work. In many cases this has meant filling the places left in industry and other occupations vacated by the men now serving in the forces, although Britain had entered the war with a higher proportion of its female population in the total workforce than any other European country. Taking account of certain exemptions (as exist for men in reserved occupations and for conscientious objectors), the new conscription will cover nearly 1.7 million single women (→ 6/2/48).

Women at work in a factory.

US joins war after Pearl Harbor raid

Hong Kong falls to Japanese offensive

South-east Asia, 31 December
Japanese forces have struck with devastating speed since 7 December when they stunned the United States by attacking the Pearl Harbor base in Hawaii. The next day the US declared war on Japan, as did Britain. Other declarations of war came almost daily, but the most significant came when Germany and Italy, supporting their Axis ally of Japan, declared war on the United States.

Winston Churchill is privately delighted, having long sought US support. But the potential long-term benefits of US participation in the war have been offset by short-term reverses as Japanese forces sweep across the Pacific and southeast Asia. In Malaya, Japan is pushing towards Kuala Lumpur and Singapore. Burma is under attack, and there have been landings in the Philippines, Wake and Guam.

Britain has already suffered serious losses. Two warships, the *Repulse* and the *Prince of Wales*, have been sunk, and on Christmas Day Hong Kong became the first British possession to see the Union Jack replaced by the emblem of the Rising Sun. Sir Mark Young, its governor, ordered all 11,000 troops under British command to lay down their arms following 18 days of fighting with intense air and artillery bombardment (→ 11/1/42).

Japanese troops enter Hong Kong after the British colony's surrender.

Indian troops fighting with Britain cross a river in Burma near Mandalay.

Make Do and Mend is the motto for the British housewife

Britain, 31 December
This has been the year when the upper classes have found themselves facing the kind of problem only too common in working-class families. A special "Make Do and Mend" department has been set up in the board of trade to publicize suggestions for patching clothes and mending curtains and bedlinen instead of replacing them with new items.

Travelling exhibitions are being planned to show how worn stockings can be cut into "clips" and made into rugs (an old tradition in northern industrial towns), prewar golfing plus-fours can be made up into overcoats, and scarves can be used to make children's frocks. Jumble sales have suddenly become popular, so much so that admission tickets are being issued for some sales. The Women's Voluntary Service is arranging "clothing exchanges" for mothers to trade in items their children have outgrown.

Wartime deprivation has found comic relief in radio programmes such as *ITMA* starring Tommy Handley. *It's That Man Again*, to give the show its full title, pokes fun at officialdom with Handley as the minister of aggravation and mysteries. "I have several hundred irritating restrictions to impose on you," said Handley in a show which proves that whatever Britons have lost during the war it is not their sense of humour (→ 3/3/42).

Now the war spreads around the world

London, 11 December
A year ago Britain and its empire stood alone against Hitler and his Italian ally, Mussolini; now, after the German invasion of the Soviet Union and Japan's attack on Pearl Harbor, the war has become one that girdles the whole globe.

In the battle of the Atlantic, US warships are already escorting convoys as far as Iceland, where the Royal Navy takes over; shipping losses of 400,000 tons a month have fallen to 100,000 tons this year.

The Italians have been expelled from Ethiopia, but in the western desert of North Africa neither Britain's Eighth Army ("the Desert Rats") nor the Axis forces under General Rommel have been able to deliver a decisive blow. Germany's drive into the Soviet Union may at last have been halted, however. Five days ago Soviet forces counterattacked, pushing the enemy back from Moscow, though Leningrad remains besieged.

Churchill told MPs today that, though a "hard period" lies ahead, the US entry into the war ensures that Britain will receive a vast increase in munitions and aid.

De Valera spurns a plea to join Allies

Dublin, 31 December
Eamon de Valera, the Eire leader, continues to maintain Irish neutrality even though the United States, the country to which he looks for traditional support, has entered the war. Believing that he would alter his stance, Winston Churchill sent a personal message to de Valera – the first since the war began – urging him to join the Allies. But the Eire premier has interpreted this as yet another move towards unity and has rejected it (→ 1/5/43).

Tommy Handley (centre), the star of radio's hit show "ITMA".

Malaya, 11 January. Kuala Lumpur, the capital, falls to the Japanese army (→ 15/2).

Belfast, 26 January. The first US troops in Europe since the First World War land in Northern Ireland (→ 5/2).

Derry City, 5 February. A US naval base is established (→ 14/1/43).

Westminster, 17 March. Coal, gas and electricity are to be rationed, MPs are told (→ 26/7).

Germany, 28 March. RAF Bomber Command signals a new policy by launching a concerted attack by 200 planes against Lübeck (→ 24/4).

New Delhi, 28 March. Indian leaders are told by the British government that they will be offered independence after the war (→ 19/9/45).

Devon, 24 April. German planes bomb Exeter in retaliation for the RAF raid on Lübeck last month (→ 5/5).

Germany, 30 May. The RAF launches its first 1,000-bomber raid, with Cologne the target (→ 31).

Oxford, 1 July. A charity to provide aid for people suffering from famine is formed.

Britain, 26 July. Rationing of sweets begins today (→ 1/2/44).

Moscow, 15 August. Winston Churchill holds his first summit meeting with Joseph Stalin, the Soviet Union's leader (→ 21/2/43).

Russia, 18 September. The largest convoy yet arrives with 27 out of 40 ships intact, two months after the disastrous PQ-17 convoy (→ 22/5/43).

North Africa, 24 October. The Eighth Army under General Bernard Montgomery launches a major offensive at El Alamein (→ 30/10).

Bordeaux, 12 December. British commandos travelling in canoes blow up six moored ships (→ 10/7/43).

Britain, 15 December. A campaign to halt the increase in venereal disease that has occurred since the war began.

London, 17 December. In a joint statement with its allies the British government condemns the anti-Semitic atrocities which it says are being perpetrated by Germany.

Burma, 19 December. British forces begin a cautious advance against Japanese troops (→ 24/3/44).

German bombers target 'Baedeker' cities

The cup that cheers: a fireman pauses during the rescue work at Exeter.

Exeter, 5 May
In the latest of the "Baedeker" raids on lightly defended English towns of historic interest, the Luftwaffe mounted a second attack on Exeter last night but with markedly less success than on the first occasion.

As well as Exeter, the Germans have hit Bath, Norwich and York with devastating effect, using high explosive, incendiaries and machine-gun fire guided by a new electronic targeting beam. The RAF has responded by transmitting a radio signal which misleads the Luftwaffe beam. In the latest raid only 13 per cent of German bombs found their target, against 50 per cent previously.

The German raids on towns featured in the Baedeker guidebook are Hitler's retaliation for the RAF's fire-bombing of Lübeck and Rostock in the last six weeks. These raids were Bomber Command's trial runs for its new policy of bombing cities in a bid to destroy German workers' morale (→ 30/5).

Allies driven back by Rommel's forces

Tobruk, Libya, 21 June
Axis forces today captured the vital North African port of Tobruk. Its loss – along with 35,000 Allied soldiers and 70 tanks – is the biggest single blow to Britain since the fall of Singapore. General Rommel's Afrika Korps has been pushing the Eighth Army back deeper into Egypt but surprised the Allies by turning back towards Tobruk in Libya. A heavy bombardment by air and artillery yesterday signalled the assault with the infantry and Panzers completing the port's capture this afternoon. The German advance is now set to continue across the desert as Rommel, "the Desert Fox", moves closer to Cairo and the Suez Canal (→ 24/10).

Maltese honoured

Valletta, Malta, 16 April
The tiny island of Malta, which has endured over a thousand German and Italian air raids in the past four months, was today awarded the George Cross – the civilian equivalent of the Victoria Cross – by King George VI in recognition of the heroism and devotion of its people. The island is less than a hundred miles (160km) from Sicily.

Singapore, the 'impregnable' naval base, surrenders to Japan

Singapore, 15 February
The Singapore base surrendered to Japan today after several confused and ineffective counter-attacks by British and Indian troops. It is the greatest military defeat in British history. The base was reputedly impregnable, but its great guns were pointing out to sea as the invaders came by land.

Unknown to the British, the Japanese, after a lightning advance down the Malay peninsula, were almost out of ammunition, though they had supremacy in the air and at sea. Lt-Gen Arthur Percival, responsible for a million civilians and 130,000 troops, was told that water supplies were running out and so surrendered to General Tomoyuki Yamashita, who has now acquired a massive arsenal of guns and ammunition (→ 19/12).

Lt-Gen Percival (second left) marches to surrender Singapore to Japan.

Battles intensify on land, sea and in the air

Air war: RAF stages 1,000-bomber raid

Germany, 31 May

More than a thousand aircraft were sent aloft by the RAF last night to devastate the city of Cologne; 1,455 tons of bombs were dropped in 90 minutes, 2,300 separate fires were started and over 3,000 buildings destroyed. Vital machine-tool and chemical plants have been crippled, and over 45,000 civilians are thought to be homeless.

Air Marshal Arthur Harris made use of every last plane in Bomber Command, from new Lancasters to ancient Whitleys; the 6,500 crewmen of the 1,047 aircraft included many who had not completed their training. The raid is seen as a test of saturation bombing tactics designed to bring the reality of total war home to Germans.

In a message to Harris, Churchill says: "This proof of the growing power of Britain's bomber force is also a herald of what Germany will receive, city by city, from now on." A message smuggled out of the Warsaw ghetto says Jews rejoiced when they heard of the raid. They see it as vengeance on Germany for Hitler's persecution of the Jews in Nazi-occupied Europe (→ 30/1/43).

The detritus of defeat: helmets and guns left by the Allies at Dieppe.

Land war: heavy Allied losses at Dieppe

Dieppe, 19 August

In just nine hours of fighting along an 11-mile stretch of the French coast at Dieppe, a 6,100-strong force of Canadians, British, Americans and Free French today lost 1,000 men killed and 2,000 taken prisoner; all their tanks and equipment were abandoned. The Royal Navy's casualties were 75 dead, 206 wounded and 269 missing; a destroyer and 33 landing craft were sunk. The RAF lost 106 planes, the Germans 48. Enemy casualties included 314 killed, 294 wounded and 37 taken prisoner and brought to England. The raid, officially no more than a "reconnaissance in force", was a disaster. Hitler, however, told his commanders: "We must realize that we are not alone in learning a lesson from Dieppe. The British have also learned. We must reckon with a totally different mode of attack and at a quite different place" (→ 12/12).

Sea war: convoy is shattered in Arctic

USSR, 10 July

The Allied convoy PQ-17 is limping into the Soviet Union's Arctic port of Murmansk after losing 24 ships of the 39 which sailed from Iceland on 27 June with vital munitions for the USSR. Of 156,492 tonnes of cargo, 99,316 tonnes were lost, including 430 of the 594 tanks on board, 210 of 297 warplanes and 3,350 of 4,246 vehicles.

The disaster has been attributed to an order which assumed that a powerful task force, headed by Germany's biggest battleship, the *Tirpitz*, had sailed to attack PQ-17. The Allies had long known of the plan for such an attack, codenamed Operation Rasselsprung [Knight's Move], and were extremely apprehensive. When the admiralty failed to get confirmation that the *Tirpitz* force was still in Norwegian ports, the order to scatter was given.

In fact Hitler, anxious not to put his most powerful ships at risk, had ordered them back to port while U-boats and dive-bombers were sent into action. For three nights and days the planes caused havoc among the defenceless merchantmen. But Sir Dudley Pound, the first sea lord, says that had the convoy not scattered the *Tirpitz* might have continued, and then all the merchant ships would have been sunk (→ 18/9).

Skirts get shorter as material gets scarce

Britain, 3 March

Skirts are several centimetres shorter than peace-time styles, and the number of buttonholes, pleats and seams has been severely restricted by new Utility regulations. After clothes rationing was introduced last year, manufacturers with limited quotas of material maximized their profits by concentrating on higher-priced items. Board of trade regulations now limit the range of materials and styles and control the level of retail prices.

A woman's tweed winter coat sells for £4/3/11 [£4.20]. For just a bit more, a man can buy a suit (if he has enough coupons), but the trousers lack turn-ups, and the jacket is single-breasted. Five centimetres (2 inches) have disappeared from shirt tails (→ 17/3).

A "Utility" suit – for 18 coupons.

Churchill wins MPs' vote of confidence

Westminster, 2 July

Accusing his critics in the House of Commons of "nagging and snarling", Churchill tonight demanded a rousing vote of confidence – and received it by 476 to 25, with 30 abstentions. He was greatly helped by the ineptitude of his chief critic, the old Chamberlainite Tory Sir John Wardlaw Milne, who called for King George VI's younger brother, the duke of Gloucester, to be appointed commander-in-chief of the army, "without, of course, administrative duties". MPs roared with derisive laughter. Churchill is none the less relieved by the vote, as there has been serious criticism of his leadership following the recent German victories in North Africa.

Sun rays compensate for shelter life for these London children.

El Alamein victory turns tide for Allies

Welfare proposed for everyone 'from cradle to grave'

A wounded gunner is helped as the battle rages in the African desert.

Montgomery: the new British hero.

Britain, 1 December

A "welfare state" caring for people "from the cradle to the grave" is proposed in a report published today. Social planning is seen as the means to build on the solidarity forged by battle and to conquer what the report identifies as the "five giants" of Want, Ignorance, Squalor, Idleness and Disease.

Sir William Beveridge, the economist who headed the committee which produced the report, wants a system of social insurance with contributions from workers, employers and the state to provide benefits for unemployment, sickness, pensions and everything from maternity to funeral grants. Family allowances would be paid to offset poverty, and

El Alamein, 30 October

After five days locked in ferocious combat on a 40-mile (64km) front, Field Marshal Rommel's mighty Afrika Korps lies battered and demoralized, its last reserves used up and its tank force shattered as Lt-Gen Bernard Montgomery, the new British commander of the Eighth Army, prepares a new offensive – Operation Supercharge.

The Eighth Army had opened its offensive on the evening of 23 October with a 15-minute artillery barrage by 1,000 guns. Then the infantry went in – the 51st Highland and the South African and New Zealand Divisions – to clear a way through the minefield for the armour. The British XXX Corps has lost 200 tanks driving a wedge into German lines, but the weight of Allied armour and the infantry's determination is winning the war of attrition. Montgomery has also been greatly helped by allied code-breaking which revealed Rommel's plans – and his weaknesses.

The fate of the Afrika Korps was, in fact, sealed seven weeks ago when Montgomery stopped Rommel in a seven-day battle at Alam Halfa ridge, near El Alamein. Until then Rommel had enjoyed three months of triumphs that caused near panic at British GHQ in Cairo, where mountains of confidential papers were burnt. Churchill had arrived in person in August to install new men, General Harold Alexander as C-in-C Middle East and Montgomery to lead the Eighth Army, with orders to destroy the enemy "at the earliest opportunity" (→ 7/11).

Beveridge: a visionary for peace.

Allied troops storm ashore in massive invasion of North Africa

Algiers, 7 November

The most formidable amphibious invasion force ever mounted – 300 warships, 370 merchant ships and 107,000 men – tonight descended upon the coast of French North Africa in an Allied bid to trap Rommel's Afrika Korps in a giant nutcracker. Operation Torch is commanded by Lt-Gen Dwight D Eisenhower, and most of his troops are also American; two British destroyers off Algiers are flying the Stars and Stripes. By playing down the British role it is hoped that the Vichy French forces in North Africa will be cooperative, but early reports suggest the Allied troops are meeting resistance at Algiers, Oran and Casablanca (→ 13/5/43).

Allied troops land as Operation Torch steps up the attack on Rommel.

"national assistance" to people who fall outside other benefits. A major element in the Beveridge vision is the creation of a "national health service".

The proposals have been warmly welcomed and build on a growing social consensus and concern that the unity shown in war should be maintained in peace. Magazines such as *Picture Post*, books, church leaders, academics and professional groups such as those representing doctors have all outlined ideas not dissimilar to those published today. The coalition government promises to give the report earnest consideration (→ 18/2/43).

German shipyards and factories reduced to a pile of rubble after bombing raids

A woman weeps in Hamburg after identifying a victim of the bombing.

Germany, 31 July

Close on one million terrified citizens have fled Germany's biggest port, Hamburg, after three devastating night raids by RAF bombers in the last five days. Over 7,000 tonnes of bombs have obliterated 10 square miles (26 sq km) of buildings and severely damaged U-boat construction yards. Water, gas and electricity supplies failed, and over 40,000 people died, many of them being sucked into the centre of firestorms rising to 1,000 degrees Celsius (1,832 degrees Fahrenheit).

The Hamburg raids came as a climax to seven months of concentrated bombing directed at a dozen cities in Germany's industrial heartland, the Ruhr. At the beginning of this year the RAF had only 260 heavy bombers. Now upwards of 700 aircraft are regularly dispatched on a single night raid.

Special bombs have been devised for specific targets. Barnes Wallis of Vickers Armstrong designed a bomb that bounces over water. This was used to breach the Mohne and Eder dams, which supply water to Ruhr industries. Over 300 million gallons of water were lost.

Pathfinder aircraft are now being used to identify the target city and drop marker bombs for the main force. Then masses of aluminium foil strips are released to confuse the enemy radar. The RAF's bomb-

ing offensive has forced Hitler to order Luftwaffe squadrons to withdraw from the eastern front; little more than 20 per cent of the Luftwaffe force is now deployed in the Soviet Union.

German sources admit that the RAF offensive has hit morale. Colonel Adolf Galland says of the Hamburg raids: "A wave of terror radiated from the suffering city and spread throughout Germany ... After Hamburg in the wide circle of the political and military command could be heard the words "the war is lost"." Albert Speer, Hitler's minister for war production, is reported to have said that six more raids on the Hamburg scale could bring Germany to its knees (→13/6/44).

Testing the "bouncing bomb".

U-boats withdrawn as Allies hit back in Atlantic battle

North Atlantic, 22 May

After a month of disastrous losses, Grand Admiral Karl Dönitz has ordered his U-boats to pull out of the North Atlantic. Only three days ago his son, Peter, perished when an RAF Liberator bomber operating from Iceland sank the U954.

In recent months, British, Canadian and American naval and air units have steadily gained the upper hand. In 1942 eight million tonnes of shipping were lost, and even as recently as March this year losses were running at almost 600,000 tonnes a month.

But now attacks on convoys by Dönitz's "Wolf Packs" are repulsed with heavy U-boat losses. Last week five of 33 U-boats were sunk in an unsuccessful attack on convoy

Dropping a depth charge at sea.

SC-130. The Allies are operating a new short-wave radar system which is able to detect a U-boat surfacing several miles away to recharge its batteries. More powerful depth charges are also being used.

These measures have been backed up by more Allied successes in breaking German codes, including one used by U-boats to communicate with their central command. The Royal Navy's codebreakers, just 24 before the war, now number 1,000 and include historians, mathematicians and linguists, some of them German refugees. Listening posts to intercept enemy signals are scattered across Britain and British territories overseas.

Italy gives up the fight

Salerno, Italy, 9 September

Allied troops aboard ships which had left Sicily for an unknown destination heard today that Italy had surrendered unconditionally – and that they were about to go ashore at Salerno, south of Naples.

These dramatic announcements came after a week of secret contacts in Lisbon between the Allies and representatives of King Victor Emmanuel and Marshal Pietro Badoglio, who ousted Mussolini in July. The British were represented by General Carton de Wiart, who had been freed from an Axis prisoner-of-war camp. An armistice was signed in Sicily a week ago but kept secret until today's amphibious operation began.

Hitler, taking an afternoon nap at his HQ in east Prussia, was roused and told the BBC had broadcast news of Italy's surrender. He

An Axis prisoner is searched.

ordered the disarming of Italian troops and their deportation to Germany for forced labour. As the Germans entered Rome, Badoglio and the Italian king fled to territory occupied by the Allies (→ 31/1/44).

'Wonder drug' is used in army hospitals

London, 31 December 1943

A life-saving drug which was used to treat Churchill's pneumonia earlier this month and is now in use in military hospitals is being imported from the United States, despite the fact that it was discovered by a British scientist, Alexander Fleming, in 1928. The patent for penicillin was lost when war came, and a shortage of microbiologists held up the drug's large-scale development. It

was first used in Britain in 1941 to treat a policeman for blood poisoning; he died because not enough was available. Factories to manufacture the drug are being built in Britain, but it may be some two years before home-produced supplies exceed imports from the US. However, enough of another "wonder drug" for treating infections, sulphanilamide, is being produced for Britain to be self-sufficient.

Row as sick Mosley is released from jail

Protests over Mosley's release.

Westminster, 1 December

After noisy protests by a group of Labour MPs, the Commons today endorsed by a substantial majority the decision by Herbert Morrison, the home secretary, to release Sir Oswald Mosley, the founder of the British Union of Fascists, who is suffering from thrombo-phlebitis. Mosley, who was interned in 1940, is back in his Oxfordshire home but must report regularly to the police. Morrison said he had been advised by doctors that Mosley's life could be put at risk by continued imprisonment. The fascist leader conducted anti-Semitic marches through Jewish parts of London's East End in the 1930s.

How the home fires keep burning as the long years of wartime just drag on

Britain, 2 December

After four years of war Britain is running out of men and women to fill the ranks of the services and run the factories. Numbers registered as unemployed in 1939 – 1,250,000 – have fallen to fewer than 60,000.

To fill a manpower gap of two million, the minister of labour, Ernest Bevin, has extended the call-up downwards to 18-year-olds and upwards to men aged 51. Conscription of women has also been extended beyond those in their twenties to women up to 50, although they can still choose between industry and service with the armed forces.

Today Bevin went further and announced that 30,000 men under 25 called up for national service will be directed to work in coal mines; they are to be selected by ballot. Coal output has fallen below the critical level of 200 million tons a year. Coal rationing was announced and then found to be unworkable; people are meanwhile urged to save fuel by bathing in no more than five inches of water.

Income tax collection began running into problems as the number of manual workers liable for tax rose from under one million before the war to over seven million. Deduction of the tax from pay packets seemed to

Bevin: extending the call-up.

be the answer until it was discovered that taking the tax in arrears, based on the previous year's assessment, could cause hardship if overtime diminished. So now it is being based on each week's pay – Pay As You Earn.

Even Christmas turkeys will be hard to find this year: each butcher with 800 registered customers will be allocated just 15 birds. Beer remains unrationed, but it has been so reduced in strength that a drinker must put down about twice as much by volume in order to keep up his alcohol intake. Still, it is not all grim news: the suicide rate has fallen from a pre-war 12.9 per 100,000 to below nine today.

Women munitions workers take a break from life on the production line.

'Forgotten army' strikes back in Burma

British jungle fighters in Burma: some attacked by land, some by air.

Imphal, India, 24 March
British, Indian and Gurkha forces have this month struck deep into Burma behind the Japanese lines, blowing up railways and bridges. In one encounter 100 Japanese were killed for the loss of one Gurkha. A glider-borne Allied force of 9,000 men, known as "Chindits" from the Burmese for "mighty lion", are being joined by Americans, Chinese and Gurkhas marching overland.

"We have inflicted complete surprise on the enemy," said Major-General Orde Wingate. "All our columns are inside the enemy's guts. The time has come to reap the fruit of the advantage we have gained." Tragically, soon after he made this statement his plane crashed in bad weather and he was killed.

The Chindits were Wingate's brainchild. British operations on the India/Burma front had had few successes, and the force became known as the "forgotten army". Wingate, described by Churchill as a "man of genius and audacity", put the Burmese theatre of war back in the headlines (→ 3/5/45).

Allied invasion of Europe draws near

London, 15 May
King George VI, with Winston Churchill and South Africa's prime minister, Field Marshal Jan Smuts, went to school today – St Paul's in London, where allied commanders have been planning Operation Overlord, the invasion of Nazi-occupied Europe. The visitors were shown a gigantic map of the Normandy beaches as General Montgomery ("Monty") explained the plan for putting eight divisions, five seaborne and three airborne, ashore in the first 48 hours.

The Germans have 60 divisions deployed along the coast to defend the Netherlands, France and Belgium. The Overlord strategy depends upon an elaborate deception operation aimed at the enemy. An entirely phantom army has been "stationed" in England opposite the Calais coast and kept busy with radio traffic for the enemy to monitor. In Stockholm, British agents have been manipulating the stock exchange to send up the value of Norwegian shares. And the day before "Monty" set out the true invasion plan he received a decrypt of Field Marshal Rommel's report to the German high command that Allied bombing of railways in northern France was disrupting supplies and his troop movements to reinforce the Calais defences (→ 6/6).

Allied forces open the road to Rome with landings at Anzio

Anzio, Italy, 31 January
When British and American forces went ashore in landing craft here last week they found the Italian coastal town of Anzio, 32 miles (51 km) south of Rome, completely deserted. The Italians had been evacuated, and the Germans had pulled out. The Allies put ashore 50,000 men and 3,000 vehicles with only 13 casualties from mines.

By landing behind enemy lines the Allies seem to have a clear road to Rome, but the US commander, Major-General John Lucas, has insisted on building up his beach defences before pushing inland as the British urge. This seems likely to give the Germans an opportunity to mobilize reserves and pin down the beach-head with artillery (→ 19/4).

British soldiers shelter in a German trench while awaiting reinforcements.

'D-Day' sees the biggest-ever seaborne invasion

The second front opens at last: Royal Marine commandos wade ashore on the beaches of Normandy to set in motion the greatest-ever invasion.

Normandy, 6 June

By dawn today 18,000 British and American airborne troops had landed in Normandy, seizing bridges and disrupting German communications. The BBC was broadcasting coded messages to the French Resistance to cut rail links, and 1,000 RAF planes were dropping 5,000 tons of bombs on German batteries.

As darkness gave way to a dull grey morning, a vast armada of 6,000 ships – men-of-war, merchantmen, barges and landing craft – could be seen rolling and heaving in the heavy seas. The Allies were going ashore to establish five beach-heads between Le Havre and the Cotentin peninsula.

This is Operation Overlord, the long-awaited Allied assault against Nazi Germany's Fortress Europe. Even at this late hour, though, the Germans still believed the "real" invasion would take place in the Pas de Calais, where Field Marshal von Rundstedt, C-in-C West, has concentrated his most powerful Panzer formations. Along with Rommel, his field commander, von Rundstedt has been duped by an elaborate deception operation, a phantom army in southern England and a stream of misleading reports from German agents who have been "turned" to serve the Allies.

On the beaches there were mixed fortunes. The British pushed inland from **Sword Beach** after repelling a Panzer attack, but their drive towards Caen was held up by tanks and trucks jamming the narrow roads. At **Juno Beach**, on Sword's right flank, the Canadians drove inland after fierce street fighting in the small town of Courseulles. The British, at **Gold Beach**, captured a pillbox and found a breakfast of sausage and hot coffee abandoned by the fleeing Germans. Further west, on **Utah Beach**, the Americans lost only six dead in clearing the beach, and the German defenders could scarcely wait to give themselves up.

But it was very different at **Omaha Beach**, where tanks were lost in heavy seas and men who reached the beach came under intense mortar and machine-gun fire. After hours of confusion the Americans recovered, and the Germans, lacking reserves, were forced to give way. By midnight, the Allies had put 155,000 troops ashore for the loss of 9,000 men.

Von Rundstedt has 60 divisions strung out across France, Belgium and the Netherlands. The Allies can muster only 37. The decisive factor will be the speed with which each side can build up its forces. Here, the Allies reckon they have the advantage with their absolute command at sea and in the air.

At this critical point, the Allies have acquired a vital piece of information. British Intelligence has decoded a Luftwaffe message reporting a critical shortage of aviation fuel. Churchill has ordered RAF Bomber Command's attacks to be diverted to Germany's vital oil installations (→8/9).

Strikes soar to mar life on home front

London, 3 December

The Home Guard mustered for its final parade in London today. King George VI took the salute as the Londoners cheered the volunteers whose disbandment symbolizes the belief that victory will be achieved.

Another emblematic change this year has been the replacement of the "black-out" of lights by the "dim-out". While servicemen are still fighting, politicians have been looking forward. A major house-building programme has been promised and an Education Act passed which creates a three-tier system of secondary education with the school-leaving age raised to 15.

Less welcome, though, has been a wave of strikes which seems certain to give 1944 a worse record for industrial unrest than many peace-time years. Three times as many days are likely to be lost this year as in 1939 – and two-thirds of all strikes were in the coal mines.

Most of the miners' grievances related to pay and conditions. In spite of their crucial role in fuelling the war industries they were, until recently, some of the worst paid workers, coming 81st in the national league table of average industrial earnings. Today, after long battles with the colliery owners and repeated government interventions, the miner is among the best paid. After the miners, workers in the engineering industry were the most strike-prone in 1944, with disputes often arising over pay scales for women performing skilled or semi-skilled jobs once reserved for men.

Nazi rockets bring new terror to London

A victim of a V1 attack on Clapham, London, is pulled from the rubble.

London, 10 November

A terrifying new weapon is being aimed at the capital and south-eastern England. Josef Goebbels, the Nazi propaganda chief, gleefully proclaims it to be Germany's second *Vergeltungswaffe*, or reprisal weapon. The V2 is a 12-tonne rocket with a speed of 3,600mph, a range of 200 miles (320 km) and a one-tonne bomb. It arrives without warning and creates widespread devastation.

The first two came down two months ago, on Friday, 8 September, at Chiswick and Epping, and thereafter began to arrive at the rate of four to six a day. But the news was suppressed; in a bid to mislead the Germans it was put about that the mysterious explosions were caused by leaks of domestic gas.

Only today has Churchill admitted to MPs that almost a hundred V2s have come down in built-up areas, after having been fired from launchers in the Netherlands. "The damage and casualties have not so far been heavy," Churchill said.

His words were not entirely reassuring. Like the V1 flying bomb, or "doodlebug" as Londoners dubbed it, the V2 is a weapon of random destruction. The first V1s arrived last June; between then and mid-September 6,725 were spotted over Britain, and 3,500 were destroyed by fighter planes or anti-aircraft guns. The death toll was a relatively low 5,475, but in London some 25,000 houses were destroyed, leading to a new wave of evacuation for the capital's children that was greater than that in the early years of the war. The V1 menace finally ended when Allied forces progressively captured the launch sites across the Channel.

Ardennes breakout surprises the Allies

Belgium, 22 December

The Allied forces on the lightly defended Ardennes front in Belgium were sent scattering in panic and confusion last week when the Germans mounted a surprise attack with two Panzer and four infantry divisions – 250,000 men and 950 tanks against 83,000 Americans with 420 tanks.

The Germans punched a huge bulge in the US lines at Bastogne and then, lunging towards the coast at Antwerp, threatened to cut off Field Marshal Montgomery's 21st Army Group from General Bradley's 12th US Army Group. To Bradley's chagrin, his forces trapped north of the bulge have been placed under Montgomery.

Though the German forces' initial thrust was devastatingly suc-

Winter war in the Ardennes.

cessful, it is doubtful whether they can keep up the momentum. They lack reinforcements, are hampered by fuel shortages, and the sleet and low cloud which protected them from Allied planes are clearing.

General George S Patton with the US Third Army, which has been engaged on the Saar front, has now swung north and is racing for Bastogne with his Sherman tanks. He reckons he can lift the siege by Christmas day. Inside the town, General Anthony C McAuliffe received a message from the Germans inviting him to surrender. He took the paper and scrawled on it: "NUTS" (→9/1/45).

A prison camp at East Ham in London provides a temporary home for Germans captured on the western front.

1945

Belgium, 9 January. The German counter-offensive in the Ardennes is defeated (→ 2/1945).

Crimea, 11 February. Winston Churchill, Franklin Roosevelt and Joseph Stalin meet at Yalta to redraw the map of post-war Europe as the Red Army advances into Germany.

Germany, February. Over 50,000 people are thought to have died in RAF raids which devastated Dresden this month (→ 24/3).

Germany, 24 March. Allied troops cross the Rhine in large numbers (→ 17/4).

Britain, 26 March. David Lloyd George, prime minister in the First World War, dies at the age of 82.

Germany, 17 April. British troops are shocked the by piles of corpses and emaciated survivors at the Belsen concentration camp (→ 30).

San Francisco, 25 April. Delegates from 46 countries meet to plan a new "United Nations" organization.

Berlin, 30 April. Adolf Hitler commits suicide (→ 7/5).

Dublin, 2 May. Eamon de Valera calls on the German envoy to condole officially on Hitler's death (→ 16).

Westminster, 23 May. The wartime coalition government resigns; a general election will take place on 5 July (→ 26/7).

Eire, 16 June. Sean Kelly is elected president (→ 6/7/46).

Denmark, 26 June. William Joyce, known for his "Lord Haw-Haw" propaganda broadcasts, is arrested and faces trial for treason.

Britain, 26 July. Labour wins a landslide victory in the general election; the result was delayed to count votes of servicemen overseas (→ 21/8).

Singapore, 12 September. Japanese forces in south-east Asia formally surrender to Lord Louis Mountbatten, the supreme Allied commander south-east Asia.

Westminster, 19 September. It is announced that India will have home rule (→ 16/5/46).

Britain, 5 November. A dock strike ends after seven weeks.

USA, 27 December. Britain is among the signatories to agreements setting up an International Monetary Fund and World Bank.

Jubilant Britons are victors in Europe

London, 8 May

After waiting all yesterday for the announcement of victory, the British people heard at 7.40 last night that today is VE (Victory in Europe) day. Dense crowds waited in the streets around Whitehall and Buckingham Palace for the prime minister's 3pm broadcast that "the German war is at an end". Hostilities would end at midnight. Sirens and hooters sounded all over the country, while bonfires were built and fancy-dress parades for children were improvised. Churches and pubs were filled to the doors. There were flags everywhere, and the government announced that bunting could be bought without coupons.

In London Churchill's car was lost in a sea of people on the way to the House of Commons. Later he appeared on a ministry balcony above Whitehall for an impromptu speech. "This is *your* victory," he told the crowds, "God bless you all!" Beside him Labour's Ernest Bevin led the crowd's singing of *For He's a Jolly Good Fellow*.

On the palace balcony King George VI and Queen Elizabeth appeared with the princesses, Elizabeth and Margaret, to a rapturous crowd. There were eight balcony appearances – some of which Churchill joined – and at nightfall the king allowed his daughters to join the throng.

At night the palace, Big Ben and the Houses of Parliament were floodlit, and searchlights illuminated the sky. Like everywhere else in Britain, London had a party mood. The streets were full of dancing and

The euphoria of victory: civilians and service personnel celebrate VE day.

singing, and chains of people doing the "Hokey-Cokey" or "Knees Up, Mother Brown" tailed behind anyone with a musical instrument. At midnight, when Big Ben sounded the hour of the official ceasefire, a

roar went up, fireworks exploded, and Thames tugs did the V-sign on their sirens. All across Britain bonfires blazed, bells pealed and people embraced complete strangers in a very unBritish manner (→ 9).

Twin advances on Berlin reveals horrors of Nazi 'death camps'

Rheims, France, 7 May

The final surrender of all forces under German command was signed here at 2.40am by General Jodl before General Bedell Smith of Eisenhower's Allied command. The surrender covers not only the western front, which has commanded most attention in Britain, but also the eastern front where the Soviet forces powered through Poland and into Germany in January.

It was the Red Army which first discovered the true bestial horror of Hitler's war when it liberated a

Nazi "death camp" for Jews at Auschwitz. Allied leaders had known from codebreaking that the Nazis were persecuting Jews on a massive scale, with millions apparently murdered. But the reality seen at Auschwitz, and again last month at Belsen when it was liberated by British troops, shocked even the most hardened of soldiers.

The final crunch that destroyed the Third Reich began on 24 March when Montgomery's armies crossed the Rhine while the Red Army, commanded by Marshal Zhukov,

crossed the Oder, poised to attack Berlin. Soviet forces were first to reach Hitler's capital, which had been subjected to sustained attack by Allied bombers. Other German cities were also hit, including Dresden, where a controversial raid and the resulting firestorm are believed to have killed over 50,000 people.

Hitler retreated to his chancellery bunker on 16 April. He committed suicide with his wife Eva Braun, formerly his mistress, on 30 April, two days after Mussolini was shot by Italian partisans (→ 8).

British troops recapture city of Rangoon

Troops of the 14th Army negotiate a river as they advance in Burma.

Rangoon, Burma, 3 May

Men of the British 14th Army today marched into Burma's capital, Rangoon – in a reminder to their fellow countrymen that, while the war may be over in Europe, it continues against Japan. The recapture of Rangoon – three years after it fell – ends General William Slim's campaign to liberate Burma, which began in February. Mandalay fell in March, and the advance has continued at lightning pace.

Elsewhere in the war against Japan the US is stepping up the offensive which it began last October with the first landing in the Philippines by an invasion force of 250,000. The Japanese counter-attack led to a three-day battle with the US Third and Seventh Fleets in and around the islands. It ended in a knock-out victory in which the Japanese lost 28 ships – including two battleships and all four remaining aircraft carriers.

In February Manila was surrounded, but 20,000 Japanese fell in its fanatical defence. Landings on Mindanao in March and Okinawa in April were accompanied by huge firebomb raids on Tokyo, Osaka and Kobe, now within range of the US's B29 Superfortresses. Japan is critically short of oil, yet there is no sign of surrender (→ 14/8).

Atom bomb ends war

Tokyo, 14 August

Emperor Hirohito today ordered all Japanese commanders to surrender their arms after two atomic bombs – the most powerful bombs the world has ever known – were dropped on Japanese cities. On 6 August Hiroshima was totally destroyed by an atomic bomb dropped by a B29 Superfortress of the US Air Force, and three days later Nagasaki was obliterated. To compound Japan's agony, the Soviet Union declared war on 9 August and attacked.

Harry Truman, who succeeded Franklin Roosevelt as US president in April, threatened other Japanese with "a rain of ruin from the air, the like of which has never been seen on this earth". The bomb, whose explosion is powered by a chain of nuclear fission in atoms of uranium 235, has the force of more than 20,000 tons of TNT. Japan claims that more than 70,000 people perished immediately, many of whom were burnt to cinders where they stood. Both cities were covered by a giant mushroom cloud of radioactive dust.

The bomb was developed by British and American scientists working in secrecy at Los Alamos, New Mexico under the codename "Manhattan Project". Research work was transferred there from Britain after the US entered the war (→ 15).

VJ Day: six years of war really are over

Londoners celebrate in Piccadilly.

London, 15 August

The surrender of Japan was announced by Clement Attlee, the new prime minister [*see opposite page*], on the wireless at midnight, with a two-day holiday to celebrate VJ day. King George VI and Queen Elizabeth, going to parliament in an open carriage, were soaked by rain. Later they made repeated appearances on the palace balcony. The crowds, bonfires, street parties and flag-decked displays of rejoicing were the equal of VE day in May, but with added thankfulness that the British, who have been fighting for six years less two weeks, have no more enemies to fight (→ 12/9).

De Valera defends Eire's war record

Dublin, 16 May

Eamon de Valera, the Irish prime minister, has given a calm and dispassionate reply to the angry attack on Eire's neutrality launched by Winston Churchill in his victory broadcast. De Valera gave credit to Churchill for successfully resisting the temptation to violate Irish neutrality, thereby advancing the cause of international morality. But he stressed that Eire's neutral stance resulted from its being a small nation which had stood alone for several hundred years against massacres and aggression (→ 16/6).

Channel Islands return to British forces after German occupation

British troops (and a policeman) return to cheers on liberated Jersey.

St Helier, Jersey, 9 May

A German soldier climbed a crane in Jersey harbour to fly a Union Jack in place of the *swastika* as the German occupation of the only British home soil to be captured during the war came to an end. The Channel Islands, which were surrendered without a shot being fired, were host to 10,000 German troops whose commander, Vice-Admiral Huffmeier, threatened to fight on. His men took no notice of his order to give only the Nazi salute to British officers. In recent weeks the islands have come close to starvation. People have been stewing rabbit skins and cabbage.

Churchill loses to a Labour landslide

Attlee is confronted by economic crisis

London, 21 August

Clement Attlee's Labour government had its rejoicings over the party's sweeping election victory last month cut short today by a body blow from the new American president, Harry S Truman. Britain faces its gravest economic crisis because, without warning, the president has put an end to the US Lend-Lease agreement with Britain, under which Britain has been receiving food imports from the US without down payment in cash.

As a result Britain now faces austerity even fiercer than that of wartime, with food, tobacco and petrol imports reduced, and British products largely reserved for export to pay for our imports. Rationing will be prolonged indefinitely; Britain's reserves are all but exhausted.

Labour won a landslide victory in last month's poll with 393 seats to 213 for the Tories, 12 Liberals and 22 Independents. The result was a surprise to all but the armed forces, who voted overwhelmingly for Labour. Their regard for Winston Churchill as a war leader was outweighed by the desire for social changes in peace. The wartime coalition government had broken up

Clement Attlee, the new prime minister after five years as number two.

on 23 May, and in an election broadcast on 4 June Churchill turned on Labour leaders who had supported him all through the war, and declared that "no socialist system can be established without a political police ... some form of Gestapo". This did more harm to the Conservatives than to Labour. People thought it ridiculous to accuse men like Attlee and Ernest Bevin, the wartime labour minister, of being no better than the Nazis.

Labour's programme for a "welfare state", with a free national health service, and for state ownership of industries such as coal and the railways reflects the discussions of post-war aims since the Beveridge Report of 1942 on how to achieve social security and a later report on full employment.

However, Labour politicians are faced with the fact that the war has bankrupted Britain. The economist J M Keynes, who is advising the treasury, calls it "a financial Dunkirk" – £4,000 million of our foreign investments have gone, exports are below half the pre-war level, civilian industries and shipping are gravely run down, and 700,000 houses in London alone need bomb damage repaired (→ 12/9).

Britain counts human, and economic, cost of its 'finest hour'

Singapore, 12 September

With the final surrender of Japanese forces in south-east Asia today, an estimate of war casualties can be given. Britain lost 420,000 members of the armed forces killed, compared with the US figure of 292,000 and the USSR's 13 million. Enemy dead are put at 3,500,000 for Germany and 2,600,000 for Japan. British civilian casualties in air raids were around 60,000 killed and 86,000 badly injured.

This, then, is the price of victory. Winston Churchill called the time when Britain stood alone its "finest hour". But now the US and the Soviet Union have emerged as the "superpowers", with Britain economically crippled – another price of victory (→ 12/1946).

One of the lucky ones: a joyful reunion for one soldier and his family.

Radio and music offer antidote to rigours of war

Britain, 31 December

The First World War is recalled as a time that inspired great poetry. "Where are the poets?" was a question much asked in the early stages of the war that ended this year. War poetry did emerge – through new names such as Keith Douglas (killed in action) and established figures such as Louis MacNeice – but there was no romanticism in this mechanized war of conscripts.

Yet the arts and entertainment played important roles in the war as escapism or inspiration. In popular terms, radio was the dominant medium of entertainment – not just comedy such as *ITMA* but cerebral programmes such as the *Brains Trust* and J B Priestley's talks. *Music While You Work* also became a national institution.

The cinema was the focus of entertainment and propaganda. The crown film unit produced documentaries such as *Target for Tonight* and *Western Approaches*, which drew enormous audiences. Laurence Olivier and Noël Coward were among major stars who gave their work a patriotic tinge in *Henry V* and *In Which We Serve* respectively.

For millions the weekly trip to the cinema was an important antidote to rationing and other wartime deprivations. So, too, was the dance hall. The arrival of US servicemen brought with it a new kind of music – the big band sound epitomized by Glenn Miller. But the most popular singer of the war was Britain's own Vera Lynn, whose songs, such as *The White Cliffs of Dover*, established her as the "forces' sweetheart".

More serious music also prospered, with record audiences for the Prom concerts and Dame Myra Hess's lunchtime recitals at the National Gallery. In the world of visual art Henry Moore painted people sheltering in the tube; he was one of over a hundred artists commissioned as official war painters.

'New towns' offer hope for war homeless

"New towns" and estates are needed to house workers and boost industry.

Westminster, December
Up to 20 "new towns" are being planned as part of the Labour government's programme to provide more housing and to revitalize industry. The New Towns Act passed this year authorizes development corporations to be formed which will create communities supposedly self-sufficient in terms of houses, jobs and public services.

Several new towns are expected to be built in south-east England to relieve pressure upon London – Stevenage, Basildon and Harlow are among possible sites. But others are intended primarily to tempt new industries to areas threatened by economic decline. Aycliffe in Darlington is likely to be the centre of one such new town with developments also planned for south Wales and central Scotland.

However it is unlikely that the first new residents will move into any of the planned developments before 1948 or 1949. In the meantime the government and local authorities face more immediate problems of housing people in cities scarred by bomb damage from the war. Hull, for instance, is estimated to need 30,000 new houses. For many, home will be one of the temporary pre-fabricated houses (known as "prefabs") now being erected in most of Britain's bomb-damaged cities (→ 18/12).

UN refuses to give membership to Eire

Ireland, 13 August
Eire has been refused admission to the United Nations Organization because of opposition from the Soviet Union. This further emphasizes the country's isolation from world affairs. The war years, known in neutral Eire as the "Emergency", have resulted in agricultural and economic crises, strikes, inflation and rising emigration. Given the state's small and ageing population, there are growing fears that the situation can only get worse.

Dissatisfaction with the Fianna Fáil government is widespread and has resulted in a proliferation of small political parties such as Clann na Talmhan, the farmers' party, which is calling for a new system of allocating land (→ 4/2/48).

Boost for the arts

London, August
The wartime funding of the arts by government will continue under the Arts Council of Great Britain, which is to be set up with a budget of £230,000. The council is the brainchild of the economist, the late Lord Keynes, who campaigned for it. Its twin objectives are to increase knowledge of the arts and to make them more accessible on the principle of "the best for the most".

'GI brides' leave Britain to begin a new life in the United States

An estimated 50,000 British GI brides were shipped out to the USA.

New York, 10 February
The first "GI brides" arrived here today to begin their new lives in the United States. As many as 50,000 British women are believed to have become engaged or married to American servicemen who were stationed in Britain during the war. "Overpaid, over-sexed and over here" was the complaint of British males. The first group of GI brides assembled at a special transit camp in Hampshire last month. There were 344 women – the youngest only 16 years old – and their 116 children. Mothers slept three to a room at the camp, with their babies beside them, before sailing in the *Queen Mary*. It is expected to take until July to transport all the women and children.

Britain's economic crisis gets worse

Housewives queue for food and coal

Britain, 27 December

Twelve cotton mills closed today and a four-day working week was announced for many factories in the English Midlands as a fuel shortage intensified. Lack of coal is forcing manufacturers to close production lines already hit hard by lack of raw materials. With queues for coal and many basic foodstuffs still rationed, it has been a bleak Christmas with little prospect of economic improvement.

A world food shortage has meant a return to wartime rations and, in some cases, tougher restrictions than were imposed during the war. In February the government announced that butter, margarine and cooking fat rations were to be reduced from eight to seven ounces per person per week. Then, in May, bread was rationed for the first time. The controls, which led to a booming black market in food and other rationed goods, were attacked by the Tory opposition leader Winston Churchill as "socialist incapacity". Labour counters by pointing to global shortages, factories and shipping destroyed by war, compounded by a lack of foreign currency (→ 22/1/47).

Petrol can be tested for a trace chemical absent from illegal supplies.

Bread was never rationed during the war, but now there are queues.

Bolton football tragedy: 33 die as barriers collapse at cup-tie

Police control the crowds while ambulancemen take away one of the victims.

Bolton, 9 March

Thirty-three football fans were killed and 500 others were badly hurt today when steel barriers collapsed at the Bolton Wanderers' ground, Burden Park, after thousands of supporters broke down fencing to get into a packed enclosure to watch the FA cup-tie with Stoke City. The home secretary, Chuter Ede, is expected to order an enquiry.

Police, who closed entrance gates nearly an hour before the trouble, were overwhelmed by the surging crowd who broke down perimeter fencing to get in. Several fans were crushed to death but further casualties were avoided when officers let fans escape by pulling down fencing around the pitch.

Cinemas boom with Britons rivalling Americans as stars

Britain, December

Cinema-going expanded hugely in the war to an average of 30 million admissions a week and the habit has stuck: a third of the population is now goes once a week, even though cinemas still have a run-down wartime look and their neon lights are banned to save fuel.

British films continue to rival American in popularity. A poll of cinemagoers names as many British stars as American in the top ten: James Mason and Stewart Granger head the actors, Margaret Lockwood the actresses, with Anna Neagle, Vivien Leigh and Patricia Roc high on the list. Hitchcock, Wilcox, Asquith, Korda and Lean head the directors. Last year's hits, *The Way to the Stars* and *Brief Encounter* are now being equalled by *A Matter of Life and Death* and *Great Expectations*(→ 11/4/47).

Full independence promised to India

London, 16 May

A plan for a united and independent India was unveiled today by Clement Attlee, the prime minister. The announcement came while Sir Stafford Cripps was in India at the head of a British mission to seek a deal that will contain the bitter divisions between the Hindu Congress and the Moslem League.

In 1935 a Government of India Bill, fiercely opposed by the Tories, virtually gave self-government to the provinces and proposed a new federal assembly at the centre, but the war has made full independence inevitable. The surrender of Singapore in February 1942 shattered British authority in India beyond repair. Although the Indian army stayed loyal, the leading nationalists, Nehru and Gandhi, were among those imprisoned for mounting a hugely popular "Quit India" campaign of civil disobedience.

If the threat of more unrest were not enough, the British have been under growing American pressure to implement the ideal of self-determination (→ 19/8).

Britons struggle against big freeze

Gangs of workers clearing snow from London's Smithfield meat market.

Dinner by candlelight becomes compulsory as shortages continue to bite.

Belts tightened as food crisis deepens

Britain, 26 February

Coal rationing is one of the options being considered by the government today as the "big freeze" goes into its fifth week. The coldest winter since 1880-81 has exacerbated fuel shortages which have already brought short-time working to many factories and steel mills. Lack of coal has also curbed supplies of electricity and gas, making over four million workers idle through power cuts. Yet coal is now piling up at the pits, unable to be moved along roads and rail lines blocked by snow.

Many shivering domestic consumers of coal have been without heat or light during the daytime for much of February. Yet some are even worse off. In Lincolnshire, Norfolk and Yorkshire the RAF is dropping food supplies for stranded villagers as well as livestock. The towns of Buxton and Bridlington have been cut off. Snowdrifts as high as 20 feet have blocked roads – the Great North Road is impassable for 22 miles – and railways. Blizzards have stopped shipping in the Channel and kept fishing fleets in port, worsening food shortages.

Emergency regulations sought to keep industry working, while offices, shops and even pubs carry on by candlelight. Weather forecasters offer no sign of an end to the sub-zero temperatures (→ 3/1947).

School leaving age is raised to fifteen

Britain, September

The new school year now beginning will not be the final year for the current generation of 14-year-olds. The minimum age to leave school is now 15, as one of the reforms of the 1944 Butler Education Act is implemented. The Act envisages raising the school leaving age to 16 at some point in the future, but no date has been set. Until now, a 1918 Act had made 14 the minimum leaving age – and most 14-year-olds did leave then (→ 26/4/48).

Planning becomes the post-war vogue

Britain, July

An Economic Planning Council has been set up this month in a move to give more coherent direction to a British economy battered by fuel shortages last winter and a run on currency reserves this summer. Its creation reflects the government's faith in "planning" as a means to combat the difficulties of the post-war years. But there is also faith in planning as a positive tool to fashion a new role for the state.

The Town and Country Planning Act requires larger local authorities to prepare comprehensive plans for their areas with powers of compulsory purchase. Local authorities will have powers to preserve historic buildings, and the government plans to levy a development charge on any increase in land values by developing the land.

The legislation stems from Labour's view that the public sector must play a greater role in shaping the economy and society than was the case before the war. Another instance of this belief is this year's Agriculture Act, which guarantees minimum prices to farmers for their products (→ 27/8).

Labour nationalizes the coal industry

London, 1 January
Cabinet ministers gathered at the headquarters of the new National Coal Board today to celebrate the fulfilment of a Labour dream: nationalization of the coal industry. But the dream could hardly have been realized at a less opportune time. The industry is struggling to meet demand, with too few miners and antiquated machinery producing too little coal. Low output, as well as low productivity, has already caused some cotton mills to begin short-time working because of fuel shortages. But Emmanuel Shinwell, the minister of fuel, insists there is no crisis (→ 1/1/48).

Coal industry under new colours.

Britain closes door on Indian empire

New Delhi, 15 August
British rule in India ended here after 163 years on the stroke of midnight last night as two new dominions, Pakistan and India, were born. A conch shell was blown in the Constituent Assembly and, as the clock ticked away the seconds to full independence, its members cheered and then pledged themselves to serve India and her people.

Lord Mountbatten, the last viceroy, immediately became governor-general of the new dominion of India. He has been rewarded with an earldom for his part in managing Britain's withdrawal.

Bells ring out for Elizabeth and Philip

The marriage of Princess Elizabeth brightens an otherwise grey outlook.

London, 20 November
The grey realities of rationing were forgotten today when Princess Elizabeth married the Duke of Edinburgh in a glittering ceremony. The bridegroom, listed as Lieutenant Philip Mountbatten on the order of service, was made Prince Philip, Duke of Edinburgh, a little earlier.

Huge crowds cheered the state coach as the princess, in an ivory dress embroidered with flowers of beads and pearls, was escorted by the Household Cavalry resplendent in scarlet tunics. After a simple service and a wedding breakfast the newlyweds left to begin their honeymoon in Hampshire (→ 14/11/48).

Edinburgh plays host to new arts festival

Edinburgh, 24 August
The first international arts festival in Britain was launched here today as a defiant gesture in the face of the prevailing austerity. Under the directorship of Rudolf Byng, the Scottish capital, decked with flags, is playing host to 800 artists from 20 countries performing music and

drama. They include the Vienna Philharmonic Orchestra under conductor Bruno Walter and the Jean-Louis Barrault theatre company from Paris. Individual stars invited include Kathleen Ferrier, pianist Artur Schnabel, and the string virtuosi Josef Szigeti, William Primrose and Pierre Fournier.

Compton sweeps into cricket record books

Compton: also a top footballer.

London, 20 September
A record-breaking summer has ended today for Denis Compton, the Middlesex and England batsman. He has scored more runs (3,816) and more centuries (18) in a single season than any other cricketer in history. His teammate, Bill Edrich, scored 3,539 runs in a hot summer which the Middlesex pair made even more uncomfortable for bowlers. Compton's cavalier attacking style captivated the crowds as much as his run-scoring. He is also a professional footballer when England's cricket team is not on tour. He plays for Arsenal and won several wartime international caps.

Divorce and babies are on the increase

Britain, December
This has been a record-breaking year in family life. Divorces have hit a new peak of 60,000 cases this year – ten times the pre-war maximum. And the birth rate has produced a "baby boom" with 20.5 births per thousand people – up a fifth over the 1939 figure.

Hasty marriages contracted during the war are now being dissolved at a rate that has alarmed church leaders. The archbishop of Canterbury blamed reforms in the divorce law while the bishop of London singled out the immoral influence of Hollywood films. Government ministers have generally adopted a more constructive approach, increasing aid to bodies such as the Marriage Guidance Council in a bid to stem the flood of divorces. Marriage itself is not declining in popularity: three in four of all people who are divorced take the plunge again.

Tired of the drab wartime Utility clothing, women love Dior's New Look, but to achieve the outer hour-glass shape it needs, they sometimes require inside help.

London, 27 January. Medical consultants threaten to boycott the national health service due to begin this year (→ 5/7).

India, 30 January. Mahatma Gandhi is assassinated.

Ireland, 4 February. De Valera loses an overall majority in the Irish general election (→ 18).

Westminster, 6 February. MPs vote to make the ATS and WAAF permanent; they will be known as the Women's Royal Army Corp and the Women's Royal Air Force.

Westminster, 16 February. The government warns Argentina not to challenge British rule in the Falkland Islands.

Westminster, 15 March. Communists and fascists are to be banned from civil service jobs vital to state security.

Brussels, 17 March. Britain joins France and the Benelux countries in forming a new defence pact.

Britain, 1 April. The electricity industry is nationalized (→ 1/5/49).

London, 26 April. A new General Certificate of Education examination is announced for England and Wales (→ 9/1948).

Britain, 13 May. Figures show the birth rate last year was the highest for 26 years.

Berlin, 30 June. The RAF joins an airlift of supplies to beat the Russian blockade of the former German capital (→ 12/5/49).

Middlesex, 4 July. Thirty-nine people die when two passenger aircraft collide near Northolt airport in Britain's worst aircraft disaster to date (→ 27/7/49).

Britain, 9 September. Footwear rationing ends (→ 15/3/49).

Westminster, 23 September. For the second session running, the House of Lords rejects the Parliament Bill curbing its powers.

Westminster, 4 November. Harold Wilson, the president of the board of trade, says many government controls over industry will be lifted.

London. 14 November. Prince Charles is born.

Dublin, 17 November. The Dáil gives a first reading to a bill under which Eire will leave the Commonwealth.

De Valera ousted after 16 years in office

Ireland, 18 February
John Costello today became head of a new coalition government, following the narrow defeat of Eamon de Valera after 16 years as Eire's prime minister.

The Fianna Fáil party faced the electorate burdened by rising emigration and a disastrous economic situation which they had done little to rectify. But de Valera's chief fear was the growing strength of the new party Clann na Poblachta. Led by Sean MacBride, a former chief of staff of the IRA, it offered an attractive blend of radical republicanism and social and economic reform, similar in fact to that offered by Fianna Fáil in 1932. De Valera appears to have taken fright at the threat posed to the ideological heartland of his own party, which lacked the energy and initiative and a vision of the future shown by MacBride.

Despite his handsome majority, de Valera decided to go to the country early in the hope of depriving Clann na Poblachta of the opportunity to improve its electoral chances in the current period of severe austerity. This error of judgement led to his defeat, although Fianna Fáil remains the largest party and Clann na Poblachta with ten seats is the junior partner in the coalition government with Fine Gael and Labour (→ 30/1/49).

Eamon de Valera badly miscalculates and loses the election to MacBride.

Troops called in to combat dock strike

Troops unload food at the docks.

Britain, 28 June
Draconian action was taken last night to deal with the dock strike when King George signed an order-in-council giving the government emergency powers to bring in troops to unload ships.

In a broadcast just before the 9 o'clock news Clement Attlee, the prime minister, said: "We must see the people are fed." He went on to rebuke the strikers: "This strike is not against capitalists and employers. It is a strike against your mates."

About 230 ships are held up by the 19,000 unofficial strikers who have been disowned by their union. Last week the ration was reduced to 6d [2.5p] worth of fresh meat and 6d worth of canned meat.

State takes over control of railways

Britain, 1 January
The passengers may not notice much difference, but from today all Britain's railways are owned by the state. Mergers had reduced the 19th-century plethora of private companies to four regional groupings by the 1920s and two world wars have left the railways increasingly dependent upon state finance to keep going. The railways were a prime target for enemy bombing in the last war and need massive investment and modernization which ministers say are way beyond the capacity of private companies to provide (→ 1/4).

'Comprehensives' aim to beat the 11-plus

London, September
A new school year is beginning and so is a new type of school. The first pupils have started term in three "comprehensive" schools now established by Middlesex County Council on the outskirts of London at Hillingdon and Potter's Bar. Other local authorities, notably the London County Council, are planning similar schools.

Comprehensive schools aim to cater for all secondary age pupils, regardless of academic ability. Elsewhere in England and Wales – the Scots have a different education system – children take an exam in the final year at primary school which determines which secondary school they attend. A varying minority of the more academically able children who "pass the 11-plus" go to grammar schools with the remainder going to secondary modern or technical schools.

A spokesman for the Middlesex County Council says: "At 11 a child may not have an examination temperament, and may fail dismally. That failure may penalize him or her for a long time, not only in denying the child grammar school and university education but shattering his or her confidence."

Another educational innovation this year was the announcement of a new General Certificate of Education (GCE) exam for 16-year-olds.

Labour constructs the 'welfare state'

Britain, December

The centrepiece of the Labour government's programme – the "welfare state" – is now in place. This year has seen the introduction of the National Health Service [*see below*], a National Assistance Act and a National Insurance scheme. Although the latter builds on 40 years' worth of social security provision, the insurance system and the health service are distinguished by a crucial new hallmark, that of

"universality". Previous schemes for unemployment or sickness insurance have hinged upon payments reflecting contributions or, if these were inadequate, a "means test" to determine assistance.

Contributions to the National Insurance scheme will still be made by employees, employers and the state, but direct taxation will be used to ensure that neither financial help in times of need nor medical care will depend upon contribu-

tions. The principle of universality means that the new services will be open to all without any variation.

National Insurance and health care are the most visible expressions of the welfare state principle that government take a greater role in social problems. This year's Children's Act on the duties of local authorities for homeless children is another manifestation, as are policies for housing, education and legal aid (→ 9/5/51).

Britain stages the Olympics, but has few gold medallists

John Mark carries the flame.

Wembley, 12 August

They were called the "austerity Olympics". The first games since the flamboyantly Nazi Olympiad of 1936 in Berlin were held without ostentation – and without new stadiums. Henley, Cowes and Bisley were used for rowing, yachting and shooting with Wembley's stadium and Empire Pool hosting the athletics and swimming. Huge crowds filled Wembley, but they had no native gold-medallists to cheer. British golds were confined to rowing (two) and yachting.

National Health Service aims to offer free medical care to all

Britain, 5 July

The National Health Service came into operation today as the flagship of the Labour government's "welfare state". It promises free health care from the cradle to the grave with treatment offered according to medical need rather than ability to pay. Dental services are included in the scheme, as is the provision of free glasses. Medicines will be prescribed free of charge.

Although the National Health Service Act became law in the autumn of 1946, it has taken until today to realize the vision of a health service open to all without charge. Aneurin Bevan, the health minister, faced strong opposition from the British Medical Association over what the doctors perceived as constraints on their freedom. Although doctors will be refused permission to establish practices in wealthy areas which have more GPs per population than poorer areas, doctors can continue their private practices.

Hospitals have also been, in effect, nationalized with control to be exercised through a network of 14 regional hospital boards in England and Wales and management committees for the individual hospitals. A similar system is being introduced in Scotland.

The medical profession has been much exercised by questions of organization, but a more immediate problem could be finance. Until now medicines, dental care and appropriate spectacles have been luxuries for many families. Demand for these services, now that they are free, is expected to be high and, some fear, limitless (→ 12/1948).

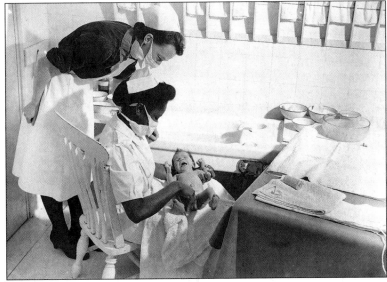

The new National Health Service offers care from cradle to grave.

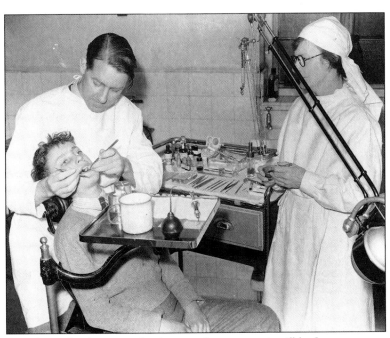

Dental care has been rare for the poor; from now on it will be free.

Second vote taken from businessmen

Westminster, December

The principle of one man, one vote, (and one woman, one vote) has now been accepted for Westminster parliaments. The Representation of the People Act passed this year ends the double voting of businessmen and some university graduates. Previously businessmen could vote in the constituencies where they lived and in the constituencies where their business was located. Universities also lose their separate seats – to be elected by graduates with their second vote – as does the City of London. However, 17 additional constituencies are to be created under the Act to reflect population movements.

Eire, 30 January. Collections are made at all Catholic churches for an "anti-partition" fund backed by all political parties (→ 8/2).

Dublin, 8 February. The government refuses to join the planned North Atlantic Treaty Organization (Nato) while Ireland is divided (→ 18/4).

Europe, 18 March. Britain is among eight countries which agree to form Nato next month.

Los Angeles, 25 March. *Hamlet* becomes the first British film to win the Oscar for the year's best movie; its director, Laurence Olivier, was also named best actor.

Britain, 24 April. Chocolate and sweets rationing ends (→ 14/7).

Britain, 1 May. The gas industry is nationalized (→ 24/2/50).

Europe, 5 May. The Council of Europe is formed with Britain and Eire among its members.

London, 9 May. Britain's first "launderette" opens for a six-month trial in Bayswater.

Westminster, 11 May. Britain formally recognizes the new Republic of Ireland (→ 2/6).

Berlin, 12 May. The USSR ends the blockade (→ 25/5/51).

Westminster, 2 June. The Ireland Act confers special status on the republic, whose citizens are not to be regarded as aliens (→ 6/6/50).

Ireland, 10 July. The last tramcar runs in Dublin.

Britain, 14 July. More rationing is announced in moves to deal with the dollar shortage (→ 26/5/50).

Britain, 4 September. The Bristol Brabazon, at 130 tons the largest airliner in the world, makes its maiden flight (→ 12/3/50).

London, 3 November. The BBC buys the Rank film studios at Shepherd's Bush to make television programmes (→ 31/12).

Westminster, 29 November. The Parliament Bill, curbing the delaying powers of the Lords, is rejected by peers, but it becomes law as MPs have passed it three times.

Britain. A Legal Aid Act passed this year helps people to obtain legal advice in and out of court.

Eire to become the Republic of Ireland

The new republic puts on a show of force after the announcement in Dublin.

Ireland, 18 April
Eire has formally become a republic and has left the Commonwealth. The prime minister, John A Costello, leader of the Fine Gael party in the coalition government, made an unexpected announcement of this plan during his visit to Canada last year, surprising his cabinet colleagues who were unaware of his intentions. With the inaugural Easter Monday parade today, the republic comes into being.

There are thought to have been several reasons for Costello's decision. He is known to have disliked the ambiguity of de Valera's External Relations Act of 1936, which left Ireland a republic in her own internal affairs while retaining the British king as a sleeping partner in external relations.

Perhaps more important, the new republic has stolen Fianna Fáil's thunder since its members have always considered themselves the only true republicans. By behaving in a manner so out of character with the performance of the party for more than a decade, Fine Gael may now be able to retrieve its fading image and appear to be a serious party concerned with the real business of politics and power.

Ireland's departure from the Commonwealth has been regretted by some, though it will probably make little difference. Britain will still treat Irish immigrants as Commonwealth citizens (→ 11/5).

Jitterbugging is the latest dance craze

Britain, December
The American GIs may have gone home, but their legacy lives on in the dance halls and popular music. It was US servicemen who brought the "swing" sound of big bands such as Glenn Miller and Tommy Dorsey to Britain during the war. Now young Britons remain in a US groove with the current craze for the "jitterbug". The more stately waltz and quickstep are not entirely out of fashion, but the jitterbug and "jiving" have grown dramatically in popularity among younger dancers. In most British towns only the cinema rivals the dance hall as a place for an evening out.

Jitterbugging and the New Look.

Clothes rationing is not all the fashion

Britain, 15 March
Clothing rationing – imposed in 1941 – ended today. Clothing coupons can be consigned to the "appropriate salvage channel", Harold Wilson, the president of the board of trade, told the Commons.

The Utility scheme – in which ready-to-wear clothes are made under a cloth quota system – will continue. Price controls on clothing, however, will stay and the government has said it is ready to freeze prices if traders start to increase them.

The end of rationing will involve a direct saving of 10,000 workers, Mr Wilson said, as department stores made hurried overnight preparations for "celebratory sales" tomorrow (→ 24/4).

Clothes come off the ration at last.

British warship in a dash for freedom

Hong Kong, 30 July
The British frigate *Amethyst* has docked here after a 140-mile [224km] dash down the Yangtse river to flee Mao Tse-tung's Communists. Caught up in the Chinese civil war between Mao and Chiang Kai-shek's Nationalists, the *Amethyst* was shelled by Communist batteries four months ago, with the loss of 43 crewmen. With fuel and rations running low, the commander, Lt-Cdr J S Kerans, had to break out. Safely at sea, he signalled the Admiralty: "No damage or casualties. God Save the King."

The pound is devalued

London, 18 September
Sterling is to be devalued by 30 per cent, the treasury announced tonight. From tomorrow one pound will be worth $2.80 as against $4.03. City firms had expected a devaluation for several weeks, as Britain's trading position worsened during the summer. The dollar deficit has grown, and in the second quarter of this year alone Britain lost £160 million of gold. However, the size of the devaluation was greater than forecast and will increase the cost of living by around 5 per cent. Banks and the stock market will be closed tomorrow by a royal proclamation which is intended to avoid panic selling.

A frantic dealer signals the cut.

Comet jets into the history of aviation

Hertfordshire, 27 July
The world's first passenger jet airliner took to the skies today after years of secret development work. The de Havilland Comet made its maiden flight from the company's works at Hatfield. The tests had begun as ground handling operations, but on his third taxi down the runway Group Captain John Cunningham allowed the aircraft to take off. BOAC has ordered 16 of the Comets (→4/9).

Tories blast African project as 'Nuts'

Westminster, 21 November
Conservative MPs tonight accused the government of wasting millions of pounds of taxpayers' money on a scheme for ground nuts in East Africa. The scheme is promoted by the government's Overseas Food Corporation. The ground nuts are meant to yield vegetable oils, thereby helping the colonies and giving Britain cheap imports, but the scheme's Tory critics claim that it costs millions more than it yields.

The Lake District becomes a national park

The Lakes' beauty: to be preserved.

Westminster, 1 April
Twelve national parks are proposed in legislation announced today in the National Parks and Access to the Countryside Bill. The parks would cover approximately 9 per cent of England and Wales – none are envisaged for Scotland or Northern Ireland. The objectives of the parks will be the potentially conflicting goals of preserving and enhancing natural beauty while also promoting public enjoyment.

It is not yet clear whether the parks will have their own planning authorities or be administered by local authorities. The relationship with farmers is also uncertain; agricultural grants to increase output could undermine the preservation of landscapes or wildlife.

British films win plaudits of Hollywood, but television poses longer-term threat

Britain, 31 December
The award of five "Oscars" to the film adaptation of William Shakespeare's famous tragedy *Hamlet* sets the seal on the new success of Britain's film industry. No British production has ever before won an Academy Award for best film, and Sir Laurence Olivier, who produced and directed it, also received the best actor award for the title role. Another British entry, *The Red Shoes*, made by Michael Powell and Emeric Pressburger, won three more awards.

Hollywood's accolade has come at a propitious time for the industry, which has recently been granted what it regards as an inadequate loan of £5 million of government money through the National Film Finance Corporation. The quota of films of British origin which the government lays down that cinemas must show was raised to 45 per cent this year.

Last year brought the director Carol Reed to prominence with *The Fallen Idol*. This year he and the writer he worked with on the earlier film, Graham Greene, followed it up with *The Third Man*, a brilliant extension of the thriller genre into high drama precisely set amid the squalor of war-battered Vienna. Two Americans, Orson Welles and Joseph Cotten, took the lead roles.

Meanwhile, under the guidance of Michael Balcon, Ealing Studios reached the heights of their own

Olivier triumphs in the title role of his award-winning "Hamlet".

invention in a genre now called "Ealing comedy". This summer saw three hilarious scripts, T E B Clarke's *Passport to Pimlico*, Compton Mackenzie's *Whisky Galore!* and Robert Hamer's *Kind Hearts and Coronets*. All three provide a feast of character acting by such stars as Stanley Holloway and Alec Guinness.

But there is competition on the horizon. When the BBC's transmitters now being built are complete, television will reach 75 per cent of the population. Viewing hours and the availability of sporting events and films to TV are still limited, but this year the BBC bought Rank's Lime Grove film studios for making programmes (→27/8/50).

Barbara Murray and Stanley Holloway star in "Passport to Pimlico".

Labour clings to power

Labour prime minister Clement Attlee addresses an election meeting.

Westminster, 24 February

Labour has clung to power in the general election yesterday, but only just. The final result emerged after hours of suspense as votes were counted in one of the closest contests for 100 years. Clement Attlee has seen his government's overall majority fall to just five – despite increasing Labour's total vote to its highest-ever figure of 13,266,592. The results are 315 Labour, 298 Conservatives. nine Liberals and three MPs from other parties.

There was an 84 per cent turnout for the poll – higher than ever before. It was a day of disaster for the Liberal Party, with 319 out of their 475 candidates losing their deposit, in what was overwhelmingly a two-horse race for power. Winston Churchill, the Conservative leader, believes that another election cannot be long delayed. "Parliament will be in an unstable condition now," he said today.

Attlee has made no public comment, but he seems likely to shelve some of the more controversial elements of the Labour programme, such as the nationalization of the cement, sugar, water and shipping industries. However, Labour is determined to complete the nationalization of iron and steel begun in the last parliament (→ 26/10/51).

Fuchs, atomic scientist, jailed for spying

Britain, 3 February

A top nuclear scientist, Dr Klaus Fuchs, was today charged with giving Russian agents secret information about how to build atomic bombs. If convicted he faces up to 14 years in prison.

Fuchs, aged 38, a German-born Communist, has been given full access to British and American research bases for seven years. It was only shortly before his arrest that the FBI of America discovered his betrayal and tipped off MI5.

The prosecution will allege that Fuchs is guilty of the "grossest treachery" and that by his betrayal he has saved the Russians years of research.

The accused scientist Klaus Fuchs.

Eighty die in worst ever civil air crash

South Wales, 12 March

A Tudor V airliner bringing rugby fans home from the Wales/Ireland international has crashed just outside Cardiff. Eighty of the 83 passengers and crew are feared dead, the highest ever death toll for a civil aircraft disaster. Sixty ambulances took the bodies to the RAF station of St Athan. No one can as yet explain the crash: the weather was clear when the Tudor V took off, only to stall and nosedive into a field shortly afterwards. It had flown without trouble, on the Berlin airlift (→ 2/5/52).

The wreck of the Tudor airliner.

English football is humiliated by USA

Brazil, 28 June

The nation that gave football to the world today suffered its greatest sporting embarrassment: the English football team lost 1-0 to the United States. Ironically, the US is almost the only significant country where football has not become the most popular sport. But its team of multi-national immigrants was still able to defeat the cream of English football – including Tom Finney and Billy Wright – at Belo Horizonte, Brazil, to send England crashing ignominiously out of the first World Cup competition it has deigned to enter.

Playwright George Bernard Shaw dies

Ireland, 2 November
The playwright and Nobel prize-winner George Bernard Shaw has died at the age of 94. Born in Dublin in 1856, he began his literary career by ghosting musical criticism and writing five unsuccessful novels. He scored his first popular success with his play *John Bull's Other Island*, which was performed in London in 1904. He went on to write over 50 plays, many of which were controversial and many of which are still regularly performed, the best known being *Pygmalion, Man and Superman, Mrs Warren's Profession, The Devil's Disciple*, and *Heartbreak House*.

In his plays Shaw often dealt with contemporary social and moral problems. An active member of the Fabian Society, he supported women's rights, the abolition of private property and campaigned for a radical change in the voting system and the reform of the English alphabet. His unorthodox views,

George Bernard Shaw: died today.

his humour and his love of paradox have become an institution and he was still writing plays up to the time of his death.

He was awarded the Nobel prize for literature in 1925.

Traffic jams are signs of motoring boom

Britain, 30 May
Record traffic jams on this Whit bank holiday were reported tonight by the motoring organizations. It is the first bank holiday since petrol rationing ended and motor manufacturers are predicting that there will now be a boom in car sales.

The number of private cars on the roads has been growing steadily

since the war. There were just over two million cars and vans registered in 1948 – little more than there had been ten years earlier – but this year's equivalent total will be between 2.25 and 2.5 million.

Petrol had been rationed for ten years and motorists celebrated its end by tearing up their coupons. But prices are expected to rise.

The post-war boom has ended petrol rationing, but started traffic jams.

Attlee warns Truman against the use of the atomic bomb in the Korean conflict

British troops march to the front line in Korea to relieve their US allies.

Washington, 8 December
Clement Attlee has won assurances from the United States that there is no intention to use the atomic bomb in the war in Korea. The British prime minister flew to meet President Harry Truman after a press conference on 30 November in which the US president appeared to consider deploying nuclear weapons in south-east Asia.

Britain has backed the US-led United Nations force which has been defending South Korea since the North Korean invasion last June. But Attlee has been alarmed

by the potential escalation of the conflict since Chinese "volunteers" entered the fray last month in support of North Korea. He demanded urgent talks with President Truman in order to argue against the use of nuclear weapons.

A bland communiqué at the end of five days of talks conceals a diplomatic triumph for the British prime minister. The text commits the US to consult its allies on the use of nuclear weapons. British sources say privately that Truman has assured Attlee that he has no plans to use the A-bomb (→ 1/5/53).

Britons are tops in newspaper league

London, December
Britons read more newspapers than any other nation in the world. Sales of national daily papers this year have reached a new record of just under 17 million copies. This is a higher proportion per head of population than in any other country and is in addition to the papers published in cities outside London and Manchester. The national distribution of newspapers – unlike, for instance, the United States where papers are generally confined to one city – gives press barons such as Beaverbrook, Rothermere and Kemsley great political power.

Coronation stone is stolen from abbey

London, 25 December
The Coronation stone, a sandstone slab weighing over 205 kg (450 pounds), was stolen today from Westminster Abbey. Scottish nationalists have claimed responsibility. Detectives in Scotland are searching for a man and woman with Scottish accents, reportedly seen near the abbey last night.

The stone, which lay underneath the Coronation Chair behind the high altar, was dragged out through a small door. It was taken from Scone in Scotland by Edward I in 1296. Historians say that England promised to return it (→ 11/4/51).

Britain, 27 January. Meat rations are reduced to the lowest levels yet – the equivalent of four ounces of rump steak a week (→ 3/7/54).

Westminster, 9 March. Herbert Morrison replaces the ailing Ernest Bevin as foreign secretary.

Scotland, 11 April. The Stone of Scone is recovered at Forfar.

Britain, 14 April. Ernest Bevin dies, aged 70.

English Channel, 16 April. The 75-man crew of the submarine HMS *Affray* are feared dead after the sub went missing.

Dublin, 8 May. An Arts Council is set up in Ireland.

Westminster, 9 May. Old age pensions will be paid at the ages of 65 and 60 for men and women respectively, not 70 and 65 as originally planned.

London, 19 May. Britain warns Iran not to seize British oil properties; eight Britons died in riots there last month (→ 23/8).

London, 25 May. Diplomats Guy Burgess and Donald Maclean disappear (→ 7/6).

Ireland, 30 May. A general election gives Fianna Fáil 69 seats, Fine Gael 40 and others 38 (→ 13/6).

Dublin, 13 June. Eamonn de Valera becomes prime minister again (→ 18/5/54).

Tehran, 23 August. British oil companies and their workers prepare to leave Iran.

London, 23 September. King George has his left lung removed in an operation at Buckingham Palace (→ 6/2/52).

Ireland, September. The Waterford Glass company begins production.

Egypt, 19 October. British troops seize the Suez Canal zone in a dispute with the Egyptian government (→ 4/12).

Ireland, 21 October. The first Wexford opera festival begins.

Britain, 24 November. Motor manufacturers Austin and Morris announce a merger.

Kent, 4 December. A bus ploughs into Royal Marine cadets at Chatham, killing 23.

Egypt, 4 December. British forces come under attack during anti-British riots; servicemen's families were evacuated last month (→ 27/7/54).

Missing diplomats suspected of spying

Donald Maclean: a Soviet spy?

Guy Burgess: another Soviet spy?

London, 7 June

Two British diplomats who served in sensitive posts in the Washington embassy have vanished in circumstances suggesting they may have been undercover Soviet spies.

Donald Maclean, aged 38, was first secretary in Washington before becoming head of the American department of the Foreign Office. Guy Burgess, aged 40, was for eight months second secretary in Washington. They disappeared from London two weeks ago. Police in Europe are looking for the men, paying special attention to the border between the British and Soviet zones in Austria. The Foreign Office has refused to speculate on their whereabouts, saying only that they have been suspended for being absent without leave.

But the US press makes no bones about the Soviet connection. The *Journal-American* predicts that the diplomats' disappearance will cause a furore over communist sympathizers in government (→ 18/9/55).

A woman's work is done in 15 hours!

London, 10 July

The average housewife works an astonishing 75-hour week – and still has to put in overtime on weekends. This picture has been built up by a Mass Observation study which looked at 700 working-class homes in the London area. It reports that "Mrs Average Housewife" has a normal working day of 15 hours. She cooks, cleans and looks after the children, and spends a quarter of her day in the kitchen. Most women do their shopping on Fridays, spending between ten shillings [50 pence] and £2. When she does get some free time, the housewife spends it reading, enjoying the radio or television or visiting the cinema (→ 16/5/52).

Ministers quit over new health charges

Westminster, 22 April

Aneurin Bevan, the minister of labour, today resigned from the government in protest at the decision to impose on adults half the cost of glasses or false teeth prescribed for them under the National Health Service. He will be joined on the back benches by Harold Wilson, until today the president of the board of trade, and John Freeman, a junior war office minister. The health charges were among measures introduced by the chancellor, Hugh Gaitskell, to meet increased defence spending (→ 30/9/52).

Bevan walks out of government.

The Stone of Scone, on which monarchs are traditionally crowned, turned up in Scotland four months after being stolen from Westminster Abbey, London, by Scottish nationalists. Scots say it was stolen from them in the 13th century. Tradition says the stone cries out against unlawful kings.

Minister ousted in church-state clash

Ireland, 11 April
Dr Noel Browne, the minister of health, has been forced to resign from the government following a clash between himself and the Catholic hierarchy over his controversial "Mother and Child" scheme.

A member of the recently formed Clann na Poblachta party, Browne became a minister on his first day in parliament, aged 32. He quickly proposed to introduce free ante- and post-natal care for mothers, as well as free medical care for all children under 16. The Catholic bishops objected at once, claiming that Catholic mothers might be exposed to gynaecological information from non-Catholic doctors. Many doctors themselves were opposed to the scheme believing that it heralded the introduction of socialized medicine.

Browne's political naivety had serious consequences. He failed to secure cabinet approval for details of his scheme, or to satisfy the demands of the hierarchy who were making strong protests to the prime minister. Finally, he decided to abide by a decision of the bishops on the compatibility of his scheme with Catholic morality.

However, the bishops denounced the scheme as being in conflict with Catholic social teaching; the prime minister, John Costello, tiring of the whole business, immediately sought Browne's resignation.

Churchill becomes premier at age of 77

Winston Churchill has never before been voted into office by the electorate.

Westminster, 26 October
At the age of 77, Winston Churchill has won his first election as prime minister. The Conservatives have been returned to office in yesterday's general election despite winning 231,067 fewer votes than Labour – 48 per cent of the poll compared to Labour's 48.8 per cent. The number of MPs for the parties is 321 Conservative, 295 Labour, 6 Liberals and 3 from other parties.

Labour used fear of unemployment and Churchill's alleged "war mongering" as weapons in its bid to retain power. The Tories countered by promising lower taxes, fewer controls and more houses. In the event, Churchill was helped by the collapse of the Liberals, who fielded candidates in only one constituency in six. Most Liberals appear to have switched to the Tories, leaving the party which led Britain into the First World War with just a handful of seats.

Labour recriminations have already begun, with left-wingers accusing the outgoing premier, Clement Attlee, of betraying socialism. But Attlee's government was exhausted as well as split. Many of its senior members had been in government for ten years and had run out of steam (→11/1951).

More Britons tune in to television age

Britain, 31 December
Television has spread this year to the north-west of England with the opening of a transmitter in the Manchester area. With broadcasts to Scotland due to begin next year, the fledgling sibling of radio is set for rapid expansion. The BBC began the world's first regular TV service in 1936, but it was suspended during the war. Until a Midlands transmitter opened two years ago viewing was confined to the London area. By last year some 344,000 homes had TV sets. This year manufacturers plan to produce 250,000 sets. By this time next year four in five of the population will be in reach of television, threatening the popularity of the cinema and radio (→1/5/53).

Tory plan for steel

Westminster, November
The new Conservative government plans to denationalize the iron and steel industry, which Labour took under state control earlier this year. Road haulage is also set for denationalization, but the Tories appear to have accepted the other major acts of nationalization undertaken by the post-war Labour government. Labour had begun to take iron and steel into state ownership before last year's election and, despite its small majority, completed the process in February (→5/4/55).

The Festival of Britain adds light, and fun, to the heart of London.

Festival promises to be a national tonic

London, 4 May
"This is no time for despondency," said King George VI as he opened the Festival of Britain on London's South Bank. One of the prime purposes of the exhibition is to dispel the gloom caused by the continuing postwar austerities. Its director, Sir Gerald Barry, calls the festival "a tonic to the nation".

A fantasy world has been created on 11 hectares [27 acres] of cleared bombsites. A "Dome of Discovery" dominates the scene and the "Skylon" hangs aloft apparently unsupported, resembling an aluminium exclamation mark. The decorative styles of the pavilions, fountains and concourses are designed to create a sense of "fun, fantasy and colour" such has not been seen in Britain since before the war. The cafés and exhibits employ furniture and fabrics in the style known as "contemporary" with bent and moulded shapes, tapering spindly legs and ball-feet.

The Royal Festival Hall gave its opening concert last night. The interior of the building has angled projecting boxes along both sides of the auditorium and forests of indoor plants – innovations that have provoked much comment. Up river at Battersea park are open-air sculpture exhibits and a funfair.

London, 31 January. Princess Elizabeth leaves for a tour of Africa (→6/2).

Windsor, 16 February. King George VI is buried (→8/12).

Britain, 21 February. Identity cards are abolished.

Westminster, 26 February. Winston Churchill tells MPs that Britain has developed its own atomic bomb (→3/10).

Britain, 30 April. The pharmaceutical industry decides to sell its products in metric units.

Wembley, 3 May. Newcastle United becomes the first team since 1891 to win the FA Cup in successive seasons, beating Arsenal 1-0.

Westminster, 16 May. Equal pay for men and women civil servants is accepted in principle by the government.

Britain, 20 June. Pedestrian crossings are to be marked by blinking orange beacons.

Dublin, 3 July. Bord Failte is established to promote tourism in the Republic of Ireland.

London, 5 July. The capital says goodbye to its last tram.

Britain, 11 July. Further details from last year's census show that one household in three lacks a bath and one in 20 has no piped water.

Northern Ireland, 26 August. A Canberra bomber returns to Aldergrove airport after the first transatlantic round-trip in a single day; it took 7 hours 59 minutes (→6/9).

Hampshire, 6 September. A prototype jet aircraft crashes at the Farnborough air show, killing 28 people (→3/4/53).

Loch Ness, 29 September. John Cobb, holder of the world land-speed record, dies in an attempt on the water-speed record.

Britain, 30 September. Left-wing supporters of Aneurin Bevan win six out of seven constituency seats on Labour's national executive (→11/11).

Britain, 11 November. Herbert Morrison beats Aneurin Bevan for the deputy leadership of the Labour Party (→14/4/54).

London, 8 December. Queen Elizabeth gives permission for next year's coronation to be televised (→24/3/53).

Britain. The first British film shot in Technicolor, *Genevieve*, has its première.

Nation mourns the king

Sandringham, 6 February

King George VI is dead and for the first time in half a century Britain is to be ruled by a queen, his elder daughter Princess Elizabeth.

As the nation mourns the man who, but for his brother Edward VIII's abdication, would have lived out his life as the duke of York, the princess, who has been holidaying in Kenya with her husband the duke of Edinburgh, is heading for home and her new responsibilities.

Born 56 years ago, the second son of King George V and christened not George but Albert, the late king had been one of the unknowns of the royal family. Unlike his flamboyant elder brother, he had an undistinguished childhood, a naval career plagued by illness and a persistent stammer that dogged his attempts at public speaking.

Yet he grew quickly into the role which had been thrust upon him, and provided a much-needed stability after King Edward's brief but turbulent reign. King George and

Smoking cut short the king's life.

Queen Elizabeth further endeared themselves to the public by their stalwart conduct during the Second World War.

A heavy smoker, the king was suffering from lung cancer. However it was a heart attack, not cancer, that killed him some time in the early hours of this morning (→16/2).

Comet begins first scheduled jet service

Comets put Britain ahead of the world with the first passenger jets.

London, 2 May

An historic first was achieved today when the British Overseas Airways Corporation (BOAC) inaugurated its passenger jet service between London and Johannesburg. This is the world's first regular scheduled airline service to be operated by a turbojet-powered aircraft – the de Havilland Comet.

The aircraft is in itself a record-maker, being the first of its kind to win a certificate of airworthiness.

At 3.12pm the Comet took off from runway 5 at London's Heathrow airport and climbed swiftly on its way to Rome, where it will make its first stop-over in the 23-hour flight to South Africa. Among those witnessing the take-off were Sir Geoffrey de Havilland and the Comet's designers, R E Bishop and R M Clarkson, all confident that today's flight puts British civil aviation ahead of its US and French competition (→26/8).

Immigration grows from West Indies

Britain, January

Increasing numbers of people are arriving to make a new life in Britain from the West Indies, India and Pakistan. As British citizens, they have free right of entry and the total arriving this year is expected to be the highest since the current wave of immigration began in 1948. A third of the new immigrants are settling in London, but there are also communities beginning to develop in parts of the West Midlands and Yorkshire.

In some cases, immigrants have been lured to Britain by the prospect of jobs in public transport and the health service. Employers such as London Transport have looked to the West Indies to overcome labour shortages for jobs such as bus conductors and station staff.

Skipper abandons battle to save ship

Falmouth, 10 January

Captain Kurt Carlsen, who for 12 days has fought to salvage his damaged and listing freighter, the *Flying Enterprise*, had to abandon ship today, forty minutes before the vessel sank. When the ship first began to break up on 28 December the crew and passengers were taken off, while Carlsen and the mate of a salvage tug stayed on board. But the towrope parted, the list increased, and today the intrepid pair climbed 'up' the side of the funnel and onto the tug's deck!

Carlsen clings to the railings.

Britain explodes its first atomic bomb

Australia, 3 October

Britain joined the atomic superpowers today when scientists exploded the first British atomic bomb at a site on the Monte Bello islands, north-west Australia. The bomb has been developed in secret over the last five years. Unlike the usual mushroom cloud that has marked US tests, the home-grown atomic weapon produced more of a raggedy-edged shape, but in all other respects it resembled its American peers.

Specialists and servicemen observed the explosion from nearby warships, and observers on a hill 100 miles away also saw it. One said, "We felt no ground shock wave, but a heavy air pressure pulse smacked the mainland four minutes and 15 seconds after the flash."

'Mousetrap' opens

London, 24 November

The noted crime writer, Agatha Christie, presented a new mystery to baffle her admirers tonight when her play *The Mousetrap* opened in London's West End. In the play, eight characters are stranded in a snowbound house; one of them is the killer, and Miss Christie keeps the audience at the Ambassadors Theatre guessing until the final scene.

Freak flash floods destroy Devon village

Workmen attempt to clear the centre of Lynmouth after the disaster.

Devon, 16 August

North Devon, well known for its holiday resorts, suffered far from summer weather today when a freak flood hit a large part of the area. Some 36 people have died, and thousands more have lost their homes as the flood devastated some 250 square miles.

Worst hit was the resort of Lynmouth – much of which was submerged when, after 23cm (9 inches) of rain fell in a single day, nearby rivers burst their banks and poured down the surrounding hills. As mud, rocks and debris smashed into their houses, many of the victims had no time to escape and were buried in their own homes.

Others died too, including three boy scouts, whose camp was overrun, a postman on his rounds and two girl hikers. The Red Cross has already begun bringing in emergency supplies of food and fresh water. Lynmouth has been declared a disaster area and a special fund has been set up for nationwide contributions to help rebuild the shattered town.

Bentley to hang for killing of policeman

London, 11 December

Derek Bentley, aged 19, will hang for the murder of a policeman, even though his accomplice Christopher Craig fired the fatal shots. At 16 Craig is too young to hang, and will be detained at "Her Majesty's pleasure" while Bentley – who allegedly urged on his partner, shouting, "Let him have it Chris!" – will face the gallows. The two men were arrested after police surrounded them on the roof of a Croydon warehouse during a bungled robbery attempt. It was then that shots were fired and PC Sidney Miles was killed (→ 28/1/53).

Bentley: sentenced to be hanged.

At least 112 are killed in three-train collision outside Harrow

Harrow, 8 October

One hundred and twelve people died today in Britain's second worst railway disaster, when the Perth to London express ploughed into the 7.31am commuter train at Harrow and Wealdstone station in north-west London. Seconds later a second express travelling north from Euston smashed into the wreckage.

The station was obliterated and emergency services fought their way through piles of debris as they battled to save the injured. Some 200 people were treated, many of whom had been crowding the platforms for the morning rush hour. Smashed carriages were piled 50 feet high; special cutting gear was used to free trapped passengers.

Rescuers hunt for survivors among the tangled wreckage of three trains.

British forces sent to fight 'Mau Mau'

Kenya, 21 October

British troops flew into the Kenyan capital of Nairobi today, an advance guard for a full-scale security operation designed to suppress the increasing violence of the country's "Mau Mau" terrorists.

Mau Mau attacks, aimed to drive the colonial government out of Kenya, have escalated sharply in recent weeks: some 40 people – both black and white – have been murdered by the self-styled freedom fighters. Social life is at a standstill, and there is some justified concern, but residents believe that the troops will right a deteriorating situation.

Hundreds die as east coast is flooded

Floods have inundated eastern England; Canvey Island above is badly hit with 125 dead and 500 missing.

Eastern England, 3 February
Hurricane-force winds combined with high tides today to swamp the sea defences along England's east coast from Lincolnshire to Kent. At least 280 people are known to have been drowned and thousands more are homeless. A major operation has been launched to save people trapped on rooftops by 2.4 metres (8 feet) of water, some in villages eight kilometres (5 miles) inland. Damage is estimated in hundreds of millions of pounds.

At Canvey Island in Essex 125 people have drowned, 500 are missing and 13,000 have been evacuated. Near Clacton, holiday chalets are under 12 feet of water and survivors are falling from rooftops into the floodwater from exhaustion.

Mablethorpe and Sutton-on-Sea have been evacuated, with hundreds still awaiting rescue: in Suffolk boats were rowed into a church to rescue 40 trapped children.

The flooding comes hard on the heels of another disaster – the January storms which caused widespread havoc.

Car ferry sinks as waves smash doors

Stranraer, 31 January
One hundred and twenty-eight people died tonight when the Irish Sea car ferry, the 2,694-ton *Princess Victoria*, sank after mountainous waves smashed in through the cargo doors. Of the 44 survivors ten were crewmen. The master, Captain James Ferguson, went down with his ship, saluting as the waves covered his head.

While the death toll is of immediate concern, an inquiry will be launched to discover just how the doors burst open. Some critics maintain that so poor was their design that this disaster was simply waiting to happen.

Further questions will cover the *Princess Victoria's* lack of proper communications equipment – she had only a limited ship-to-shore radio – and of lifeboats. Many passengers died in their life jackets after being forced to jump overboard and swim through the waves to life rafts (→ 25/2).

British expedition conquers Mount Everest

Safely down: Edmund Hillary (left), John Hunt and Tenzing Norgay.

Nepal, 1 June
Mount Everest, at 29,028 feet the world's highest peak, has been conquered at last. Two days ago, at 11.30am, New Zealander Edmund Hillary and Sherpa Tenzing Norgay stood on the summit, planted their respective flags, plus that of the United Nations, and spent 15 minutes taking photographs and eating mint cake. The British expedition, led by Sir John Hunt, had made one earlier attempt, which was defeated by bad weather. Now the peak has been scaled – a fitting prelude to tomorrow's coronation.

Elizabeth II crowned at Westminster

Huge crowds cheer the young monarch

PLondon, 2 June

Vivat Regina! A new Elizabethan age began today with the coronation of Queen Elizabeth II in Westminster abbey. Crowds thronged the London streets, defying the rain for a glimpse of their new young monarch, and the abbey itself brimmed with heads of state, prime ministers and other dignitaries gathered from every corner of the earth. London was witnessing its greatest celebration since the end of the Second World War.

In a ceremony dating back to the Middle Ages, Princess Elizabeth was anointed with holy oil by the archbishop of Canterbury, then presented with the symbols of her authority – the orb, the sceptre, the rod of mercy and the ring of sapphires and rubies. Then the archbishop raised the crown of St Edward above her head, lowered it and proclaimed, "God save the Queen".

As the peers and dignitaries echoed the cry, and trumpets and bells echoed across the capital, the guns of the Tower of London fired their salute. Then Prince Philip led forward his fellow peers in the formal act of homage to the woman who is not only his Queen but also his wife. Afterwards the crowd had its reward – a procession of carriages that took the Queen to Buckingham Palace (→ 3/2/54).

A new Elizabethan age begins: the queen is crowned in Westminster abbey.

Pomp and ceremony captured on television

London, 2 June

Thousands packed the streets of London today to watch the coronation, but tens of thousands more, many of them viewing for the first time, saw the ceremony on that new technological miracle – the television. Indeed, at a time when the monarchy, as much as any institution, must come to terms with the modern world, the televising of the coronation has been heralded as a practical step in that direction.

Television, invented in the 1920s, was launched as a public service in the 1930s but suspended during the Second World War. Since then the BBC has relaunched its service, but the purchase of sets has remained gradual. The coronation changed all that. It has captured the public interest more than any other postwar event, and the decision to permit cameras into the abbey was welcomed by the thousands who would have had no other chance to witness the pageantry and ceremony. Britain, it is said, is a democracy; television will undoubtedly make it even more so (→ 13/11).

Scientists discover the secrets of DNA

Cambridge, 25 April

The British bio-physicist Francis Crick and the American virochemist James Watson, have identified what many are describing as the secret of life itself: the genetic material DNA, or deoxyribonucleic acid; its molecule, the carrier of genetic inheritance, bears the shape of a double helix. The discovery comes as the climax of years of work by a whole community of international scientists, but much of the credit must go to these two inspired young scientists.

At last! Newly knighted jockey Sir Gordon Richards finally wins the Derby at his 28th attempt.

At last! After years of trying, Stanley Matthews finally wins the FA Cup with Blackpool.

Christie to hang for murder of his wife and three others

London, 25 June

John Christie was sentenced to death today for strangling four women, one of them his wife, and hiding their bodies in his house at 10 Rillington Place in Notting Hill. Three of the women were prostitutes with whom he had attempted sexual intercourse after making them unconscious with coal gas.

The balding, bespectacled clerk's plea of insanity was dismissed by the jury. The judge described the case as a "horrible one and a horrifying one".

Three years ago Christie was the key witness against Timothy Evans, who was hanged for his wife's murder. Now Evans's family has asked for a review (→ 15/7).

Christie: did he kill Evans's wife?

Hard-drinking poet dies at age of 39

New York, 9 November

Dylan Thomas died at the age of 39 here today at the beginning of a lecture tour. His wild, hard-drinking behaviour has made him better known for his life than for his poems. Just before leaving London for the United States he delivered the manuscript of a radio script, after losing it and then retrieving it from a Soho pub. Called *Under Milk Wood*, it is the account of a day in the life of a sleepy Welsh seaside village. His *Collected Poems* came out last year.

Costello forms his second Irish coalition

John Costello receives his seal of office from President Sean O'Kelly.

Ireland, 2 June
John Costello, the Fine Gael leader, has put together his second coalition government after preventing the return of Fianna Fail at the polls. The outgoing administration had pursued a deflationary economic programme that was deeply unpopular. Its finance minister, Sean McEntee, had been seen as the natural successor to Eamon de Valera, whose days as leader of Fianna Fail are numbered; but, as a result of the electoral defeat, McEntee has given way to Sean Lemass.

The new administration is made up of members of Fine Gael, Labour and Clann na Talmhan, a traditional party representing farmers which has intermittently enjoyed a minority representation in the Dáil. It also has the tacit support of Clann na Poblachta, an active participant in Costello's first coalition government, formed in 1948.

Significantly, Costello's former finance minister, Patrick McGilligan, has taken the job of attorney general, and Gerard Sweetman, a vigorous conservative, has gone to the department of finance.

Ireland faces a serious balance of payments problem, isolation from markets in Europe and America, a stagnant manufacturing sector, and a general lack of confidence. These difficulties, together with rampant emigration, present the new coalition government with a formidable challenge (→ 14/12/55).

Bannister runs a record four-minute mile

Oxford, 6 May
Roger Bannister, a medical student aged 25, entered the history books this afternoon when he became the first man to run a mile in under four minutes. The four-minute mile had become the most sought-after goal for middle-distance athletes, with intense competition to be the first to break the barrier. Australia's John Landy had come close – and so today Bannister, aided by his pacemakers Chris Chataway and Chris Brasher, set out to try to break the record. In spite of a cool wind at Oxford University's Iffley Road track, they succeeded in achieving their target: Bannister broke the tape at three minutes 59.4 seconds.

Roger Bannister runs into history.

Bevan quits in row over foreign policy

London, 14 April
Aneurin Bevan resigned from the shadow cabinet today in protest at Labour's support for the rearming of West Germany. Often regarded as a maverick, the Welsh firebrand is not alone in his opposition to the creation of a new Wehrmacht. He has more than 100 parliamentary supporters and there is a general feeling of uneasiness in the country about giving guns back to the Germans so soon after their "permanent" demobilization.

However, the rearmament issue is only part of a growing internal conflict facing the Labour Party. In addition to the "Bevanites" in parliament, Bevan has strong support within constituency parties, trade unions and the party's national executive committee for more left-wing policies.

Rabbits wiped out

Britain, 1 July
Britain's rabbits are on the road to extinction. Over the last year the virus myxomatosis has infected 90 per cent of burrows in southern England alone. Farmers say that the virus is a vital aid to pest control, since rabbits destroy crops worth £50 million each year. Scientists, however, are warning that this epidemic, if unchecked, will badly disturb the balance of nature (→ 19).

British troops open fire on Greek riots

Cyprus, 18 December
British troops shot dead two Cypriot youths today when nationalist demonstrators campaigning for union with Greece besieged the police station at Limassol. At the height of the protests, which spread across the island, the Union Jack outside the police station was torn down and briefly replaced by the Greek flag. In all, 42 Greek Cypriots were arrested. The riots followed an announcement by the United Nations that it has put off a demand by the Athens government that Cyprus be allowed to exercise the right of self-determination (→ 13/9/55).

Books go up in flames as rationing ends

Not only ration books went up: women celebrated with balloons.

London, 3 July

Men and women ceremonially tore up their ration books in Trafalgar Square last night as the government announced the end of all rationing after 14 years. Clothes and sweet rationing were ended in 1949. Meat was the last to go; already the butchers are predicting price rises.

Smithfield market opened at midnight, instead of 6am, for the first time since the war and porters handled huge sides of beef, some weighing 400 pounds. "We haven't seen the like since 1939," a market spokesman said. "It's extraordinarily good quality, too." When the rationing of clothes ended, the government threatened to freeze prices if they began to increase. Now regulation has been left to the National Federation of Housewives, whose members were seen patrolling butchers' shops with notebooks today. "If we find that prices are not falling we will hold protest meetings," they warned.

At several Conservative Association meetings ration books were burned as relics of the dark days of 1947 when an economic crisis forced rationing back to wartime levels and the meat ration was reduced to a shilling a week.

Eighteen-year-old Lester Piggott is led in after winning the Derby.

Metal fatigue was cause of jet deaths

Farnborough, 19 October

Experts based at the Royal Aircraft Establishment here may have identified the cause of a series of recent disasters involving Comet jets.

Wreckage from a jet that crashed off the island of Elba on 11 January – after which all Comets were grounded – shows that metal fatigue weakened the cabin roof containing the radio direction-finding aerial. The roof broke up in flight, bringing about the accident, which left 35 people dead. Today's report will be passed to investigators of two other crashes involving Comets – that of 2 May last year at Calcutta, which claimed 43 lives, and that of 9 April this year near Naples, in which 14 passengers and crew were killed (→ 17/3/57).

Building of houses breaks all records

Britain, 31 December

In what is seen as a triumph for the housing minister, Harold Macmillan, a record number of new houses – 354,000 – have been constructed this year. Three years ago the Conservative Party conference called for 300,000 houses to be built annually; the total in 1951 was just over 200,000 and falling.

Macmillan introduced a range of measures to encourage all forms of housing, including higher subsidies and fewer restrictions on obtaining mortgages. But in particular he put much greater emphasis on private house-building than had been the case under the Labour government. Almost 30 per cent of new houses completed this year were built by the private sector.

Royal tour comes up trumps down under

The Queen and Duke are warmly received on their first tour of Australia.

Australia, 3 February

The Queen arrived in sun-drenched Sydney this morning for the first visit to Australia by a reigning British monarch. She was accompanied by the duke of Edinburgh. Their liner, the *Gothic*, edged into the harbour through a line of some 500 small craft. The Queen was clearly excited by the warmth of the welcome as she stood on the bridge waving to port and starboard. As the *Gothic* dropped anchor at Athol Bight, the headlands were covered with cheering, flag-waving people.

In the past month she has enjoyed equally rapturous receptions in New Zealand. "I want to show that the crown is not merely an abstract symbol of our unity but a personal and living bond between you and me," she said in her Christmas Day broadcast – the first to be delivered from outside Britain.

Eden leads Tories to election victory

Anthony Eden salutes the crowds.

Westminster, 26 May 1955

Sir Anthony Eden – who succeeded Sir Winston Churchill as prime minister on 6 April – has led the Conservatives to victory in a general election. The handsome Eden, who has long lived in the shadow of the great warrior-statesman, is now prime minister in his own right. With an overall majority of 58 seats, he has broken the stalemate created by the close results of the 1950 and 1951 elections.

Eden appears to have got his timing right, winning a confidence vote from the nation that will allow him to attack the economic problems and the industrial unrest, which grow more menacing every day. He has also been given a strong mandate for the East-West diplomatic talks scheduled for this summer.

One of the pleasures of the election has been to see the 80-year-old Churchill, relieved of the cares of office, successfully defending his Woodford constituency with boyish enjoyment. There is less joy for the defeated Labour Party, however, with rumours abounding of a bitter rift over the right of succession to the ageing Clement Attlee, who prefers Hugh Gaitskell to the deputy leader, Herbert Morrison. Others favour the radical Aneurin Bevan (→ 7/12).

Troops on stand-by as strikes worsen

London, 31 May

Troops are to be put on stand-by following the granting of emergency powers to the government to cope with the worsening effects of the rail and dock strikes. Privy councillors were summoned to Balmoral today for a special meeting at which the Queen signed the proclamation of a state of emergency.

Gwilym Lloyd George, the home secretary, insisted tonight that the emergency powers will not be used to break the strikes but will enable the government to maintain public order and to make sure that food supplies get through. A total of 125,000 men are now on strike and travel, exports and the unloading of food are severely affected (→ 14/6).

Air will be cleaner in smokeless zones

Westminster, 27 July

The Clean Air Bill is published today. It is an attempt to banish forever the London pea-souper whose last major appearance in December 1952 brought the capital to a halt and killed 4,000 people. If passed, the bill will restrict the use of coal on domestic fires, establish smokeless zones and raise the chimneys of power stations. It should cut dramatically deaths from bronchitis and other respiratory complaints.

Attlee steps down as leader of Labour Party

Sir Winston Churchill, now in his eighties, finally departs from office.

Clement Attlee decides to resign.

London, 7 December

Within eight months the two wartime leaders Winston Churchill and Clement Attlee have left frontline politics. Churchill resigned as premier in April and today his wartime deputy and peacetime opponent, Attlee, announced his departure in typically modest fashion.

"Before you turn to important business I have a personal statement," he told Labour colleagues. "I want to end uncertainty over the future leadership. I am resigning." He is 72 and his greatest legacy is perhaps the "welfare state" forged during his premiership between 1945 and 1951 (→ 14).

Toothpaste ad heralds new age of TV

London, 22 September
Amid much speechifying and trumpeting, commercial television started broadcasting tonight, providing London viewers with an alternative to BBC television for the first time.

Offerings from the two London commercial contractors, Associated Rediffusion and the Associated Broadcasting Company, included such standard fare as a variety show, drama excerpts linked by the actor Robert Morley, and a boxing match from Shoreditch.

The real difference lay in the six minutes of advertisements, which, as the first to be screened on TV, were the target of much controversy. In the event they proved tasteful if anticlimactic. They began with one for Gibbs SR toothpaste.

The BBC went on air half an hour earlier. Its answer to commercial television's opening speeches from the Guildhall was *The Donald*

Cleaner teeth, and a clean break with the past for commercial TV.

Duck Story. But what really stole its rival's thunder was a drama on steam radio – the death in a fire of Grace Archer, a leading character in *The Archers*. The timetabling on ITV's big night, the BBC would have its audience believe, was sheer coincidence (→ 11/12/56).

The romance is over: Princess Margaret announces she will not marry Townsend

London, 31 October
The threat of a scandal within the royal family was laid to rest tonight when Princess Margaret announced that her romance with Group Captain Peter Townsend is at an end. While the princess, at 25, has the right to marry whomever she wishes, she has chosen to place national duty before personal emotion. It is less than 20 years since her uncle, Edward VIII, chose a very different course; his niece has other priorities. Her love for the former Battle of Britain hero became public two years ago. No one doubted their affection, nor were there any criticisms of the character of the 40-year-old former equerry to King George VI.

But Townsend is a divorced man, and as such is ineligible to marry a royal princess. Margaret could have chosen a civil marriage, but that would have effectively placed her outside her family. To general relief, her head has triumphed over her heart (→ 6/5/60).

Before the end: Townsend stands unobtrusively behind Princess Margaret.

Ireland is admitted to the United Nations

Ireland, 14 December
The Republic of Ireland has been admitted to membership of the United Nations. It is felt that the timing of Ireland's entry will enable it to play an active part in influencing the United Nations policy of general decolonization.

This significant change in Ireland's status, comparable in importance, perhaps, to the declaration of Ireland as a republic in 1949, oc-curs during the second inter-party government under the premiership of John Costello. His minister for external affairs, Liam Cosgrave, the son of the country's first leader after independence, has made a dignified and impressive speech to the assembly. He will receive able support from several outstanding officials in his department, including Conor Cruise O'Brien and F H Boland (→ 12/12/56).

Ex-model to hang for lover's murder

London, 21 June
Ruth Ellis, the blonde model who has been convicted of the murder of her boyfriend David Blakely, a racing driver, will hang for her crime. An Old Bailey jury of ten men and two women took only 25 minutes to find Ellis guilty, rejecting her defence that it was a "crime of passion", and affirming that jealousy can never justify murder. Ellis displayed no emotion as she heard the verdict, although she plans an appeal. Women are rarely hanged in Britain, and the case will give fresh impetus to the campaign against capital punishment (→ 13/7).

Swaggering 'Teddy Boys' invite trouble

"Teds": setting a new fashion.

Bath, 28 May
Groups of raucous "Teddy Boys" are attracting attention across Britain. But their flamboyant imitation of "Edwardian" fashion – slicked-back hair, long coats with velvet collars and "drainpipe" trousers – is not the only cause of interest. Several cities have reported disturbances as violence flares between rival gangs of teenage youths. In Bath, for instance, 16 "Teds" were arrested tonight after trouble at a dance hall. Their behaviour often matches their extravagant clothes, but the swaggering "Teds" say they are being blamed for trouble which others provoke. The older generation is not amused.

Crisis in Cyprus is worsened by strike

Cyprus, 13 September
The crisis in the British colony of Cyprus escalated today when the nationalist group EOKA brought out the island's workers on a general strike. Illegal processions and demonstrations and fighting between the Greek and Turkish communities stretched police and military resources, and hundreds were arrested. Orders to shoot to kill if necessary did not have to be used, although soldiers of the Royal Inniskillings used bayonets to disperse a huge mob that had erected a barricade on the road between Lysi and Nicosia (→ 29/11).

Makarios deported by British authorities

Cyprus, 9 March
Archbishop Makarios, the leader of the Greek Cypriot community, was deported to the Seychelles today by the British authorities. Described by the governor, Sir John Harding, as "a major obstacle to a return to peaceful conditions", Makarios is the figurehead of his people's demands for independence, as important as the elusive General Grivas, the head of the terrorist organization EOKA. Indeed, Makarios is regarded as the inspiration for and a leading member of EOKA, which has threatened a massive bombing campaign in retaliation for the deportation (→ 9/8/57).

EOKA suspects under guard.

Controversial play shakes up the stage

Kitchen sink drama has arrived.

London, 13 May
Look Back In Anger, written by an unknown actor, John Osborne, is hailed today by the critic Kenneth Tynan as "the best young play of its decade" and its hero, the ranting Jimmy Porter, as "the completest young pup since Hamlet" and the spokesman for the generation now in its twenties. The play is one of the first to be staged at the Royal Court theatre under the new regime of George Devine, after some 25 theatres had turned it down. The theatre's publicity names Osborne as one of the "Angry Young Men". Older critics have asked what he and his hero are so angry about.

Britain mourns its first movie mogul

London, 23 January
Sir Alexander Korda, the nearest thing Britain has known to a movie mogul in the Hollywood style, died today aged 62. A Hungarian, he began making films in a shed in his twenties but failed in Hollywood before creating London Films in 1932. He gambled everything on *The Private Life of Henry VIII* – which made his and Charles Laughton's fortunes. He built Denham studios in 1936 and produced H G Wells's *Things to Come*, *The Ghost Goes West*, *The Scarlet Pimpernel*, *The Four Feathers*, and after 1945 *Anna Karenina* and *Richard III*. He made and lost £2 million in films.

First African colony promised freedom

London, 18 September
The Gold Coast is to be Britain's first black colony in Africa to win its freedom. It was announced today that the colony will become independent on 6 March next year. The first leader of the new nation will be Kwame Nkrumah, the head of the Convention People's Party, who led his party to victory in elections in 1951. Nigeria and Sierra Leone are two other West African colonies expected to follow the Gold Coast towards independence. Their peaceful progress contrasts with the continuing violence in Kenya and uncertainty in the Central African Federation (→ 6/3/57).

Missing frogman near Soviet ship, government admits

Britain, 14 May
The British government said today that a frogman missing since last month had been doing "underwater tests" near the cruiser carrying the Soviet leaders Nikita Khrushchev and Nikolai Bulganin during their visit to Britain. The government had earlier denied that any such activity had been in progress near the *Ordzhonikidze* and two escort ships in Portsmouth harbour, but has now agreed that Commander Lionel "Buster" Crabbe was testing "certain equipment". Crabbe disappeared during the operation and is presumed drowned. Soviet newspapers have accused Britain of "shameful underwater espionage" and "dirty work by enemies of international cooperation".

The Soviet delegation spent eight days here for talks about "peaceful coexistence". Bulganin is the Soviet premier, but most interest was focused on the ebullient Khrushchev. In March he electrified the Soviet Communist Party's 20th congress by a speech in which he denounced his predecessor, Joseph Stalin, as a despotic and criminal murderer. During his British visit Khrushchev clashed with George Brown, a Labour leader. "I'd vote Tory," the Soviet leader said afterwards (→ 26/6/57).

July 27. Jim Laker walks off at Old Trafford as the first cricketer to take all ten wickets in a test innings, finishing with 19 for 88 in the match against Australia.

British opinion divided as crisis erupts in Suez

Nasser sees off Britain and France.

London, 3 November

The Suez invasion begun by Anglo-French forces on 31 October has divided opinion in Britain. Two junior ministers, Anthony Nutting and Edward Boyle, have resigned and, while there have been no resignations from the cabinet, R A ("Rab") Butler and Sir Walter Monckton are said to have been opposed to the attack on Egypt.

The Labour Party has joined the Liberals and dissident Tories to mount an attack on the government under the slogan "Law not War". Hugh Gaitskell, the Labour leader, has been passionate in his criticism of the prime minister, Sir Anthony Eden, and in a broadcast tonight appealed for his overthrow. But there has been equally fierce criticism of Labour for allegedly damaging national unity at a time when the forces are risking their lives.

The Foreign Office, alarmed by international criticism, is opposed to the invasion. The Treasury is fearful of US hostility. The newspapers are split: most support Eden, but the *Observer* and the *Manchester Guardian* describe his actions as "gangsterism" (→8).

Eden blunders over Suez.

US forces Allies to cease fire in Suez

Suez Canal Zone, 8 November

The Anglo-French attempt to seize the Suez Canal from Egypt and topple Colonel Nasser from power has failed. All military operations were halted at midnight under the terms of the ceasefire imposed by the United Nations.

There is no doubt that the invading force could have gone on to take the entire canal zone – most of the Egyptian air force has been destroyed and those army units that resisted have been pushed aside – but Britain was unable to withstand American pressure. In spite of what Sir Anthony Eden understood to be the tacit approval of John Foster Dulles, the US secretary of state, President Eisenhower reacted furiously to the invasion. His ministers and diplomats have put enormous pressure on Britain to withdraw, and the Americans were crucial in forcing through the ceasefire resolution at the UN.

Even more important, "Ike", for so long a friend of Britain, made it clear that sterling, under attack from all sides, would receive no support from the United States. The crunch came yesterday when the Treasury informed the chancellor, Harold Macmillan, that Britain needed a loan of a billion dollars if the pound was not to be devalued.

Washington's answer to his plea for help was emphatic: no money without a ceasefire. The cabinet had no choice but to accept. Britain is no longer a world power (→19).

Buildings are set ablaze as the British and French storm into Port Said.

With the fighting over, British paras patrol unconcerned through Port Said.

Strain of Suez crisis takes toll on Eden

London, 19 November

Sir Anthony Eden, worn out by the strain of the Suez affair, is to fly to Jamaica and rest there for three weeks. A communiqué, issued at midnight by the prime minister's office, announced that the leader of the House of Commons, "Rab" Butler, will run the cabinet while Sir Anthony is away.

The question that must be asked is: will he ever return to power? He has suffered a terrible international disaster and has inflicted divisive wounds on Britain. There is no doubt about his moral and physical courage, but even before Suez there were signs that his health was giving way.

In 1953 he suffered an attack of the jaundice that has troubled him for some time; he had three gall-bladder operations that year. There is speculation that his ill-health may have undermined his political judgement. Certainly, he became obsessed with toppling Nasser, regarding the Egyptian strongman as a Middle Eastern Hitler. It was an obsession that clouded his thinking at a dangerous time.

His departure will do little to ease the controversy provoked by Suez. Despite the denials of the foreign secretary, Selwyn Lloyd, many people in the United States believe that Britain and France colluded with Israel to allow the Israeli army to invade Egypt and so give Britain and France the excuse to intervene (→21).

Macmillan replaces Eden as Tory leader

Surprise choice: Macmillan, seen here with the chief whip, Edward Heath.

Westminster, 9 January

The ailing Sir Anthony Eden, his once glittering career ruined by the Suez débâcle, has resigned as prime minister, and the chancellor, Harold Macmillan, aged 62, has been appointed to succeed him.

While Eden's departure had been expected, the appointment of Macmillan had not. It is the outcome of a bitter struggle within the Tory Party. The man marked down to succeed was "Rab" Butler, Eden's deputy, but he was strongly opposed by some Tory MPs because

of his lack of enthusiasm for the Suez enterprise.

Butler is deeply disappointed but would only comment in his usual enigmatic fashion that "if my services are of value, they will be at Mr Macmillan's disposal". At first hawkish over Suez, the new prime minister's attitude changed to that of a dove when the financial situation became serious. He has good personal and business connections in the United States and he sees the repair of Anglo-American relations as his first task (→ 20/7).

IRA maintains new violence campaign

Dublin, 5 July

Eamon de Valera, who became the Irish premier again after the general election in March, has today moved against the Irish Republican Army by using part of the Offences Against the State Act of 1940.

Tough emergency measures will involve using the Curragh military camp as a detention centre. However it is by no means clear that this will stem the IRA's renewed campaign of violence against military targets in Northern Ireland which began last December. De Valera's decision was in part politically motivated. In the election, Sinn Féin emerged from the wilderness and won four seats (→ 9/10/58).

Britain says 'No' to Common Market

Rome, 25 March

The European Economic Community came into being today with the signing of the Treaty of Rome by "the Six": France, West Germany, Italy, Belgium, Holland and Luxembourg. The aim of this "Common Market" is the free movement of people, goods and money among the member states.

Britain has decided not to join for traditional British reasons: its ties to the Commonwealth and its suspicion of European entanglements. It also fears that the EEC will develop a supra-national authority that will erode Britain's sovereignty over domestic affairs. The government is hoping to establish a wider, but less formalized European Free Trade Area (→ 20/11/59).

Airliners grounded

Manchester, 17 March

Following a crash last week at Manchester's Ringway airport, in which 22 people died, British European Airways has grounded all its oldest Viscount turbo-prop airliners. Passengers due to fly out on five scheduled flights from London have been left stranded. Experts are now blaming the recent crash on a mechanical fault in the Viscount's wing flaps (→ 4/10/58).

One way of trying to acquire riches is to invest in the new premium bonds; prizes of up to 1,000 are on offer, picked by a machine called "Ernie".

Legalization urged of homosexual acts

Britain, 4 September

Homosexual acts between consenting adults should no longer be a criminal offence, according to a government report published today. The committee, chaired by Sir John Wolfenden, also proposes new laws on soliciting to clear prostitutes from the streets, but does not seek to ban "the oldest profession". Sir John, who is vice-chancellor of Reading University, argues that the law should allow individual freedom of choice and action in matters of private morality. By "adult" the committee means anyone over the age of 21. Reform of the homosexual laws would remove a common cause of blackmail. The government will await public reaction before initiating any legislation.

Death toll mounts as Asian flu hits UK

Britain, 23 September

The Ministry of Health has tried to allay public alarm over the present outbreak of Asian influenza, stressing that it is a mild one. But attacks have been complicated by pneumonia and bronchitis. Deaths from influenza in 160 large towns in England and Wales rose from 8 to 47 in the week ending 14 September. Children are particularly vulnerable and many are staying away from school.

Lewisham train crash kills more than 90

A scene of unutterable chaos greets rescuers at the site of the crash.

London, 4 December

Two trains packed with commuters and Christmas shoppers crashed in thick fog at Lewisham, south London, this evening. It is feared that over 90 people are dead and some 200 injured, many still trapped in the wreckage. It appears that the driver of the 4.56 steam express from Cannon Street to Ramsgate failed to see two stop signals. His fireman shouted a warning and he applied the emergency brake – but it was too late. His locomotive slammed into the rear of the stationary 5.18 Charing Cross to Hayes electric train.

The electric train, its brakes on, telescoped and, while the steam locomotive stayed on the tracks, its tender reared up and brought down the supports of a bridge carrying a loop line over the track. The 350-ton bridge crashed onto the already mangled carriages. Two minutes later the driver of another train on the loop line, moving slowly up to a red light, saw a gaping hole in the track. He halted with his leading coach tilted over the wreckage.

Tonight heavy lifting gear looms through the fog as members of the emergency services and the Royal Engineers struggle to lift girders and untangle the telescoped carriages, while stretcher-bearers carry away the dead and injured. This accident will boost the campaign for the introduction of an automatic warning system.

Severe fire causes nuclear plant scare

Cumberland, 17 October

Britain's fledgling atomic industry has suffered its most serious accident to date. Fuel rods in one of the 152-metre (500-foot) chimneys at the Windscale atomic works overheated, releasing large amounts of radioactive material into the atmosphere. The Atomic Energy Authority stresses that no one was injured and that most of the radioactive material has been blown out to sea. The chimney where the fire began has been shut down, while the rest of the plant, which makes plutonium for the military, is back in production. None the less sales of milk from a large area around Windscale have been banned, since the milk contains up to six times the legal limit of radioiodine.

Women among 'life peers' to join Lords

London, 30 October

Women will be included in a new category of "life peers" to be admitted to the House of Lords, it was announced today by the leader of the upper house, the earl of Home. Formerly, entrance to the house has been restricted to male bearers of hereditary titles, but it will now be revitalized by an infusion of new blood. Other reforms will streamline the day-to-day procedures of the Lords (→ 21/10/58).

The latest music rocks around the clock

London, December

A craze for "rock and roll" has swept Britain this year. Its birthplace was the coffee bars of London's Soho district. Tommy Hicks, a 20-year-old merchant seaman, acquired a new surname (Steele) and a new career (singer) after being discovered singing in the "Two I's" coffee bar. Hits such as *Singing the Blues* demonstrated that Britons could rock just as well as the Americans who inspired the new musical fashion.

Television has recognized and exploited the popularity of rock with the BBC's *Six-Five Special*, but the major stars remain American. Bill Haley and his group, the Comets, were enthusiastically mobbed when he toured Britain in February; his audiences jived in the aisles, just as they had done during the first rock films. Elvis Presley – well known from such films as *Loving You* – has been the biggest record-seller.

A distinctive variant of rock has emerged in the "skiffle" sound of the former jazzman Lonnie Donegan. Cheap guitars and even washboards have enabled hundreds of amateurs to form their own skiffle or rock groups.

Haley is good, but rather old.

Steele is good, and younger.

'Busby Babes' die in plane tragedy

The wrecked plane in which England's finest football team was travelling.

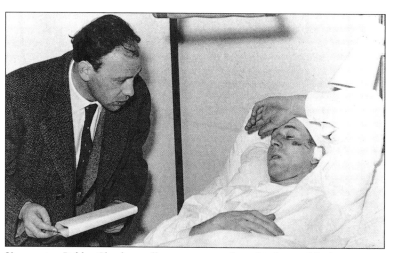

Young star Bobby Charlton talks to pressmen from his hospital bed.

Munich, 6 February

Manchester United football club's bid for the European Cup has ended in tragedy. Seven members of arguably the finest team in England – nicknamed the "Busby Babes" after their manager Matt Busby – have been killed in a plane crash at Munich airport. The tragic accident, in which eight journalists and three of the club's staff also died, happened as the team began the last leg of its journey home from Belgrade, where they qualified for the European Cup semi-finals.

The Munich runway was covered with snow, and the pilot of the BEA Ambassador had to abort his first take-off. At the second attempt the plane failed to gain height, hitting a fence and then an airport building before breaking in two. The survivors, many of them badly injured, have been taken to a Munich hospital. Among the most seriously hurt are Busby himself, the England left-half Duncan Edwards and fellow England player John Berry.

Of the players reported killed four were full internationals. They were the Manchester captain Roger Byrne (28), Tommy Taylor (25) and David Pegg (22), who played for England; and Bill Whelan (22), who had four caps for the Irish Republic (→ 21).

Nuclear disarmers march 50 miles to weapons headquarters

Aldermaston, 7 April

To the sounds of a skiffle group playing "When The Saints Go Marching In" 3,000 people marched past the gates of the Atomic Weapons Research Establishment at Aldermaston today and called for Britain, Russia and the United States to stop the manufacture, testing and storage of nuclear weapons.

The Campaign for Nuclear Disarmament, formed this year, claimed that 12,000 supporters attended the final rally and that 600 hardcore marchers had walked the entire 50 miles from London.

There were speeches from Stuart Morris of the Peace Pledge Union and the US pacifist Beyard Rustin. At one point marchers attacked a car of people who accused them, through a loudspeaker, of "playing Khrushchev's game" (→ 3/10/60).

Footsore anti-nuclear marchers hope to influence government policy.

Treasury ministers quit in benefits row

Westminster, 7 January
The chancellor of the exchequer, Peter Thorneycroft, and his two junior treasury ministers, Enoch Powell and Nigel Birch, resigned yesterday when their proposals to slash expenditure to curb inflation were turned down by the cabinet. Their proposals, which included abolishing the family allowance for the second child, were said by the prime minister to be "neither politically nor socially desirable". As he set out on a Commonwealth tour this morning, Macmillan was asked about the loss of his treasury team. He replied: "I thought that the best thing to do was to settle up these little local difficulties and then turn to the wider vision of the Commonwealth" (→ 8/10/59).

Britain and Iceland start war over cod

North Sea, 2 September
Britain and Iceland are at loggerheads over fishing rights in the North Sea after two Icelandic gunboats seized a Grimsby trawler today. Although the Royal Navy has freed the trawler, the *Northern Foam*, this "cod war" is unlikely to end here. The Reykjavik government is determined to maintain its newly declared 12-mile (19.2-km) limit around Iceland (→ 6/5/59).

'Grand Old Man' of English music dies

London, 26 August
Dr Ralph Vaughan Williams, the most "English" composer of his time, went on producing important works to the end. His last four symphonies were written between the ages of 76 and 85 – the last, his ninth, premiered only four months before his death today. He loved and used English folk song but also wrote for films such as *Scott of the Antarctic*. His "Fantasias" were popular, but he departed from the pastoral vein in his tough and dissonant fourth symphony. "I don't know whether I like it," he said. "But that is what I meant."

Race riots break out in two English cities

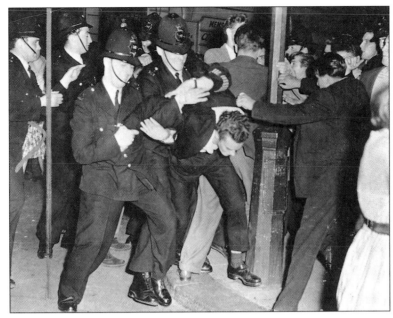
Policemen struggle with crowds as racial violence flares in Notting Hill.

London, 9 September
Petrol bombs and thousands of milk bottles were thrown at police in London last night, after white youths taunted black immigrants with racist slogans. Several people were badly hurt and 59 are being charged with weapons offences.

A white gang had been abusing black people at a house in Blenheim Crescent, Notting Hill Gate, when the immigrants replied with a hail of milk bottles and a petrol bomb. Several black men then attacked the whites with iron bars. In nearby Bayswater black men were ambushed leaving a club. Police detectives from the Special Branch think that right-wing extremists may have started the trouble.

In another incident today, at a Nottingham magistrates' court, a television cameraman was accused of starting a riot which led to a clash between white and black communities in Ann's Well Road and five people being imprisoned. The prosecution said the cameraman had attempted to reconstruct a previous fight. After he lit a magnesium flare "the mock fight, presumably staged for the benefit of the cameras, developed into something more serious" (→ 15).

The last debs are presented to the Queen

The palace feels debs are archaic.

Edinburgh, 3 July
A youthful, if perhaps archaic, ritual came to an end today when the Queen received the last debutantes to be presented at court. Miss Fiona Macrae curtseyed her way into royal history at Holyrood Palace, four months after the last debutantes had been presented at Buckingham Palace. Debs' dances, debs' delights and the whole paraphernalia of "coming out", so much a part of upper-class life, are unlikely to vanish, but this rite of passage will now have to do without royal patronage. The duke of Edinburgh played a part in ending the tradition, which he believes conflicts with the modern image sought by royalty.

LP, STD and Zeta: useful inventions enter British life

Britain, December
It has been an exciting year for scientific developments in Britain. The year opened with the announcement of experiments with a machine called "Zeta", which is reported to offer the possibility of harnessing atomic power to provide cheap or even free energy.

It is too soon to say whether this attractive theoretical vision is realistic. However, some other innovations of 1958 are already in production – including long-playing 33rpm records (LPs), a Lotus car with a glassfibre shell, and the "stereophonic" record players or amplifiers. A different kind of revolution in communications was initiated this month when the Queen made the first telephone call in a new "subscriber trunk dialling" (STD) system. On 5 December she dialled directly from Bristol to Edinburgh without her call having to be made via an operator. The Post Office says that the whole of Britain will be connected to the new STD system.

Potentially the most spectacular development is what is called a "hovercraft". This is a new form of vehicle that floats above the ground on a cushion of air and can therefore travel across water or land. It was invented by Christopher Cockerell, a Suffolk boat-builder (→ 16/4/59).

Trying out the new "stereo".

Dublin, 8 January. Eamon de Valera says he will quit as prime minister and run for the Irish presidency (→ 23/6).

Surrey, 22 January. Mike Hawthorn, the British world champion racing driver, dies in a car crash at Guildford.

Britain, 22 January. New figures show that two-thirds of Britons now have television sets (→ 17/9).

Moscow, 21 February. Harold Macmillan, the British prime minister, arrives for talks with Soviet leaders (→ 29/3/60).

London, 23 February. A peace agreement is reach on the future government of Cyprus (→ 27/10).

Southern Rhodesia, 27 Feb. A state of emergency is declared in the British colony.

Britain, 27 May. Filter-tip cigarettes have helped tobacco manufacturers maintain sales after recent reports linking smoking and lung cancer.

Ireland, 23 June. Sean Lemass becomes head of the government (→ 25).

London, 7 July. Hugh Carleton-Greene is chosen to be BBC director-general.

Norwich, 28 July. The first postal codes and postal sorting machines are introduced.

Birmingham, 18 August. The "Mini" motor car is launched (→ 8/11).

London, 24 August. The House of Fraser wins a takeover battle with Debenham's for Harrod's department store.

Westminster, 27 October. The Queen's speech opening parliament promises independence for Cyprus and Nigeria (→ 16/8/60).

London, 19 November. The Queen's head is to appear on bank notes for the first time (→ 8/2/60).

Scotland, 17 November. Duty-free areas are introduced at Prestwick and Renfrew airports; Heathrow plans similar facilities (→ 22/2/60).

Stockholm, 20 November. The European Free Trade Association (EFTA) is formed by Britain and six other nations as an alternative to the six-nation European Economic Community, or Common Market (→ 14/1/63).

Westminster. The National Insurance Act introduces a graduated pension scheme.

De Valera becomes president of Ireland

Dublin, 25 June

After a lifetime in active politics, Eamon de Valera has been elected president of the Republic of Ireland. Under the constitution which he created, he moves now to a non-political, head-of-state position.

Sean Lemass replaced Eamon de Valera as leader of Fianna Fáil and head of the government two days ago, advocating a change of focus towards a more pragmatic set of priorities mainly concerned with trade and the economy. Inevitably, there will be less emphasis on civil war politics, on the reunification of Ireland and on the restoration of the Irish language (→ 6/10/61).

De Valera: the new Irish president.

Film industry suffers as television booms

The goggle-box takes over Britain.

Britain, 17 September

The British cinema industry is being hit hard by TV. The people who used to take pleasure in going out to lose themselves in the glamour and the adventure of the movies now stay at home and watch the "goggle-box". The Rank Organization revealed today that cinema attendances slumped from 1.396 million in 1950 to 1.101 million in 1956 and they are still dwindling. Even fiercer competition is promised by the BBC's purchase of 20 American films for TV (→ 8/2/61).

Invention takes off on a cushion of air

Isle of Wight, 16 April

The hovercraft – a revolutionary vehicle that travels on a cushion of air – has just floated off the drawing board and into reality.

Unveiled last year by its inventor, the Suffolk boat-builder Christopher Cockerell, the hovercraft at once attracted the interest of the National Research and Development Corporation. Now a two-ton hovercraft is under construction by Saunders Roe on the Isle of Wight. Future plans include a 100-ton vehicle for passengers and one of 10,000 tons for freight (→ 20/7/62).

Icelandic cod war hits stormy waters

North Sea, 6 May

The so-called "cod war" between Britain and Iceland is becoming increasingly violent. During a recent stand-off 20 live rounds were fired by an Icelandic gunboat at a Hull trawler, the *Arctic Viking*. Though they were just warning shots, one shell missed the trawler by a mere 3 yards. Britain has today protested vigorously to the Icelandic government about this "dangerous and unseamanlike" action.

Over five million teenagers make their mark on the decade

Britain, January

Most areas of Britain have enjoyed more affluence during this decade than ever before – and among the beneficiaries are the nation's teenagers. As a group, "teenagers" did not exist before the 1950s. Now there are fashions, music and consumer products produced specifically for a teenage market said to be worth £500 million a year.

Many of the first influences were American – actors such as Marlon Brando and James Dean or singers such as Elvis Presley. But native stars such as Cliff Richard through TV shows like *Oh Boy* have built on the earlier trad jazz and skiffle crazes to eclipse most of the Americans, at least in the home market. Films such as *Expresso Bongo* highlight the distinctive teenage culture that is emerging in Britain.

Oh Boy! Worth £500 million a year, Britain's young are taken seriously.

Mac's majority keeps the Tories in power

Westminster, 8 October
Harold Macmillan, campaigning on the slogan "You've never had it so good", has brought the Tories home with a thumping majority of 102 in the general election. The result is unique this century as the Tories have increased their majority twice in a row: from 20 in 1951 to 62 in 1955 and 102 today. The final tally of seats is expected to be Conservatives and Unionists 365, Labour 258, Liberals 6, Others 1.

"Supermac" is highly delighted with the result, although he has dismissed it offhandedly, saying: "It has gone off rather well." It did not go off at all well for the Liberals, who had such high hopes of success under their new leader, Jo Grimond. They doubled their votes but failed to win any more seats. Among their candidates were two former presidents of the Oxford Union, Jeremy Thorpe, who was elected, and Robin Day, who lost.

The Labour Party ended the day in disarray, racked with divisions and totally defeated. Hugh Gaitskell conceded defeat early in the vote-counting, bitterly blaming the squabbling between the left and right of his party. Privately he agreed with the prime minister, who commented: "I think the class war is now obsolete."

The election has, in fact, been a triumph for the unflappable prime minister, who, although patrician in style, has learnt how to appeal to the man in the street as well as to the City of London (→ 3/11/60).

Macmillan on the stump: affluent voters have returned him to power.

Irish trade unions form new group

Dublin, 24 September
The Irish Congress of Trade Unions held its inaugural conference today. Last February the Congress of Irish Unions and the Irish Trade Union Congress voted to unite.

This represents the healing of a rift in the trade union movement that has existed since 1945 when the Irish Transport and General Workers' Union, together with a number of smaller unions, seceded from the ICTU to establish their own Congress of Irish Unions.

Report slams new buildings as 'ugly'

London, 18 December
The "drabness", "mediocrity" and "deplorably low standards" of modern inner-city architecture were attacked in the annual report of the Royal Fine Art Commission today. Ugly nuclear power stations in regions of natural beauty and spreading suburbs were also targets for criticism. The commission, whose members include John Betjeman and Henry Moore, concluded that without a plan the outlook for cities was "poor"(→ 2/6/60).

Motoring boom fuelled by first motorway and the introduction of the £500 'Mini'

Motorways seem certain to become part of the new British landscape.

Britain, 8 November
Sightseers flocked to Britain's new motorway, the M1, on the first Sunday since it opened last week. An eight-mile by-pass for Preston was opened last year as the first stretch of motorway in Britain, but the new M1 north of Watford towards the Midlands is the first extensive stretch of proper motorway.

Its completion marks the climax of a decade of astonishing growth in motoring, which has seen the number of private cars and vans in Britain more than double from the total of 2,307,000 that were registered in 1950. This growth was boosted still further by the launch this year of the British Motor Corporation's new "Mini" car. It went on sale in August at no more than £500 including purchase tax. Its designer, Alec Issigonis, has produced a revolutionary design by mounting the engine sideways.

In many ways the Mini is an austere creation – instruments are sparse, doors are opened by strings, windows slide open – but the sprightly engine and the car's smallness make it a highly convenient vehicle for driving in town. Less welcome consequences of motoring's boom years are the introduction of parking restrictions such as yellow lines (→ 3/1/61).

Designer Alec Issigonis with two of the first of his revolutionary Minis.

PM's talk of change angers South Africa

Cape Town, 3 February
Harold Macmillan angered members of the South African parliament when he declared in Cape Town today: "The wind of change is blowing through this continent and, whether we like it or not, this growth of national consciousness is a political fact." They did not like it at all, and many accused the British prime minister of meddling.

Now at a crucial stage of his African tour, Macmillan said that the great issue was whether Asia and Africa swung to communism or to the West and he urged South Africa to adopt policies to promote racial equality. The premier, Hendrik Verwoerd, was loudly applauded when he retorted: "There has to be justice not only for the black man but also for the white man." Britain has been bending with the "winds of change". Ghana is due to become a republic this year, Nigeria is to be independent and Kenya will be given a power-sharing constitution. Since 1945 some 500 million people in former British colonies have become self-governing (→ 9/5).

Space-tracking station sets a new record

Jodrell Bank telescope sets record.

Cheshire, 14 March
The radio telescope at Jodrell Bank has set a record in space-tracking, making contact with the American satellite Pioneer 5 over a distance of 407,000 miles (651,000km).

The first contact came yesterday when the probe was 350,000 miles away. A spokesman said: "We sent a signal out at 2pm which switched on the transmitter in the satellite and we tracked it for the next half-hour before turning it off."

The previous record – about 290,000 miles – was achieved when the Soviet Union contacted Lunik 3, which photographed the dark side of the moon last year.

New talent revives Irish film industry

Ireland, 5 February
President Eamon de Valera and the Irish prime minister, Sean Lemass, have both attended the première this evening of the first full-length feature film to be made in the Irish language. It is entitled *Mise Eire* (*I am Ireland*).

The creation of George Morrison – an international film archivist of some distinction – with Irish folk music orchestrated by Sean O'Riada, *Mise Eire* will give Irish audiences their first opportunity to see a film about their recent past. The period covered is the civil war and the war of independence. It is also hoped that the film, which was made in collaboration with Gael-Linn, will help in a campaign to promote the Irish language.

Atlantic record set by lone yachtsman

Francis Chichester nears New York.

New York, 21 July
Francis Chichester has set a new record for sailing across the Atlantic. He arrived in New York today in his yacht *Gypsy Moth II* just 40 days after starting his solo voyage from Plymouth. Chichester, who is 58 years old and has had lung cancer for the last two years, was often beset by hurricane-force winds. Clothes kept in the lockers were tossed about so much that holes were worn in them. The dinner jacket he planned to wear in the evenings went mouldy (→ 27/8/66).

May 6. Princess Margaret waves to the crowds from the balcony of Buckingham Palace following her wedding to the photographer Antony Armstrong-Jones, here standing between the Queen and Queen Mother.

Irish soldiers killed in Congo troubles

Ireland, 8 November

Ireland's involvement in United Nations peacekeeping in the Congo has resulted in the tragic deaths of ten soldiers in an ambush at Niemba. A wave of sadness, mingled with pride, has swept Ireland at this first international sacrifice in the cause of world peace. It is widely seen as the mark of Ireland's emergence from its isolation after the Second World War.

The decision to commit military forces to the peacekeeping effort in central Africa, which required special Dáil legislation, also involved General Sean MacEoin, and, at the diplomatic level, the controversial work in Katanga of Conor Cruise O'Brien (→ 1/12/61)

Surge in gambling

Britain, December

The passing of the Betting and Gaming Act, designed to set the British love of a flutter within a legal framework, has led to a great surge in gambling, with betting shops and gambling clubs springing up to replace the street-corner bookies. The growing craze for bingo is astonishing. Many disused churches and cinemas are being converted into bingo halls.

'Lady Chatterley' is cleared of obscenity

Queues form to buy "Lady Chatterley's Lover" after the jury's decision.

London, 2 November

Lady Chatterley's Lover, the long-banned novel by D.H. Lawrence, has emerged from the shadows and into the bookshops, thanks to today's landmark decision by an Old Bailey jury, who declared that the work, prosecuted under last year's Obscene Publications Act, was not obscene. As of today copies of the 3/6d [17.5p] Penguin paperback will be freely available.

The "Lady C" trial has been a test case for the new act, the first of its kind since 1857, and is designed to draw a line between "filth" and work that, though controversial, is of real literary merit. Too often, the literary baby has been washed away with the "dirty" bathwater.

In many ways the trial pitted the old Britain against the new, with experts from both sides putting forward their own sincerely held beliefs. It has not only been a case of what makes "literature", but of the direction of national morality. The old brigade may complain, but the Old Bailey jury has voted for the future (→ 10).

National Service's passing-out parade

Britain, 31 December

National service – a rite of passage that has been losing its popularity among British males – came to an end today when 2,049 young men became the last to receive their call-up cards. Since national service began in 1939, 5,300,000 scruffy civilians have been squarebashed into men by bellowing sergeants. All but 50 of today's batch are destined for the army; others will join the RAF. The privates will discover the joys of Brasso and blanco on two weeks' basic training in Aldershot, while the RAF recruits will fall in at Cardington, Bedfordshire.

The last of the batch go on parade.

Working-class realism takes the centre stage in films and plays

London, December

Working-class realism, pioneered at the Royal Court theatre, has all but ousted traditional drawing room comedy from the West End, banishing "posh" diction in favour of regional accents and manners.

The Court has produced Arnold Wesker's plays *Roots*, which focuses on farmworkers in Norfolk, and *The Kitchen*, set below stairs in a restaurant. Harold Pinter with *The Caretaker*, about a devious tramp, Shelagh Delaney with *A Taste of Honey*, set in deprived Salford, and Keith Waterhouse with *Billy Liar*, the dreams of a Leeds undertaker's assistant, are among the new wave of playwrights, while the cinema has produced *Room at the Top* and *Saturday Night and Sunday Morning* in the same vein.

Albert Finney on the make in "Saturday Night and Sunday Morning".

Labour leaders are split over the bomb

Scarborough, 3 October

A furious row erupted at the Labour Party conference here today over nuclear disarmament. During the debate the party leader, Hugh Gaitskell, launched a fierce attack on the supporters of the Campaign for Nuclear Disarmament, calling them "pacifists, unilateralists and fellow travellers". Close to tears, he told a largely hostile conference: "There are some of us who will fight, fight and fight again to bring back sanity and honesty to the party we love." Despite his plea, the major unions voted with the unilateralists to "ban the bomb". Ignoring all other differences, the party is now split from top to bottom on this one issue (→ 12/9/61).

Britain, 3 January. The one millionth Morris Minor is produced (→ 10/7/62).

Britain, 8 January. Five people, including the Canadian businessman Gordon Lonsdale, are arrested as spies (→ 8/5/).

Britain, 30 January. An oral contraceptive pill becomes available in Britain (→ 4/12).

Ireland, 31 January. The West Clare railway, made famous in song by Percy French, closes.

London, 8 February. The BBC says it is to drop the radio programme *Children's Hour* because television has cut its audiences (→ 31/12).

London, 15 March. South Africa says it will leave the Commonwealth after becoming a republic in May (→ 24/10).

Paris, 28 April. It is revealed that Britain has applied to join the Common Market (→ 4/8).

Wembley, 6 May. Tottenham Hotspur become the first team this century to complete the league and FA Cup "double".

Britain, 18 May. New universities are to be built at Colchester, Canterbury and Coventry.

Canterbury, 27 June. Michael Ramsey becomes the 100th archbishop of Canterbury.

London, 28 June. A judge says that a ballot by the Electrical Trades Union was illegal because it was rigged by communists.

London, 14 July. Yuri Gagarin, the first spaceman, receives an ecstatic welcome from crowds as he begins a visit to Britain.

Westminster, 4 August. MPs approve the government's bid to join the Common Market.

Sussex, 28 August. The earliest known Roman mosaics are uncovered at Fishbourne, near Chichester.

London, 12 September. Nobel prize winner Bertrand Russell and playwright Arnold Wesker are jailed for inciting a breach of the peace in their campaign for nuclear disarmament (→ 18).

Malta, 24 October. The island becomes independent (→ 27/10/64).

Britain, 4 December. The oral contraceptive pill is to become available on the NHS (→ 12/1967).

Dublin, 31 December. Radio Eireann begins a television service (→ 27/6/62).

Mass arrests at big ban-the-bomb demo

London, 18 September
More than 800 people were arrested today in the biggest, most violent ban-the-bomb demonstration so far seen in London. Among those held by police were Canon John Collins, the chairman of the Campaign for Nuclear Disarmament, the playwright John Osborne, the jazz singer George Melly and the actress Vanessa Redgrave.

At one point over 15,000 protestors jammed Trafalgar Square, on a day that saw the Russians explode the 12th nuclear bomb in the present series of tests. The clashes came as 3,000 police struggled to arrest demonstrators staging "sit-down" protests. Last week the No-

bel prizewinning philosopher Bertrand Russell, a prominent member of CND, was jailed for inciting a breach of the peace.

Formed just over three and a half years ago, CND has gained the support of between a quarter and a third of the public, according to opinion polls. Last year it was a major factor in persuading the Labour Party's annual conference to back unilateral nuclear disarmament. But the determination of the Tory government to maintain its independent deterrent has led some CND supporters to form a Committee of 100, which urges civil disobedience rather than seeking to woo political parties (→ 20/2/62).

Part of a crowd estimated at 15,000 stage a "sit-down" nuclear protest.

Labour peer battles for Commons seat

Benn fights against being a peer.

Westminster, 8 May
Anthony Wedgwood Benn, who has just doubled his majority in the by-election at Bristol South-east, was refused admission to the House of Commons today when he arrived to claim his seat. His problem is that the by-election was caused by his own elevation to the peerage as Viscount Stansgate on the death of his father last year. As a peer, he cannot sit in the Commons.

The reluctant Labour lord was barred from the Commons by the principal doorkeeper, a formidable former regimental sergeant major, who told him that, if necessary, force would be used to keep him out. He must now await the passage of a law enabling peers to renounce their titles (→ 30/5/63).

Brainwashed spy is jailed for 42 years

London, 8 May
An ex-diplomat was given a record 42-year jail term at the Old Bailey today. For nine and a half years the self-confessed spy, 38-year-old George Blake, is said to have passed all the documents he could to the Russians while working in Germany and the Lebanon. Lord Chief Justice Parker said his treachery had "rendered much of this country's efforts useless". Blake was captured by the communists in the Korean war when he was vice-consul in Seoul. He was held for three years and is thought to have been brainwashed (→ 22/10/62).

English women finalists at Wimbledon

Mortimer (right) wins Wimbledon.

Wimbledon, 8 July
For the first time since 1914 the All-England Lawn Tennis and Croquet Club of Wimbledon today staged an all-English final for its ladies' singles championship. It ensured the first home win since Dorothy Round's in 1937.

Christine Truman, just 20, was favoured to beat her compatriot, Angela Mortimer, for the title. But Mortimer's patience eventually won the day against the greater power of Truman, who appeared to have been hampered by a fall in the first half of a closely fought match. Mortimer, in her second Wimbledon singles final, finally won in three sets by 4-6, 6-4, 7-5.

Government tightens immigration control

Westminster, 1 November
The government, concerned about the ability of Britain to absorb the increasing number of immigrants from the Commonwealth, is to introduce a Commonwealth Immigration Bill which will impose some restrictions on their numbers. More than 21,000 arrived last year and 100,000 are expected this year.

Under the terms of the bill Commonwealth citizens will be able to apply for an entry voucher if they have a job to come to, or if they possess skills or educational qualifications likely to be useful in the United Kingdom. They may also be allowed to enter as part of a quota, the size of which will be decided at any given time by the government. There will be no restrictions on immigrants who can support themselves by private means.

The bill, seen against the background of the racial disturbances in Nottingham and London's Notting Hill, is bound to cause great political controversy. The Labour and Liberal parties are certain to oppose it on the ground of racial discrimination because it will hardly affect white Commonwealth immigrants. At the same time the Labour Party is bound to be embarrassed by the hostile attitude of its working-class supporters to coloured immigrants who are seen to be competing for jobs and houses (→ 2/7/62).

Seeking a new life: West Indian immigrants arrive in Southampton.

Irish diplomat sacked

Conor Cruise O'Brien talks to Irish UN troops in breakaway Katanga.

Ireland, 1 December
In an atmosphere of intense controversy, the secondment of Conor Cruise O'Brien from the department of external affairs to the United Nations, as special representative in Katanga, has been ended. He has been recalled to the Irish foreign service by the minister for external affairs, but is unlikely to accept this move, and will almost certainly resign.

He has been the victim of personal vilification, mainly directed at his left-wing views, in an attempt to prevent him from implementing the United Nations mandate in the Congo – part of which involved the removal of all foreign military and paramilitary personnel, including mercenaries and foreign political advisers.

Although complex, the situation has involved at least two countries, France and Britain, in activities designed deliberately to frustrate the objectives of the UN while at the same time maintaining formal support for that organization. They allowed United Nations resolutions aimed at ending the conflict to pass, but then took action to stop their implementation. They also actively worked to ensure the removal of Conor Cruise O'Brien from the key position he occupied, a move to which the Irish government has reluctantly agreed.

'Beyond the Fringe' is satirical success

Britain, December
Four university graduates, appearing on stage without scenery or special costumes, have brought a new brand of satirical humour to London's West End this year with their revue, *Beyond the Fringe*. The quartet – Alan Bennett, Peter Cook, Jonathan Miller and Dudley Moore – find humour in politics, the Church, the Second World War and even death. The revue's successful transfer from the Edinburgh Festival has been followed by the launch of a new satirical magazine, *Private Eye*, which revives the tradition of lampooning public figures.

Sean Lemass set to head minority rule

Ireland, 6 October
In his first electoral test as leader of Fianna Fáil, Sean Lemass has demonstrated that he is an indifferent votegetter, but he has managed to form a minority government with the support of independents.

After the baleful years of the fifties, with high emigration, serious balance of payments problems and poor economic growth, the country is beginning to show signs of recovery and Sean Lemass, widely regarded as having the right mixture of business opportunism and caution, is seen as the right leader for the new decade (→ 26/2/62).

Eighty-two people were killed in Ireland's worst air crash, when this chartered DC6 of President Air Lines crashed into the Shannon estuary.

Liverpool, January. The Beatles, a local rock group, are refused a contract by the Decca record company (→4/11/63).

Essex, 11 February. A schoolboy claims a world record after dancing "the Twist" nonstop for 33 hours.

London, 17 February. James Hanratty is sentenced to death for murdering Michael Gregsten on the A6 last year, after the longest murder trial in British history.

London, 20 February. Six anti-nuclear protesters are jailed under the Official Secrets Act (→8/8/63).

Northern Ireland, 26 February. The IRA announces a ceasefire after a five-year campaign of violence (→25/3/63).

Kent, 15 March. The Liberals overturn a huge Tory majority to win the Orpington by-election (→13/7).

London, 2 April. The first push-button-controlled pedestrian "Panda" crossings are introduced.

West Sussex, 23 April. Stirling Moss, the racing driver, is seriously injured in a crash at Goodwood.

Brighton, 3 June. The first legal casino in Britain opens.

Britain, 27 June. A second BBC television channel is urged by a government committee (→11/7).

Belfast, 10 July. A motorway opens to Lisburn, the first in Ireland (→22/8/63).

Cornwall, 11 July. The first live television pictures are beamed across the Atlantic via the Telstar satellite and a terminal at Goonhilly Downs (→19/1/63).

London, 9 August. Sir Laurence Olivier is named as the first director of the National Theatre (→22/10/63).

Britain, 19 September. A royal commission recommends the creation of a "press council".

London, 8 October. Judge Elizabeth Lane becomes the first female judge to sit in the High Court (→1970).

Westminster, 8 November. A junior minister, Thomas Galbraith, resigns after his letters to the spy, William Vassall, are published (→11/5/63).

Bermuda, 21 December. The US agrees to sell Polaris missiles to Britain.

Mac purges his cabinet

Westminster, 13 July

Harold Macmillan, renowned as "Supermac", is now being called "Mac the Knife" after his ruthless purge of his ministers tonight. The prime minister has sacked seven of his most senior colleagues – one-third of the cabinet. It is a bloodletting on a scale without equal in modern political life.

The casualties, headed by Selwyn Lloyd, the chancellor of the exchequer, Lord Kilmuir, the lord chancellor, and Harold Watkinson, the minister of defence, seem to have had little notice of their dismissals, which followed 24 hours after another huge Tory voting collapse in by-election polling.

The view in Westminster is that the prime minister, normally so unflappable, has been panicked into extreme action in order to save his government, which is under pressure from many quarters. Rising unemployment, the pay pause, Britain's failure to keep up with her economic rivals, especially resurgent Germany and Japan, have all eroded Tory support among its traditional sympathizers.

It was the Orpington by-election in March, when a Tory majority of nearly 15,000 was turned into a Liberal win by 7,800, which sound-

"Mac the Knife" draws blood.

ed the alarm. There is a smell of Tory fear in the air and it is doubtful if Macmillan's explanation of his purge – "we need a broad reconstruction" – will wash. Observers see it more as a firing squad to encourage the others (→14/2/63).

Civil servant spy jailed for 18 years

London, 22 October

A 38-year-old admiralty clerk and son of a vicar, who was "entrapped by his lust", was jailed for 18 years today for spying for the USSR.

While working at the British embassy in Moscow, William Vassall was photographed at a homosexual party and blackmailed. Back in London he used a tiny camera to photograph "highly important" documents and was paid enough to double his salary. The Attorney-General, Sir John Hobson, said: "Entrapped by his lust he had neither the moral fibre nor the patriotism to alter his conduct" (→8/11).

Sporting changes

London, July

The Gentlemen and the Players will meet this month for the 137th, and last, time. The annual match between the nation's top amateur and professional cricketers has been ended by the cricket authorities at Lord's on the grounds that it is anachronistic. In another portent of professional dominance, players in the most popular winter game, football, have won their campaign against the minimum wage.

Britten's 'War Requiem' marks the opening of Coventry Cathedral

The interior of the new Coventry Cathedral, risen from the ashes of 1940.

Coventry, 30 May

Benjamin Britten's sombre new *War Requiem* was given its first performance here tonight as part of the inauguration of Coventry's new cathedral. The stone building, joined to the black ruins of the old, which was destroyed by German bombers in November 1940, was designed by Sir Basil Spence and is dominated by works by contemporary artists: a vast window of richly coloured glass by John Piper, a giant tapestry of Christ Enthroned by Graham Sutherland and, beside the entrance steps, Jacob Epstein's huge sculpture of St Michael, the cathedral patron saint, triumphing over the Devil. Building took six years. Britten's setting of the requiem mass alternating with First World War poems by Wilfrid Owen has already been hailed as a major masterpiece (→4/12/76).

First hovercraft passenger service opens

The first passengers reach the shore after a hover trip at up to 56mph.

Rhyl, 20 July

The world's first ever passenger hovercraft service opened today, running from Rhyl to Wallasey across the estuary of the River Dee. It carried 24 passengers, plus 8,000 letters and cards. The hovercraft was invented in 1953 by Christopher Cockerell, who was knighted for his efforts. Designed to operate over water, rough or swampy ground, or flat land surfaces, the craft rides on a cushion of air, generated by downwards-directed fans and driven by a gas turbine or diesel engine. It is hoped that their commercial use may be extended to longer journeys (→ 30/4/66).

Immigrants rush to beat midnight deadline

Westminster, 2 July

The new rules restricting the right of Commonwealth citizens to enter the United Kingdom became effective at midnight last night. The advent of the restrictions has led to a last-minute flood of immigrants and there have been some remarkable scenes at ports and airports. Among the luckiest were 74 Jamaicans without the newly required work permits whose plane was delayed by bad weather. They landed at Belfast 56 minutes after the new rules were applied but were allowed to stay. Others were less lucky. Three Pakistanis were sent home from London and several Indians and Adenis are being held awaiting repatriation (→ 22/2/68).

007 James Bond makes his screen debut

The name is Bond, James Bond.

London, 30 October

The exotic adventures and hair's-breadth escapes from implausible villains by novelist Ian Fleming's hero, James Bond, might have been thought unfilmable. But *Dr No* is proving that assumption wrong.

The terrors of the Caribbean island of Crab Key, where Dr No resides, are handled with nonchalant ease by Sean Connery as Agent 007. The direction by Terence Young is smooth and efficient, above the average for British thrillers. Fleming has written 12 James Bond novels and plans are afoot to film *From Russia With Love* and *Goldfinger*.

Paris, 14 January. President de Gaulle dashes Britain's hopes of joining the European Economic Community (→ 16/5/67).

London, 18 January. Hugh Gaitskell, the Labour leader, dies aged 56 (→ 14/2).

London, 4 February. Two journalists are jailed for refusing to disclose the sources of their stories.

Westminster, 22 March. John Profumo, the war minister, tells MPs there was "no impropriety" in his friendship with a model, Christine Keeler (→ 5/6).

Belfast, 25 March. Captain Terence O'Neill becomes prime minister of Northern Ireland (→ 28/10/64).

Moscow, 11 May. Greville Wynne, a British businessman, is jailed for spying (→ 1/7).

Westminster, 30 May. A Peerage Bill is published which will enable peers such as Viscount Stansgate (Anthony Wedgwood Benn) to renounce their titles.

London, 9 July. Ninety-four people are arrested after protests against a visit by the Greek king and queen.

Westminster, 22 July. An independent commission into slum housing is announced.

Moscow, 8 August. A treaty is signed banning nuclear tests in the atmosphere (→ 17/6/80).

London, 26 September. A report on the Profumo scandal by top judge Lord Denning says security had not been endangered but criticizes how ministers handled the affair. →

Scarborough, 3 October. Harold Wilson commits Labour to a new scientific revolution.

Westminster, 10 October. Harold Macmillan announces his resignation as prime minister because of illness (→ 18).

Westminster, 20 October. Iain Macleod and Enoch Powell refuse to serve in the cabinet under Lord Home (→ 8/11).

Kinross, 8 November. Sir Alec Douglas-Home, having renounced his earldom, wins a by-election in order to join the House of Commons (→ 16/10/64).

London, 6 December. Christine Keeler is jailed for perjury and conspiracy to pervert the course of justice.

Wilson elected as new Labour leader

Westminster, 14 February

Harold Wilson has today emerged the victor in a bruising battle for the leadership of the Labour Party following the death of Hugh Gaitskell. After James Callaghan was eliminated from the contest in a preliminary vote, the choice was between the wily Wilson and the temperamental George Brown, who was the deputy leader of the party under Mr Gaitskell. After much infighting Wilson eventually won comfortably with 144 votes against 103. Aged 46, he is the youngest leader in the history of the Labour Party. "My mandate", he says, "is to lead the party to victory in the coming election and that is what I intend to do" (→ 10/10).

Harold Wilson is Labour's choice.

Politicians upset by lampooning 'TW3'

Britain, 19 January

Public houses will empty earlier than usual tonight, conversation will stop in millions of homes. The reason? A late-night, live television show called *That Was The Week That Was*. Its brand of irreverent humour has upset politicians and troubled the BBC governors but also attracted audiences of up to 12 million since it began last month. Religion, royalty, politics and sex were previously taboo in comedy shows on TV, but they are staple ingredients of "TW3", which is fronted by David Frost (→ 17/1/64). ▷

War minister quits after sex and spy revelations

Profumo, dressed for state pomp.

London, 5 June
John Profumo, the secretary of state for war, resigned from office today, confirming one detail of a long-simmering scandal involving sex, high society and national security. He admitted "with deep remorse" that ten weeks ago he lied to the Commons in saying that there had been "no impropriety whatever" in his relationship with attractive young "model" Christine Keeler, at the time a missing witness in an Old Bailey trial.

For months there have been hints, like this version of "She Was Poor But She Was Honest" on the satirical TV show TW3: "See him in the House of Commons/Making laws to put the blame/While the object of his passion/Walks the street to hide her shame."

The scandal now rocking Mr Macmillan's government first emerged when a West End osteopath and artist, Stephen Ward, facing charges of living off immoral earnings, claimed that Profumo had used his flat to meet Keeler. Ward had a country cottage on Lord Astor's Cliveden estate and it was there, Ward claimed, that Profumo first saw 21-year-old Keeler naked in the swimming pool.

But the scandal does not just involve sex and high society – after Profumo's first statement he and and his wife, the actress Valerie Hobson, went to the races with the Queen Mother – spying is said to be involved, too. Another of Keeler's lovers is the Soviet naval attaché Captain Eugene Ivanov and there are rumours that Ward is in the pay of MI5.

To spice this brew still further another of Keeler's lovers recently attempted to shoot her, and her flatmate is Ward's mistress, an 18-year-old blonde model Mandy Rice Davies, who was previously mistress to the notorious slum landlord Peter Rachman.

Mr Macmillan has written to Profumo saying: "This is a great tragedy for you." He hopes the confession and resignation will end the matter. It seems unlikely (→3/8).

Keeler, undressed for the camera.

Ward takes fatal overdose after vice trial

London, 3 August
Dr Stephen Ward, the artist and osteopath at the centre of the high-society sex scandal, is dead. He had been in a coma for three days after overdosing on sleeping pills on the final day of his trial.

While unconscious he was found guilty of living off immoral earnings, a charge he firmly denied. He claimed he was a victim of a campaign of vilification and that the authorities were determined to destroy him for his part in the Profumo affair.

The trial revealed a twilight world where the rich and famous consort with drug addicts, callgirls like Christine Keeler and others of dubious morality. Members of the public queued for hours to hear details of orgies, two-way mirrors and black magic rituals.

Ward, the son of a vicar, admitted to being a connoisseur of love-making and a "thoroughly immoral man" but strenuously denied he had ever taken money for prostitution. However, in his hour of need, high society deserted him (→26/9).

Ward, deserted by his high-society friends, hemmed in by officials.

Sex scandal investigated by Lord Denning

Mandy Rice-Davies leaves the Old Bailey after giving evidence.

London, 26 September
It must have been the first time ever that hundreds of people scrabbled for copies of a government report when it went on sale at midnight. But this was the Denning report on the Profumo affair and there was always hope of fresh revelations. Who, for example, was the eminent figure who served at dinner parties naked except for a mask?

Sensation-seekers, however, had to content themselves with learning that Harold Macmillan and his ministers were condemned for failing to deal with the affair even when it was affecting public confidence, but that security was not endangered. The man in the mask was interviewed but Denning declared he was not a minister.

Fall-out from the affair continues. Police are investigating the confessions of two prostitutes, Vicky Barrett and Ronna Ricardo, that they lied when giving evidence against Stephen Ward; evidence of perjury has also emerged in the trial of "Lucky" Gordon, Christine Keeler's boyfriend (→6/12).

Train robbers steal more than a million

Buckinghamshire, 8 August

A gang of highly organized thieves netted the biggest haul ever taken in a British robbery today when they stopped a Royal Mail train and stole 120 mailbags holding well over £1 million worth of banknotes. At least 15 men, armed and masked, carried out what has been dubbed the Great Train Robbery, but police suspect that so carefully planned a crime must have had inside help. No firearms were used but the driver, Jack Mills, aged 58, was severely beaten during the raid, which depended on split-second timing (→ 27/3/64).

Driver Jack Mills was clubbed.

Complete outsider becomes new Tory PM

Westminster, 18 October

The unlikely figure of the 14th Earl of Home is to be Britain's next prime minister. His name emerged from the mysterious Tory process of "consultation" following the resignation of the ailing, dispirited Harold Macmillan during the party conference at Blackpool last week. Lord Home, a cricket-loving Old Etonian, will renounce his title in order to sit in the Commons.

Behind the smooth announcement that he has been appointed by the queen on the advice of Mr Macmillan and after consulting Sir Winston Churchill and other elder statesmen, lies a tale of intrigue and skulduggery. It was expected that "Rab" Butler, the deputy premier, would get the job but Macmillan, an old foe of the urbane Butler, plotted from his hospital bed to have him excluded.

Lord Hailsham and Reginald

Home: like a rabbit from a hat.

Maudling were also found wanting by the Tory "magic circle" and Macmillan produced Alec Douglas Home, as he will be called, like a rabbit from a hat (→ 20).

Nuffield, the creator of Morris cars, dies

London, 22 August

Lord Nuffield, the farmer's son who became to Britain what Henry Ford was to America, has died at the age of 84. His was a remarkable success story. Born William Morris, he worked in a cycle repair shop in Oxford, set up his own business and then turned to making cycles. He progressed to motorcycles and, in 1912, produced his first car. He saw the potential of the family car and made a fortune from classics like the Morris Oxford. His MG sports cars enjoyed worldwide acclaim.

In later life he developed a second career, giving away the £27 million he had accumulated in the first. His greatest gift was the Nuffield Foundation (→ 24/11/65).

Rail branch lines axed by Beeching

London, 27 March

The nation's rail network is to be savagely pruned under proposals contained in *The Reshaping of British Railways*, by Dr Beeching, who was brought in as chairman of the British Railways Board to increase efficiency. The proposed cuts are certain to raise fierce opposition. They will slash the rail network by a quarter, close 2,128 stations, scrap 8,000 coaches and axe 67,700 jobs. There will be no passenger services north of Inverness and most branch lines in north and central Wales and the West Country will close (→ 16/2/65).

Report urges spread of higher education

Westminster, 23 October

A massive expansion of higher education is called for in a report published today by a government-appointed committee under Lord Robbins. The report says that higher education should be available to all those qualified to benefit from it. It proposes six new universities – in addition to the four approved two years ago – and the expansion of existing universities, plus university status for ten colleges of advanced technology (→ 1/1965).

Bishop of Woolwich causes unholy row

London, 31 December

The press, secular and religious alike, has been unusually riven with arguments about the nature of God ever since the Bishop of Woolwich, Dr John Robinson, published a slim paperback entitled *Honest to God* earlier this year. In it he says the traditional ways of conceiving of God, as "up there" above the clouds and later "out there" beyond the universe, like a mental vision of an Old Man in the Sky, are nowadays obstacles to faith. God as "a sort of celestial Big Brother" must give way to God as "ultimate reality" and the ground of all being. But as to how this is to be imagined, the bishop remains obscure.

Screaming pop fans go wild as 'Beatlemania' sweeps Britain

London, 4 November

The indisputable stars of the Royal Variety Show tonight were four young men from Liverpool. "Rattle your jewels," said John Lennon as the Beatles rocked their way to another triumph. Their first record made only a modest impact last year, but this year has seen a string of number ones such as *She Loves You* and *I Wanna Hold Your Hand*.

Most of their songs are composed by two members of the group, John Lennon and Paul McCartney – but the music can rarely be heard above the screams of fans in the grip of "Beatlemania". Roads and airports have been blocked by fans clamouring to see the "Fab Four", who next year plan to take their music to America (→ 8/2/64).

The "Fab Four" celebrate the news that "She Loves You" has sold a million.

'Third Man' named in spy controversy

London, 1 July

The government admitted today in a House of Commons statement that "Kim" Philby, the former foreign office colleague of the traitors Burgess and Maclean, was, after all, the "Third Man". It was he who tipped off Maclean, through Burgess, that he had been discovered. Both then fled to the Soviet Union.

Philby was named by Labour MP Marcus Lipton in 1955 but he was cleared by Harold Macmillan, then foreign secretary. Philby was forced to resign from the Foreign Office in 1951 and became a foreign correspondent in Beirut. He vanished in January and is now assumed to be in Moscow (→ 22/4/64).

Philby: Moscow's secret servant.

Curtain goes up on 'National' actors

London, 22 October

The National Theatre Company's first performance took place tonight at its temporary home, the Old Vic. Laurence Olivier directed *Hamlet* with Peter O'Toole in the title role leading a company mainly of young actors who have yet to make their names. It is nearly 60 years since the first practical proposals for a national theatre: after many false starts an architect, Denys Lasdun, has been appointed and a site – the fifth – has been chosen, on the South Bank. Parliament in 1949 voted £1 million to build the theatre.

1964

London, 13 January. Designer Mary Quant says Paris fashions are out of date (→ 12/1964).

Britain, 17 January. The top TV programme is *Steptoe and Son* (→ 21/4).

London, 6 February. Britain and France agree to build a Channel tunnel (→ 20/1/75).

New York, 8 February. The Beatles arrive at the start of their first US tour (→ 30/6/67).

Ireland, 20 March. Playwright Brendan Behan dies.

Aylesbury, 27 March. Ten men are convicted for their part in last year's Great Train Robbery.

Britain, 28 March. Radio Caroline begins pop music transmissions from a ship in the North Sea.

London, 31 March. Single service ministries are abolished and become part of the ministry of defence.

London, 9 April. Labour wins the first elections for the new Greater London Council.

Britain, 21 April. BBC-2 goes on the air; *Play School* is its first programme (→ 8/2/65).

Berlin, 22 April. Greville Wynne is freed by the Russians in a spy swap deal for Gordon Lonsdale (→ 23/7/65).

Co Down, 2 July. The Ulster Folk Museum opens at Cultra.

Westminster, 28 July. Winston Churchill leaves the House of Commons for the last time (→ 24/1/65).

Britain, 29 July. The first clinic offering family planning advice to unmarried women opens (→ 12/1967).

London, 21 August. Three women are found guilty of indecency for wearing "topless" dresses.

South-east Asia, 3 September. Britain agrees to back Malaysian forces against Indonesian aggression.

Britain, 15 September. The *Daily Herald* ceases publication, to be replaced by *The Sun*.

Belfast, 28 October. Rioting begins in Catholic areas after a republican flag is removed by the police (→ 9/2/65).

London, 27 October. Harold Wilson warns Southern Rhodesia against a unilateral declaration of independence (→ 11/11/65).

Mods and Rockers run riot on South Coast

Mods charge across Margate sands in pursuit of the retreating Rockers.

Margate, 18 May

Rival gangs of teenage Mods and Rockers clashed again this weekend at a number of South Coast resorts. Members of the teen cults fought, terrorized holidaymakers and ran riot in an orgy of vandalism that brought chaos and violence to the Whitsun break.

Fights broke out in Southend, Bournemouth and Clacton, but the resorts worst hit were Brighton, where police dispersed a mob of 600 youths and arrested 76, and Margate, where two teenagers were stabbed and 51 arrests were made.

Jailing four of the rioters, and imposing fines that totalled £1,900, the magistrate echoed the views of many when he dismissed the brawlers as "little sawdust Caesars". One paid his fine by cheque, a gesture that seemed to sum up what many see as a culture that gives its youngsters too much money and too little responsibility.

Mods – sharp-suited, scooter-riding, and consumers of "purple hearts", that is, amphetamines – and Rockers – who prefer leather jackets, motorcycles and alcohol – have hit the headlines this summer with a series of beachfront battles. This weekend has seen the worst violence yet, and Home Secretary Henry Brooke has promised action.

Press baron Beaverbrook dies, aged 85

Beaverbrook (l): newspaper tycoon.

London, 9 June

Lord Beaverbrook, the Canadian-born press baron, died of cancer today. He was 85. A bishop's son, he made his first fortune with deals which owed more to buccaneering zeal than evangelical spirit. He arrived in London like a whirlwind, throwing himself into politics and using his *Express* newspapers to "cause trouble".

He knew he was dying and met death with customary bravery. Two weeks ago he made a supreme effort to attend his birthday party at the Dorchester. He moved his friends to tears when he said he would soon become an apprentice again, whether in heaven or hell he did not know.

Labour back in power

Westminster, 16 October

The Labour Party has won the general election – but by the thinnest of margins. Labour has 317 seats, the Tories 303, the Liberals 9. Counting the Speaker's seat this gives the new prime minister, Harold Wilson, an overall majority of only 4. It was uncertain until the last votes were counted late this afternoon which party would emerge the victor.

But Wilson is delighted. "Nice place we've got here," he said as he stepped inside 10 Downing Street. He led his party to victory with the promise of "purposive planning" and benefited from his pipe-puffing wisdom, which came over well on the new electoral weapon of television. His rival's cadaverous features showed up to poor advantage and he could not rid himself of the tag of "14th earl of Home" despite his neat retaliatory crack that his opponent was presumably the 14th Mr Wilson.

What remains to be seen now is whether Wilson, with such a small majority, can run the country in the face of hostile opposition in the House of Commons (→ 22/7/65).

Harold Wilson and George Brown had high hopes despite a slim majority.

Doors close at the 'Ever-open' Theatre

London 31 October 1964

The permissive society, as it is being called, has made the once-naughty Windmill Theatre redundant. The home of stage nudity since before the Second World War, its proud boast throughout the wartime air raids was "We Never Closed". Now its nude tableaux are not titillating enough to save it.

The Windmill's great days were immediately after the war when a new wave of comedians, including Peter Sellers and Tony Hancock, appeared between the nude scenes attempting to distract the patrons from the Windmill girls.

Capital punishment is to be abolished

Westminster, 21 December

In a free vote today the House of Commons abolished the death penalty for murder by the overwhelming majority of 355 to 170. This does not mean there will never be another hanging in Britain, for the effect of the measure will be reviewed in five years' time and there are certain offences, such as treachery, for which death remains the penalty. The House of Lords also has to give its decision on the bill, but such is the anti-hanging feeling in the Commons that it is unlikely the trap will ever be sprung on another murderer (→ 18/12/69).

Vocal younger generation cuts loose to forge a fashionable, swinging Britain

Britain, December

Whether it is a reaction to the austerity of the years after the Second World War, the growth of the baby boom generation, or the flowering of Mr Macmillan's "never had it so good" society, today the keyword is youth. And Britain, often seen as a backwater in the face of the ever-faster spread of American culture, is setting the pace.

Traditionalists may (and do) decry what they see as an increasingly permissive society, but it is the young, whose spending power has made them an unprecedentedly important force in the market place, who are calling all the cultural and social shots.

Britain's new standards can be seen in every walk of life. In the world of rock music the fabulously successful Beatles have exported their own brand of charm to the United States, where it has taken the country by storm and paved the way for what Americans are already calling the "British invasion". In fashion, where Mary Quant's designs have made every smart young (and not so young) woman into a "swinging dollybird", Britain is setting the rules.

Carnaby Street, for many people as much a concept of trendy living as a sidestreet in London's West End, is equally popular among the boys, with designers like John Stephen showing that staid old Savile Row has no monopoly on fashionable tailoring. The new develop-

Mary Quant, with the architect, Alexander Plunket Greene.

ments represent an end to the drabness of the Fifties. The old conformity has been replaced by a new way of life, dictated not by the old establishment, but by a more vocal, energetic and creative young.

Pop culture is the new thing. The outrageous styles which are on display in the boutiques, the pacy lyrics of the new rock songs, the irreverent pirate radio stations, the discotheques filled with what the press are calling a "new aristocracy" of pop stars, model girls, photographers and other young and chic professionals, lively shops such as Habitat, providing a shortcut to the latest lifestyles – everything is combining to promote a new, "swinging" Britain.

Dancing to "Sounds Incorporated" on the TV show "Ready Steady Go".

Historic Irish meetings

The first meeting between the Irish prime ministers of the north and south.

Dublin, 9 February

In the second of two historic meetings between the prime ministers of Northern Ireland and the Irish Republic, Sean Lemass here met Captain Terence O'Neill to continue discussions begun last month when he paid a visit to Stormont Castle.

Lemass's motives, in responding to O'Neill's cross-border initiative, are essentially economic. Setting aside completely the united Ireland objectives of his predecessor, he is seeking to achieve modest coopera-

tion in trade, energy and tourism. Captain O'Neill, although more cautious in his view of the political wisdom of meeting his opposite number in the south, has continued with the talks in the belief that a new and more liberal climate must develop between north and south. But he faces a hardline attitude from northern Unionists and is unlikely to win the support of the Catholic minority who believe themselves to be victims of sectarian discrimination (→16/11).

Labour backs one education for all

Westminster, January

The 11-plus exam is to end. Tony Crosland, the education secretary, this month asked local authorities to produce plans for "comprehensive" secondary schools to cater for pupils of all abilities.

Labour has long campaigned for an end to the 11-plus exam, which allocates children to grammar or secondary modern schools. One in ten pupils in England and Wales attend comprehensive schools already, but the government wants the schools to cater for a majority of pupils within a decade. Several forms of comprehensives are being mooted, but none will appease Tory critics who want to preserve the grammar schools (→10/9/66).

TV curbs smoking

London, 8 February

Cigarette advertising is to vanish from the television screen, health minister Kenneth Robinson announced today. Although critics call the ban illogical – press and billboard advertising are to continue as usual – the government has singled out television as especially effective in targetting the young and vulnerable (→30/7).

World bids a sad farewell to Winston Churchill with state funeral

Churchill's coffin is taken by barge on his last journey along the Thames.

Oxfordshire, 30 January

Sir Winston Churchill, who died six days ago at the age of 90, has been laid to rest in a village churchyard near his family's home at Blenheim Palace. Today's modest graveside ceremony stood in stark contrast to the last few days of national mourning on the grand scale, led by Queen Elizabeth II.

Hundreds of thousands of people filed past Sir Winston's coffin over the three days that he lay in state in Westminster Hall, whilst representatives of 110 nations attended the state funeral service in St Paul's Cathedral, London. Some 350 million people in Europe alone watched on television. Tributes have meanwhile poured in from around the world to the man whom the Pope, for one, has called the "indefatigable champion of freedom".

Edward Heath elected as new Tory leader

London, 27 July

The Tory Party today elected Edward Heath as its new leader in place of Sir Alec Douglas-Home. Heath owes much to his predecessor – for Sir Alec, appalled at the plotting that led to his own "emergence" as leader, instituted the system by which Heath was elected.

Heath received 150 votes against 133 for the favourite, Reginald Maudling, and 15 for Enoch Powell. At 49 years, he is the youngest Tory leader for a century. A grammar school boy, he represents a shift to the middle class in the leadership of the Tory Party, which has for so long been an aristocratic prerogative (→31/3/66).

Mr Heath collects a bouquet.

Child murder on the Moors shocks nation as crimes of violence soar to new levels

Cheshire, 28 October

Two people have been charged with the murder of Lesley Ann Downey, a ten-year-old girl whose body was found on Saddleworth Moor 13 days ago. Angry crowds tried to attack the cars carrying Ian Brady, aged 27, and Myra Hindley, aged 23, as they left court after the hearing today. A police search continues for other bodies on the moors. The "moors murder" is a case that has shocked the nation.

It is part of an upward spiral of violence in Britain over the last ten years. Until the mid-1950s violent crime increased by around six per cent a year; since then, the rate of increase has been 11 per cent. The number of offences of violence has rocketed from 5,869 in 1955 to 15,976 last year. And the percentage increases among young people between the ages of 14 and 21 has been proportionately greater than in the population as a whole.

"Law and order" is becoming a more prominent political issue. By a piquant irony, the Murder Bill to abolish the death penalty for a trial period of five years completed its final parliamentary stages today. Its measures are expected to become law next month (→6/5/66).

Last African colony rebels against Britain

Rhodesia, 11 November

Rhodesia, Britain's last colony in Africa, is on a war footing tonight after Ian Smith, the prime minister, issued a long-expected unilateral declaration of independence.

Echoing the 18th-century American Declaration he said: "It may become necessary for a people to assume .... the separate and equal status to which they are entitled ..." But in this case the "people" are not the four million Africans in the colony but the 220,000 whites.

Smith has been threatening UDI since last year but it became inevitable after the May election when there was a 30 per cent swing in favour of the "cowboy" Rhodesian Front party, committed to keeping power in white hands in order to maintain "civilized standards".

Mr Smith has assumed wide powers to impose rationing and censorship and has sacked the governor, Sir Humphrey Gibbs. Britain has cut all ties with the rebel regime and promises to impose sanctions but is in a dilemma. Commonwealth countries are calling for decisive action to crush the rebel regime but a majority of the British might well oppose such measures against their "kith and kin" (→16).

Volunteers help with the search for more bodies on Saddleworth Moor.

The Beatles received MBE's from the Queen for their services to music. Unknown to her they smoked cannabis in the Buckingham Palace loo.

First Irish premier, 'WT', dies aged 89

Ireland, 16 November

Ireland's first prime minister, William Thomas Cosgrave, has died. Born in Dublin in 1880, he fought in the 1916 rebellion and was later imprisoned.

He supported the 1921 treaty, was minister for local government in the first Dail and president of the second Dail. After the deaths of Arthur Griffith and Michael Collins, he was effectively head of the government and led each administration until Fianna Fail came to power in 1932. A conservative and hardline leader, he never again achieved power. He retired from politics in 1944 (→14/12).

Housewife launches a 'clean-up' of TV

Birmingham, 29 November

Mrs Mary Whitehouse, whose "Clean Up TV" campaign has been combating what she sees as immorality on television for the past 18 months, launched a new pressure group today. The National Viewers' and Listeners' Association is to pursue identical aims to CUTV, targeting what Mrs Whitehouse calls the "bad taste and irresponsibility" of the BBC. The corporation dismisses her as at best a self-appointed censor, and at worst a crank, but Mrs Whitehouse says she has 500,000 supporters, dedicated to fighting the evils of today's "permissive society" (→3/7/67).

England surge to dramatic World Cup win

Hurst leaps above the goalkeeper on his way to a World Cup hat trick.

Wembley, 30 July
England won football's World Cup in a pulsating match at Wembley stadium today. The nation where football began has thus won the sport's supreme international competition for the first time.

Sixteen nations competed in the finals, which were staged in England for the first time. Matches were held in several parts of the country before today's Wembley final. It was Portugal whom England had to overcome to reach the final – and they did so in a classic encounter starring two of the tournament's top stars, Bobby Charlton and Eusebio. West Germany were the other finalists, having beaten the Soviet Union in the second semi-final.

The Germans took an early lead in today's final, but goals from the West Ham pair, Geoff Hurst and Martin Peters, put England into a lead that they held until the dying seconds. Then a West German equalizer took the game into extra time – and controversy. A shot by Hurst bounced down from the bar just behind the line, according to the linesman but not the Germans. However, a third goal by Hurst dispelled the doubts to seal England's triumph, 4-2. Even the laconic manager, Alf Ramsey, smiled.

Church heads meet after 400-year rift

Rome, 23 March
The heads of the Roman Catholic and Anglican communions today met officially for the first time in 400 years. Pope Paul VI received Dr Michael Ramsey, the Archbishop of Canterbury, with the "kiss of peace" in the Sistine Chapel and talked of "a bridge of respect, of esteem and of charity" being rebuilt between the two confessions. During his visit Ramsey will discuss various issues that still divide Canterbury and Rome in the hope of moving towards greater unity. But opponents are never far away: three British ministers here have dubbed Dr Ramsey "a traitor to Protestant Britain".

Archbishop meets pope in Rome.

Economic troubles hit the newly elected Labour government

Wilson playing street football; some critics see his policies as an own goal.

London, 20 July
The worsening economic situation has forced the government to impose a freeze on pay and dividends. It will last for six months and be followed by another six months of severe restraint. Announcing these and other crisis measures today, Harold Wilson said that "the time has come to call a halt" to runaway inflation.

While the prime minister's actions may make economic sense, they have created political turmoil. The cabinet is split and the unions furious. George Brown is threatening to join Frank Cousins, the former transport workers' leader, in resigning. Cousins was formerly the minister of technology (→ 19/11/67).

Coal tip buries Welsh schoolchildren

Jack Lynch, former footballer, is voted new Irish premier

Aberfan, 27 October

Aberfan, the Welsh mining village that has lost a whole generation of children in a disaster that has appalled the world, today began the task of burying its dead. The funeral was held of 82 of the 116 children and 28 adults who died on 21 October when the massive, waterlogged coal tip that for decades had hung precariously above the village engulfed the local school, leaving a trail of destruction in its wake.

A ten-year-old survivor recalled the scene: "We heard a noise and saw all the stuff flying about. The desks were falling about and the children were shouting and screaming. We couldn't see anything." No-one yet knows exactly why the tip collapsed – the best guess is that an underground spring loosened the piles of waste, creating what Lord Robens, the Coal Board chairman, called "a water bomb" – but around midmorning the huge pile began its fatal slide towards the school. Tens of thousands of tons of slurry, which had collected over

The Aberfan school was directly in line with the avalanche of slurry.

years of mining, rolled over the school, demolishing it in a matter of seconds. A high-level inquiry into the incident has been ordered.

Hundreds of rescuers, many of them parents, fought to uncover the victims. The headmistress was among the lucky survivors; the deputy head was found dead, the bodies of five children in his arms. As prime minister Harold Wilson, who visited the site, put it, "I don't think any of us can find words to describe this tragedy."

Dublin, 9 Nov

Sean Lemass, the Irish prime minister, has resigned as the leader of the Fianna Fail party and has been succeeded in the post by his minister for finance, Jack Lynch. Born in Cork and a former footballer, the softly-spoken Lynch was not considered to be a likely candidate for prime minister. But he emerged as a practical compromise choice between the two more aggressive candidates, Charles Haughey and George Colley.

The personalities and political styles of the three men are very different but their policies are firmly those of their erstwhile leader, Sean Lemass. Lynch is expected to be a quietist leader, with no strong views on policy. This was epitomised in his winning style – an outsider quietly romping home on the rails (→ 6/2/67).

Moors Murderers are to be jailed for life

First Nationalist MP is elected in Wales

Westminster, 21 July

Gwynfor Evans, the first Welsh Nationalist member of the House of Commons, took his seat today as victor in the by-election at Carmarthen. There was a nice bit of by-play when he was sworn in. He had been expected to refuse to take the oath in English but did so without demur. However, he then asked if he could repeat the ceremony in Welsh. Mr Speaker refused. Why not? asked Evans. Because other people would not know what you were saying, said Mr Speaker.

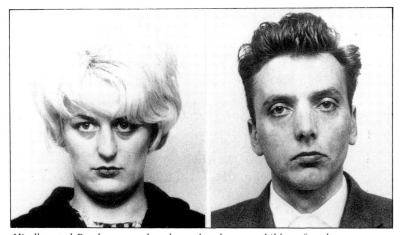

Hindley and Brady tortured and murdered young children for pleasure.

Jack Lynch takes over as premier.

Chester, 6 May

A man and a woman were sentenced to life imprisonment today for the torture and murder of two children and a teenage boy. The all-male jury was visibly harrowed by a recording of the torments one of the victims was subjected to before she was killed.

Known as the Moors Murderers because the bodies were buried on the Pennine moors, the killers –

Myra Hindley, aged 24, and Ian Brady, aged 28 – were found out when Hindley's brother-in-law called the police after he saw Edward Evans, aged 17, killed with an axe.

Nude photographs of the victims and tape-recordings of the killings were traced through a left-luggage ticket found in Hindley's prayer-book. The two other victims were Lesley Ann Downey, aged ten, and John Kilbride, aged 12.

Biggest gas field discovered in North Sea

London, 2 June

Philips Petroleum today claimed to have "struck it rich" in the North Sea, drilling into a huge gas field off the mouth of the Humber. A test well is showing a gas flow of up to 480,000 cubic metres (17 million cubic feet) a day, which is 3.5 per cent of Britain's daily gas needs.

This discovery, taken in conjunction with a Shell/Esso announcement last month of a "significant" find in a nearby area means that this region is as rich in gas as the BP field further north. If trade expectations are fulfilled all Britain's gas will one day be provided from the North Sea (→ 20/6/69).

1967

Leaking oil tanker bombed to save coast

Land's End, 30 March
Fighter aircraft blasted the wreck of the oil tanker *Torrey Canyon* again today in a final attempt to burn off the oil that has fouled 100 miles of coastline in what has been described as "the greatest peace-time threat to Britain". Fighters have dropped 48 incendiary bombs and some 5,500 litres (1,200 gallons) of napalm on the remains of the 61,000-tonne tanker, which was wrecked on the Seven Stones Reef between Land's End and the Scilly Isles, carrying 100,000 tonnes of oil. Tomorrow divers will check that no oil remains on board.

The prime minister, Harold Wilson, held a mini-cabinet meeting to deal with this threat to the West Country tourist industry.

The broken wreck has been bombed.

Scotland's Celtic clinch European Cup win

Lisbon, 25 May
Scottish pride was triumphantly reasserted tonight when Glasgow Celtic became the first football team from the British Isles to win the European Champions' Cup. So Scotland, smarting from the English triumph at last year's World Cup, has won the supreme soccer competition between the league champions of all the major European countries.

On a sweltering night in the Portuguese capital, Celtic were soon one goal adrift in their final against Internazionale of Milan. The Scots conceded an early penalty and were faced with a struggle against a team renowned for one of the strongest defences in Europe. However, with nearly 60 minutes gone, Tommy Gemmell equalized and the Scots pressed home their attacks against a team that could no longer rely solely on defence.

With eight minutes to go, Celtic's non-stop attack finally found a hole in Inter's defence with Steve Chalmers claiming what turned out to be the winning goal. Celtic's captain Billy McNeill hoisted the huge trophy and Lisbon tonight belongs to Jock Stein's green-and-white army of fans.

Wilson snubbed by de Gaulle over EEC

Paris, 16 May
President de Gaulle of France told members of the press today that there are "formidable obstacles" to Britain's application to join the European Economic Community (EEC). France will say "oui" only when the British prove that they have begun to think like good Europeans. Apparently it would also help if the "special relationship" between England and the US ceased. The prime minister, Harold Wilson, has put a brave face on this. He told MPs that the application will be vigorously pursued. After all, his government secured a huge majority in favour of this move: 488 votes for and only 62 against.

'Sergeant Pepper' is success for Beatles

Liverpool, 30 June
The Cavern, where the Beatles first honed their musical skills, may have become a shrine for their fans, but the simple rock tunes of those years are another world compared to the virtuosity of the group's latest LP, *Sergeant Pepper's Lonely Hearts' Club Band*. The album incorporates a range of styles and influences – from vaudeville to drugs – to produce a revolutionary thematic LP that has been widely praised by critics. The group gave up touring last year (→ 1/1968).

Campbell dies attempting to break world water speed record

Donald Campbell: "She's going!"

Coniston, 4 January
Donald Campbell's brave attempt to break the world water speed record has ended in tragedy. His craft, the jet-powered *Bluebird*, somersaulted and disintegrated today on Coniston Water as Campbell chased his own record of 276.33 mph (444.71 kph). His last words on the radio link were: "She's going – she's going. I'm almost on my back." He was within a fraction of a second of achieving his goal. Frogmen have recovered Campbell's helmet, shoes, oxygen mask and teddy bear mascot, but there is no sign of the body. The search has now been called off.

"Bluebird" plunges into the water.

The pound is devalued

Westminster, 19 November
The government, facing economic disaster with labour troubles, a massive foreign trade deficit and a heavy run on sterling, has been forced to devalue the pound. It goes down from 2.80 dollars to 2.40, a fall of 14.3 per cent. This move is a blow for James Callaghan, the chancellor, who said that devaluation was "a flight into escapism".

The prime minister, on the other hand, seems positively chirpy. In a television address he presented devaluation and the tightening of the credit squeeze as the key to economic expansion. The move does not mean, he said, "that the pound here in Britain in your pocket or purse or in your bank has been devalued".

James Callaghan, the chancellor.

Flower power blooms among the hippies

London, 31 December
It has been the year of "flower power". It has bloomed at hippy festivals, such as that at Woburn in August, and has its own language, fashions and lifestyles. Drugs are part of this world, and icons, including some members of the Rolling Stones, have fallen foul of the law. If the rest of the world finds the drugs, the music and the notion of "love" as a cure for the world's ills somewhat hard to take, then the "hippies" who preach this new gospel are equally convinced that they are right. The hippie revolution springs from the USA. Now it is here too, fuelled by the psychedelic hallucinogen LSD and serenaded by rock music. The generation gap has never been wider (→27/9/68).

Rolling Stones Mick Jagger (l) and Keith Richards: drugs charges.

Abortion and sex laws made more liberal

Britain, December
The more liberal and permissive attitudes to sexual behaviour that have characterized the 1960s have culminated in three significant new acts of Parliament becoming law this year.

The first was the Abortion Act, piloted through Parliament by a young Liberal MP, David Steel, but backed by the government and many Conservatives. This allows women to have abortions if two doctors confirm that this is necessary on medical or psychological grounds. The National Health Service (Family Planning) Act, which

allows local authorities to provide contraceptives and contraceptive advice, was the second. Birth control clinics now anticipate that increasing numbers of women will choose the contraceptive "pill", which is becoming more widely available.

The third was the Sexual Offences Act, which (in England and Wales) allows homosexual acts to take place between two consenting adults in private. Previously, these had been criminal acts. However, the age of consent for homosexuals is to be 21, not the 16 allowed for heterosexual intercourse (→1/4/74).

Hippy pop festivals have a fair share of fights and drugs among the love.

As traffic increases so does the need for extra road safety. The breathalyser is the latest attack on drunks behind the wheel.

Scots join the bandwagon of nationalism

Scotland, 2 November
Scotland, officially part of the United Kingdom since the 1707 Act of Union, showed that lust for independence never dies, even after nearly three centuries, when the Scottish Nationalist Party (SNP)

today won its first seat in Westminster since 1945. In the by-election at Hamilton, Winifred Ewing took the seat for the SNP, which was formed in 1934 with the aim of separating Scotland from the UK and establishing a national assembly.

British troops leave Aden after 128 years

Aden, 30 November
Exultant Arabs celebrated in the streets of the port city of Aden today as the last British troops left for home. Few will regret leaving a posting that for the last year has become increasingly hostile. It was

the final chapter in a 128-year-old story, which started when in 1839 the British East India Company seized the port to protect its routes to the East and has ended with the creation of the People's Republic of South Yemen.

Goodbye to steam, but hello Concord

Toulouse, 11 December
In the year that Britain bade farewell to its last steam-hauled mainline passenger trains, the nation has taken a significant step towards a new era of air travel. The first prototype of the world's first faster-than-sound passenger airline was rolled out of its hangar today at Toulouse in France. The Concord (or Concorde to the French) is a triumph of international collaboration as well as aviation technology; it is being developed jointly by aircraft manufacturers in France and Britain (→9/4/69).

1968

Powell speech stirs row over immigration

London, 6 May

Enoch Powell's views on the danger of Britain being flooded by immigrants won support today from a Gallup poll which showed that 74 per cent of the population is broadly sympathetic to his argument that Britain must be "mad, literally mad as a nation" to allow 50,000 dependants of immigrants into the country each year.

Powell was sacked from his position as Tory shadow defence minister by the Opposition leader, Edward Heath, last week following an apocalyptic speech in Birmingham in which Powell said: "As I look ahead I am filled with foreboding. Like the Roman, I seem to see the River Tiber foaming with much blood."

The classical allusion may have made Powell's warning excessively dramatic but he insists he chose his words carefully and denies he is being irresponsible or seeking to incite racial prejudice. The speech took other senior Tories by surprise, although a number of them share his views, and reaction to it was immediate, triggering a fierce controversy over race relations that is still raging some time later.

Powell has been condemned as a racist, both by liberals and representatives of the immigrant communities, but there have been marches and demonstrations in his support and politicians of all parties are uneasily aware that he reflects the fears of very many people (→ 26/11).

Smithfield porters show support.

Enoch Powell: rivers of blood.

George Brown quits the foreign office

Westminster, 15 March

George Brown, the tempestuous deputy leader of the Labour Party, today carried out what he has often threatened – he quit the government. He departed blaming Harold Wilson for running a dictatorial administration, although most of his former colleagues think the prime minister has shown great patience. Brown, who lost a leadership contest to Wilson in 1963, was initially the minister for economic affairs before becoming foreign secretary. A man of undoubted energy and originality, his fiery personality and sometimes erratic behaviour have led to his departure (→ 18/5/70).

Twice world motor racing champ dies

West Germany, 7 April

Champion racing driver Jim Clark was killed instantly in a horrifying crash on the Hockenheim circuit today when he lost control of his Lotus on a fast straight and slammed into trees at 125 mph. Clark, son of a farmer from the Scottish border country, won the Formula One championship twice and was leading this year's championship. He won a remarkable 25 races in only seven seasons and was regarded by his fellow drivers as the best of his generation.

Three die as London tower block collapses

Ronan Point after the collapse.

London, 16 May

One of London's newest tower blocks, the 22-storey Ronan Point, in Newham, east London, collapsed today, killing three residents. The immediate cause of the disaster was a gas explosion in a flat built on the corner of the 18th floor, but poor building work coupled with essential design faults in the fast-track "system building" design – used in many of London's modern towers – meant that every single flat on the corner crumbled. It was as if a house of cards had been dislodged. A full-scale inquiry has been ordered and the Greater London Council is considering banning any further "system-built" blocks.

The wreckage of Jim Clark's car.

Police break up Ulster civil rights march

Derry, 6 October
Rioting broke out in the Catholic Bogside area of Londonderry overnight after police dispersed a banned march staged by the Northern Ireland Civil Rights Association. The Unionist government objected to the provocative route, from a Protestant area into the walled city, and when police baton-charged the marchers, Gerry Fitt, the Westminster MP for West Belfast, was one of 88 people injured.

Only about 400 attended the march, which was mainly to protest against the Unionist city council's failure to provide Catholic housing, but there was anger throughout the nationalist community at what was seen as police over-reaction. The marchers offered little resistance as police attacked them with batons and the first water-cannon to be deployed on the streets of Ulster. While most photographers fled, an

RUC men club a demonstrator.

Irish television cameraman continued filming, capturing scenes of RUC brutality which have alerted world opinion to the Ulster civil rights campaign (→ 22/11).

Student sit-ins spread across the country

Students at Hornsey College of Art demand a say in running the college.

London, 31 May
As student sit-ins spread through universities and colleges, the latest flashpoint emerged in north London today when angry students at the Hornsey College of Art have declared "a state of anarchy".

Following the example of such institutions as the London School of Economics, which in turn has echoed a movement first seen in the USA and, earlier this month, the bloody clashes on the streets of

Paris, the Hornsey students have abandoned debate, turning instead to direct action in their bid to revolutionize the way in which their college is administered.

They want a complete shake-up both of teaching in the college and of the way student affairs are conducted. They have taken over the college buildings, evicted the principal, Harold Shelton, and declared that they will sit in until all their demands are met (→ 3/2/69).

'Hair' is well and truly let down in the West End after censorship laws abolished

London, 27 September
Tonight, one day after the censorship of the Lord Chamberlain over the theatre was abolished, the hippie musical *Hair* did not so much open as hit London like a "happening". The show is a deafening, "tribal love-rock musical" that celebrates "doing your own thing".

The cast, when they were not swinging from the balconies or the proscenium or pelting the audience with confetti or with a resounding fusillade of *the* four-letter word, swung to the tribal rock beat of Galt MacDermot's exciting score, in numbers like "Good morning Starshine!" At the first-act curtain they took all their clothes off under a huge blanket and stood there confronting the audience. It demonstrated that once they had taken their clothes off, there was not much more even they could do.

The show was created by two New York actors, Gerome Ragni and James Rado, inspired by seeing a flower-people's "Be-in" in Central Park, against the war in Vietnam. It was first staged in New York's East Village. One song is in praise of:

Hair like Jesus wore it
Hallelujah I adore it. (→ 21/9/69)

"Hair" explodes onto the London stage with fun, songs and full nudity.

South Africa blocks cricket tour by MCC

Bloemfontein, 17 September
John Vorster, South Africa's prime minister, has cancelled this winter's MCC tour of South Africa because Basil D'Oliviera, England's Cape Coloured all-rounder, has been chosen to replace the injured Tom Cartwright. In a statement read out at a meeting of the Nationalist Party here today, Vorster claimed that the touring party was "no longer a cricket team but a team of troublemakers for South Africa's separate development policies". The omission of D'Oliviera from the team chosen last month was greeted by protests from both anti-apartheid groups and cricket fans; when Cartwright fell out, his selection became inevitable (→ 5/11/69).

Top fashion model Twiggy is thin, pale, gauche and young. Her look seems to sum up an era and millions of girls copy it.

1969

London, 1 January. Rupert Murdoch wins a takeover battle against Robert Maxwell for the *News of the World*.

Kenya, 1 January. Thousands of Asians holding UK passports are expected to leave for Britain shortly.

Westminster, 23 January. A proposal to cut legal penalties for smoking cannabis is rejected by the government.

London, 3 February. Student protests close the London School of Economics.

Northern Ireland, 24 February. In a general election Unionist supporters of the pro-reform premier, Terence O'Neill, win 27 seats compared to 12 for his Unionist opponents (→ 18/4).

Northern Ireland, 18 April. Nationalist Bernadette Devlin wins a Mid-Ulster by-election at the age of 21 (→ 1/5).

Northern Ireland, 1 May. James Chichester-Clark becomes prime minister (→ 16/8).

North Sea, 20 June. High-grade crude oil is found (→ 19/10/70).

Lancashire, 12 July. Tony Jacklin becomes the first British golfer to win the Open championship since 1951.

Moscow, 24 July. Jailed Briton Gerald Brooke is freed in a swap for two Soviet spies (→ 24/9/71).

Isle of Wight, 31 August. Bob Dylan stars in a pop festival that draws 150,000 fans.

London, 16 September. "Biba", a fashionable boutique, opens as a department store.

London, 21 September. Police storm a hippie "squat" at 144 Piccadilly.

Belfast, 28 September. Troops erect a "peace wall" between the warring communities (→ 12/10).

Twickenham, 5 November. Anti-apartheid demonstrators invade the pitch during a game by the touring South African Springboks (→ 22/5/70).

London, 13 November. A woman has quintuplets after fertility drug treatment.

Westminster, 18 December. The experimental ban on capital punishment is made permanent.

Westminster, 18 December. The formation of a part-time Ulster Defence Regiment is approved (→ 29/3/70).

Concorde makes supersonic maiden flight

"Wizard flight": Britain's Concorde prototype takes off for the first time.

Bristol, 9 April
The British Concorde has made its first flight. Concorde 002, the fruit of £360 million of investment, took off from Filton, Bristol, on a 21-minute flight in which the supersonic aircraft's four Rolls-Royce Olympus engines managed a modest 202 mph (323 kph). Brian Trubshaw, today's pilot, was none the less delighted and said he had a "wizard flight". Britain and France – whose own Concorde (001) took off a month ago – hope to sell 400 of the craft, netting some £4,000 million by the 1980s. The lucrative United States market could prove a problem, however: noise levels recorded today were twice those permitted in the US (→ 23/1/70).

Labour backs down over union reforms

Westminster, 18 June
Harold Wilson has been forced to abandon the Industrial Relations Act in the face of opposition within the cabinet and the trade union movement. The act, designed to implement the recommendations of the employment secretary Barbara Castle's white paper, *In Place of Strife*, would have given the government legal powers to cope with strikes. Opposition to it, led by James Callaghan, has proved too strong and at a meeting today the prime minister was forced to agree to the formula of a "solemn and binding agreement" by which the TUC will monitor disputes.

Easier end planned for unhappy couples

London, 13 June
An easier end to unhappy marriages came a step nearer today when the Divorce Reform Bill was given its third reading. It will mean that a divorce can be obtained after two years' separation with mutual consent or after five years apart without. Opposition to the bill has centred on fears for the financial position of women – Lady Summerskill has called it a "Casanova's Charter" – and it will not be implemented before further legislation has been passed giving women a bigger stake in matrimonial assets.

Derry marchers are caught in ambush

Londonderry, 4 January
Defenceless students dived through hedges and jumped into a river to escape stones and screaming loyalist attackers at Burntollet bridge, south of Derry today, as they neared the end of their four-day civil rights march across Northern Ireland. Although the 70 marchers had a heavy police escort, no effective action was taken against the ambush by about 200 Protestants blocking the main road and occupying the hillside. Sweeping reforms of housing and local government were announced last month (→ 24/2).

East End Kray twins face long jail term

London, 5 March
Gangland twins Ronald and Reginald Kray, who were said to have terrorized the East End, were given life sentences today for murder. Mr Justice Melford Stevenson said they should not be released for 30 years. Four members of their "firm" were also convicted.

The 35-year-old brothers gained a reputation for violence, as well as a cult following in the club world. They were arrested after George Cornell, aged 38, was shot in the head at the Blind Beggar pub and Jack "The Hat" McVitie, also 38, was lured to a flat and then stabbed in the face, chest and throat.

July 5. The Beatles may have stopped performing, but Mick Jagger struts on, leading the Rolling Stones in a free concert at London's Hyde Park.

British troops are deployed to control Ulster riots

Rioters and police confront each other near a Catholic barricade in Belfast.

With little idea what has caused the riots, British troops stand bemused.

Northern Ireland, 16 August
British troops have been welcomed in Catholic areas of Londonderry and Belfast, standing in for a police force exhausted by sectarian riots. Ten people have been killed and over 100 wounded by gunfire in two days that recall the worst periods of the 1920s.

Housewives offered cups of tea as 600 soldiers of the Light Infantry mounted guard moved in to the Catholic Falls Road district of Belfast, which had been attacked by armed Protestant gangs. The IRA could only muster six guns in west Belfast and were taunted in graffiti: "IRA – I Ran Away". Altogether 500 houses, mostly belonging to Catholics, were destroyed.

Riots flared in Londonderry on 12 August after a controversial decision to permit the annual Apprentice Boys' parade by Protestants near the Catholic Bogside. Barricades were erected, marking out a "Free Derry" area, and a panic reaction to the threatened deployment of the partisan "B Special" police reservists drove matters to a head. As agreed by Stormont and Westminster, 400 men of the Prince of Wales' Own Yorkshire regiment took up positions around the Bogside at 5pm on 14 August. They remain, under the army GOC, General Ian Freeland, as part of a "temporary" operation, with instructions to act impartially.

Fears for the safety of Catholics led the Irish prime minister, Jack Lynch, to broadcast a statement in which he said that Dublin "can no longer stand by". In practice, this has meant ordering field hospitals to the border, near Derry; but hopes and fears have been raised on all sides (→ 28/9).

Army uses tear gas on Protestant crowd

Northern Ireland, 12 October
Three people were killed – including the first security force victim in the current violence – and 66 were injured in a weekend of Protestant mayhem, following an announcement that the "B Special" police reserves were to be abolished and the Royal Ulster Constabulary reorganized. Protestant reaction was quick and violent. Shots rang out during angry confrontations in the Shankill district yesterday and Constable Victor Arbuckle fell dead, the 11th victim of the violence. After 20 soldiers were hurt during attacks with petrol bombs, the army was issued with instructions to shoot back at snipers and bombers. At the height of the riots, tear gas was fired at a stone-throwing mob of 500 Protestants. Further troop reinforcements have brought their numbers to 9,000 (→ 12/12).

Some rioters wore gas masks.

Nationalist MP jailed for inciting a riot

Devlin MP breaks rocks to throw.

Londonderry, 12 December
Bernadette Devlin, who in April became at 22 the youngest MP for nearly 200 years, was today sentenced to six months' imprisonment in Derry for incitement to riot during "the battle of the Bogside" in August. She was freed on bail pending an appeal.

A diminutive figure in a miniskirt, she was cheered from the courthouse by supporters singing "We Shall Overcome". Her lawyer claimed that she had acted from the highest motives, comparable to "the roles of Joan of Arc and Florence Nightingale", with concern for the safety of women and children. She won a by-election as an anti-Unionist unity candidate by 4,000 votes, but is bitterly disliked by Protestants who are unhappy about police reforms introduced by the British government (→ 18).

Britain, 9 January. "Hong Kong flu" claims 2,850 lives this week.

London, 23 January. The first "jumbo" jet, a Boeing 747 of Pan Am, lands at Heathrow airport (→ 21/1/76).

Britain, 2 February. Bertrand Russell, the passionate liberal philosopher, dies aged 97.

Westminster, 9 February. Parliament says that men and women will receive equal pay by 1976 (→ 6/3/71).

Britain, 16 March. The *New English Bible*, published today, is a sell-out.

Derry City, 29 March. Troops seal off the Catholic Bogside area after riots (→ 16/4).

Northern Ireland, 16 April. Britain announces plans to send an extra 500 troops to join the 6,000 already here; the Unionist Reverend Ian Paisley wins the Bannside by-election (→ 31/7).

London, 18 May. A general election is called (→ 19/6).

London, 22 May. The MCC, under government pressure, cancels the South African cricket tour of England.

Dublin, 28 May. Charles Haughey and Neil Blaney, former cabinet ministers of the Republic, face arms smuggling charges (→ 23/10).

Britain, 22 June. Female ministers are to be ordained in the Methodist Church.

Luxembourg, 30 June. Britain, Ireland, Denmark and Norway open talks on entry into the Common Market (→ 24/6/71).

London, 17 July. A new sex comedy by Kenneth Tynan, *Oh! Calcutta!*, opens.

Westminster, 20 July. Iain MacLeod, the chancellor of the exchequer, dies suddenly.

Belfast, 2 August. The army begins using rubber bullets.

Cumbria, 24 August. A part of Windscale nuclear power station is closed due to a radioactive leak.

Beirut, 30 September. The British government exchanges Leila Khaled, a Palestinian terrorist, for British hostages seized by Palestinian hijackers.

North Sea, 19 October. BP has struck oil (→ 3/11/75).

Germany, 26 December. The 22-year-old Olympic athlete Lillian Board dies of cancer in a Bavarian clinic.

Damages paid to thalidomide victims

London, 23 March

Damages totalling £370,000 were awarded in the high court today to 18 children born with defects caused by their mothers taking the drug thalidomide while pregnant. The judgement was against Distillers (Biochemicals), which sold the drug under licence to Germany.

The amounts awarded depend on the severity of the disability, with five children born with tiny "flipper" arms winning £28,800 each. The figure includes damages to parents for shock and loss of earnings.

The case follows a long investigation and campaign by the *Sunday Times* which was fiercely contested through the courts by the Distillers company (→ 29/11/72).

Jacklin wins the US Open championship

Minneapolis, USA, 21 June

Tony Jacklin drove, chipped and putted his way into golfing history today when he became only the third player to hold the British and US Open championships at the same time. His victory in the US Open today – the first by a Briton for 50 years – follows success in the British one last July.

Jacklin won by seven strokes in sweltering heat. He was the only golfer to beat par in all four rounds of the tournament. His prize is £12,500 but is worth far more in terms of commercial contracts that await the new double champion.

Jacklin in the rough on the 17th.

Election win for Heath

Edward Heath, the jubilant winner.

Westminster, 19 June

After a big political upset, Edward Heath arrived at Downing Street tonight as Britain's new prime minister. The Conservatives confounded opinion pollsters to achieve 68 net gains in yesterday's general election, sweeping to office with a 4.7 per cent swing from a shell-shocked Labour Party. Until the campaign's final days Harold Wilson had appeared to be heading for a third successive election victory.

Labour had recovered from the rows over union policy last year and edged into an opinion poll lead last month. This lead soared to as high as 12.5 per cent at one point during a campaign fought mostly in warm sunshine.

Wilson mounted a relaxed, almost presidential campaign. Heath doggedly battled away on rising prices and union power, with few signs of encouragement until a balance of payments deficit announced 72 hours before polling day took the gloss off Labour's claims to economic recovery. Then the final opinion poll became the first to show a swing to the Tories.

Labour apathy was as much a factor as any late swing to the Conservatives, however, with voter turn-out down to 70 per cent. Final figures are 330 Conservatives, 287 Labour, 6 Liberals and 1 Scottish Nationalist (→ 4/3/74).

'Women's Lib' becomes a powerful force

Britain

Women's rights made two tangible advances this year in terms of law reform while finding a new champion in Germaine Greer, the author of *The Female Eunuch*.

The legal advances came in the form of two acts of parliament. The Matrimonial Property Act laid down that a wife's work – whether in jobs outside the home or as a housewife within it – was to be regarded as an equal contribution with that of the husband if, in the event of divorce, the family home had to be divided.

The Equal Pay Act also passed through its parliamentary stages this year. It does not come fully into practice for five years, and even then there are loopholes, but it does finally establish the principle of equal pay for equal work.

Feminists have welcomed both of these new acts, which continue a process of reform which gathered momentum during the Sixties in areas such as abortion, divorce and contraception. The availability of the contraceptive pill came to sym-

Ardent feminist: Germaine Greer.

bolize a new liberation for women, which Germaine Greer advances in her bestselling book. A university lecturer, she challenges the masculine world with an erudite critique of the way it stereotypes women's roles. Even so, "women's lib" as a movement is in its infancy here compared with more strident campaigns in the United States (→ 9/2).

'Fabulous four' to go separate ways

Liverpool, 9 April
Sad-faced youngsters dressed in mourning black here today at the news that this city's favourite sons – the Beatles – are splitting up and going their separate ways. The sadness will be echoed wherever the fabulous four's music is played – that is, in every corner of the globe.

Paul McCartney – who is now reputed to be at loggerheads with his co-Beatle John Lennon – issued in the high court the writ that ended the partnership, which had recently been under strain from business squabbles within the Beatles' multi-million pound Apple Corporation (→ 8/12/80).

Kidnappers release British diplomat

Toronto, 13 December
For the British diplomat James Cross the ordeal by kidnap ended today when he was released by French-Canadian terrorists of the Quebec Liberation Front (FLQ). Cross had been held for two months – and there were grave concerns for his safety when the body of Pierre Laporte, the Quebec minister of labour, who had been kidnapped at the same time, was found in the boot of a car. Cross is with a Cuban diplomat until his kidnappers reach Havana, under an agreement reached with the Canadian police. He told the Canadian prime minister, Pierre Trudeau, by telephone: "The nightmare is over."

Northern Ireland erupts in chaos

Army's honeymoon with Catholics ends

Belfast, 31 July
The killing by troops of an alleged petrol bomber, Danny O'Hagan, during rioting in north Belfast has marked the conclusion of a year-long honeymoon between the British Army and the Roman Catholic community. O'Hagan was the first to die following a warning by General Ian Freeland, the army GOC, that petrol bombers would be shot.

Relations have worsened since the jailing on 26 June of Bernadette Devlin, the civil rights leader, for her part in the August 1969 riots in Derry, and a 35-hour curfew of the Lower Falls area this month after six Protestants and a Catholic had been killed in skirmishes.

A house-to-house search involving 3,000 soldiers turned up 107 firearms, 250 pounds of explosives, 100 home-made bombs and 21,000 rounds of ammunition. It was regarded as counter-productive, however, in terms of antagonizing an entire Catholic population.

The deteriorating relations have been exploited by the Provisional IRA which was formed in January, having split from the Official IRA in a clash over political or military strategies. The new "provisional" executive has dedicated itself to making Northern Ireland ungovernable, and with finance from overseas, as well as from the Republic, has already been responsible for more than 40 bombings (→ 21/8).

British military police patrol the Falls Road area after a night of violence.

Gerry Fitt leads new Ulster reform party

Belfast, 21 August
A new party for moderate nationalists, the Social Democratic and Labour Party (SDLP), was launched today by Gerry Fitt, the Westminster MP for West Belfast, and six prominent Stormont MPs, including John Hume. The party is a radical supporter of civil rights, believing that the unity of Ireland can be achieved only through the consent of the majority of the people.

The new party reflects the volatility of politics here. In April the Rev Ian Paisley and a Democratic Unionist colleague won Stormont by-elections, followed by Paisley's election to Westminster in June. And in April the Alliance Party was formed, aimed at liberal Protestants and Catholics (→ 9/2/71).

Ian Paisley: Protestant Unionist.

Haughey is not guilty in Irish gun trial

Dublin, 23 October
The former government minister Charles Haughey, together with three other defendants, has been acquitted of conspiring to import arms into the republic. It was alleged that their intention – not sanctioned by the government – was to send the arms to the beleaguered Roman Catholic minority in the north of Ireland. Immediately after the verdict, Haughey issued a challenge to the Fianna Fáil party leader, Jack Lynch, whose action in dismissing Haughey from his government last May had led to the trial. The case has attracted enormous public attention. Charges against a second former senior minister, Neil Blaney, were dropped at a preliminary hearing. The trial which followed was aborted, due to inadmissible evidence about one of the defendants, and a new trial was ordered. During that, conflict of evidence between Charles Haughey and his former government colleague James Gibbons clearly indicated that one of the two men was committing perjury.

January 9. Flames and smoke, fanned by gale-force winds, cause serious damage to the Starlight theatre on Eastbourne's 100-year-old pier.

1971

'Angry Brigade' bombs minister's home

London, 14 January

An anonymous letter sent to several Fleet Street newspapers claims that an extremist group calling itself the Angry Brigade was responsible for planting two terrorist bombs at the home of a cabinet minister two days ago. The bombs exploded outside the Hertfordshire home of Robert Carr, the employment secretary. He and his wife and younger daughter were in the house at the time. They escaped unhurt, but windows were shattered, and the front door was blown out.

The Angry Brigade has previously claimed responsibility for three other terrorist attacks in London – the machine-gunning of the Spanish embassy and bombs at the Miss World contest and the department of employment offices in Westminster. Robert Carr, although a liberal Tory, has been at the centre of controversy because he is spear-

Carr's Daimler after the blast.

heading the proposals of Edward Heath's government for curbing trade union power. Leaders of all political parties have condemned the attacks.

Football crowd barriers collapse, killing 66

The buckled barriers at Ibrox Park, where 66 people were crushed to death.

Glasgow, 2 January

Crowd barriers collapsed today at Ibrox Park stadium, sending football fans tumbling down terraces amid a tangle of twisted metal. Sixty-six people died and hundreds were injured in Britain's worst soccer disaster – and the second at Ibrox Park this century. In 1902 20 people died when a terrace collapsed during an international.

Today's tragedy occurred shortly after Glasgow Rangers, the home team, had equalized against their closest and fiercest rivals, Glasgow Celtic. As the capacity crowd pushed forwards, some barriers gave way, hurling fans onto those at the front. Some fans found safety on the pitch, but others were crushed by the weight of bodies falling helplessly on top of them.

An inquiry into safety at major sporting venues seems certain to be announced by either central or local government.

Faulkner becomes Stormont premier

Belfast, 21 March

Brian Faulkner was elected today as prime minister of Northern Ireland after Major James Chichester-Clark had resigned "in order to underline the seriousness of the situation". Faulkner, a former commerce minister, takes over at a time of turmoil, after the murder of three off-duty Scottish soldiers and a march by shipyard men demanding the introduction of internment without trial. London's agreement to send 1,000 more troops was insufficient to save Chichester-Clark, who was regarded as too soft in his dealings with Westminster.

Brian Faulkner selects his cabinet.

British currency gets decimal point

Britain, 15 February

Britons bade a reluctant farewell to the venerable system of pounds, shillings and pence today and began the struggle to understand decimal coinage. Gone are the half-crown [12.5p] and the florin [10p], and the wholly illogical system in which 240 pennies equal one pound.

The chairman of the decimal currency board, Lord Fiske, is content that things are going well; but many are finding it hard to cope with the new currency which includes a minute and anachronistic half-pence piece, which is roughly the equivalent of the chunky and trusted old copper penny.

Soviets oust Britons in tit-for-tat move

Moscow, 8 October

Five Britons are to be expelled from the USSR, the Soviet authorities announced today. A further 13 have been refused entry into the country.

The move comes as no surprise. On 24 September the foreign secretary, Sir Alec Douglas-Home, announced the expulsion of 100 Soviet diplomats and officials – who, he said, had turned London into a "hive of Russian intelligence activity". A tit-for-tat response by the other side is usual in these cases.

The British move was taken at a time of strained Anglo-Soviet ties, partly prompted by the decision in June to grant asylum to the Soviet space expert Anatol Fedoseyev, a big prize for the West. The revelations of another defector, the KGB agent Oleg Lyalin, led to the September expulsions (→ 21/11/79).

Britain agrees to terms to join EEC

Westminster, 24 June

After a year of negotiations, the government announced today that it had agreed terms to join the European Economic Community (EEC) or Common Market. "We have a very satisfactory deal," said Geoffrey Rippon, the minister in charge of the EEC negotiations.

Rippon told MPs that transitional arrangements would safeguard the interests of both British and Commonwealth farmers. And he defended the annual cost of membership – £100 million in 1973 rising to £200 in 1977. The European policy is a linchpin of Edward Heath's strategy. It was the British prime minister's talks with President Pompidou of France last month which resolved many of the difficulties. Now Heath has to win the consent of parliament (→ 28/10).

Riots flare in Ulster after IRA suspects are interned in massive terrorist crackdown

Sinn Féin supporters make their protest against internment outside Whitehall.

Shipbuilding hit by 'lame duck' policy

Glasgow, 14 June

No government money is to be made available to help Upper Clyde Shipbuilders stave off liquidation. The announcement was made today by John Davies, the trade and industry secretary. His declaration was attacked in the House of Commons by Tony Benn, who as Labour's technology minister had put £20 million into the company.

Edward Heath's government was elected on a manifesto promising non-intervention in industry; it was made clear that "lame ducks"

would not be saved. Although ministers back-tracked from this policy following the collapse of Rolls-Royce in February, no reprieve is envisaged for the shipbuilders. Davies insists that public money should not be pumped into ailing or bankrupt industries.

Four thousand jobs are directly threatened at Upper Clyde Shipbuilders, and there is talk of a "work-in" by a labour force convinced that the yard – where many of Britain's most famous ships were built – can still be profitable.

Northern Ireland, 11 August

Violence has erupted on the streets of Belfast in the 48 hours following the re-introduction of internment without trial. Twenty-one civilians – including a priest giving the last rites – and two soldiers have been killed and some 300 houses destroyed by fire. An estimated 7,000 refugees have fled to the Republic.

All 342 terrorist suspects seized on 9 August were nationalists. Of these 116 have already been released, many of them non-violent civil rights activists. Even though the round-up, code-named Operation Demetrius, was brought forward a day as a consequence of riots, many IRA leaders escaped the net. The Northern Ireland prime minister, Brian Faulkner, claimed success in his efforts to "flush out the gunmen". But it has also provoked the moderate Social Democratic and Labour Party to boycott all government bodies in protest (→ 16).

Suspects face rough internment in Ulster

Belfast, 16 November

Nationalists reacted angrily today to the findings of the Compton commission, appointed to investigate allegations of torture of internees in Northern Ireland. Sir Edmund Compton, the ombudsman, found no evidence of brutality by police interrogators. Five interrogation techniques developed by the army in Aden and Cyprus were investigated, involving hooding of suspects, exposure to continuous noise, standing against a wall supported by the fingertips and deprivation of sleep and food. All the detainees except one refused to give evidence, on the grounds that the commission sat in private (→ 20/12).

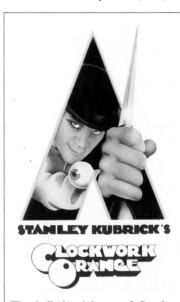

The balletic violence of Stanley Kubrick's "Clockwork Orange" has been thrilling cinemagoers.

British engineering takes a bashing with the collapse of Rolls-Royce.

All-out miners' strike puts Britain in dark

Police work goes on by candlelight despite the cuts in power supply.

Miners' wives join the protest, which has led to nationwide blackouts.

London, 16 February
With most power stations working below capacity and 12 completely shut down by fuel shortages, Britain has been hit by electricity blackouts lasting nine hours. Militant miners are picketing power stations in order to impede deliveries; at Longannet, near Edinburgh, three policemen were injured on Monday when 2,000 miners fought police to stop deliveries of oil. In London, miners have hired boats to picket Thames-side power stations.

Operating under the government's state of emergency, which was proclaimed last week, industry is working a three-day week, and families are being urged to heat only one room in their homes. It is reckoned that industry has laid off over one million workers.

In a move widely interpreted as a sign of the government's weakening resolve, Edward Heath, the prime minister, has appointed a high court judge, Lord Wilberforce, to lead a three-man inquiry into the miners' claim for a pay increase which would be substantially above the Coal Board's pre-strike offer of £2 a week (→ 18).

Britain signs on dotted line to join EEC

Brussels, 22 January
Britain, Ireland, Denmark and Norway signed a treaty here today agreeing to join the European Economic Community next January. Although the European Community Bill has yet to be accepted by the British parliament, MPs backed the principle of membership last October by a majority of 112. Opponents from both sides of the house plan to fight the bill all the way, with Labour more seriously split than the Conservatives. Edward Heath, the prime minister, remains confident of success. Ten years ago President de Gaulle thwarted his negotiations to join. Today, not even a bag of printer's ink thrown at him by a demonstrator could mar his satisfaction (→ 11/5).

An ink-spattered Edward Heath.

Maudling quits in financial scandal

Westminster, 18 July
Reginald Maudling, the home secretary, resigned today because of his connection with a Yorkshire architect, John Poulson, who is facing corruption charges. Bankruptcy hearings have raised wider allegations of corruption. With a police inquiry inevitable, Maudling decided that he had to quit, since the home secretary has ministerial responsibility for the police. It has not been alleged that Maudling has done anything improper, but he was involved with a Poulson company during his time in opposition. Although he received no payment himself, his children and a theatre charity with which his wife is connected did benefit.

Allegations force Maudling to quit.

Calculations at the press of a button

Cambridgeshire, 31 December
It weighs 70 grams (2.5 oz), it is 50mm (2in) wide and less than 10mm thick, and it is, says its inventor, Clive Sinclair, the world's first true pocket calculator. He is off to New York to put the £79 Sinclair Executive on sale there for $195. Sinclair, who left school with "A" levels in maths and physics, has turned out a whole string of innovations in his works, an old flour mill, at St Ives. The Executive has four tiny mercury cells, as used in hearing aids, which drive a 7,000-unit micro-chip.

Civil rights marchers are shot dead

Wages frozen and price rises halted

Westminster, 6 November

Wages and prices are to be frozen for 90 days, the prime minister told MPs today. The standstill, which also covers dividends and rents, could be extended for a further 60 days under emergency legislation which amounts to a major U-turn by the Heath government.

Edward Heath was elected on a platform that included the rejection of statutory wage controls, but rising prices, a worsening balance of payments deficit and increasing numbers of strikes produced a sterling crisis this summer. Talks with unions and industry have failed to produce a voluntary agreement to curb inflation (→ 1/5/73).

Derry City, 30 January

Paratroopers opened fire on an illegal civil rights march in Derry today, killing 13 civilians and injuring 29 in what has already been dubbed another "Bloody Sunday". Army claims that the soldiers were fired upon, and that some of the victims were carrying nail bombs, have been hotly disputed.

About 15,000 took part in the march against internment. Near the city centre, water cannon and tear gas were used before men of the 1st Paratroop Regiment opened fire on fleeing marchers. The killings followed an intense IRA bombing campaign in Belfast. In reprisal, a Protestant bomb in December killed 15 in a Catholic pub (→ 2/2).

Two of the victims of "Bloody Sunday" lie dead on a deserted Bogside street.

Amin expels Asians

Kampala, 6 August

Uganda's industrious and prosperous Asians were faced with imminent expulsion to Britain today when the country's brutal military dictator, General Idi Amin, alleged that they were "sabotaging the economy" and said that he was getting rid of all those with British passports, an estimated 50,000, or virtually the whole community. When Uganda, Kenya and Tanganyika became independent ten years ago, the Asians were reassured by being given British passports, although without the automatic right to come to Britain.

Direct rule imposed in Northern Ireland

Shipyard workers in Belfast protest at the imposition of direct rule for Ulster.

Belfast, 24 March

The Northern Ireland government of Brian Faulkner resigned today in protest at Edward Heath's demand for security responsibility to be transferred to Westminster. Stormont will be suspended from 28 March, and William Whitelaw has been appointed secretary of state for the province, ending 51 years of self-government.

London is responding to increasing signs that Stormont is losing the war against the paramilitaries. On 4 March two women died in the bombing of the Abercorn restau-

rant in Belfast, and after six people had died in a Donegal Street blast loyalists threatened all-out warfare against the IRA. Summoned to London, Faulkner was stunned by Heath's demands for a referendum on the border, steps to end internment and moves towards power-sharing, but only refused to give way on security. The Heath government has distanced itself from Stormont ever since Bloody Sunday [*see above*], and security chiefs believed that their policies would not be acceptable as long as they were associated with the Unionist regime (→ 28).

British army ends IRA 'no-go' areas

Derry City, 31 July

Army bulldozers today demolished barricades which had turned parts of Derry into "no-go" areas for a year. Some 5,000 of the 21,000 troops in Northern Ireland assisted in the operation, in which two civilians died. There was little resistance from the IRA, many of whose leaders are in the Republic. The show of force followed a "Bloody Friday" in Belfast on 21 July, when 11 died in 21 IRA explosions. Two weeks earlier a 14-day IRA truce had broken down (→ 9/8).

Anti-terrorist laws extended in Ireland

Dublin, 1 December

Two bombs have exploded in the centre of the city, one outside Liberty Hall and the other in Marlborough Street, killing two people and injuring 127. The explosions occurred during a parliamentary debate on an amendment to the Offences Against the State Act, giving greater powers of arrest and detention to the police. It was expected that the Fianna Fáil government would be defeated, leading to a general election. In the event Fine Gael dropped its opposition, and the legislation was passed (→ 28/1/73).

Women rush to buy the first issue of "Cosmopolitan", a monthly magazine promising articles on life, love, sex and money.

London devastated by IRA bombing

London, 8 March

The IRA brought its bombing campaign to the heart of London today when cars parked outside the Old Bailey and Scotland Yard exploded, killing one man and injuring 244. Most injuries were caused by flying glass which sliced through the busy streets. There would have been many more casualties if the police had not acted on a telephoned warning and defused two other car bombs.

It is thought that the bombs were planted to mark the referendum being held in Northern Ireland to decide if the people want to remain part of the United Kingdom. Most Catholics are boycotting the poll, but the IRA's actions leave no doubt about its intention not only to continue its campaign of violence in Ireland but also to spread it to the mainland.

It is pointed out that last year's attack on the Parachute Regiment's mess at Aldershot was carried out by the Official IRA as a specific act of revenge for "Bloody Sunday", when the "Paras" shot dead 13 demonstrators in Derry. Today's bombs were planted by the Provisional IRA, which is responsible for most of the current violence. Ten people have been arrested tonight at Heathrow airport (→ 9).

Council of Ireland created at Sunningdale

Faulkner (l) and Cosgrave making history as north and south are linked.

Berkshire, 9 December

An historic four-day conference at Sunningdale was concluded today with an agreement between the British, Irish and Northern Ireland governments to set up a council of Ireland, a consultative body linking Belfast and Dublin for the first time since partition.

The council provides an Irish dimension, as demanded by nationalists, to the accord reached on 21 November between the Northern Ireland parties and the Ulster secretary William Whitelaw on a new power-sharing executive for the province. The Sunningdale agreement ties the Republic to recognition of the fact that there can be no change in Northern Ireland's status without majority consent.

The council, consisting of seven ministers from Belfast and Dublin, will be mainly concerned with co-operative ventures in areas like trade and tourism. But loyalist politicians, absent from the conference, have promised to resist any Dublin involvement in the affairs of Northern Ireland (→ 22/1/74).

Thirty holidaymakers die as flames destroy Isle of Man complex

Holidaymakers watch in horror as flames and smoke engulf Summerland.

Douglas, Isle of Man, 2 August

The £2 million Summerland entertainment complex at Douglas, on the Isle of Man, was packed with holidaymakers when fire broke out in the upper storeys tonight. Within minutes the restaurant, solarium, discothèque and theatre were engulfed in a raging inferno that killed 30 people and injured at least 80 others. Many have severe burns; others were trampled in the panic. "I was knocked down in the stampede," a woman survivor said. "I was flat on my stomach, and there was a kiddie underneath me."

Hours after the fire had been extinguished a pall of black smoke hung over the devastation. Fire investigators are seeking to establish both the cause of the fire and the reason why it spread so fast.

Distillers is banned from supermarkets in thalidomide row

London, 5 January

In a new twist to the dispute over the controversial thalidomide drug, goods produced by the Distillers Company, the drink and pharmaceuticals giant, are being banned from some supermarket shelves because of the delay in settling compensation claims. The boycott, by David Greig and Redmans, will affect well known brands of whisky, gin, vodka and brandy.

Cases involving Distillers (Biochemicals), which marketed the drug in Britain, are still before the courts, but Distillers has offered £11.25 million to thalidomide victims and their families, and the government has given £3 million to help cover the cost of home care.

The drug had been in use for several years before it was discovered that when it was taken as a sedative during pregnancy a woman was at risk of giving birth to a deformed baby.

Three-day working week introduced

Westminster, 17 December

Most British workers face a three-day week in the New Year under a package of measures announced today to combat what the government called "the gravest situation by far since the end of the war". Public spending will be cut, a speed limit of 50mph imposed, television blacked-out at 10.30pm and credit controls will be tightened in a mini-budget which comes barely one month after last month's state of emergency and rises in bank rate.

Edward Heath's government is under attack both at home and abroad. At home, industrial unrest over stage three of the government's prices and incomes policy has been compounded by more particular grievances. Power workers, miners and railwaymen are among groups currently imposing overtime bans or other restrictions. Coal supplies to power stations are already down 40 per cent.

These difficulties have been intensified by the Arab-Israeli war last October. Supplies of oil –

Motorists join the queue for petrol as the shortage of oil worsens.

which provides 50 per cent of Britain's energy – have been cut by 15 per cent, causing long queues for petrol and the distribution of ration books. More ominous for the government is the prospect of the im-port bill for oil quadrupling at a time when the balance of payments is already grim. If the industrial rows are not solved quickly, it is likely that the Conservatives will call an election (→ 26/6/74).

Britain and Iceland clash in fishing row

An Icelandic boat pulls alongside a British fishing vessel as a warning.

Reykjavik, 21 May

The British frigate *Cleopatra* and the Icelandic gunboat *Thor* spent much of today shadow-boxing in the disputed 50-mile (80-km) fishing zone around Iceland. The *Thor*, which had been shadowing the British fishing fleet, suddenly made off to harass a West German trawler, and the *Cleopatra* followed. With only 4 miles between the two ships, the *Thor* spun round and headed for the *Cleopatra*; when she came within a quarter of a mile, the *Cleopatra* made off. The *Thor* later reappeared and, closing to 100 yards (91m), sent a large wave against the *Cleopatra's* starboard side. As darkness fell the two ships were still dodging and weaving (→ 19/2/76).

BBC feels waves as rival radio goes on air

London, 8 October

The BBC's 50-year-old monopoly of radio broadcasting was broken today when the all-news station LBC – the London Broadcasting Company – went on the air using a temporary aerial slung from the smoke stacks of a Thames-side power station and studios off Fleet Street in a square near Dr Samuel Johnson's house, now a museum.

Tomorrow Capital Radio, a pop music station to rival the BBC's Radio One, will start broadcasting. Both will look to advertising for revenue. LBC has set out to build up a newsgathering network of contributors at home and overseas, but doubts have been expressed as to whether it can pull in the £1 million a year gross on which its ambitious plans are based.

May 5. A triumphant Bobby Kerr, captain of second division Sunderland, lifts the FA cup after their shock 1-0 victory over mighty Leeds United.

Labour in power after two elections

Heath loses after miners' challenge

Westminster, 4 March

Harold Wilson is back in Downing Street tonight, promising to put Britain back to work. He heads a minority government after the general election held on 28 February rebounded on the outgoing prime minister, Edward Heath, who had run an anti-union campaign on the issue of "Who governs Britain?".

Not the Conservatives, came the answer, although for four days the fate of Heath's government hung in the balance as he sought a pact with Jeremy Thorpe's resurgent Liberals. In the election, Labour won 301 seats, the Conservatives 297 and the Liberals 14; nine went to Scottish and Welsh Nationalists and 12 to Northern Ireland.

Talks between Heath and Thorpe failed, in spite of the offer of a cabinet post for the Liberal leader, so Harold Wilson begins his third term as premier. He is expected to end the four-week pit strike and to lift the state of emergency, including the three-day week. Tory hopes in the campaign were undermined by a disclosure that official figures for miners' pay were incorrect, improving the cause of the strikers and of Labour, which argued that it was best able to end the rash of industrial disputes (→10/10).

Harold Wilson congratulating his staff at Labour Party headquarters.

Tiny majority returns Wilson to No 10

Westminster, 11 October

Harold Wilson has won his fourth general election out of five contests, but his majority is just three seats over all other parties in yesterday's poll. The totals are Labour 319, Conservatives 276, Liberals 13, Nationalists 14 and others 13.

Labour had ruled for seven months as a minority government, using the time to promote an aura of stability after the trauma of the three-day week and miners' strike.

A voluntary "social contract" with the unions was cited as an alternative to the Tory reliance on legislation to curb inflation and strikes. Denis Healey, the new chancellor, boosted pensions and said that difficulties with the balance of payments had eased. Edward Heath warned about rising inflation but failed to shake off the legacy of last winter. Now he faces trouble within his party, after three defeats in four as Conservative leader (→11/2/75).

Huge explosion kills 29 at the Flixborough chemical plant

The acrid smoke and rubble are all that remain of the chemical plant.

Humberside, 1 June

At 4.35 this afternoon the village of Flixborough (population 200) was devastated by violent explosions at a nearby chemical plant which for years has been the community's main source of employment.

Twenty-nine people were killed, about a hundred stone-built cottages were wrecked, the factory was left a grotesque tangle of blackened steel girders, and an acrid cloud is drifting across the countryside. All those who died were working close to the central control room when a red warning light came on, and the factory hooter sounded. The next moment two tremendous blasts tore the factory apart.

Counties all change for a more efficient local government

London, 1 April
The biggest shake-up in local government for almost a century comes into effect today with the redrawing of almost all county boundaries along the lines set out by Lord Redcliffe-Maud and his commission. Town charters dating from the Middle Ages and counties recorded in the Domesday Book have had their ancient identities erased. Only ten of 45 English counties and one of 13 in Wales remain unchanged.

Yorkshire and Lincolnshire, England's two largest counties, lose their distinctive ridings ("thirdings", from Old Norse). Part of Yorkshire's East Riding is joined to part of Lincolnshire over the river Humber to become Humberside. Four English counties disappear completely: Cumberland, Huntingdonshire, Westmorland and Rutland, the smallest (pop 19,000), which is joined to Leicestershire.

Another innovation is the creation of "metropolitan counties" – conurbations based on six large cities. The wide-ranging reforms are accompanied by new regulations for the payment of councillors for attending meetings and carrying out other council duties. It is claimed that local government will become more efficient, but cynics point out that today is April Fools' Day (→ 31/3/86).

IRA blasts Birmingham

One of the busy pubs bombed by the IRA in a night of carnage and destruction.

Birmingham, 21 November
The IRA's three-year-long mainland bombing campaign moved into a new dimension of terror tonight when two Birmingham pubs packed with young drinkers were wrecked; 17 people were killed and more than 120 injured.

When the timed bombs went off simultaneously in the Mulberry Bush and the Tavern in the Town, tons of rubble crashed down on the drinkers. Firemen worked with bare hands to extricate the hundreds trapped beneath beams and masonry. Passing taxis joined ambulances to ferry the injured to the city's hospitals. It is believed that the outrage was planned as revenge for the authorities' ban on the staging of a "hero's" funeral for James McDade, who blew himself up in Coventry last week while putting together a home-made bomb.

In Northern Ireland intelligence sources reported in August 1971 that the IRA was believed to be planning to bring the bombing campaign to England. Two months later the observation platform of the Post Office Tower in London was wrecked by a bomb. Since then all parts of the tower have been closed to the public (→ 29).

Strike puts an end to power-sharing

Belfast, 28 May
Northern Ireland's power-sharing executive collapsed today after a 14-day strike by loyalists opposed to the inclusion of nationalists in the government and to the Council of Ireland [*see page 1172*]. There had been fears that power cuts could lead to sewage in the streets. The executive's leader, Brian Faulkner, quit after failing to persuade SDLP colleagues to negotiate with the strikers. London gave little support to the executive. On 25 May Harold Wilson called the strikers "spongers" on British democracy, which hardened their resolve (→ 17/6).

'Lucky' Lord Lucan wanted for murder

London, 12 November
A distraught young woman appeared in the doorway of a Belgravia pub crying: "He's murdered my nanny! My children! My children!" The woman, suffering from head injuries, was Lady Lucan, the wife of Richard John Bingham, the earl of Lucan, known ironically as "Lucky Lucan" for his heavy losses at London's gaming tables. Lady Lucan said that her husband had battered the nanny, Sandra Rivett, aged 29, in the basement of their home and then attacked her when she came into the room. Lucan is being sought by police to face a murder charge (→ 19/6/75).

Lucky Lucan: wanted by police.

Missing MP found alive down under

Sydney, Australia, 24 December
Britain's missing Labour MP, John Stonehouse, is being questioned by police here. He vanished after an inquiry began into the affairs of a Bangladeshi bank of which he was chairman. Later his clothes were found on a Miami beach. But it was not long before stories emerged from Australia about a man resembling Stonehouse, said to be accompanied by the MP's secretary, Sheila Buckley. Police arrested him, saying that they had seized a false passport. Stonehouse says that he had wanted to start a new life down under.

Morecambe and Wise: the inimitable comedy duo whose zany sense of fun and the ridiculous pulls in television audiences of at least 20 million.

London, 16 January. The IRA ends its 25-day truce (→ 5/4).

London, 20 January. The government abandons plans for a Channel tunnel (→ 20/1/86).

Britain, 13 February. Miners accept a pay rise of 35 per cent.

Glasgow, 15 March. Troops clear the 70,000 tonnes of refuse which have built up during the nine-week dustmen's strike.

Britain, 3 April. The National Health Service admits that over half of the 5,000 paying beds in hospitals have been closed in an attempt to phase out private patients.

Belfast, 5 April. Nine people die and 79 are injured in bomb blasts (→ 4/5).

Westminster, 26 April. Members of the Labour Party vote 2-1 to leave the European Economic Community.

Northern Ireland, 4 May. Ulster Unionists win in elections to the Ulster Convention (→ 29/8).

Britain, 13 May. Inflation reaches 21 per cent (→ 11/7).

St Ives, Cornwall, 21 May. Barbara Hepworth, the sculptor, dies in a fire at her studio, at the age of 72.

Westminster, 9 June. Proceedings in the House of Commons are broadcast live on radio for the first time (→ 21/11/89).

London, 19 June. A jury finds the missing peer, Lord Lucan, guilty of the murder of Sandra Rivett, his children's nanny.

Britain, 21 August. Unemployment figures reach 1.25 million (→ 22/4/80).

Northern Ireland, 2 October. Protestant revenge killings for IRA atrocities leave 11 people dead (→ 3).

Dublin, 3 October. The Irish government refuses to free three imprisoned IRA members in exchange for the Dutch businessman Tiede Herrema, who was kidnapped today (→ 31).

Belfast, 31 October. The provisional Sinn Fein leader Seamus McCusker is shot dead by the official IRA (→ 7/11).

North Sea, 1 November. Three people die and six are injured in a blaze aboard the Ekofisk A oil rig.

Co Kildare, 7 November. Tiede Herrema is freed after being held for 36 days (→ 12/12).

Thatcher is first woman to lead party

Westminster, 11 February
Margaret Thatcher today became the first woman to lead a British political party. She beat four rivals to clinch the leadership of the Conservative Party, but the real battle was a week ago. It was then that the 49-year-old former education secretary unexpectedly beat Edward Heath by 130 votes to 119. That vote was too close to be decisive, except for Heath, who stood down after more than nine years as leader. William Whitelaw joined the race, but Mrs Thatcher's momentum was unstoppable; she won 146 votes to Whitelaw's 79. Nobody else got more than 20 (→ 5/4/76).

A triumphant Margaret Thatcher.

Inflation reaches a record 25 per cent

Britain, 11 July
Pay rises are to be limited to £6 a week under a policy unveiled today. People earning more than £8,500 a year will get nothing at all, and firms will be penalized if they pass on higher wage costs in higher prices. Harold Wilson, the prime minister, called the plans "rough justice" but said they were essential to cut inflation, now running at 25 per cent a year. The "social contract" with the unions has failed to curb huge pay rises, which have taken over from imports as the main cause of inflation (→ 13/7/77).

Thirty-four passengers killed in Underground crash at Moorgate

Firemen struggle to find survivors in the wreckage of the underground train.

London, 28 February
In the worst ever accident on the London Underground, 34 passengers and a driver were killed at Moorgate station when a crowded train crashed at full speed into a dead-end tunnel. The driver, Leslie Newson, aged 56, was bringing his 8.37am train from Drayton Park alongside platform nine when, instead of braking, he accelerated into a 72-metre (80-yard) blind tunnel, crashed through sand piles and overrode the buffers. The first three of the train's six coaches crumpled into a tangled mass of steel; 4.5 metres of the leading carriage were compacted into 60 centimetres. Teams of doctors and firemen spent the day in the dust and heat of the wreckage struggling to reach those who were still alive (→ 18/11/87).

Women win important rights on equality

London, 31 December
Britain has marked International Women's Year, which ends today, with two major pieces of legislation to advance the status of women. The Sex Discrimination Act makes it an offence to discriminate against women in employment, education, training and trade union activities, and in the supply of goods, facilities and services.

A potentially controversial aspect of the act is the ban on discrimination in advertisements for job vacancies. It seems certain that it will no longer be possible to advertise for, say, a fireman, a doorman or even a female secretary. Some occupations – in mining, prisons, religious orders and midwifery – have been exempted. An equal opportunities commission has been set up to look for offenders and take them to court.

The Equal Pay Act is the latest in a number of measures over the years which have sought to remove pay differentials between men and women, with varying degrees of success. The new act does not give women equality in pensions, taxes or social security (→ 18/11/87).

Charlie Chaplin swaps his bowler for a top hat and a knighthood.

Britons vote to stay in Common Market

The first results of the referendum are shown at London's Waldorf hotel.

Britain, 6 June

The people of Britain have voted overwhelmingly to stay in the European Economic Community. Final figures released tonight show that in yesterday's unprecedented referendum those voting "Yes" to Europe totalled 67.2 per cent of the poll. There were pro-European majorities in all parts of the United Kingdom, with only the Shetlands and Western Isles saying "No".

It was the first referendum in British history. It also saw the abandonment of collective cabinet responsibility as ministers were allowed to campaign for opposing policies. The official government line was to recommend a vote in favour on the basis of what Harold Wilson called the improved terms of membership which he had negotiated at an EEC summit in Dublin. But seven of the 23-strong cabinet backed opposition to membership, as Wilson knew they would; the referendum was designed as much to keep Labour intact as to offer a democratic right to vote. The campaign cut across party lines, with the former Tory premier Edward Heath sharing platforms with Labour's Roy Jenkins and other pro-Europeans against such unlikely political bedfellows as Tony Benn and Enoch Powell (→ 3/1/77).

British elms struck by a deadly fungus

London, 30 October

A devastating fungus is spreading through the forests of England, destroying the country's elm trees. Already, according to the Forestry Commission, 6.5 million trees have died. Known as Dutch elm disease, it was identified in France in 1918, in the United States in 1933 and in Britain in the 1960s. The fungus is believed to be transmitted by the elm bark beetle, and there is no known cure; to prevent, or slow down, the spread of the disease, infected trees are cut down and then burnt. The elm is a valuable timber tree, being a tough, durable hardwood favoured by carpenters.

Thousands of elm trees are felled.

North Sea gold is just flowing ashore

Britain's first production platform.

Edinburgh, 3 November

Britain's currency took the first step towards becoming a "petropound" today, when the Queen inaugurated an underwater pipeline to bring North Sea oil ashore from BP's Forties Field. The pipeline runs for 100 miles (160km) on the seabed and then 127 miles underground to the Grangemouth refinery on the Firth of Forth. When the Forties comes into full production the pipeline will carry 400,000 barrels a day, about one quarter of the country's oil needs. Proved reserves are valued at £200,000 million; to exploit them engineers are operating in rough seas and harsh conditions on so far unexplored frontiers of technology (→ 30/4/77).

'Dev', a nationalist first and last, dies

Dublin, 29 August

Eamon de Valera, the former president of Ireland – the man who, in his life and character, had become the embodiment of Ireland in the first half of the 20th century – died today, aged 92. The fact that he was born in New York, the son of a Spanish father and an Irish mother, saved him from execution in 1916, though he was a leader of the Easter rising. He went on to become an astute and vigorous Irish republican leader, and from the time of his accession to power in 1932 until his death he overshadowed Irish public life (→ 2/10/75).

IRA gunmen hold husband and wife hostage in Balcombe Street

Armed police cover the flat which was under siege in Balcombe Street.

London, 12 December

IRA gunmen who had been holding a middle-aged couple hostage in their Balcombe Street home for six days surrendered peacefully today as members of the SAS prepared to storm the flat. The siege began when the four men, believed to have been part of the gang which has been terrorizing the West End, burst into Mr and Mrs Matthews' flat, following a car chase in which shots were fired when the gang was recognized by one of the policemen swamping London. They are now being questioned about the murders of a policeman and of Ross McWhirter, the editor of the *Guinness Book of Records* (→ 7/1/76).

James Callaghan, 64, is elected by Labour Party as the successor to Harold Wilson

Wilson resigns as prime minister.

Callaghan takes over at No 10.

Westminster, 5 April
James Callaghan is the new prime minister. Just three weeks after Harold Wilson unexpectedly announced his resignation, he gives way to an older man – the 64-year-old Callaghan, who held off a strong challenge from Michael Foot by 176 votes to 137. Previous rounds in the contest had eliminated Roy Jenkins, Tony Crosland, Tony Benn and Denis Healey.

No major change in government policy is expected, with Healey staying at the treasury to deal with the worsening economic crisis. Sterling is fragile, but the political cost of harsh economic medicine could be high. The government has a wafer-thin majority which could be eroded altogether through by-election losses. The strong leadership challenge of Michael Foot also indicates the growing strength of Labour's left-wing.

However, speculation about the cabinet is still secondary at Westminster to that concerning the reasons for Wilson's resignation. He says that he told the Queen last December, and had decided to go back in March 1974. Thirty years on the front bench was enough, he said, but voluntary retirement from the top in apparently full health is very rare in politics (→ 24/3/77).

UK guilty of torture

Strasbourg, France, 2 September
Britain was accused today of "inhumane treatment and torture" in its war against terrorist violence in Northern Ireland. A commission set up under the European Economic Community found that the "deep interrogation" techniques routinely used during the questioning of IRA suspects constituted a clear breach of human rights.

The British government has reacted angrily to reports that the Irish Republic plans to press these charges further. Dublin is asking that all allegations of torture should be heard by the European court of human rights (→ 19/1/78).

Oct 24. James Hunt: world motor-racing champion by a point.

Thorpe quits amid homosexual claims

Westminster, 10 May
Jeremy Thorpe has quit as Liberal leader after weeks of Westminster gossip. Thorpe, who is 47, said today that he could no longer stand "a sustained press witchhunt and campaign of denigration". He denied claims by an unemployed male model that they had had a homosexual relationship. "No man can effectively lead a party if the greater part of his time has to be devoted to answering allegations and countering plots and intrigues," said Thorpe, who was offered a cabinet post by Edward Heath in 1974 during moves to form a coalition government (→ 27/10/77).

Jeremy Thorpe: forced to resign.

Scots drink all day

Glasgow, 16 December
Although MPs today voted their approval "in principle" for the setting up of separate Scots and Welsh parliaments, few expect that these changes will ever be enacted. But for citizens north of the border, at any rate, there is one consolation prize: from now on, unlike the English, they will have the right to drink all day. As a result of section 64, subsection 3, of the Licensing (Scotland) Act, which is now safely on the statute book, pubs in certain places where there is strong local demand and no pressing official objections will be free to stay open from 11am to 11pm (→ 2/3/79).

Belfast women launch a peace campaign

Women and children of Belfast march for an end to the violence in their city.

Belfast, 8 August
The deaths of three Catholic children, run down by a hijacked car in west Belfast, has inspired the so-called "Peace People" to launch a campaign against violence from all sides. Mairéad Corrigan, the sister of the children's injured mother, Anne Maguire, joined Betty Williams and a journalist, Ciaran McKeown, to organize a peace march to the Shankhill Road, the traditional home of Belfast unionism.

The hijacked car's IRA driver had been shot dead by his army pursuers. Because of the tragic circumstances the peace women have won enormous public sympathy at a time when the political situation in the province looks gloomy. The constitutional convention, elected last year to advise on new political structures for Northern Ireland, broke up in March after MPs rejected a majority report calling for a reversion to an old-style Stormont, without power-sharing. On 21 July the new British ambassador to Dublin, Sir Christopher Ewart-Biggs, and his secretary died when an IRA landmine exploded under his armoured Jaguar (→ 27/11).

Britain borrows to prop up the pound

Blackpool, 28 September
James Callaghan bluntly warned the Labour party conference here today that Britain could no longer cut taxes and boost public spending. "You cannot spend your way out of a recession," said the prime minister, just 24 hours after the slide in the value of sterling had forced Denis Healey, the chancellor, to turn back at Heathrow from a planned trip to an international finance conference.

Despite swingeing public spending cuts and higher interest rates announced in July, sterling has continued to fall, plummeting by four cents against the dollar on Monday to a record low of $1.63. Alerted by the Bank of England to the run on reserves, Healey returned to the treasury where he is orchestrating an application for a massive loan of £2.3 billion from the International Monetary Fund (IMF).

The chancellor was later given a rough reception at the party conference, but this is just a foretaste of battles to come. The IMF loan to prop up the pound will entail further public spending cuts, much to the dismay of Labour left-wingers who accuse Healey and Callaghan of betraying socialism by implementing monetarist policies (→ 22/5/85).

Scorching hot sun breaks all records

Cooling off in Trafalgar Square.

London, 31 August
Cricket-loving crowds at Lord's cheered today when rain briefly stopped play in a crucial county match. It was the first break for weeks in Britain's cloudless, record-breaking summer. The heatwave, unrivalled since accurate records began, has delighted most people, filling parks and beaches with sunbathers. But it has forced the government to give the popular sports minister, Denis Howell, a second job: "minister for drought". Millions in Wales and the southwest are without water (→ 1/9).

National Theatre opens on South Bank

London, 25 October 1976
Britain's new National Theatre building was opened by the Queen tonight – the culmination of a campaign that began in 1907, when the actor-playwright Harley Granville-Barker and the critic William Archer published their *Scheme for a National Theatre* and won support from campaigners like Bernard Shaw. Denys Lasdun, the new building's architect, was the fifth to draw up plans for national theatres on as many sites. The result is a concrete structure resembling a liner and containing three auditoriums: the open-stage Olivier, the proscenium Lyttleton theatre and the Cottesloe studio space.

The Queen was welcomed by Sir Laurence Olivier (a peer who refuses to use his title in the theatre) on the stage which bears his name. He created the National Theatre as an illustrious company at the Old Vic in 1963 and gave way to Peter Hall as director in 1973 after much ill-health. "To those who follow I wish joy eternal of all of it," he said in what may be his last appearance on the stage.

The first productions in the two main auditoriums were *Hamlet* in the Lyttleton and *Tamburlaine the Great* in the Olivier, both starring Albert Finney and directed by Peter Hall. The building is not yet finished, and the Cottesloe is due to open next spring. The total cost of the building, met by the government and the Greater London Council, is running at £16 million, and the finishing and equipping of it is plagued by union disputes.

The sky is lit up with fireworks as the long-awaited National Theatre opens.

Liberals honour deal with Labour Party

David Steel, the Liberal leader.

Westminster, 24 March
Thirteen Liberal MPs tonight kept alive the Labour government by opposing a motion of "no confidence" tabled by the Conservatives. The vote was the first fruit of a "Lib-Lab pact" agreed between James Callaghan and David Steel, who succeeded Jeremy Thorpe as Liberal leader last year. It helps the government to buy time until the economy improves, and it gives the Liberals a toehold in government. Liberals will have a veto, in theory, over future cabinet proposals.

The pact dashed Tory hopes, which had soared when Nationalist MPs declared their intention to vote against Labour. By-election losses have cut the government's overall majority to just one, excluding the speaker and his deputies. Margaret Thatcher, the Conservative leader, mocked her party rivals as "timid men fearful of the fate they know awaits them". David Steel backs the pact as both a means of achieving greater influence for his party and a move towards electoral reform. But with his party in the electoral doldrums, he is also playing for time (→ 25/5/78).

Fianna Fáil party wins Irish elections

Ireland, 26 June
In the most substantial election reversal in Irish political history, Fianna Fáil, led by Jack Lynch, has been returned to power while the former coalition government has suffered a humiliating defeat. Three outgoing ministers (among them Conor Cruise O'Brien) have lost their seats. Liam Cosgrave has resigned as leader of Fine Gael, and Brendan Corish has resigned as leader of the Labour Party. The Fianna Fáil party worked hard for its victory, and fought a hard, intelligent and carefully prepared campaign. A detailed manifesto included specific promises. The most attractive, to a population crippled by inflation, was the removal of the rates paid by householders. Jack Lynch's personal appeal to voters was also a major factor in securing the result (→ 7/12/79).

Pickets turn violent at Grunwick strike

North London, 20 June
Police came under vicious attack today as they moved in to arrest 17 bottle-throwing pickets at the Grunwick film-processing laboratories, where a long-running strike has been fanned by left-wing political groups into a focus for increasingly violent protest.

Initially the dispute was about achieving union recognition for the plant's poorly paid, mainly Asian workforce. That has now become a secondary issue as TV teams arrive from all over the world to film the daily confrontations.

Oil rig blows sky high in North Sea

Attempts to quell the fire continue.

Aberdeen, 30 April
Eight days after the Bravo oil rig blew up in Norway's Ekofisk Field, a huge 1,000-square-mile slick is threatening wildlife and fishing along most of Scotland's eastern coastline. Only wind change now looks likely to avert a major ecological disaster. Over a hundred platform workers were safely evacuated when oil gushed 45 metres (150 feet) into the air during an attempted drilling-valve change. Twenty-eight million litres of crude then escaped before experts succeeded in applying an effective seal. Norway has called it the worst pollution catastrophe since North Sea oil-prospecting began (→ 27/6/78).

April 2. Red Rum, the crowd's favourite, returns to the winner's enclosure after becoming the first horse to win the Grand National hat trick.

Queen celebrates her silver jubilee

London, 7 June

The Queen lit a giant bonfire in Windsor Great Park tonight to launch a week of celebrations for her silver jubilee. As the flames leapt high above the trees, 100 other congratulatory beacons, from Land's End in Cornwall to Saxavord in the Shetland Isles, sparked into life. Many were on the same sites as the fires commanded in 1588 by Elizabeth I to mark the defeat of the Spanish Armada.

But although the country is almost universally happy to congratulate Elizabeth II on completing the first quarter-century of her reign, there is widespread recognition that not everything has gone well for Britain in the 25 years since she ascended the throne.

During that period virtually all the former colonies that made up the British Empire have achieved independence, and although Britain remains a nuclear power and, after a couple of false starts, is now con-

The Queen and the lord mayor of London on a jubilee "walkabout".

firmed as a member of the European Community, few would yet argue that this provides a fully satisfactory alternative role.

Although the country basked in unparalleled prosperity during the

1950s and 1960s, it has undoubtedly slipped several places down the world's economic league tables and is currently suffering very high unemployment, inflation and idle production capacity (→ 30/6/81).

Cricket crisis as Packer wins case

London, 25 November

Cricket's establishment today lost a legal battle to punish top players for joining a series of unofficial internationals planned by the Australian publisher Kerry Packer. The high court in London ruled that a proposed ban on players taking part in Packer's "cricket circus" was an unreasonable, and therefore illegal, restraint of trade.

Tony Greig and Ian Chappell, two former captains of England and Australia, head 35 test cricketers who have signed contracts with Packer for a series of matches in Australia this winter. This private venture is seen as a direct challenge to the future of test cricket.

Jubilant Wade wins glory at Wimbledon

Wimbledon, 1 July

The Queen's silver jubilee year saw an appropriate victory for patriots in the ladies' tennis final at Wimbledon today. Virginia Wade recovered from losing the first set to Betty Stove of the Netherlands to become the first British champion since Ann Jones in 1969. The Queen was present to witness her country's triumph in Wimbledon's own centenary year. Another Briton led the parade of former winners – Kitty Godfree, who was the champion in 1924 (→ 8/7/78).

Laker's 'no-frills' Skytrain leaves runway

The first Skytrain, Gatwick to New York, is waved off by Freddie Laker.

Gatwick airport, 26 September

More than 270 passengers queued for 24 hours to buy seats on the first cut-price Skytrain service to New York. They paid just £59 for a "no-frills" flight, while the cheapest regular single fare is £186.

As they filed on board, Freddie Laker, the man who made it all possible, personally thanked them all for "helping to prove me right"

in his belief that there is a profitable mass market in air travel at rock-bottom prices.

For an extra £1.75 they were able to enjoy a meal of paté, beef, apple pie, cheese and a small bottle of red wine. Although Laker has now successfully got his airline off the ground, the big carriers are expected to redouble their efforts to put him out of business (→ 7/2/82).

Economic statistics show steep decline

Birmingham, 31 December

For the first time since the invention of the internal combustion engine, Britain imported more cars this year than it made itself. This depressing statistic marks yet another significant milestone in the long history of industrial decline.

The drastic oil-price rise in the early 1970s and the resulting worldwide recession cruelly exposed the weaknesses of the country's manufacturing base. In trade after trade, from textiles and shoes through steel and heavy engineering to the new growth sectors of electronics and computers, the once dominant British market share has steadily dwindled. In many sectors, imports now dwarf home production.

Government efforts to reverse this trend have had only limited success. Despite the stepping up of governmental "trade and industry" support by 44 per cent this decade, to its present annual level of £2.6 billion, there is little sign of widespread revival. Nearly two million people are currently without work, a figure not seen since the 1930s.

Wade well on her way to winning.

Belfast, 25 February. In the wake of last week's restaurant bombing, the leading republican Gerry Adams is charged with membership of the IRA (→ 6/9).

London, 25 March. Oxford win the Boat Race after the Cambridge boat sinks a mile from the finish (→ 4/4/81).

London, 25 May. David Steel, the Liberal leader, says that the Lib-Lab pact will end with the current parliamentary session (→ 4/5/79).

Devon, 3 June. Jeremy Thorpe, the former Liberal leader, is interviewed by detectives investigating a plot to kill a former male model, Norman Scott (→ 4/8).

Wimbledon, 8 July. Bjorn Borg wins his third Wimbledon singles title (→ 7/7/85).

Westminster, 21 July. The government announces a new pay-increase guideline of 15 per cent; the unions reject it as unrealistic (→ 11/1978).

Somerset, 4 August. Jeremy Thorpe is accused with three others of plotting to kill Norman Scott (→ 20/11).

Manchester, 31 August. The *Express* newspaper group announces plans to launch a new national daily, possibly to be called the *Daily Star*.

Belfast, 6 September. Gerry Adams is released from jail after a judge rules that there is insufficient evidence to prove that he is a member of the IRA (→ 17/12).

London, 29 September. A Bulgarian defector, Georgi Markov, who died after being stabbed by an umbrella point, is believed to have been poisoned.

London, 23 October. The government plans to replace GCE "O" Level and CSE examinations with a single exam, the GCSE (→ 29/7/88).

Somerset, 20 November. Committal proceedings against Jeremy Thorpe, for allegedly plotting to murder Norman Scott, begin at Minehead (→ 13/12).

London, 30 November. Publication of *The Times* and the *Sunday Times* is suspended indefinitely, owing to industrial action.

London, 17 December. Police step up security as the IRA begins a Christmas bombing campaign (→ 30/3/79).

Britain found guilty of inhumane action

Strasbourg, France, 19 January
Britain has been found guilty of using interrogation techniques that were "inhumane and degrading, in breach of Article 3 of the Human Rights Convention" in Northern Ireland. But the judges of the European Court of Human Rights threw out, by 13 votes to four, the much more serious charges of torture which the government of the Irish Republic has been trying to establish for the past two years. Dublin reacted angrily to the decision and issued a long statement justifying its acrimonious pursuit of the case, on which it is believed to have spent over £300,000.

Cricket newcomer Ian Botham a star

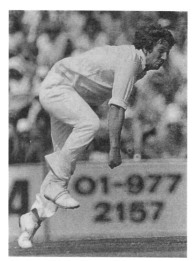

Botham is the hero of the test.

London, 19 June
English cricket has a new star. In the test against Pakistan which ended at Lord's today, Ian Botham achieved the finest all-round performance ever recorded by an England player. Botham, who is 22, struck his third century in seven test matches before his medium-fast swing bowling produced figures of eight wickets for 34 runs in Pakistan's second innings: the best analysis since Jim Laker took all ten Australian wickets in an innings in 1956. The Somerset all-rounder has now captured five wickets in an innings five times in his first seven test matches (→ 21/7/81).

World's first 'test-tube baby' is delivered

Manchester, 26 July
The world's first "test-tube baby" was born just before midnight tonight at Oldham General Hospital, in Greater Manchester. The baby girl's successful delivery, by Caesarean section, marks a potentially enormous step forward in the ability of medical science not only to treat infertility, which was the immediate objective, but also, more controversially, to establish much greater control over the whole process of human reproduction.

Meanwhile Dr Patrick Steptoe, who was responsible for both the delivery and a large part of the 12-year research programme which made it possible, said: "All examinations showed that the baby is quite normal." Mrs Lesley Brown, her mother, was said to be "enjoying a well earned sleep".

The embryo which became baby Louise had been implanted in Mrs

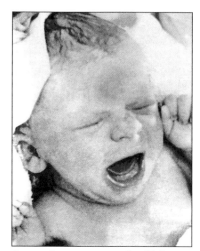

Louise Brown screams healthily.

Brown's womb last November after one of her eggs was fertilized under laboratory conditions by her husband's sperm. Mrs Brown was sterile because of blocked fallopian tubes (→ 26/3/82).

Belfast bomb kills at least 14 in restaurant

Northern Ireland, 18 February
Twenty IRA suspects were arrested in Belfast today following yesterday's terrorist attack on the Le Mons restaurant, ten miles east of the city. Blast incendiaries turned the restaurant into an inferno, killing 14 people at a dog-club dinner and injuring many more. Unusually, the IRA issued an abject apology, accepting that its nine-minute warning was "totally inadequate". But it went on to claim that "all killings stem from British ... denial of Irish sovereignty".

Several hotels in Northern Ireland were attacked during a two-week IRA blitz before Christmas aimed at destroying the remaining tourist trade (→ 25).

Mrs Bridges (Angela Baddeley), Hudson (Gordon Jackson), Rose (Jean Marsh): below-stairs stars of the ITV series "Upstairs Downstairs".

North Sea gives UK oil self-sufficiency

Aberdeen, 27 June

Oil output from the North Sea has exceeded one million barrels a day for the first time. The latest monthly production figures show that Britain is now the 16th biggest oil-producing nation and is set to become totally self-sufficient within two years. Current liftings, running at the rate of 56 million tonnes a year, represent 60 per cent of demand. But new discoveries are being made all the time, and Britain will soon be able not only to meet all its own needs but also to become a substantial exporter (→ 27/3/80).

Princess announces intention to divorce

The royal couple in happier times.

London, 10 May

Princess Margaret, the Queen's younger sister, is seeking a divorce from her husband, the earl of Snowdon. The couple have been separated for the past two years, and it is expected that the two children of the marriage will continue, as at present, to live with their mother.

Under the proposed settlement Lord Snowdon will receive a house in central London. He has already resumed his former career as a successful photographer. The princess plans to continue her public engagements. Her official position will be unaffected by the split.

Former Liberal leader goes on trial

Jeremy Thorpe, looking drawn and tired, takes a walk with his wife, Marion.

Minehead, Somerset, 13 December

Jeremy Thorpe, the former leader of the Liberal Party, was today committed for trial at the Old Bailey charged, with three other men, with conspiracy and incitement to murder. The alleged victim of the conspiracy and murder plot was Norman Scott, a former male model who has alleged that he and Thorpe once had a homosexual relationship. Thorpe, who has always denied this allegation, said in court: "I plead not guilty and will vigorously defend this matter."

The magistrates told that Thorpe allegedly paid £5,000 for Scott to be shot, decided that there was a *prima facie* case to be answered. Thorpe resigned as party leader in 1976 because of press speculation about Scott (→ 22/6/79).

More seek sun, fun and cheap holidays

Heathrow airport, 31 December

Airlines, charter firms, package-tour operators, cross-Channel ferries and the whole range of travel agents all report yet another near-record year as more and more Britons seek their annual dose of sea, sun and getting away from it all.

Officially a holiday is defined as any four nights or more away from home that are not spent on business. On that basis Britons took 48 million of them in 1978, almost equalling the 49 million peak recorded in 1973. An ever-increasing number of holidays are spent abroad. Some nine million holidaymakers crossed the Atlantic, the North Sea or the Channel this year – up from seven million in 1971, and from just two million in 1951. By far the most popular destination is still Spain, which attracts 30 per cent of all these tourists.

Union clashes with government over a 15 per cent pay rise

Dagenham, Essex, November

A 17 per cent pay rise has been agreed by the Ford motor company, effectively torpedoing the government's hopes of imposing a 15 per cent pay norm on British industry this year. This policy was rejected by both the TUC and the Labour Party conferences this autumn, although the Labour government had already signalled that it was determined to maintain its tough anti-inflationary stance.

Car workers at Ford were the first major group to challenge the policy, with a claim for a minimum pay rise of £20 a week. By the end of September all 23 plants were at a standstill. The 17 per cent pay deal conceded by the Ford management sets a benchmark for other industries far in excess of what the government insists will be imposed on public sector workers. The success of the Ford strike will encourage other workers to adopt militant tactics. James Callaghan, the prime minister, said this month that this winter will be "make or break" for his government (→ 14/2/79).

Punk faces the future without Sex Pistols

Britain, 31 December

The outlook for punk is not good: the year ends amidst persistent rumours that the archetypal punk band, the Sex Pistols, is soon to split up. Things certainly look bleak for their bassist, Sid Vicious, currently facing police charges in New York for the murder of his girlfriend, Nancy Spungen, last October.

Punks dressed in all their finery.

Maybe punk can survive the Pistols' demise: it has, after all, been around for a while. It first hit the headlines in 1976 and has since won the notoriety that it always craved. Its acolytes like their music simple, loud, fast and aggressive. One- or two-minute songs are thrashed out by the likes of the Clash, Sham 69 and Generation X with a commitment and fury totally at odds with the disco music of the charts.

Yet punk is more than the music alone. It offers teenagers what they have always sought from rock: a vehicle for their wish to rebel. Committed to "anarchy", punks set out to shock, with their dyed Mohican hairstyles, torn mohair sweaters, bondage gear and spitting at the stage during gigs – and that is just the girls.

Britain in grip of political turmoil

Britons suffer harsh winter of discontent

London, 14 February

Union leaders and ministers today announced a St Valentine's day agreement in a bid to end the "winter of discontent" caused by a rash of strikes. What began in January as a strike by lorry drivers for a 25 per cent claim escalated into a wave of action that has seen rubbish pile up in streets, food and petrol supplies disrupted, patients turned away from hospitals and even the dead left unburied.

The settlement of the strike by petrol-tanker drivers only opened the floodgates for others, as the drivers' 14 per cent pay deal shattered the government's 5 per cent pay norm. Disputes spread to the public sector, causing widespread chaos. With James Callaghan, the prime minister, at a summit in the West Indies, Margaret Thatcher, the Tory leader, moved to attack union power. "A boneless wonder" was her verdict on today's deal.

Labour is doomed by devolution issue

Westminster, 28 March

Two Irish MPs abstained tonight and brought down the Labour government. James Callaghan lost a no-confidence motion by a single vote – 311 to 310 – and becomes the first prime minister to be defeated on such a motion since 1924.

Callaghan's parliamentary problems became acute on 2 March when devolution referendums were held in Wales and Scotland. Since the ending of the Lib-Lab pact last year the government had relied on Nationalist MPs for its majority. Voters in Wales rejected devolution and while those in Scotland were narrowly in favour of a Scottish Assembly they failed to achieve the required 40 per cent figure. When the government rejected pleas by Scottish Nationalist MPs to push ahead regardless, the Nationalists withdrew their support. With one Labour MP absent through illness, the government was doomed (→ 29).

Piles of uncollected rubbish fill the streets as the strike continues.

Thatcher victorious in general election

London, 4 May

Margaret Thatcher today became the first woman to be prime minister of Britain. She moved into Downing Street following the Conservatives' victory in yesterday's election, promising that "where there is discord may we bring harmony". The final figures are Conservatives 339, Labour 269, Liberal 11, Nationalists 4, others 13.

Labour has slumped to 36.9 per cent of the vote – its lowest since 1931. The Tories had two million more voters with 43.9 per cent of the poll, with particularly high swings in their favour in southern England. Although the Tory lead in the opinion polls was cut during the campaign, the legacy of the "winter of discontent" proved impossible for James Callaghan, the outgoing premier, to shake off (→ 12/6).

Winning wave from Mrs Thatcher.

Change of direction signalled at No 10

Westminster, 12 June

Margaret Thatcher's government has lost little time in signalling a change in economic direction. The first budget introduced today by Sir Geoffrey Howe, the chancellor of the exchequer, slashes income tax, boosts indirect taxes such as VAT and attacks public spending. Controls on pay, prices and dividends are to be scrapped, while a range of measures is planned to offer incentives to businessmen. The budget has the hallmark of the "enterprise culture" espoused by monetarist Tories such as Sir Keith Joseph.

Mrs Thatcher believes that her election victory last month is a watershed in post-war politics. The old Keynesian primacy of public spending, the power of the unions and the corporatism of the welfare state are all blamed for contributing to economic decline (→ 10/10/80).

Oil-tanker blast kills 49 in Ireland

Bantry Bay, Co Cork, 8 January
A series of explosions tore apart an oil tanker early this morning, claiming the lives of 49 people. The ship, owned by the Total oil company, was unloading her 120,000-ton cargo when the first blast turned her into a fireball and shook the whole town. Seven of the victims were shore-workers. Witnesses said that the tanker had discharged half her load when she exploded without warning. Tugs fought the blaze but were forced to retreat by spreading patches of burning oil. Total officials are mystified as to the possible cause of the disaster.

Charles Haughey is elected as Irish PM

Ireland, 7 December
Charles Haughey, the former minister of health, has defeated George Colley for leadership of the Fianna Fáil party, following the surprise resignation of Jack Lynch, and is now prime minister. A controversial figure, he stood trial in 1970 for importing arms, and was acquitted.

Haughey remained on the back benches of the party until 1975, when Jack Lynch, then in opposition, was persuaded to bring him on to the front bench as spokesman on health (→ 30/6/81).

February 9: Trevor Francis joins Nottingham Forest as the first ever £1 million footballer.

IRA kills public figures

Airey Neave's car, blown up as it left the House of Commons' car park.

Mullaghmore, Co Sligo, 27 August
Shock and outrage have greeted the murder today of Earl Mountbatten of Burma, formerly supreme Allied commander in South-east Asia, the last viceroy of India and a cousin of the Queen. In a day of horrific IRA carnage 15 soldiers also died in a massive blast at Warrenpoint, Co Down. The 79-year-old earl, who was holidaying at his Irish home, Classiebawn Castle, died instantly when an IRA bomb ripped apart his boat, the *Shadow V*. His grandson Nicholas, aged 14, and a boatman of 17 also died in the blast. For the second time in five months a respected public figure has died at the hands of the IRA. On 30 March Airey Neave, the hardline Tory spokesman on Northern Ireland who was a close aide of Margaret Thatcher, died when a bomb blew up under his car as it left the Commons's car park (→ 23/11).

'Yorkshire Ripper' claims his twelfth victim

Bradford, 2 September
The murder of Barbara Leach, aged 20, a student at Bradford University, brings to 12 the total of women killed by the man known as "the Yorkshire Ripper". The grisly nickname derives from the bizarre way in which he mutilates his victims' bodies. The body of the Ripper's 12th victim was found on the borders of the city's red-light district, but unlike most of the previous victims in a reign of terror that has lasted four years, Barbara Leach was not a prostitute. Detectives leading one of the biggest manhunts ever mounted in Britain warn that after this seemingly random attack no woman can be safe alone on the streets at night (→ 2/10).

Royal art adviser was 'Fourth Man'

Anthony Blunt – the fourth man.

Westminster, 21 November
Sir Anthony Blunt, the art adviser to the Queen and a guru to generations of art students, was a Russian spy, the prime minister told shocked members of parliament today. In a written answer, Margaret Thatcher named Blunt as the fourth man in the Burgess, Maclean and Philby spy ring. She said that he had been investigated in 1964 and after being granted immunity from prosecution had admitted his role as a long-term Soviet agent, talent-spotting for the KGB in pre-war Cambridge. Blunt, who is in hiding abroad, has been stripped of his knighthood (→ 26/3/83).

Irish Catholics rejoice as the pope makes a peace visit to Ireland

Dublin, 30 September
No pop star could have expected a more rousing welcome than that which Pope John Paul II received today from the Irish nation. One and a quarter million people came to Phoenix Park to watch his plane arrive at Dublin airport. Two hours later he said Mass in the park with 40 cardinals and bishops. He then conducted a huge service outside Drogheda where the congregation included 250,000 from Northern Ireland. The pope's message was peace. "On my knees I beg you," he said, "to turn away from violence. Further violence will only drag down to ruin the land you claim to love and the values you claim to cherish" (→ 29/5/82).

Pope John Paul II brings his message of peace to the Catholics of Ireland.

Oil-rig tragedy kills 100

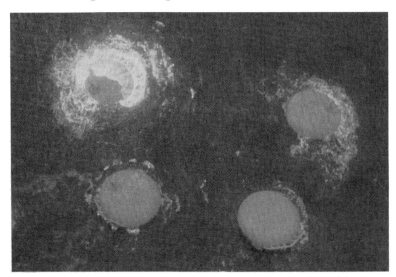

The upturned feet of four of its legs mark the capsized rig's position.

North Sea, 27 March

An oil platform capsized in stormy seas today, leaving half the 200 men aboard feared dead. It took just 15 minutes for the Alexander Kielland, a semi-submersible platform, to disappear beneath the waves after one of its five massive air-filled steel legs was broken, presumably by a wave. It was a floating hotel for North Sea rig workers, about 50 of whom were in the cinema at the time. Many must have drowned, but rescuers hope some will have survived in air pockets.

Phillips Petroleum, the owners of the Alexander Kielland, said: "We fear a great disaster." Helicopters, planes and at least 13 ships have gone to the rescue. Seven people are known to have died, and bodies have been seen hundreds of metres away. Some survivors were flown ashore, others given emergency treatment on a production platform nearby. Tom Greenwood, a survivor, saw disaster strike at 6.30pm: "Metal screeched as it began to keel over. Suddenly men were cut and bleeding" (→ 6/7/88).

Fury as missile base opens in Greenham

Berkshire, 17 June

Anti-nuclear protesters, mostly women, are gathering in response to the news that US-owned cruise missiles are to be based at the US Air Force airfield at Greenham, and later at Molesworth in Cambridgeshire. The missiles are among 160 to be based in Britain after NATO's decision to counter the Soviet SS-20 rockets being moved into Eastern Europe. Britain is the first NATO country to accept cruise missiles on its land (→ 12/12/82).

Heart attack kills chiller master Hitch

Bel Air, California, 29 April

Alfred Hitchcock, the Leytonstone greengrocer's son who became one of film's great masters of suspense, died today, aged 80. He made the first British talkie, *Blackmail*, in 1929, and successes such as *The Lady Vanishes* and *The Thirty-Nine Steps* followed. He moved to Hollywood and won an Oscar for his first film there, *Rebecca*. Later chillers included *Rear Window*, *Psycho* and *The Birds*. "Hitch", knighted four months ago, could be glimpsed briefly in most of his films.

Thatcher says 'the lady's not for turning' as ministers squabble

Strikers, including "flying pickets" from Corby, are pushed aside at the steel stockists John Lee Co in Grantham, Lincs – Mrs Thatcher's home town.

Brighton, 10 October

Margaret Thatcher today made clear her determination not to abandon her tough economic policies in the face of rising unemployment and increasing divisions within the cabinet. She told the Tory conference here that there would be no policy U-turns like those of Edward Heath in the 1970s. "You turn if you like," she said. "The lady's not for turning."

Unemployment is now over two million, and there have been bitter strikes involving steelworkers, who are in one of the heavy industries most hit by the current recession. More liberal (or "wet") members of the cabinet, such as James Prior, Peter Walker and Francis Pym, are resisting treasury demands – backed by Mrs Thatcher – for savage cuts in public spending (→ 15).

Iranian embassy stormed by SAS

Kensington, London, 5 May
Television viewers watched a real-life thriller this evening as the Special Air Service stormed the terrorist-held Iranian embassy and released 19 hostages. Cameras had been trained on the elegant Regency terrace overlooking Hyde Park since the siege began six days ago, when five gunmen captured the embassy staff and demanded the release of political prisoners in Iran. Suddenly, the news emerged that the terrorists had shot dead one hostage and were threatening to kill another every half-hour.

Within minutes, men in black uniforms and balaclavas, carrying sub-machine guns, had leapt onto the balcony and attached explosives to the windows, while their comrades abseiled from the roof to break in from the rear. When the charge went off, the SAS men ran inside, threw stun grenades and hunted down the terrorists, who had opened fire on their captives.

The SAS gives cover as a hostage is guided to safety during the siege.

One Iranian diplomat was killed and another badly wounded.

The terrorist leader would have killed one SAS man had he not been tackled by PC Trevor Lock, who had been on duty when the gunmen first invaded the embassy. Four of the five terrorists were shot dead by the SAS, who bundled the hostages to safety. The fifth survived after women hostages had pleaded for his life.

Foot leads the way for Labour Party

Westminster, 10 November
Michael Foot tonight became the new leader of the Labour Party, following the resignation of the former premier, James Callaghan, last month. Foot, a 67-year-old left-winger, defeated Denis Healey, the combative standard-bearer of the right in Labour's increasingly bitter sectarian divisions, by 139 votes to 129 in a ballot of Labour MPs. Tory ministers are surprised and delighted. Foot, a former Fleet Street editor, is an engaging, cultured man, but they believe that as a nuclear disarmer with relatively limited experience of high office he is a vulnerable opponent. Healey is a former chancellor and defence secretary with a populist appeal that the Tories feared (→ 9/5/83).

Foot gives a wave as the new leader.

Obsessive fan shoots John Lennon at point-blank range

New York, 8 December
John Lennon, whose music inspired a generation, was shot dead tonight by a crazed fan. The former Beatle, aged 40, had been at a recording session and was walking into the Dakota building with his wife Yoko Ono when Mark Chapman, to whom Lennon had given his autograph earlier in the day, came up to him and fired five shots at point-blank range from a .38 revolver.

As word of the shooting spread, fans began a vigil outside the Dakota. Lennon was rushed to Roosevelt hospital for surgery but never recovered. His killer, meanwhile, read *The Catcher in the Rye* while waiting to be arrested. He is being held under high security in Tombs prison. Police say that Chapman flew from Hawaii, where he bought the gun, and stalked Lennon for three days before shooting him.

Golding steals Booker prize from Burgess

Burgess: a master of language.

London, 21 October
Two of Britain's small number of literary titans fought it out for this year's Booker prize for fiction. William Golding, a veteran of 69 with *Lord of the Flies* and *Free Fall* to his credit, published *Rites of Passage*, the account of a voyage to Australia in a converted wooden warship, written by a young man setting out for a colonial post. The writing in period idiom is a *tour de force*. Against it was ranged the latest meaty novel from the prolific Anthony Burgess. *Earthly Powers* is also a *tour de force* about an attempt to canonize a pope, narrated by a homosexual novelist. It was a close contest between top-class entries. Golding just won.

Sebastian Coe (c), disappointed by a silver medal in the Olympic 800m, pushes himself to his limit to win the gold medal in the 1,500m final.

Britain suffers worst riots of century

All is quiet on Mayall Road, Brixton, after a night of violence and terror.

Police struggle with a rioter as the streets of Toxteth erupt in violence.

SDP takes shape

London, 25 January

At Limehouse today a time-bomb was placed under British politics by four former Labour cabinet ministers. "The gang of four", as Roy Jenkins, Shirley Williams, David Owen and William Rodgers are nicknamed, issued a statement attacking Labour for drifting towards extremism. They were stung into action by a special Labour Party conference this month at Wembley which gave more power to unions and party activists in selecting leaders and MPs. The proposed Council for Social Democracy could become a fully fledged party.

July 29. A fairytale wedding for the Prince of Wales, who married Lady Diana Spencer in St Paul's Cathedral today (→ 21/6/82).

Liverpool, 13 July

As shopkeepers in Liverpool, London, Hull, Wolverhampton, Reading, Birmingham, Preston and Chester shovel up the broken glass from their shopfronts, and bulldozers clear the barricades of cars and rubbish from the streets, Britain reflects on its worse week of rioting this century.

Trouble began in the Liverpool ghetto of Toxteth on 4 July when black and white youths attacked the police. Next day the police withdrew from the area, admitting that the mob had got "out of control". By the week's end there was rioting and looting in eleven different inner city areas, reaching its climax on 10 July, "Britain's night of anarchy".

This week's riots were far more extensive than April's riot at Brixton, in south London, when what began as a confrontation between black youths and police cracking down on street crime turned into a two-night orgy of looting, vandalism and arson as young blacks and whites – mostly unemployed – attacked the police.

Government spokesmen affirm that they will not permit any "no-go" areas – where police cannot go in Britain – and dismiss the political significance of much of this week's anarchy as "copy-cat" riots. Community leaders disagree, pointing to the high levels of poverty and unemployment and to the perception of young blacks that they are harassed by the police for being both young and black (→ 29/9/85).

Disco fire kills 49

Dublin, 14 February

Ireland is in shock and mourning after 49 Dubliners, mostly teenagers, burnt to death in a disco fire during a St Valentine's day dance. A further 130 who survived are in hospital with severe burns. The ceiling of the Stardust Club was made of plastic, the emergency exit doors were blocked, and there were iron bars on the windows to prevent people from coming in without paying. Once the ceiling caught fire the flames spread. The ceiling melted onto the victims, who were trapped in the building, as the exit was blocked by panicking crowds.

FitzGerald is new premier of Ireland

Ireland, 30 June

Following a general election, Dr Garret FitzGerald has taken office as prime minister at the head of a precarious Fine Gael/Labour Party coalition government which depends on the support of three Independent deputies.

It has been a troubled year for the out-going Fianna Fáil government, beset by difficulties caused by the IRA prisoners' hunger strike in Northern Ireland. Added to this has been the exposure of serious deficiencies in economic forecasting, reinforcing vigorous criticism by the opposition of the government's prodigality (→ 12/1982).

IRA hunger strike ends

Belfast, 3 October

Six republicans ended a seven-month hunger-strike campaign in the Maze prison today as it became clear that their families would intervene to save their lives. There were also signs that the government would concede some of their demands. The campaign began after the withdrawal in 1976 of the special status for terrorists. Prisoners refused to wear uniform and smeared excrement around their cells. Bobby Sands, aged 27, began his fast on 1 March. Sands, elected as Sinn Féin MP for Fermanagh and South Tyrone on 9 April, became the first striker to achieve IRA martyrdom on 5 May (→ 14/11).

Marchers rally in support of the IRA hunger strikers in the Maze prison.

Sutcliffe confesses to 'Ripper' murders

London, 29 April

Peter Sutcliffe, a 34-year-old Bradford lorry driver with a neat beard and an impassive stare, stood in the dock at the Old Bailey today and admitted that he was "the Yorkshire Ripper". In his four-year reign of terror he had killed 13 women and attempted to kill another seven, mostly prostitutes. He denies murder but admits manslaughter on the grounds of diminished responsibility. Behind him sat two survivors of his attacks. In front of Sutcliffe were laid out the Ripper's tools: knives, drills, hammers and screwdrivers. His wife, Sonia, only a metre away, looked as impassive as her husband (→ 24/5/89).

Peter Sutcliffe on his wedding day.

Blank shots fired at Queen in the Mall

London, 30 June

As the Queen rode side-saddle down the Mall for the Trooping of the Colour, six shots range out from the crowd, fired by an unemployed youth, Marcus Sargeant. Police and guardsmen disarmed him while the Queen, recovering from the shock, patted her black mare Burmese on the neck to reassure her, then continued on to Horseguards' Parade.

The shots, it later turned out, were blanks. Sargeant – who has been charged under the Treason Act – told Special Branch officers that his action was a protest against unemployment (→ 7/7/82).

Penlee lifeboatmen perish in rescue bid

Cornwall, 20 December

Eight lifeboatmen – all unpaid volunteers – perished today off Land's End with four shipwrecked sailors whom they had rescued. The lifeboat was launched from the tiny fishing village of Mousehole, two miles from Penzance, into hurricane-lashed seas to answer an SOS call from the 1,400-tonne coaster *Union Star*, dashed on rocks.

Though the men took four crew members off the stricken ship, the lifeboat was crushed against the *Union Star* by 18-metre (60-foot) waves before it could take off the remaining eight.

Crippled Irish novelist Christy Brown dies

The talented artist Christy Brown.

Co Kerry, 7 September

Christy Brown, one of Ireland's authentic novelists despite having cerebral palsy from birth, died here today at the age of 48. He was one of a family of 13 and had the full use of only one of his limbs, his left foot. He grew up in Dublin, where his father was a bricklayer. He learned to draw and paint with his foot before he could talk. In 1954 he wrote the moving account of his struggles, *My Left Foot*, and in 1970 an autobiographical novel, *Down All Our Days*, which had all the tang and unsentimentality of the Dublin slums.

July. The Humber Bridge, the world's longest single-span suspension bridge, under construction since January 1980, is officially opened.

Britain at war in the Falkland Islands

The "General Belgrano" lists and sinks after the British submarine attack.

A survivor from HMS "Sheffield".

South Atlantic, 4 May

The harsh realities of modern war were brought home to the British task force today when the destroyer HMS *Sheffield* sank after being hit by an Exocet missile which had been launched from a Super Etendard fighter flying beneath the fleet's radar screen. Captain James "Sam" Salt only had time to shout "Take cover" before the missile struck.

The rocket's unexpended fuel set fire to the *Sheffield's* plastic and aluminium fittings, and the "Shiny Sheff" was blotted out by poisonous black fumes. Other ships sent their fire-fighting teams, but the fires were too fierce. The battle to save her went on for five hours; she was taken in tow, but, as if tired of the struggle, she rolled over and sank. Twenty of her crew were killed.

This setback is a major blow to Britain's attempt to regain the Falkland Islands – long claimed by their nearest neighbour, Argentina, and invaded last month. It follows the sinking of the Argentinian cruiser *General Belgrano* by the nuclear-powered submarine HMS *Conqueror*, and the recapture of South Georgia, a Falklands dependency, by Royal Marine commandos. When Margaret Thatcher, the prime minister, announced the news that South Georgia had been taken she cried "Rejoice", but the threat of the radar-guided Exocets, which can be launched more than 20 miles (32km) from their targets and skim the waves at speeds of 700mph (1,125kph), will ensure that regaining the Falklands will be no walkover despite the great success of the Harrier jump-jets in protecting the task force.

Politically, the sinking of the *Sheffield* – the first loss of a major British warship for 37 years – has sent tremors round Westminster, with some Tory MPs demanding the bombing of Argentina. Cooler heads argue that this would harm the justice of Britain's cause (→ 22).

Argentinians surrender as British forces regain Port Stanley

Port Stanley, 14 June

Fighting in the Falklands ended today with the surrender of Major-General Menendez, the Argentinian commander, and tonight the Union flag flies over Port Stanley once more. The end came when British troops, fighting hand to hand, broke through the last ring of defences at Tumbledown mountain, and the Argentinians began to leave their well prepared defences and stream back to the port.

White flags were blossoming like flowers, and a Spanish-speaking British officer got through to Menendez by radio and convinced him of the hopelessness of his situation. Shortly afterwards Major-General Jeremy Moore, Land Forces Commander, signalled London: "The Falkland Islands are once more under the government desired by their inhabitants. God save the Queen."

His news was received with rejoicing in the House of Commons, and Margaret Thatcher said that the victory had been won by an operation which was "boldly planned, bravely executed and brilliantly accomplished". However, there can be no doubt that this campaign, fought 8,000 miles away, was balanced on a knife edge. The loss of the *Atlantic Conveyor* and her supplies was a disaster, and it is unlikely that the task force could have continued the fight much longer. The known death toll is 255 British and 652 Argentinian (→ 22/7).

The British flag flies at Port Stanley.

Pope's visit to Britain ends 450-year rift

Canterbury, 29 May
Pope John Paul II, on an historic visit to Britain, prayed in Canterbury Cathedral today with the archbishop of Canterbury, Dr Robert Runcie. It was the most dramatic gesture of reconciliation between the Anglican and Roman Catholic Churches since Henry VIII's split with Rome 450 years ago.

One of Henry's descendants, the Prince of Wales, was there to represent the Queen, the supreme head of the Church of England, and emotions spilt over in tears and applause as the pope stepped out of the sunshine into the cool nave to a fanfare of trumpets. The pope and the archbishop announced the creation of a commission to study the reunification of the churches.

Historic moment: Archbishop Robert Runcie (l) prays with the pope.

FitzGerald returns as PM after hectic year

Ireland, December
Following the second of two elections this year, political stability has been restored by a coalition between Fine Gael and the Labour Party, with Garret FitzGerald as prime minister.

The first election took place in March after a particularly harsh budget brought in by the 1981/2 coalition government, also led by Dr FitzGerald. Neither of the two main parties achieved a majority, but Charles Haughey managed to secure the support of left-wing deputies, and he and his Fianna Fáil party were therefore able to form a government.

That administration then faced a period of severe economic crisis and was weakened by political scandals,

Haughey campaigning in Dublin.

dissension, the death of one deputy and the serious illness of another. Defeat in a no-confidence motion brought about by FitzGerald ended one of the unhappiest years in Irish politics (→ 10/3/87).

Uninvited visitor in Queen's bedroom

London, 7 July
Michael Fagan, a 35-year-old unemployed Irishman, climbed into Buckingham Palace early today, took a bottle of wine and made his way to the Queen's bedroom, where he woke her by drawing the curtains and then sitting on her bed to chat about his family.

He sat there for at least eight minutes, and it was not until he asked for a cigarette that the Queen was able to alert the switchboard. Fagan was then escorted from the bedroom by a footman and arrested by embarrassed policemen. Heads will undoubtedly roll (→ 12/10/86).

Women lead peaceful anti-missile protest at Greenham Common

Non-violent protesters plan the next move outside the missile base.

Berkshire, 12 December
Greenham Common airbase was ringed by 20,000 women holding hands today to "embrace the base" in protest at the proposed siting there of 96 US cruise missiles. The women, mostly from the "Peace Camp" they have established on common ground outside the base, have been staging a vigil here since September. The council has twice tried to evict them but has failed.

Their demonstration went off peacefully today, with stirring anti-war songs and a great shout of "Freedom" as the circle was completed. Tomorrow they plan to blockade the base and confront US servicemen (→ 1/4/83).

Laker's dream dies as airline collapses

Gatwick airport, 7 February
Sir Freddie Laker, the pioneer of cut-price air travel, is "in a state of misery" following the collapse three days ago of Laker Airways. He cannot even take heart from the offers of help which are pouring in. One businessman, who argued that Sir Freddie has done more for enterprise in Britain than anyone else in the past 25 years, offered £1 million. Prince Michael of Kent sent a telegram offering his support. But the banks have decided otherwise.

TV's fourth channel sparks early row

London, 2 December
The new ITV Channel Four has run into trouble only a month after it started transmitting. William Whitelaw, the home secretary, tonight expressed concern at the "bad language, political bias and many other undesirable qualities" which he says that people have found in its programmes. The channel was set up to cater for minorities, but some viewers are shocked by explicit discussion of subjects such as homosexuality and feminism (→ 17/1/83).

The spectacular flood barrier across the river Thames is completed.

Britain, 1 February. ITV's breakfast television programme, TV-am, goes on the air (→ 5/4/87).

Britain, 3 February. Unemployment figures reach an all-time high of 3,224,715 (→ 18/6/87).

London, 26 March. Anthony Blunt, the Queen's former art adviser and a Russian spy, dies.

Berkshire, 1 April. Thousands of CND supporters form a 14-mile-long human chain linking Greenham to Burghfield in protest at the cruise missile base.

Westminster, 9 May. Margaret Thatcher calls a general election for 9 June (→ 10/6).

Westminster, 12 June. Michael Foot resigns as leader of the Labour Party (→ 13).

Westminster, 13 June. Roy Jenkins resigns as leader of the SDP; he suggests Dr David Owen as his successor (→ 2/10).

Westminster, 14 September. John Selwyn Gummer succeeds Cecil Parkinson as chairman of the Conservative Party (→ 5/10).

Westminster, 2 October. Neil Kinnock is the new leader of the Labour Party; his deputy is Roy Hattersley.→

London, 5 October. Cecil Parkinson admits having had a relationship with his secretary, Sara Keays (→ 14).

Westminster, 16 October. Norman Tebbit succeeds Cecil Parkinson as secretary for trade and industry.

Belfast, 12 November. Gerry Adams is elected leader of Sinn Féin (→ 22).

Liverpool, 18 November. Janet Walton, a 31-year-old, gives birth to sextuplets, all girls.

Northern Ireland, 22 November. The Unionist Party pulls out of the Ulster Assembly after three church elders were shot dead in South Armagh last Sunday (→ 4/12).

London, 26 November. Over £25 million in gold bars is stolen from Heathrow airport in one of the UK's biggest robberies.

Northern Ireland, 4 December. Allegations of a "shoot-to-kill" policy are raised after the deaths of two IRA gunmen in an SAS ambush (→ 17).

London, 17 December. The IRA steps up its Christmas bombing campaign with a bomb in Harrods (→ 14/3/84).

Irish wonder-horse Shergar is snatched

Shergar: where is he now?

Co Kildare, 9 February

Shergar, the winner of the Epsom and Irish Derbies and worth more than £10 million at stud, has been stolen from the Ballymany Stud near Newbridge. Details of the theft are unclear, and the mystery is not made easier by the fact that nine hours elapsed before the police were alerted.

There are rumours both that he has been killed and that he has been seen in dozens of little villages. It is known, however, that a ransom demand for £2 million has been made by telephone. Suspicion is hardening that the wonder-horse, owned by a syndicate headed by the Aga Khan, has been taken not by a man of the turf but by the IRA.

Cereal, eggs, toast and breakfast TV

London, 17 January

Early-morning television began today with the BBC's "Breakfast Time", presented by Selina Scott and Frank Bough. Despite some moans that people do not want, or need, TV with their cornflakes, the BBC is confident that breakfast TV is here to stay. Next month ITV's early morning show, TV-am, headed by "the Famous Five" – David Frost, Robert Kee, Angela Rippon, Anna Ford and Michael Parkinson – goes on the air (→ 1/2).

Thatcher back in power

Westminster, 10 June

The Conservative vote fell in the general election yesterday, but Margaret Thatcher is back in power with the Tories' largest majority since 1935 – 144 over all other parties. The scale of her triumph was largely the result of a split in the anti-Tory vote, with the Liberal-Social Democratic Alliance on 25.4 per cent of the poll coming close to pipping Labour (27.6 per cent) as runner-up. But the Alliance was better at securing votes than seats. The final results are Conservatives 397, Labour 209, Alliance 23, Nationalist 4, Others 17.

In spite of high unemployment, a victory for the Tories never seemed in doubt during the campaign. The Tory party managers contrasted Mrs Thatcher, the Falklands victor, with Michael Foot, the CND-supporting Labour leader. Labour's manifesto did little to deflect attacks on its alleged extremism, promising to leave the Common Market and more nationalization. The result is a disaster for Labour – its worst share of the vote since the 1920s, and virtually wiped out in southern England. Foot and Roy Jenkins, the Social Democratic leader, intend to resign (→ 12).

Mrs Thatcher campaigning on home ground in Finchley in the election run-up.

IRA hurt at hands of Belfast 'supergrass'

Belfast, 5 August

The longest – 117 days – and most expensive trial in Irish legal history ended today with the conviction of 35 IRA members on the word of Christopher Black, aged 29, a north Belfast man who turned "supergrass". He gave police extensive inside details of the IRA which seriously undermined its activity.

Black is one of six "converted terrorists", both republican and loyalist, who have named their accomplices in return for immunity and new identities for themselves and their families. So far about 80 have been convicted, and up to 220 suspects are in custody awaiting trial on the evidence of about 14 new "supergrasses" (→ 25/9).

August 14. The British athlete Daley Thompson wins the gold medal in the first World Championship decathlon in Helsinki.

Over 130 break out of Belfast prison

Belfast, 25 September
One hundred and thirty-four jailed IRA members escaped today from the high security Maze prison, 12 miles south of Belfast. It is the biggest jailbreak in British history. A prison warder was stabbed to death, another was shot in the head, and a policeman and a prisoner were wounded. Official sources said that 15 prisoners were recaptured near the prison.

Prisoners on cleaning duty in one of the H-blocks produced guns and overpowered warders before hijacking a meals lorry and driving to the main gates in warders' uniforms. A warder was stabbed during a struggle, and the prisoners made off on foot or in hijacked cars. Locals said that five were recaptured almost immediately, and four were caught trying to cross the river Lagan. Prison staff are unarmed, although H-blocks have the highest proportion of "lifers" in the world – 230 out of 850. Three-quarters of the province's 2,500 prisoners are classified as terrorists (→ 12/11).

Irish people vote to restrict abortions

Ireland, September
A referendum to ensure that abortion would never be legalized, by approving the insertion of a clause into the constitution giving the foetus equal rights to that of the mother, has been carried. Support for it came largely from rural areas.

The so-called "pro-life" amendment is the result of a long, bitter and divisive campaign. It began when members of a right-wing "pro-life" group approached the leaders of the two main political parties, Charles Haughey and Garret FitzGerald, seeking assurances by way of a national referendum that abortion (already illegal) could never be introduced. Both agreed.

Through three divisive general elections the matter remained unresolved. Finally Dr FitzGerald, as prime minister, concluded the business by giving in to pressure and agreeing to a definitive wording which the most eminent lawyers of the day argued over for some time. Eventually an amendment was put before the people and carried.

Kinnock and Owen plot Tories' downfall

Brighton, 2 October
Neil Kinnock, a 41-year-old left-winger who has never held office in government, was today chosen to be the Labour Party's new leader. His defeated rival, Roy Hattersley, is to become deputy leader in what the party hopes will be the "dream ticket" to recover from the débâcle of its second successive general election defeat. But Kinnock faces major internal and external problems. The Labour Party is still split between left and right, with constituency activists – and some unions – markedly to the left of the parliamentary leaders. And he also has the challenge of the Social Democrats, now led by the former Labour foreign secretary David Owen, who succeeded Roy Jenkins after the election (→ 27/1/86).

A new future for Labour: Kinnock (centre) and Hattersley (left) taste victory.

Burrell collection finds striking new home

The Burrell gallery: both the building and its contents have won awards.

Glasgow
The Burrell collection, which has been waiting for a home since 1944 when it was presented to the city by Sir William Burrell, has one at last. The new gallery, which won a competition for its architects Britt Andreson, John Munier and Barry Gasson, has already won awards as both a museum and a building. The Burrell collection is mainly of artefacts from ancient civilizations and mediaeval Europe. It furthers the revival of Glasgow as a home of the arts. The Citizens' theatre in the Gorbals has won international renown under Giles Havergal for its revivals of classic plays.

Parkinson quits in secretary sex scandal

Lancashire, 14 October
Cecil Parkinson, who as party chairman was the architect of the Conservative election victory in June, has resigned from the cabinet following revelations of an affair with his secretary, Sara Keays. She is expecting his child in January, and this week, during the party conference at Blackpool, she gave *The Times* an interview in which she claimed that Parkinson had broken a promise to marry her. He had told Margaret Thatcher of the scandal in June; she saw no reason for him to quit and appointed him trade and industry secretary. Now that it is public he has decided to go (→ 16).

Cecil Parkinson and Sara Keays – no longer romantically involved.

Violence sours pit strike

Riot police charge to disperse the pickets at Orgreave coking plant.

South Yorkshire, 29 May
In the bitterest confrontation yet of the three-month-old coal strike, 41 policemen and 28 miners were injured today outside the Orgreave coking plant here. The police wore full riot gear for the first time and only restored order after repeated mounted charges.

The picketing miners were trying to stop convoys of lorries taking coke from the plant to a steelworks. The NUM president, Arthur Scargill, claimed that South Yorkshire was like a "police state which you might expect to see in Chile but not here". The strike began in opposition to a 5.2 per cent pay offer and a programme of pit closures. Much of the violence so far has been concentrated in Nottinghamshire, where the miners have continued working in defiance of "flying pickets" of Yorkshire miners who in turn were defying a high-court injunction restricting them to their own area. The personal animosity between the coal board's chairman, Ian MacGregor, and Scargill, as well as the gulf between their positions – 20 pit closures and 20,000 job losses against no closures and no job losses – makes a speedy end to the strike unlikely (→ 30).

Hong Kong part of Anglo-Chinese deal

Beijing, 26 September
An agreement was initialled here today which allows China to resume sovereignty of the British colony of Hong Kong in 1997 when the lease negotiated in the 19th century expires. The communist leaders of China have promised that the free-enterprise system and lifestyle established in Hong Kong will "remain unchanged for 50 years" after the date of the transfer of power. Hong Kong is to be a special administrative region of the People's Republic of China, with various rights and individual freedoms which will be enshrined in a new "basic law" (→ 22/12/89).

Britain's ice-dancing duo, Jayne Torvill and Christopher Dean, skate superbly to win the Olympic gold for ice-dancing.

Fire from the skies sets off York blaze

York, 9 July
A thunderbolt, traditionally a sign of divine wrath, struck 700-year-old York Minster today, causing fire damage estimated at £1 million. The archbishop of York dismissed the suggestion that the wrath was directed at the liberal and controversial Dr David Jenkins, who was consecrated last week as bishop of Durham, and Dr Robert Runcie, the archbishop of Canterbury, saw a miracle in that only the south transept was destroyed, and the famous Rose Window survived. Many of the treasures were saved, and insurance will cover rebuilding costs.

Flames engulf York Minster.

Concern grows over spread of HIV virus

Tyne and Wear, 18 November
Two people have died of Aids after being infected by blood transfusions. One was Terence McStay, a haemophiliac who received contaminated American plasma. The 35-year-old laboratory worker was treated in Newcastle. Homosexuals, hard-drug users and other high-risk groups will now be banned as blood donors; within 12 months blood imports will end, and blood tests for Aids are being developed. In April it was announced that the virus which causes Aids, HIV, had been independently identified by American and French researchers (→ 15/3/85).

IRA bomb blasts Tory conference HQ

Scientists face a difficult future as funding cuts bite

The bomb-shattered Grand hotel.

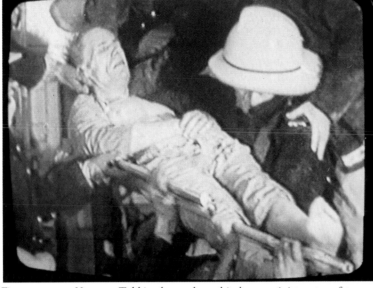

Fireman carry Norman Tebbit, the trade and industry minister, to safety.

Britain

Science is in crisis. While a cost-cutting government demands that funding is concentrated on areas which promise practical benefits, its popularity is slipping. Science's transformation of daily life is now taken for granted, and it is increasingly seen as the source of many current problems, from acid rain to the vanishing ozone layer.

The power of science can be seen in the achievements of molecular biology. On the one hand it promises cures for genetically based diseases like sickle-cell anaemia, and the cheap production of insulin; on the other

Brighton, 12 October

Margaret Thatcher today made a defiant speech to the Conservative conference just hours after she had narrowly escaped death when an IRA bomb ripped apart the Grand hotel in the early hours of the morning. Five people were killed, including one MP, Sir Anthony Berry, and the wife of the party's chief whip, John Wakeham. More than 30 people were injured, many seriously, after being pulled from the

rubble by firemen. The bomb exploded at 2.54am in the hotel, which was being used by most members of the cabinet during this week's party conference. It ripped a huge gash down the front of the building on the seafront. Four floors of the hotel were shattered by the blast, caused by a bomb weighing 9 kilos (20 pounds).

The prime minister had a lucky escape. She was still awake, having been working on today's speech to

the conference. Two minutes before the bomb exploded she had been in a bathroom which was to be wrecked by the explosion. Some of her colleagues were less fortunate. Norman Tebbit, the industry minister, was pulled from the wreckage by firemen after several hours. His wife was also hurt. The IRA admitted responsibility for the bomb, adding: "Today we were unlucky, but remember we have only to be lucky once" (→28/2/85).

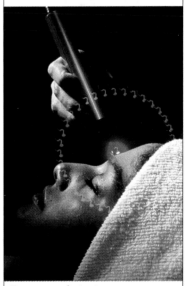

Lasers revolutionize surgery.

Innocent woman PC shot dead by Libyans outside embassy

Shots from the Libyan embassy leave Yvonne Fletcher fatally wounded.

London, 22 April

The anonymous Libyan who shot dead Yvonne Fletcher, the young policewoman, has seven days to leave the country, together with the rest of the students and professional diplomats living in the embassy in St James's Square. WPC Fletcher was killed five days ago while on duty at a demonstration outside the "People's Bureau"; however, her abandoned hat remains on the pavement, a poignant reminder for the millions who have followed this siege on TV.

Britain has now severed diplomatic relations with Colonel Gadaffi's Libya, and British diplomats in Tripoli have been warned to "consider their safety". As the Libyans are likely to remove vital evidence, the identity of WPC Fletcher's killer may never be known (→ 27).

loom spectres like sheep being engineered to produce pharmaceuticals in their milk.

Science has been the victim of successful developments like the computer's silicon chip, which first appeared on the mass market about ten years ago, powering a pocket calculator that cost around £70. Now it is in everything, from nuclear weapons to watches, and the same computing power costs £7.

Science may have caused pollution, but it alone can clear it up, maybe using discoveries made by financially starved pure researchers.

Twin tragedies shake British football

Onlookers watch horrified as the stands at Bradford City go up in flames.

People lie dead or dying in the wake of rioting by Liverpool soccer fans.

Brussels, 29 May

Forty-one Italian and Belgian soccer supporters were killed tonight when Liverpool fans went on the rampage against followers of the rival Juventus team at Heysel stadium, and a wall and a safety fence at the stadium collapsed. The disaster comes only 18 days after a fire swept through the main stand of Bradford City football club during a match against Lincoln City, killing 40 people. At Bradford, as at Heysel, most of the dead were trampled in the panic.

With the tragedy at Heysel, Britain's reputation in European football has reached its nadir. Even as Belgian police and ambulance personel tried to revive victims, Liverpool fans were still attacking the Italian supporters with bottles, iron bars and flagpoles. In the end police commanders had to call in mounted police and paratroopers.

The image of drunken and chauvinistic British football hooligans is familiar to every European country, and many now expect that British teams will be banned from European football.

The prime minister, Margaret Thatcher, who watched today's events live on televison, said that those responsible had brought "shame and dishonour" to the community. Some of her opponents argue that Mrs Thatcher's own brand of anti-European chauvinism has done as much to contribute to the hooliganism as the beer (→ 30).

Church 'diplomat' wins release of hostages

Tripoli, 6 February

Four Britons held prisoner in Libya for eight months have been freed. They were handed over today to Terry Waite, the archbishop of Canterbury's special envoy. All four – Robin Plummer, a British Telecom engineer; Michael Berdinner, a university lecturer; Alan Russell, an English teacher, and Malcolm Anderson, an engineer – were arrested last May in reaction to the "siege" of the Libyan embassy in London, following the shooting of a policewoman and several protesting Libyan exiles. Only two – Anderson and Russell – have been charged, Russell receiving a three-year sentence for "breaches of security".

There were fears that Waite's mission would fail after Jana, the Libyan news agency accused Mrs Thatcher of trying to hamper the release by unveiling a memorial to WPC Yvonne Fletcher and going ahead with the trial in Manchester of four Libyans on bomb charges. But Libya now says that the releases will go ahead as planned.

For Terry Waite – a gentle giant – the releases are seen as a triumph for his own personal brand of un-official diplomacy, at a time when Britain has no diplomatic contacts with Libya (→ 21/1/87).

July 4. First-class maths honours for Ruth Lawrence, aged 13, who took her degree in two years.

Miners' strike ends to cries of 'scab!'

The year-long national strike is over.

South Wales, 6 March
Welsh miners marched back to work today to the sound of brass band after their year-long strike against redundancies. It is the end of their industry, but like their English and Scottish comrades they display dignity in defeat. It was not only the longest coal strike in British history but also the most bitter. The early violence at the Orgreave coking plant in South Yorkshire, where one miner died and hundreds were injured and arrested, set the tone. To add to the bitterness – and the violence – Nottinghamshire miners refused to strike and formed a rival to the National Union of Mineworkers: the Union of Democratic Mineworkers.

'Live Aid' rocks to help feed the world

London, 13 July
£40 million was raised for the hungry of Ethiopia today at the biggest rock concert ever produced. The concert, Live Aid, was organized by the Dublin-born rock star Bob Geldof, whose Band Aid single *Do They Know It's Christmas?* raised tens of thousands of pounds for Ethiopia's starving people.

Live Aid was held at two venues, Wembley stadium in London and the JFK stadium in Philadelphia. Over one and a half billion people in some 160 countries watched on television while the giants of rock, Mick Jagger, David Bowie, Queen and Dire Straits, urged fans to donate their cash (→ 17/7).

Thousands pack Wembley stadium.

Anglo-Irish deal signed

Ulster Unionists demonstrating against the Anglo-Irish agreement.

Belfast, 15 November
The prime ministers of the United Kingdom and of the Republic of Ireland today signed an agreement that all sides regard as momentous. The Anglo-Irish Agreement allows the Irish government the right to discuss virtually all aspects of life in Northern Ireland and sets up a secretariat to be staffed by civil servants from London and Dublin.

Unionist politicians in Northern Ireland have reacted with fury to the agreement, failing to be mollified by the Dublin government's acknowledgement that Irish unity could be achieved only "with the consent of a majority of the people of Northern Ireland". Mass demonstrations are planned in Belfast in protest at the agreement, which was signed today at Hillsborough by Margaret Thatcher and Garret FitzGerald. Some Irish Nationalists are also unhappy, castigating the Dublin government for giving up its traditional belief in Irish unity.

Mrs Thatcher said today that the agreement recognizes the interests of both the Protestant majority and the Catholic minority in Northern Ireland. The failure to make political headway within Northern Ireland, and increasing cooperation between security forces on both sides of the border, provided the background to today's deal. Talks at an inter-governmental council had also brought the two governments closer together (→ 11/12).

Holiday tragedy at Manchester airport

Manchester, 22 August
Fifty-four passengers were killed today when an engine on a British Airtours Boeing 737 exploded and the plane burst into flames just as it was about to take off. The pilot attempted to abort take-off after the explosion, but in vain. Eighty passengers escaped down the chutes; the rest died in the inferno.

The crash has turned this August into the worst month for airline crashes ever recorded. So far 711 passengers have died: 517 in Tokyo, 140 at Dallas, Texas, and now 54 at Manchester.

PC is hacked to death in Tottenham riots

London, 7 October
A former community policeman was hacked to death on a north London housing estate today, in the most vicious rioting that British police have ever experienced.

The riots – on the Broadwater Farm estate in Tottenham, an inner city council project that belies its name – were sparked off by the death of a middle-aged black woman, Mrs Cynthia Jarrett, who died of a heart attack during a police raid. Within hours police had been called to the estate by fake "999" calls and been ambushed by a hail of bricks and petrol bombs, and – for the first time in an inner city riot – by gunshots. From 6.30pm until long after midnight both black and white youths fought bloody battles with more than 500 police in riot gear. The dead policeman has been named as PC Keith Blakelock, aged 40. Four more policeman have been wounded by gunshots, and over two hundred others have been injured.

A Tory MP, John Wheeler, dismissed claims that the riot stemmed from either social deprivation or insensitive policing. The Labour home affairs spokesman, Gerald Kaufman, has called for a full inquiry. "This is not the England we should be living in," he said.

Sir Clive Sinclair test drives his latest invention, the C5.

Northern Ireland, 24 January. Unionists are re-elected in 14 of 15 seats contested on the Anglo-Irish agreement (→ 23/6).

Westminster, 28 January. The rates system will be replaced with a "community charge" (→ 20/9/89).

London, 16 February. Police clash with pickets at the new News International plant at Wapping. The trouble is over the move of the production of the *Sunday Times* and *News of the World* there (→ 5/2/87).

Australia, 2 March. The Queen signs the Australia Bill severing constitutional ties with Britain.

London, 29 March. The first test-tube quintuplets are born.

Lebanon, 17 April. Three British hostages are murdered in retaliation for British participation in the US air strike against Libya.

Belfast, 24 June. The Reverend Ian Paisley is forcibly removed from the Ulster Assembly after it is dissolved (→ 12/7).

Atlantic Ocean, 29 June. Richard Branson in the *Virgin Atlantic Challenger II* completes a record crossing.

Northern Ireland, 12 July. Over a hundred are injured in Orange day clashes between Catholics and Protestants (→ 13/8).

Westminster, 23 July. Prince Andrew, the duke of York, marries Sarah Ferguson.

Dublin, 13 August. Gerard O'Reilly, an IRA suspect, is freed because of an error in his extradition warrant (→ 8/5/87).

Sunderland, 8 September. Nissan, the Japanese car manufacturers, opens a factory.

China, 12 October. The Queen begins the first state visit by a British monarch.

Westminster, 21 November. A "safe-sex" campaign is launched in a bid to stop the spread of Aids (→ 4/5/87).

London, 1 December. A department of trade and industry inquiry opens into the shares of Guinness, the beer and spirits group (→ 9/1/87).

Manchester, 19 December. John Stalker resigns from the police force.

Britain, 29 December. Harold Macmillan, the earl of Stockton and a former prime minister, dies aged 92.

Leon Brittan resigns as trade and industry secretary over leaks in 'Westland' affair

Leon Brittan resigns over a leak ...

... and so does Michael Heseltine.

Westminster, 27 January
Margaret Thatcher has survived the greatest threat so far to her 11-year leadership of the Conservative Party. After a month in which two cabinet ministers have resigned – ostensibly over the future of the Westland helicopter company but in reality about her style of government – the prime minister has survived a debate today in the Commons which even she had thought could end in her resignation.

The fuse in the Westland affair was lit by Michael Heseltine, who walked out of a cabinet meeting on 9 January to announce his resigna-

tion. The defence secretary had been locked in an increasingly public dispute with Leon Brittan, the trade and industry secretary, about official policy towards the Yeovil-based Westland company. But then Heseltine widened the assault by talking of "a breakdown of constitutional government".

Three days ago Brittan resigned, taking responsibility for the role of his press secretary in leaking part of a letter from a government law officer that had been critical of Heseltine. The role of Downing Street staff in the leak is what made Mrs Thatcher vulnerable (→ 12/6/87).

Northern Ireland is to lose its assembly

London, 23 June
The government has today dissolved the Northern Ireland assembly, which had degenerated after four years into a unionist forum for attacking the Anglo-Irish Agreement signed last year.

The Northern Ireland secretary, James Prior, wanted the assembly to be the basis of "rolling devolution" leading to self-government. Any application for devolution needed the support of 70 per cent of the membership – 55 out of 78 – so that unionists needed nationalist backing. The SDLP won 14 assembly seats, to Sinn Féin's five, but never took them up because Prior's plan had no role for Dublin (→ 24).

Irish reject divorce

Dublin, 26 June
A referendum to amend the constitution and allow a limited form of divorce has been overwhelmingly defeated. Opinion polls predicted a "yes" vote, but in the closing stages of the campaign it became clear that the opposition of the Roman Catholic Church, coupled with apparent confusion about the benefits to which the divorced wife would be entitled, had caused the public – particularly women – to change its mind.

Britain and France move a little closer as 'Chunnel' gets go-ahead

Pipe-line dreams become a reality as Britain and France agree to a tunnel.

Lille, France, 20 January
After nearly two hundred years of bickering and false starts, Britain and France have finally agreed to link their two countries with a pair of undersea rail tunnels, expected to cost around £5 billion. The first passengers through the Channel tunnel from Folkestone to Sangatte are scheduled to make the London/Paris trip in April 1993. Margaret Thatcher and President François Mitterrand made the historic announcement today in Lille.

The all-rail solution was decided on after various alternatives, like a multi-lane road bridge, were rejected as too hazardous or too expensive. But it is hoped that it may be possible to add a road tunnel early in the 21st century (→ 8/3/89).

Greater London loses its local council

The staff of the former Greater London Council (GLC) pose for a last photo.

London, 31 March
The Greater London Council, which always claimed to be the world's largest local authority, was abolished tonight, along with the metropolitan county councils of Greater Manchester, Merseyside, Tyne & Wear, South Yorkshire, West Yorkshire and West Midlands. Responsibility for planning, coordinating and servicing large parts of Britain's capital city will in future be divided among its 42 constituent boroughs.

This decision brings to an end a long simmering conflict between the prime minister, Margaret Thatcher, and the GLC's outspoken and irreverent chairman, Ken Livingstone, who deliberately set out to become the voice of the ultra-radical (or, as most Conservatives put it, "loony") left wing of the Labour Party. He delighted in both mocking and flouting government intentions at every turn.

But it was his attitude to spending public money that set him on the final collision course with central authority. Local government budgets, of which London's was by far the largest, account for up to a quarter of national expenditure, and during the early 1980s the treasury became determined to bring this under effective ministerial control. The final straw was Livingstone's popular "Fares Fair" cheap fare policy for London Transport, which involved lavish subsidies. When the courts declared these illegal, the GLC's fate was sealed.

Manchester deputy is taken off inquiry

Belfast, 30 June
John Stalker, Manchester's deputy chief constable, has been suspended from duty pending investigation of his alleged association with "known criminals". This further clouds the future of the controversial inquiry he has been conducting for the past two years into the possible existence of a deliberate police "shoot-to-kill" policy in Northern Ireland.

Stalker's attempts to clarify the deaths of various IRA suspects have frequently brought him into conflict with the Royal Ulster Constabulary. He is believed to have been on the verge of significant discoveries in May when he was sent on indefinite leave (→ 19/12).

John Stalker: policy investigation.

Moore, poet of the human figure, dies

Henry Moore: international fame.

Hertfordshire, 31 August
Henry Moore, the sculptor who has the biggest international reputation of any living British artist, died today at his home in the village of Much Hadham.

Born a Yorkshire miner's son, he carved directly in stone and enjoyed what he called the "hard navvying" involved. He sought inspiration not from Graeco-Roman sculpture but from primitive, particularly Mexican, art, which suggested the theme of the reclining figure which he explored all his life. He sometimes set his works in the open landscape. His drawings of people sleeping in the London Underground during the Blitz first made him popular.

Rich pickings for 'Yuppies' in City boom

"Big Bang": new technology comes to the floor of the Stock Exchange.

London, 27 October
"Big Bang" day, marking the wholesale deregulation of London's many interlocking financial markets, started with a damp squib. The £20 million of new stock-market computers broke down under the early flood of orders.

But that failure, which was quickly corrected, only momentarily obscured the extent of the revolution undergone by the City. From a network of small, gentlemanly firms and partnerships, where the wealth enjoyed by the favoured participants was protected by a centuries-old system of price-fixing agreements and cartels, it has become overnight an international casino where many of the world's most astute (and highly paid) brains compete for profits.

In preparation for this opportunity, a formidable roster of international banks and brokerage firms has set up shop in Britain, often paying astronomical sums in both salaries and purchase fees to buy the way in. The resulting proliferation of bright young people earning six- and even seven-figure salaries has necessitated a new collective noun: these "Yuppies" (from the acronym YUP – Young Urban Professional) now confidently expect to rule the world.

Car ferry sinks; 200 die

Zeebrugge, Belgium, 6 March
Disaster was inevitable when the bow doors of a car ferry were left open, allowing the sea to flood into the car deck as the ship left this Belgian port tonight. The *Herald of Free Enterprise* rolled over and sank, drowning 200 passengers and crew in the North Sea.

Disaster came so swiftly that there was no time for a "Mayday" distress call to be sent out, but Dutch and Belgian helicopters were swiftly on the scene, plucking many passengers from the sea. Survivors told of horror and heroism as victims clung to fixed furniture before slipping into the water; of selfless acts of courage by the crew; and of a man who formed a human bridge to allow passengers to climb to safety through broken windows.

Rescue workers search for survivors.

Hostage-rescuer Waite is seized in Beirut

Fears are growing for the safety of Terry Waite, the archbishop's envoy.

Beirut, 21 January
Terry Waite, the archbishop of Canterbury's special representative in Lebanon, failed to return from a mission to rescue hostages here today and is now believed to be a hostage himself. The tall, bearded Waite dismissed his Druze escorts before setting off to negotiate with Hezbollah ("the Party of God") which is thought to be holding the hostages. He insisted that he was safe and would be taken to see Westerners being held prisoners.

The Druze are concerned for his safety. Their leader, Walid Jumblatt, has contacted the Shia Moslems asking for news. With no sign of Waite's return, most Western observers are convinced that Waite is now a "star hostage".

More knowledgeable experts believe that Waite's name is tainted in the Middle East by his involvement in the "Irangate" affair. In Hezbollah thought he is associated with Colonel Oliver North and the CIA, and more than likely he is being held, like the other hostages, in a terrorist cell in the teeming downtown quarter of this war-torn and divided city (→ 30/8/90).

Thatcher is elected for her third term

Westminster, 12 June
Margaret Thatcher has become the first prime minister this century to win three successive general elections. Despite some jitters, and a glitzy campaign by Neil Kinnock's red-rose-wearing Labour Party, the Conservatives yesterday won an overall majority of 100. The final results: Conservatives 375, Labour 229, Alliance 22, Nationalists 6, Others 18. One consolation for Kinnock is that Labour is further ahead of the Alliance, with 30.8 per cent of the votes against 22.6. David Steel, the Liberal leader, plans to call for a merger with the other half of the Alliance, the Social Democrats led by David Owen (→ 6/8).

U2 recalls the glory days of British rock

United States, April
The Dublin-based band U2 has scaled another rock-music peak by appearing on the cover of *Time* this month, an accolade shared only with the Beatles and The Who.

Gone are the heady days of the Sixties when British bands dominated the American charts, although three years ago the English seemed back on top when Culture Club, Duran Duran and The Police all received Grammy Awards.

Two years ago the baton of acclaim crossed the Irish Sea when *Rolling Stone* hailed U2 as "the band of the eighties".

Dublin's greatest export: U2.

'Black Monday' hits the financial world

London, 19 October

London's Stock Exchange reeled under a tidal wave of selling today as more than £50 billion was wiped off the value of shares in publicly quoted companies. Selling continued from the moment that dealers reached their desks at 7am today, and the Exchange was still in tumult at the close.

London's disastrous day echoed a similar panic on Wall Street last Friday and heavy selling in Tokyo. The Hong Kong market is to remain closed all week. In New York, the Dow Jones industrial average fell 508 points to 1,739, wiping 22.5 per cent off share values. The fall was almost double that experienced on the first day of the great crash of 1929 and was described by the chairman, John Phelan, as "the nearest thing to a financial meltdown I've ever come across."

The crash is blamed on the United States budget, trade deficits, rising interest rates and computerized "program trading".

England lashed by worst storm of century

The morning after the storm the full extent of the damage can be seen.

Southern England, 16 October

A full-scale hurricane hit southern England today, killing at least 17 people and leaving a swathe of damage and destruction from Dorset to East Anglia. Damage is estimated at £300 million: roads and railway lines have been blocked by countless fallen trees, hotels and houses have collapsed, and thousands of homes are without power and likely to remain so for days. In London, the hospital casualty wards were crowded with victims of flying debris; the fire brigade dealt with 6,000 emergency calls, and Kew Gardens lost a third of its trees. The meteorological office is under fire for having failed to predict the extraordinary storm. Only hours before the disaster hit the country, a TV forecaster laughed off what turned out to be an accurate prediction by an anxious viewer.

IRA bombers blast Armistice parade

Co Fermanagh, 8 November

The IRA exploded a huge bomb in a disused school at Enniskillen this morning, killing 11 people as they assembled for the annual Armistice day parade. A further 63 were injured, several critically. A claim by the IRA that the army triggered off the bomb with a scanning device was dismissed contemptuously by the Northern Ireland secretary, Tom King. Gordon Wilson, aged 60, was buried under the rubble with his daughter Marie. Father and daughter held hands, but Marie died five hours after being freed. Even so, her father was prepared to forgive her killers. "I shall pray for those people," he said (→ 28/1/88).

Enniskillen mourns its dead.

North-south divide widens as southern house prices soar sky high

London, 24 September

Never was the "north-south divide" in Britain better demonstrated than in a review of house prices published today showing that the price of a typical semi-detached house in London has leapt by 26.8 per cent – £53 a day – in the past year. Such is the escalation in property values that any northerner or midlander finding work in London will need a pay rise of at least 25 per cent to maintain living standards.

House prices in London now cost five and a half times salaries; in the midlands two and a half; in the north two and a third. Some hard-pressed southerners are now commuting to London from newly bought homes in the north.

Gunman runs amok in Berkshire town

Berkshire, 20 August

Bearing an automatic rifle and other weapons from his collection, Michael Ryan, aged 27, walked almost casually through the sleepy market town of Hungerford today, leaving 14 people dead and 15 wounded before, cornered by police in his old school, he shot himself.

Ryan's orgy of slaughter began in nearby Savernake Forest, where he shot a woman who was with her two children. He drove home and shot his mother and set light to their home before he set out again on foot, killing indiscriminately – anyone who came in his sights.

Thirty killed in an horrific Underground blaze at King's Cross

The horrifying reality of the fire damage is seen at King's Cross Underground.

London, 18 November

Commuters heading home for the weekend were engulfed in a blazing inferno when a flash fire ripped through King's Cross tube station tonight, killing 30 people. The ferocity of the blaze was such that only seven survivors were treated in nearby University College hospital for severe flash burns.

The fire began on a wooden escalator which carried travellers into the blazing ticket hall. An accumulation of inflammable fluff under the escalator is being blamed, together with staff cuts and poor training. Despite a previous recommendation, no sprinkler system is in operation at King's Cross.

1988

IRA bomb trio gunned down by SAS team

Sean Savage (l), Mairéad Farrell (c) and Danny McCann: all shot dead.

Gibraltar, 7 March 1988

Three well-known IRA terrorists, Sean Savage, Danny McCann and Mairéad Farrell, were shot dead here today by undercover SAS men. The three, admitted by the IRA in Belfast tonight to be an "active service unit", had been trailed across the Spanish border, and it is believed that they were planning to bomb the Changing of the Guard ceremony, which is watched by large crowds. In the House of Commons, Sir Geoffrey Howe, the foreign secretary, said that when the three were challenged "they made movements which led the military personnel operating in support of the Gibraltar police to conclude that their own lives and the lives of others were under threat. In the light of this response, they were shot dead." This version is disputed by some eye-witnesses of the event, who say that the SAS men opened fire without warning (→ 16).

Prince Charles slams modern architecture

London, 28 October

Prince Charles lambasted Britain's modern architects tonight in an *Omnibus* TV programme which he wrote and narrated himself. He did not pull his punches. The British library, he said, was "like an academy for secret police"; the National Theatre, like "a nuclear power station in the middle of London"; and St Paul's was surrounded by a "jostling scrum of skyscrapers". He said that he had discovered on his travels that many people are "appalled by what we have done to so many of our towns since the war". Architects, still smarting under his description of the proposed extension to the National Gallery as a "monstrous carbuncle", will take no comfort from this new attack, although laymen might.

Licensing laws give drinkers more time

London, 20 May

There will be celebratory drinks for those who hate to hear a landlord call "time, gentlemen, please", for under the Licensing Act, which received the royal assent today, 65,000 pubs in England and Wales will be able to stay open from 11am to 11pm on weekdays, with more restricted hours on Sundays. How many pubs will take advantage of the new freedom remains to be seen. Many publicans are unhappy at the thought of all the extra wages they will have to pay to keep their houses open for such long hours.

Death toll mounts to 150 in oil rig blaze

North Sea, 6 July

It is feared that more than 150 men died tonight when the Piper Alpha oil rig positioned 120 miles east of Wick blew up with an explosion which one survivor said was "like an atom bomb going off". Only about 70 of the rig's workers are thought to have survived the blast and the inferno which brought the sea near to boiling-point.

One man told how some gave up and waited for death while others jumped 12 metres into the scalding sea to be picked up by rescue boats, themselves in danger of bursting into flames. Many men were trapped in the crew's quarters which now lie on the seabed in a tangle of wreckage. Survivors speak of a scream of gas before the explosion.

Fires still rage on Piper Alpha.

Physicist interprets the 'History of Time'

Stephen Hawking: time historian.

Cambridge, 31 December

Stephen Hawking, possibly the greatest physicist since Einstein, has seen his layman's guide to the mystery of time and the universe top the non-fiction bestseller list every week since it was published. This is despite the fact that *A Brief History of Time* is no easy reading. Dr Hawking, who is 46, is professor of mathematics at Cambridge University. For the last 20 years he has been confined to a wheelchair by motor neurone disease. He lectures, dictates and converses by means of a computer with synthetic voice operated by two fingers of one hand – all that he can move.

Anglicans debate women bishops

London, 1 August

The bitterness and confusion which persists among Anglicans over the position of women within the church was demonstrated by two contrary votes at the Lambeth conference today. The assembled bishops first agreed overwhelmingly, by 423 votes to 28, that the consecration of women as bishops could not be prevented. But the archbishop of Sydney then found much support for another motion arguing that it would "destroy our unity" and "the credibility of the office of bishop". He lost by 277 to 187, but his supporters point out that if the votes of the American delegation are discounted a majority of bishops in the rest of the world is against the consecration of women.

Edwina quits with egg on her face

Westminster, 16 December

Edwina Currie, the junior health minister, resigned today after two weeks of controversy caused by her claim that most British eggs are infected with salmonella. Egg sales plummeted, flocks were slaughtered and farmers outraged. Today she bowed to the storm and left; it had been one rumpus too far for a controversial politician. As a health minister she had said that northerners died of "ignorance and crisps" and that cervical cancer was the result of being too sexually active – "nuns don't get it," she said.

Outspoken Edwina is forced to quit.

Pan Am jet disaster over Lockerbie

Dumfries and Galloway, 22 Dec

A Pan American jumbo jet blew up in mid-air last night, raining debris on a swathe of border country. The fuselage crashed into the heart of the quiet market town of Lockerbie, vaporizing several houses and gutting others. All 259 passengers and crew died, along with 11 people on the ground. Shocked citizens spoke of a fireball falling from the sky. "The whole sky lit up and it was virtually raining fire," said one, Mike Carnahan.

Flight 103 had originated in Frankfurt, and after stopping at Heathrow was on its way to New York. Most of the passengers were Americans, among them servicemen and 38 students from Syracuse University, flying home to join their families for Christmas.

There has been no official explanation yet for the tragedy, but the suddenness of the catastrophic break-up of an aircraft as strong as a Boeing 747 – it simply vanished

Lockerbie surveys the damage and loss of life after last night's horrific plane crash over the town. All that remains of one street is a huge charred crater.

from the radar screens – points to sabotage by bomb. Ever since the US cruiser *Vincennes* mistakenly shot down an Iranian Airbus last July killing 286 people, a revenge attack has been feared and expected. It has emerged that US embassies had been warned that a Pan Am flight could be the target for a terrorist bomb attack.

National curriculum imposed in schools

Westminster, 29 July

Schools in England and Wales face their biggest shake-up since the 1944 Education Act. Under the Education Reform Bill which received the royal assent today a national curriculum will be laid down for all state schools detailing not only which subjects must be taught but also the elements within those subjects. The new curriculum will be introduced progressively over the next few years and will be backed by attainment targets and regular testing for children at the ages of seven, 11, 14 and 16. This represents an unprecedented shift towards centralized power in education, away from the classroom and local authorities.

The role of local education authorities is certainly under attack with provision for schools to opt out of councils' control. Ministers see this power – to be decided by parental ballot – as a counter to what they regard as the "loony left" policies of Labour councils. Similar opting-out provisions are to be introduced in Scotland.

Train crash tragedy at Clapham Junction

Rescue workers battle to free trapped passengers from the twisted wreckage.

London, 12 December

Two trains packed with rush-hour commuters ran into each other this morning at Clapham Junction, the world's busiest junction. Seconds later an empty train piled into the wreckage, and only instant reaction by a guard stopped a fourth train adding to the carnage of Britain's worst railway disaster for more than 20 years. The death toll has reached 36, and more than a hun-

dred are injured. Rescue workers had to prise the mangled trains apart to get to trapped passengers. Doctors crawled through wreckage administering transfusions and painkillers to the injured until they could be cut free.

Signal failure seems to have been the cause of the tragedy. British Rail admits: "The fail-safe mechanism did not work." There is to be a public inquiry.

Thirty die when jet hits motorway just short of the airport

The wreckage of the Boeing 737.

Leicestershire, 9 January
Motorists on the M1 watched terrified tonight as a Boeing 737 airliner smashed into an embankment, scattering burning debris across three lanes. The crash took place near the village of Kegworth, between Nottingham and Leicester.

The new British Midland plane, on a flight from Heathrow to Belfast, had already reported engine difficulties and was heading for an emergency landing at East Midlands airport. At least 30 of the 125 passengers and crew have died, but 70 have been rescued, some after being trapped for two hours (→ 11).

Pact helps Haughey to survive again

Dublin, July
Charles Haughey has finally been elected prime minister, with the support of the Progressive Democrats, and his Fianna Fáil party has entered into its first coalition government. The results of the election held on 15 June had been inconclusive, with no one party able to form a government. Mr Haughey, having failed for the fifth time to gain an overall majority, was unwillingly forced into coalition discussions with the Progressive Democrats, a party led by Fianna Fáil dissidents (→ 9/11/90).

Death threat to Rushdie

Tehran, 14 February
The execution of a British author, Salman Rushdie, was ordered here today by the Iranian leader Ayatollah Khomeini. In a radio broadcast he declared: "I inform the proud Moslem people of the world that the author of *The Satanic Verses* book, which is against Islam, the Prophet and the Koran, and all those involved in its publication who were aware of its content, are sentenced to death."

The novel, published last year, has sold 40,000 copies and been publicly burnt in Britain at large rallies, and last weekend five people died in a demonstration against it in Pakistan. Its title refers to verses cut from the Koran by the Prophet as Satan-inspired; in one, prostitutes play out a fantasy that they are the Prophet's wives.

Rushdie, a Booker prize-winner who was born in India but lives in Britain, said: "It is not true that

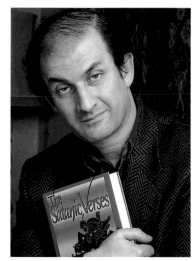

A death threat hangs over Rushdie.

this book is a blasphemy against Islam. I doubt very much that Khomeini has read it. It concerns the struggle between the secular and the religious views of life." He is seeking police protection.

Thousands of Scots fail to pay 'poll tax'

Strathclyde, 20 September
The community charge is meeting severe problems in Scotland. Today almost 300,000 people in the large Strathclyde region were said not to have paid it. The "poll tax" was introduced here, but not in England and Wales, in April. In Glasgow almost almost one in three adults are in arrears. These difficulties with a tax championed by Margaret

Thatcher in the face of widespread opposition are a source of glee for the Scottish Nationalists and other political opponents. But Labour's Scottish spokesman, Donald Dewar, scorned the idea that the defaulters were "a determined army marching in support of a non-payment campaign". They were, he said "the victims of circumstance, oppressed by poverty" (→ 2/3/90).

Lives at risk as ambulance crews strike

Police take over as ambulance men.

London, 23 October
Londoners calling for an ambulance are likely to get the police from today. This morning ambulance crews began a work-to-rule in support of a pay claim, and management promptly stopped their pay and declared them "off duty".

The union accused the management of being intimidated by the government, while the management claims that the crews are in breach of contract. Both sides say that they want talks before someone dies. Although the police are supported by the Red Cross and St John's Ambulance Brigade, their equipment and training are vastly inferior (→ 21/11).

Disaster hits FA Cup semi-final

Sheffield, 15 April

The city of Liverpool is in deep mourning tonight after the death of 94 Liverpool football fans, one aged only ten, in Britain's worst-ever sporting disaster. The tragedy happened at an FA Cup semi-final between Liverpool and Nottingham Forest when the police ordered one of the gates of the Hillsborough stadium in Sheffield to be opened to allow more Liverpool fans onto terraces that were already packed. As they rushed in those at the front were crushed; as well as the dead, 170 were injured.

One shocked supporter, Wayne Adams, aged 17, said: "I realized it was serious when I saw one of the lasses standing near me just turn blue. She went down. She was dead. That was it." Badly injured supporters were passed over the fence to the pitch; some lucky ones scrambled to safety on the balcony above.

Within minutes play had stopped, and the pitch became like a battlefield with police, ambulancemen and fans working frantically to revive the dying and cope with countless broken arms and legs. Nottingham and Liverpool supporters alike willed the rescuers on. Applause broke out as a man seemed to stir as he was given the kiss of life while an ambulanceman pummelled his heart, but it died away as his head sagged in death (→ 4/8).

Some fans are hauled to safety and escape the desperate crush which follows.

Over two million pay their respects at Anfield in a week of mourning.

Lawson resigns in a bitter public clash with prime minister

Westminster, 26 October

Nigel Lawson tonight resigned as chancellor of the exchequer after a day of drama at Westminster. The man whom Margaret Thatcher had called her "brilliant" and "unassailable" chancellor walked out after two confrontations with the prime minister at Downing Street.

In the morning Lawson told her that his position was being undermined by sniping from Sir Alan Walters, her personal economic adviser. Sack him or I go, Lawson warned. Mrs Thatcher answered questions in the House of Commons in the afternoon about Sir Alan's position, but pointedly declined to disown Sir Alan's criticisms of her chancellor.

It was the final straw for the chancellor, who, after seeing the prime minister once more, handed in his resignation. "Successful conduct of economic policy is possible only if there is full agreement between the prime minister and the chancellor of the exchequer," says Lawson in his letter of resignation, with the obvious implication that this was not so with Mrs Thatcher. The two had disagreed in particular over Lawson's support for Britain joining the European monetary system as soon as possible.

Revellers drown on Thames river boat

London, 20 August

An all-night birthday party on a Thames pleasure boat ended in tragedy in the early hours of this morning, with at least 26 drowned.

It was just before 2am when the 90-tonne pleasure cruiser *Marchioness* was hit by an 1,880-tonne ocean-going dredger, the *Bowbelle*, and sank within seconds. "It was like a tank running over a mini" said Ken Dwan, a director of the owners of the *Marchioness*.

There were about 150 fashionable young people on the boat – photographers, models and City workers; so far 76 of them are known to have survived, but the final death toll could top 60.

Free after 14 years: 'the Guildford Four' walk away from prison

London, 19 October

Four alleged terrorists, found guilty in 1975 of a pub bombing in Guildford, had their convictions overturned by the court of appeal today on the grounds that the evidence against them had been based on police lies and fabricated confessions.

Known as "the Guildford Four", Gerard Conlon, aged 35, Carole Richardson, aged 32, Patrick Armstrong, aged 39, and Paul Hill, aged 35, had been the focus of a lengthy campaign. In January the appeal court was ordered to review their convictions, and in May inquiries by the Avon and Somerset police showed that detectives had tampered with evidence. Another bombing case – that of the Maguires – also involves dubious evidence.

Gerard Conlon, free after 14 years, raises a fist to the ecstatic crowd.

1990

Prison erupts in an 'explosion of evil'

Manchester, 6 April

The mutiny at Strangeways prison, now in its sixth day with prisoners still occupying two wings of the vast Victorian prison was described today by its Governor, Brendan O'Friel, as "an explosion of evil". He said that the destruction within the prison was of a magnitude hard to comprehend. Fires have been started, roof slates ripped off for use as missiles and facilities destroyed. The riot, obviously planned, erupted in the prison chapel. The rioters are protesting about overcrowding and being "banged up" for as long as 23 hours a day in their cells.

Guinness sentences

London, 28 August

The Guinness takeover scandal ended with fines and prison sentences for three of Britain's top businessmen today. Ernest Saunders, the former chairman of the brewing company, was jailed for five years for "dishonesty on a massive scale". The stockbroker Tony Parnes, who collapsed in the dock, received 18 months. Gerald Ronson, the garage and property tycoon, was jailed for a year and fined £5 million. Sir Jack Lyons, who was also found guilty, was judged to be too ill to be sentenced today.

Western hostages take the centre stage as British troops move into Persian Gulf

Persian Gulf, 23 August

The build-up of troops comprising the "Desert Shield" force to combat Saddam Hussein's aggression in the Gulf is taking place slowly but surely. The Americans already have 30,000 soldiers plus aircraft in Saudi Arabia. Warships are moving into position in the Gulf. One RAF squadron of Tornadoes has arrived, and more men, ships and planes are in the pipeline.

Meanwhile Saddam is twisting and turning in his attempt to avoid conflict with the United Nations while holding on to Kuwait. His latest ploy is to appear on Baghdad television with British hostages. Describing them as his "guests", he said that they were "heroes of the peace" who would prevent a war by their presence in Iraq. Dressed in a grey civilian suit, he was all oleaginous charm as he attempted to ruffle the hair of six-year-old Stuart Lockwood and ask him if he was getting enough cornflakes. Stuart, arms folded defiantly, squirmed at the dictator's touch. Saddam appears to have thought that he could allay fears for the hostages' safety, but his handling of a frightened little boy has served only to underline their peril (→ 28).

Young Stuart Lockwood shies away from Iraq's President Saddam Hussein.

Poll-tax protesters do battle with police on streets of London

Police in riot gear clash with political extremists on the poll-tax march.

London, 31 March

A full-scale riot raged through the West End last night, following a rally in Trafalgar Square by some 300,000 people protesting against the introduction of the poll tax. The demonstrators chanted: "We won't pay" and listened to the Labour MP Tony Benn call for civil disobedience to make it unworkable.

Trouble broke out when violent elements in the largely peaceful crowd clashed with the police. Cars and buildings were set on fire and shopfronts smashed, and, as mounted police dispersed the crowds, the rioting moved on to Soho where tourists were caught up in the violence, which lasted until midnight. Many people were injured, and 341 arrests were made (→ 1/3/91).

Hostile challenge ousts Thatcher as Tory leader

Howe and Heseltine take up the challenge

Turning against his team captain: Sir Geoffrey in the House of Commons.

Westminster, 14 November
Michael Heseltine today declared his intention to fight Margaret Thatcher for the leadership of the Conservative Party. His challenge came within 24 hours of an outspoken attack on the Thatcher style of government by the man who had been her longest serving cabinet minister, Sir Geoffrey Howe.

Sir Geoffrey had resigned as deputy prime minister on 1 November, and yesterday he told MPs that Mrs Thatcher had a "nightmare" vision of Europe which was running "increasingly serious risks for the future of our nation". He said that colleagues were undermined and added: "It's rather like sending your opening batsmen to the crease only for them to find, the moment the first balls are bowled, that their bats have been broken before the game by the team captain."

Heseltine cites cabinet disunity and Europe as reasons for his challenge, nearly four years after he quit the cabinet in the "Westland" crisis. He plans to make reform of the poll tax an issue ($\rightarrow$ 22).

Thatcher resigns; enter Hurd and Major

Westminster, 22 November
Shortly after nine o'clock this morning Britain's first woman prime minister announced her intention to resign. "It's a funny old world," said Margaret Thatcher just two days after she had failed by only four votes to win a sufficient margin of victory over Michael Heseltine. She was attending a summit in Paris when the result of the first ballot was announced and initially signalled her determination to fight on. Frantic discussions went on all day yesterday, with a majority of cabinet colleagues saying that they no longer felt she could beat her former defence secretary. Douglas Hurd, the foreign secretary, and John Major, the chancellor, have now joined the fight for the succession ($\rightarrow$ 27).

The boy from Brixton makes it to the top

Westminster, 27 November
John Major is to be Britain's next prime minister. At 47, he is the youngest this century and has had a meteoric rise; he became an MP in 1979 and only joined the cabinet three years ago. He also has an unlikely background for a Tory leader: he left school at 16, without any O-levels, and was out of work for a time in Brixton, south London, before beginning a banking career.

Major won 185 votes for the Tory leadership against 131 for Michael Heseltine and 56 for Douglas Hurd. It was two votes short of outright victory under party rules, but Heseltine said that he would withdraw in the interests of party unity, and so did Hurd ($\rightarrow$ 28/6/91).

John Major, the new prime minister.

July 4. Tears of despair from Paul "Gazza" Gascoigne as England's World Cup chances are dashed when Germany win 4-3.

Hostage is freed from 'ultimate despair'

Dublin, 30 August 1990
Brian Keenan, freed after four years and four months as a hostage of Islamic Jihad terrorists in Beirut, came home to a joyous reception today bearing the news that at least one of the British hostages, John McCarthy, is alive. Keenan said that it was McCarthy's sense of humour which kept them sane.

The 39-year-old teacher, pale and haggard and on the verge of tears, gave a moving description of the ordeal he shared with his fellow captives: "Hostage is a crucifying aloneness ... it is a silent screaming slide into the bowels of ultimate despair. Hostage is a man hanging by his fingernails over the edge of chaos, feeling his fingers slowly straightening" ($\rightarrow$ 19/11/91).

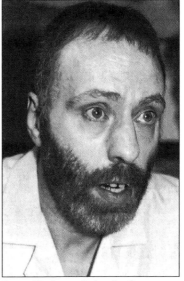

Brian Keenan: glad to be free.

Irish get their first woman president

Dublin, 9 November
Mary Robinson has become the first woman president of Ireland. A doctor's daughter from Ballina, in Co Mayo, she had a distinguished academic career and later became one of the country's best known constitutional lawyers. Elected to the senate at the age of 25, she campaigned for the introduction of family planning legislation – a controversial issue at the time.

Many people see her victory as representing the image of a new Ireland. She is seen to speak not only for women but also for minority groups and the disadvantaged, for whom much of her work as a lawyer has been carried out.

British troops move into Gulf war zone

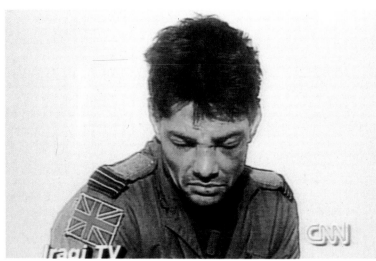

Lieutenant John Peters, a captured RAF pilot, as seen on Iraqi television.

Saudi Arabia, 17 January
The awesome power of modern weaponry was unleashed on the Iraqi capital, Baghdad, last night as the talking ended, the deadlines ran out, and Operation Desert Storm was launched with the aim of retaking Kuwait from Saddam Hussein.

A single F-117 Stealth fighter began the attack by destroying a telecommunications centre with a 2,000-lb (909-kg) "smart" bomb.

This was followed by Tomahawk cruise missiles, bombers, radar-jamming planes, Wild Weasel missiles and RAF Tornadoes which made dangerous, low-level sorties against Iraqi airfields. Britain has contributed 25,000 men to the 700,000-strong Allied force, about half of which is American, as well as four warships and 60 strike aircraft. "It is a battle that must be fought," said John Major (→ 8/4).

'Birmingham Six' cheered as they walk free

A jubilant "Birmingham Six" greet the crowds outside the Old Bailey.

London, 14 March
For 16 years six men were imprisoned for the IRA-inspired bombing of a pub in Birmingham. Today they walked free into the arms of their ecstatic supporters after the appeal court acknowledged that they had been convicted on faulty scientific evidence and forced confessions. The release of "the Birmingham

Six" – Hugh Callaghan, Richard McIlkenny, Paddy Hill, Billy Power, Gerry Hunter and Johnny Walker – has led to calls for the resignation of Lord Lane, who denied their appeal three years ago. The home secretary, Kenneth Baker, has acknowledged that this is the third gross injustice involving Irish people in 18 months (→ 25).

Downing Street hit by IRA mortar bomb

London, 7 February
The IRA attempted to assassinate John Major and the cabinet today when it fired a mortar bomb into the garden of No 10 Downing Street. It exploded just 12 metres from where the prime minister was chairing a war cabinet meeting.

The mortars – two others fell harmlessly 100 metres away – were fired through the roof of a white Transit van parked in Whitehall just after a man had jumped out and escaped on a motorcycle.

"I think we had better start again somewhere else," Mr Major is said to have remarked (→ 18).

Belfast is patrolled

Belfast, 15 November
Hundreds of extra troops have been drafted into Belfast to combat a new wave of sectarian murders. Seven people have been killed in 36 hours, prompting fears of an IRA and loyalist paramilitary tit-for-tat campaign before Christmas. Most of the loyalist murders are claimed by the outlawed Ulster Defence Association (UDA).

British troop numbers have been boosted by 300, including 100 sent from England, plus 1,400 part-time members of the Ulster Defence Regiment (UDR). Nationalists are unhappy about the UDR presence, saying that they are mistrusted by Roman Catholics and should be confined to loyalist streets.

Britain's first woman astronaut, Helen Sharman, out of orbit.

World watches as Western hostages freed

A sigh of relief as Waite is freed.

McCarthy waves: glad to be free.

Wiltshire, 19 November
A big man came home today. Five years ago Terry Waite, as special envoy for the archbishop of Canterbury, was working to free Western hostages held in Lebanon. Then he was kidnapped himself.

He limped down the plane steps at RAF Lyneham – the effect of being chained to a wall for nearly five years – but his forceful and moving account of his captivity showed that his spirit and his Christian faith were unbroken. He told of how in his darkest days he had been sustained by a postcard from an unknown well-wisher, showing a picture of an earlier imprisoned Christian – John Bunyan. Waite is the sixth hostage to be released this year since the freeing of the journalist John McCarthy (held for five years) in August. McCarthy came out with the news that Waite and others were well and a letter from the Islamic Jihad for the UN secretary, Javier Perez de Cuellar. It became clear that Israel held the key to breaking the Western hostage log-jam, since Hizbollah wanted its people out of Israeli jails.

No one is revealing the backstage deals, but gradually the hostages were freed, including the courageous Jacke Mann, a 77-year-old Spitfire pilot who survived two-and-a-half years on a chain. Three Americans are still held in Beirut, including Terry Anderson who has been there for six years.

Longest post-war recession grips UK

Britain, 19 December
A rise in German interest rates announced by the Bundesbank today was not the Christmas present which British ministers wanted. Several other European countries raised their rates in line with those of Germany, thus intensifying the pressure on sterling while making it more difficult for Britain to reduce interest rates to boost the economy.

Norman Lamont, the chancellor, has spent much of the year saying that recovery was just around the corner, and in August the Bank of England agreed that the worst of the recession was over. But recovery has proved elusive, and the current recession has now lasted longer than any other since the slump of the 1930s.

In this week alone there have been figures showing that manufacturing output fell again in October; that unemployment has risen to more than 2.5 million; and that housing repossessions, as people are unable to pay their mortgages, are expected to rise to 80,000 this year. A gloomy forecast from the previously upbeat Confederation of British Industry, and few signs of a Christmas boom in the shops, have dented hopes that consumer demand would spearhead economic recovery. Exports, too, are flagging as economic problems mount in the United States and Germany.

Indebted publisher meets watery end

Maxwell: the "Mirror's" hero is dead.

Canary Islands, 5 November
Did he jump or was he pushed? That is the question that may never be answered about the dead publishing tycoon Robert Maxwell, whose naked body was found today floating in the sea 20 miles southeast of Tenerife a few hours after disappearing from his luxury yacht *Lady Ghislaine*.

Those favouring suicide point to the increasing problems facing his debt-laden empire, which owes the banks an estimated £2.6 billion. Others claim that he was far too arrogant to take his own life and favour a murder scenario.

Flamboyant Freddie succumbs to Aids

London, 24 November
One of the most extravagant figures in the pop world died of Aids today. Freddie Mercury, the lead singer of Queen, was the driving force behind a band that stayed at the top throughout the 1970s and 1980s. Despite being firmly in the high-risk category for Aids, as both a bisexual and a heavy drug user, he shrugged off his alarming weight-loss of recent months and denied having Aids until yesterday.

Queen produced the first video to promote a single – *Bohemian Rhapsody* – in 1975 and embarked on a series of flamboyant tours; in 1985 it stole the show at the Live Aid concert. A bright light has gone out in the pop firmament.

Flamboyant Freddie on stage.

Major makes stand at Maastricht talks

Netherlands, 11 December
John Major, the prime minister, today hailed an agreement between European leaders as "game, set and match" for Britain. Leaders of the 12 nations in the European Community finally reached agreement on closer economic and monetary union in the early hours of today at their summit in Maastricht. Britain was allowed to defer a decision on a single currency and to opt out of a proposed "social chapter" of the treaty. But the Maastricht treaty still moves to what it calls "ever closer union" and extends central powers of the commission. It has to be ratified by each country.

Nov 2. Australia beat England 12-6 to win the Rugby World Cup in a fiercely fought contest.

London, 4 January. Britain's first "Moslem parliament" is inaugurated.

London, 29 January. The Department of Health reports a 50% rise in cases of AIDS acquired through heterosexual intercourse between 1990 and 1991.

London, 25 March. United Newspapers announces the closure of *Punch* magazine after 150 years of publication.

Melbourne, 25 March. Pakistan defeat England by 22 runs to win the cricket World Cup.

Britain, 26 March. The country suffers its worst drought since that recorded in 1745.

London, 10 April. An IRA car bomb kills three people in the City (→27/8).

London, 19 April. Comedian Frankie Howerd (b 1917) dies.

Madrid, 28 April. British artist Francis Bacon (b 28/10/1909) dies.

Berkshire, 3 June. Actor Robert Morley (b 26/5/1908) dies.

Wimbledon, 5 July. Andre Agassi and Steffi Graff win the tennis singles finals.

London, 20 July. Kevin Maxwell is ordered to pay £406.5 million in damages.

Barcelona, 8 August. British athletes win a total of 20 medals, including five golds, at the Summer Olympics.

Budapest, 16 August. British driver Nigel Mansell becomes the Formula One motor-racing world champion.

Britain, 30 September. The Royal Mint introduces the new, smaller 10 pence coin.

London, 13 October. The Booker Prize is awarded jointly to Michael Ondaatje and Barry Unsworth.

New York, 4 November. Elton John signs a £26 million deal with Time-Warner.

London, 25 November. Agatha Christie's play *The Mousetrap* celebrates its 40th anniversary in the West End.

London, 9 December. Buckingham Palace announces that the Prince and Princess of Wales are to separate after 11 years of marriage.

Balmoral, 12 December. Princess Anne marries Commander Tim Laurence.

Reading, 25 December. Monica Dickens, author of *One Pair of Hands*, (b 10/5/1915) dies.

Fourth straight win for Conservatives

London, 10 April

John Major has won an unexpected election victory, despite a lacklustre campaign during which he often looked more like the leader of the opposition than the prime minister. Meanwhile, Labour's Neil Kinnock attended a series of slick rallies, avoiding gaffes and becoming more leaderlike with every day. At the last minute, however, voters shied away from the widely predicted prospect of a Labour/Liberal Democrat coalition. And they voted with their wallets: the Conservatives were the only party to pledge not to raise income tax. The Tories now have a relatively comfortable parliamentary majority of more than 20 seats (→18/7).

John Major's enthusiastic supporters express their satisfaction after the vote.

Kevin, Ian Maxwell charged with fraud

London, 18 June

Police made early morning raids on the homes of Kevin and Ian Maxwell, sons of the late publisher Robert Maxwell. Both men were arrested and charged with fraud offences involving a combined total of at least £140 million. As they left the court after being released on bail, Kevin Maxwell said: "After seven months of trial by rumour, of trial by innuendo, of trial by selective press leaks, and of prejudicial media reporting, I am really looking forward to being able to defend myself in a court of law" (→20/7).

20 April. Comedian Benny Hill, born in Southampton in 1924, dies of a heart attack in London.

Hong Kong's last governor moves in

Hong Kong, 9 July

Chris Patten, Hong Kong's newly appointed governor, issued a manifesto today as he took office. He wants the colony, due to be handed back to communist China at the end of his tenure in 1997, to have a more accessible and democratic government, an aim that is sure to annoy Peking. He then went walkabout in the crowded heart of his domain. Surrounded by a scrum of newsmen and bodyguards, the grinning governor squeezed his way through the narrow alleys of the Mong Kok red-light district.

Lloyd's of London posts huge losses

London, 24 June

Lloyd's today revealed a loss of £2.06 billion, the worst in its 300-year history, for 1989, when the insurance market was hit by huge claims from four disasters: the *Exxon Valdez* oil spill, Hurricane Hugo, the San Francisco earthquake and the Phillips Petroleum explosion in Texas.

Individual Lloyd's investors, known as 'Names', have a completely unlimited liability to make good the losses. Many therefore face utter financial ruin. They will probably take legal action against Lloyd's.

Scotsman John Smith takes over Labour

London, 18 July

John Smith scored a decisive victory over his only challenger, Bryan Gould, today to become the 14th leader of the Labour Party. He won 91 per cent of the votes: Margaret Beckett was elected deputy leader. Smith, former shadow chancellor, faces a formidable task to revive the party after the election defeat and resignation of Neil Kinnock. He told Labour activists that he intends to democratize the party and win back the support of women. "The party of change must be ready to change itself", he said (→21/7/94).

30 June. Margaret Thatcher is introduced to the House of Lords today as Baroness Thatcher.

Ulster strife claims its 3,000th victim

Belfast, 27 August

A grim milestone was reached in Northern Ireland today when 19-year-old Hugh McKibben became the 3,000th victim of the Troubles. Sectarian violence has claimed on average a life every three days in the past 23 years since John Gallagher, a 30-year-old Catholic, was shot dead by the now-disbanded B Specials during riots in Armagh.

McKibben's death is thought to stem from a dispute between rival factions of the Irish People's Liberation Organisation, a republican splinter group. The security forces were not involved, and the IRA denies responsibility (→24/4/93).

Heritage minister David Mellor quits government over sex scandal

London, 24 September

David Mellor, the heritage secretary and one of John Major's closest friends, resigned tonight. Mellor's problems began with revelations of his affair with actress Antonia de Sancha. He survived the scandal, but a libel case brought by Mona Bauwens, daughter of a PLO official, against a newspaper finished him off. Bauwens, who had invited the Mellor family to holiday with her in Spain, argued that the paper had suggested she was not fit to be seen in decent company. Although the jury failed to reach a verdict, Mellor's judgement in accepting a free holiday from Bauwens was so fiercely questioned in court that his resignation became inevitable.

Mellor, dubbed "Minister for Fun", has admitted an affair with an actress.

Monetary chaos after Britain leaves ERM

London, 18 September

Britain's decision, announced two days ago, to quit the European Exchange Rate Mechanism and allow sterling to float has plunged the markets into chaos.

The admission of defeat by Prime Minister John Major and Chancellor Norman Lamont, after a battle against speculators which is estimated to have cost Britain £15 billion, had also led to harsh words between Britain and Germany. Lamont blamed Bonn's economic policies for the fall of the pound and "many of the tensions within the ERM".

Mystery of Mona Lisa's smile solved?

London, 13 December

British psychiatrist Digby Quested believes he has finally explained the enigmatic quality of Mona Lisa's smile. "The key to the mystery is", he says, "that it is a mirror image." Mona Lisa's smile is more pronounced on the left side, as is common in forced smiles. Had Leonardo da Vinci not painted the portrait as if it were a reflection, the smile would have appeared more natural and sincere. Earlier investigations had shown that Mona Lisa's features matched exactly those of a self-portrait by Leonardo, and X-rays revealed a beard beneath the surface of the painting.

Furious miners force Major to back down

London, 21 October

The government was forced to grant major concessions to the miners in order to ensure victory in a rowdy Commons debate on pit closures tonight. Even so, it scraped home by just 13 votes.

The debate took place against a background of a march through London by thousands of miners and their supporters, all protesting against government plans to close 10 coal mines. Michael Heseltine, the trade and industry minister, has now pledged to save some of the threatened mines.

1992 was 'annus horribilis', says Queen Elizabeth

London, 24 November

The Queen, speaking with evident sadness and a voice weakened by smoke from the fire that devastated Windsor Castle just four days ago, told guests at a Guildhall banquet tonight, planned as a celebration of her 40th anniversary on the throne, that 1992 had been an "annus horribilis". It is "not a year on which I shall look back with undiluted pleasure", she added.

She did not refer directly to the succession of royal disasters in a year which saw the divorce of the Princess Royal, the separation of the Duke and Duchess of York and

A fire last week damaged Windsor Castle, one of the Queen's favourites.

the marital difficulties of the Prince and Princess of Wales. As the year ends, the criticism of the royal family grows more insistent. The Queen now faces demands to use some of her fortune to help pay for repairs to Windsor Castle and to pay income tax just like her subjects. Referring to the tabloid newspapers which have hounded her family throughout 1992, she said: "We are all part of the same fabric of our national society, and that scrutiny can be just as effective if it is made, by one party or another, with a touch of gentleness, good humour and understanding" (→12/12).

Major pollution alert as oil tanker is wrecked off Shetland Isles

It is now questioned why the Braer took this notoriously hazardous route.

Sumburgh Head, 6 January

Oil poured from the stricken tanker *Braer* throughout the night as she threatened to break up in the hurricane-force winds which drove her onto the rocks of this dangerous southern tip of the Shetland Isles. Pollution experts who have rushed to the scene remain powerless to deal with more than 84,000 tonnes of light crude which has begun to foul the coastline of one of Britain's most precious wildlife sanctuaries. Some scientists fear that a major ecological disaster is in the making, while others believe that storm-force winds and the tide could break up the oil, allowing it to be dispersed fairly quickly (→15).

Briton is first woman to be Concorde pilot

London, 25 March

Barbara Harmer, aged 39, became civil aviation's first woman supersonic pilot today when she flew as first officer of Concorde.

It was, she said after the flight, "the achievement of a long-held ambition". She began her career as an air traffic controller, learning to fly privately. She became a flying instructor to get a commercial licence before joining British Caledonian to pilot BAC One Elevens and later converting to long-haul DC-10s. She is one of 40 women pilots currently employed by British Airways.

The Grand National ends in disarray

Liverpool, 3 April

Aintree racecourse officials have declared this year's chaotic Grand National void. John White, whose mount, Esha Ness, came in first, was in tears. The trouble began when animal-rights demonstrators ran onto the course just before the off. When calm was finally restored, the jittery horses broke through the tape in a false start. On the second attempt there was another false start, but the front runners carried on, believing that the shouts of officials trying to stop the race were simply those of protesters.

Bosnia plan is dead, Lord Owen concedes

Geneva, 17 June

A dispirited Lord Owen conceded today that his peace plan for Bosnia, based on the division of the country into 10 semi-autonomous regions, is utterly dead.

The clearly frustrated British mediator could only urge President Alija Izetbegovic of Bosnia to accept the plan proposed by his victorious enemies, the Serbs and the Croats. That plan calls for partitioning Bosnia into three ethnically homogeneous states, with the Muslims getting only 10 per cent of the total territory (→5/1/94).

Royal Navy to bear brunt of force cuts

London, 5 July

The Royal Navy is to suffer draconian cuts in a reassessment of Britain's defence commitments following the collapse of the Soviet Union. The destroyer and frigate force will be cut from 40 to about 35 units. The Upholder class of four diesel-electric submarines, which cost £900 million to build, will be sold, leased or moth-balled. The RAF will also suffer, with the loss of a Tornado F3 squadron.

The cuts, announced in a white paper, *Defending our Future*, will meet Treasury demands for £1 billion in military savings.

12 July. Andrew Lloyd Webber's musical, "Sunset Boulevard", with Patti LuPone as an ageing Hollywood star, has taken the West End by storm.

Maastricht treaty is ratified by Britain

London, 2 August
Britain today took a big step towards far closer relations with its European neighbours.

The United Kingdom has at last ratified the Maastricht treaty, 20 months after it was negotiated. The final obstacle was removed when Lord Rees-Mogg abandoned his court case against its legality. A four-page instrument of ratification, written on vellum and signed by the Queen, had already been flown to Rome – where the European Community began – and as soon as the Rees-Mogg case ended it was deposited with the foreign ministry there.

Last month, Prime Minister John Major was forced to resort to a vote of confidence in the House of Commons over the Maastricht Bill, threatening to seek the dissolution of parliament and call a general election if the government lost. The threat brought the Tory Euro-rebels back into line. Forced to make a choice between an election in which the Tories would have faced defeat and giving Major the authority to proceed with the ratification process, their resistance crumbled and the prime minister won his vote of confidence.

The irony is that after its politically divisive progress through both houses of parliament, many Euro-sceptics now regard the treaty, in the words of Norman Lamont, as "a bit of a fossil".

Historic Ulster declaration signed

London, 15 December.
The British and Irish prime ministers, John Major and Albert Reynolds, today signed a historic declaration designed to bring peace to Northern Ireland. The vital document, agreed after much hard bargaining, holds out the prospect of Sinn Fein joining talks on the future of the province, if the IRA renounces violence forever. It was generally welcomed in Westminster, although the Unionist firebrand Ian Paisley denounced it out of hand. The question of continued bloodshed or peace is now in the hands of the men of violence, republican and loyalist (→31/8/94).

Neo-Nazi's election unleashes a storm

London, 19 September
Riot police broke up fighting between anti-Nazis and members of the British National Party in the East End today in clashes reminiscent of pre-war battles against Mosley's Fascists. The violence, in the heart of the Bengali community, follows Derek Beackon's election as the country's first BNP councillor, in a by-election at Millwall. Beackon benefited from local belief that the Bengalis are given preferential treatment in housing and also from divisions between his Labour and Liberal Democrat opponents.

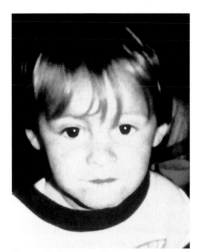
Premiers John Major and Albert Reynolds appeal to the men of violence.

Two boys found guilty of toddler's murder

Preston, 24 November
After a harrowing trial, two 11-year-old boys, the youngest murderers in modern British legal history, were found guilty of killing two-year-old James Bulger and ordered to be detained for "very, very many years". The boys lured the toddler away from his mother during a shopping trip. They proceeded to drag him through Liverpool before beating him to death on a railway line. Throughout the trial, the boys had been known as Child A and Child B, but the judge, Michael Morland, today gave permission for their names, Jon Venables and Robert Thompson, to be revealed.

James Bulger was beaten to death.

A woman to head Britain's security services

London, 1 October
Pauline Neville-Jones, a career diplomat, is to chair the Joint Intelligence Committee, whose task is to evaluate intelligence from MI5, MI6, Government Communications Headquarters and the Defence Ministry and to advise the prime minister of potential threats to British political, economic and military security.

As is becoming customary, she was introduced to the press. Neville-Jones, the second woman to fill a top intelligence job (Stella Rimington is head of MI5), will continue in her present post as head of the Defence and Overseas Secretariat in the Cabinet Office.

Pauline Neville-Jones faces the press.

30 July. Linford Christie of Britain (centre) easily outruns Americans Carl Lewis (left) and John Drummond to win the 100 metres event at Gateshead.

London, 5 January. Lieut-Gen Sir Michael Rose is appointed to lead UN forces in Bosnia (→23/1/95).

London, 5 January. Cricket commentator Brian Johnston (b 24/6/1912) dies.

Westminster, 14 January. The Duchess of Kent is the first member of the royal family to become a Roman Catholic in modern times.

Manchester, 20 January. Football manager Sir Matt Busby (b 26/5/1909) dies.

London, 31 January. BMW agrees to pay $800 million for an 80 per cent share in Rover.

Westminster, 21 February. MPs vote to lower the age of consent for homosexuals from 21 to 18.

Twickenham, 19 March. Wales win the Five Nations rugby championship.

Mull of Kintyre, 2 June. Twenty-five senior anti-terrorist officials are killed in a helicopter crash.

Britain, 12 June. In European Parliament elections, Tories win only 18 seats to Labour's 62.

London, 29 July. Former Labour leader Neil Kinnock is appointed an EU commissioner.

Britain. 29 August. The Sunday Trading Act, allowing shops to open legally on Sunday for the first time in Britain, comes into effect.

Berlin, 8 September. The last British forces leave Berlin.

London, 27 September. A four-month series of rail strikes ends.

Belfast, 13 October. Ulster's three main loyalist terrorist groups announce a ceasefire.

Israel, 31 October. The Duke of Edinburgh becomes the first member of the royal family to visit Israel.

Mansfield, Notts, 1 November. Sydney Dernley, Britain's last surviving executioner, dies aged 73.

Belfast, 9 December. The first formal talks between British officials and Sinn Fein representatives in 22 years begin (→15/1/95).

London, 11 December. A man wins £17.8 million in the National Lottery's first big jackpot.

Dublin, 15 December. John Bruton is elected premier a month after the fall of Albert Reynolds's government.

Queen and Mitterrand open Chunnel

Coquelles, France, 6 May
After two centuries of schemes, eight years of technological and political struggle and billions of pounds, a dream became reality as Queen Elizabeth and President Francois Mitterrand cut red, white and blue ribbons to inaugurate the Channel Tunnel. The Queen, having first opened the Eurostar terminal at Waterloo, passed through the tunnel to Coquelles, where the trains carrying the two heads of state met nose to nose. After a colourful ceremony, the Queen and the French president sat in the royal Rolls Royce as it was carried back to England on Le Shuttle for another opening ceremony.

A dream comes true at last for women priests

Bristol, 12 March
The first women priests in the long history of the Church of England were ordained in Bristol Cathedral today. A total of 32 women were ordained by the Bishop of Bristol, who spoke of the women's "significant journey". The two-hour service took on an atmosphere of rapturous celebration, and as the last "Amen" signalled the completion of their formal consecration there were extraordinary scenes. Applause rang round the cathedral's gothic arches and several of the new priests cried with joy.

6 June. Queen Elizabeth travels to Bayeux cemetery in Normandy to pay tribute to the British soldiers killed during Operation Overlord 50 years ago.

Major's 'Back to Basics' row grows

London, 10 January
The prime minister is desperately trying to patch together his crumbling "Back to Basics" campaign. John Major has made this campaign, which calls for a return to old-fashioned family values, a central part of government policy.

Major has just lost two ministers: Lord Caithness, who resigned following the suicide of his wife, and Tim Yeo, the environment minister who quit after the revelation that he had fathered a child as a result of an affair with Tory councillor Julia Stent. Yeo tried to hang on to his job but was forced into resignation under pressure from his South Suffolk constituency party.

Westminster is buzzing with stories of other improprieties. Major has called for an end to the moral witch hunt against Tories who behave foolishly. He said that "Back to Basics" is not about the sexual morality of individuals and has denied he was preaching at single mothers. The nation is not convinced.

Tony Blair wins race to lead Labour Party

London, 21 July
Tony Blair has been elected leader of the Labour Party in a landslide, winning more than half the votes in all three sections of the party: the MPs, the constituencies and the trade unions. He easily beat John Prescott, who, in a separate vote, was elected deputy leader.

Blair, at 41, is the party's youngest leader ever. He is a modernist, far removed from the dinosaurs of old-fashioned socialism, and he regards his victory as a mandate to continue the reforms started by his predecessor, John Smith, who died in May. In a speech tonight, he told a triumphant meeting he would not rest until he had put Labour "in its rightful place – in government again" (→29/4/95).

11 August. Actor Peter Cushing (b 26/5/1913) dies of cancer.

The IRA opens a door to Ulster peace

Belfast, 31 August
After 25 years of bloodshed, the IRA has announced a "complete cessation of military operations". The way now seems open to a political settlement of this savage sectarian conflict. Sinn Fein leader Gerry Adams, who persuaded IRA hardliners to accept last year's Downing Street Declaration, said: "We have taken a great step by removing the republican gun from Irish politics."

However, one major problem has already surfaced. The IRA document speaks of a "cessation" of military operations but does not use the word "permanent", a condition laid down in the declaration as a prerequisite for Sinn Fein to join talks on Northern Ireland's future. The British government has demanded clarification from the IRA. Irish Prime Minister Albert Reynolds, who has done much to bring about peace, has reassured John Major that although the word "permanent" was not in the statement, other phrases showed that the republican movement was now committed to a democratic peace process. "As

New-style graffiti on the streets of Northern Ireland.

far as we are concerned, the long nightmare is over," he said. The reaction of the Protestant community is less ecstatic. Ian Paisley said the IRA's "war machine" could be turned on at any time, and there is scepticism about the worth of the IRA's word. Major must convince the loyalists that they have not been sold out in some secret deal (→13/10).

South Africa back in the Commonwealth

Westminster, 20 July
The Queen Mother joined heads of state and politicians from all around the world in Westminster Abbey today to celebrate South Africa's return to the Commonwealth after 33 years in the wilderness. There was a mood of happiness in the abbey, which, at one stage, was filled with the joyful sound of South African township jazz.

Archbishop Desmond Tutu compared the return, which follows the election in May of Nelson Mandela as South Africa's first black president, with the tale of the prodigal son. He said South Africa had squandered her riches during the dark years of apartheid, but international pressures and the struggles of her own people had finally brought the country back to its senses. "Like a prodigal, she has returned home and is getting a right royal welcome and can only say 'Wow'," he said. Tomorrow, the South Africans return to Lord's for their first Test match in England in 24 years (→26/3/95).

Millions chase National Lottery's first jackpot

London, 19 November
The winning number in Britain's first National Lottery came up in a TV extravaganza tonight as gambling fever seized the nation, but no single ticket holder claimed the jackpot. Instead, the £15.8 million prize was shared by seven punters.

However, many more people than expected won the guaranteed minimum prize of £10. But what the gamblers wanted was the big prize. Camelot, the organizers, estimate that about 25 million people had bet by tonight's deadline, putting £45 million in the kitty (→11/12).

20 October. The Queen and President Yeltsin at the Bolshoi Theatre during the first visit to Moscow by a British monarch since the Russian Revolution.

Belfast, 15 January. The British army ends 25 years of daylight street patrols.

London, 14 February. 95 years after his death, a stained-glass memorial window to Oscar Wilde is unveiled in Poets' Corner, Westminster Abbey.

Belfast, 10 May. The British government holds the first ministerial talks with Sinn Féin since 1972.

Old Trafford, 21 May. Wigan beat Leeds 69-12 to complete a grand slam of Rugby League trophies: Premiership, League Championship, Challenge Cup and Regal Trophy.

Westminster, 24 May. Harold Wilson, Labour prime minister 1964–70 and 1974–6, (b 11/3/1916) dies aged 79.

Salamanca, Spain, 18 July. British athlete Jonathan Edwards sets a new world triple jump record of 17.98 metres.

England and Wales, 6 August. Licensing laws are relaxed, allowing pubs to open on Sundays from noon onwards.

London, 18 August. The largest traditional Hindu stone temple outside India opens in Neasden.

London, 31 August. The Meteorological Office announces that August has been the hottest month since 1659.

Coldstream, 9 October. Sir Alec Douglas-Home, Conservative prime minister 1963–4, (b 2/7/1903) dies aged 92.

Kyle of Lochalsh, 15 October. A bridge between Skye and the mainland is opened.

London, 28 November. John Major and John Bruton issue a joint communiqué pledging to begin all-party talks in N. Ireland and to create an international body to decommission terrorist arms (→15/12).

Singapore, 2 December. Rogue trader Nick Leeson is sentenced to six-and-a-half years in prison. He was extradited from Germany and yesterday pleaded guilty to fraud and forgery.

Belfast, 15 December. The arms decommissioning panel, headed by former US senator George Mitchell, begins work.

London, 20 December. Buckingham Palace confirms that the Queen has written to the Prince and Princess of Wales, urging them to divorce.

Dublin, 21 December. Jack Charlton resigns, ending his phenomenally successful period in charge of the Irish national football team.

Peace plan for N. Ireland

Belfast, 22 February
The British and Irish prime ministers, John Major and John Bruton, today published a joint framework for all-party talks on a new political settlement in Northern Ireland. It proposes the creation of a "North-South body" with "executive, harmonising or consultative functions" and responsibility for agreed areas on an all-Ireland basis, and an elected devolved Northern Ireland assembly. It also suggests that the Dublin government will amend the Irish Constitution to remove its territorial claim to Northern Ireland. Sinn Féin leader Gerry Adams welcomed the document, saying "its ethos is for one Ireland". The Unionist response was dismissive: Peter Robinson of the Democratic Unionists said "Ulster has been served with an eviction notice to leave the UK". At a press conference today Major declared that nothing in the document would be imposed and Bruton said the document was designed to "create new structures to which both communities in Northern Ireland will be able to give an equal sense of allegiance".

Labour drop Clause 4

London, 29 April
Tony Blair won a significant battle today in his drive to "modernise" the Labour Party in pursuit of victory in the next general election. A special conference voted to replace the venerable Clause 4 of the Labour Party constitution – which committed Labour to strive for "common ownership of the means of production, distribution and exchange" – with a more general set of "aims and values". The new clause commits the Party to working for a just society, an open democracy, a dynamic economy and a healthy environment. The change was backed by 65.23 per cent of votes. Earlier this week, Blair said "we are witnessing a new Labour Party being born".

Tony Blair (right) with Tom Sawyer, General Secretary of the Labour Party.

Protests fail to stop live animal exports

Dover, 20 April
Six lorries carrying calves and lambs for slaughter were today shipped from Dover to Dieppe, France, in the first livestock exports from the port for six months. Port authorities had banned such exports in the face of sometimes violent animal rights protests. But on 12 April the High Court ruled that the Dover ban and similar ones at other ports were discriminatory against the livestock trade and should be lifted. Since last October a popular movement against the export of live animals for slaughter has attracted an unlikely alliance of outspoken campaigners and respectable members of the middle classes; police and protestors clashed regularly.

Major's poll win boosts authority

London, 4 July
Prime Minister John Major today won the contest for leadership of the Conservative Party in a bid to end speculation about challenges to his authority. By 218 votes to 89 he defeated John Redwood, who thereupon resigned as Secretary of State for Wales. Major has been under fire following the Conservatives' dismal showing in opinion polls and their disastrous performance in local elections in April and May.

Dealer behind Barings collapse is held

Nick Leeson following his arrest.

Frankfurt, 2 March
Nick Leeson, the 28-year-old British financial dealer whose multi-million pound losses brought down Baring's Bank last month, was arrested by German police today. Leeson's unauthorised dealings on the Singapore futures market plunged Baring's, Britain's oldest merchant bank, £850 million in debt. When the size of the catastrophe became apparent, he went into hiding with his wife Lisa on 23 February. The couple flew to Europe, apparently heading for Britain in the hope of facing trial there rather than in Singapore. Baring's was placed in administration on 26 February after the Bank of England refused to put together a rescue package. It seems likely that it will be bought – including its vast debts – by the Dutch ING group.

8 May. Thousands watch the Red Arrows on the 50th anniversary of VE Day.

Diana speaks out

London, 20 November
Her Royal Highness Princess Diana last night admitted adultery and cast doubt on whether her husband Prince Charles would ever become King. In a stunningly frank interview for the BBC TV programme *Panorama*, the Princess said of army officer James Hewitt "Yes, I adored him. Yes, I was in love with him". Referring to her husband's infidelity with Camilla Parker-Bowles, she said: "There were three of us in this marriage, so it

The Princess of Wales interviewed.

was a little bit crowded". When interviewer Martin Bashir asked if Charles would become King, the Princess said: "I don't think any us know the answer to that". She added: "The top job, as I call it, would bring enormous limitations to him, and I don't know whether he could adapt to that".

In the most astonishing royal statement since Edward VIII's abdication speech in 1936, Diana also admitted to having suffered from postnatal depression and bulimia. She said she did not think that "the Establishment" wanted her to become Queen "because I do things differently, because I don't follow the rule book, because I lead from the heart, not the head", adding "I would like to be Queen in people's hearts". The broadcast must surely have brought closer the divorce of the Prince and Princess of Wales. Buckingham Palace has refused to comment.

Tories reeling after double poll defeat

Westminster, 5 May
There is renewed talk of deposing John Major as Conservative Party leader this morning after voters in yesterday's local elections deserted the Tories. They lost control of 62 councils in England and Wales, leaving them in power in just eight, while Labour gained 44 to hold power in 155, and the Liberal Democrats gained 14 to have power in 44 councils. If the voting pattern is repeated in the general election,

Labour will win by a landslide. It follows the Tories' humiliation in the Scottish local elections on 6 April, when the Party failed to gain control of a single one of the 29 unitary authorities that will be set up in April 1996. Former Conservative Party chairman Sir Norman Fowler called on MPs to demonstrate their loyalty to Major, saying "Unless we can address the unity issue, then I am afraid the outlook is bleak".

29 November. Damien Hirst wins the Turner Prize with *Mother and Child, Divided*, two sheep pickled in a tank of formaldehyde.

Irish leader calls for talks before decommissioning

Dublin, 12 November
Tensions are running high between the British and Irish governments over the faltering Northern Ireland peace process and in particular over whether all-party talks – including republican Sinn Féin – should start before the Irish Republican Army and other paramilitary groups have begun decommissioning their weapons. John Bruton yesterday called on the Westminster government to give the go-ahead to talks in advance of IRA decommissioning, but today John Major said such a move would be a "reckless short-term gesture". Both sides are keen to make progress on the issue before the planned visit to Northern Ireland of US President Bill Clinton on 30 November (→28/11).

Narrow majority for Irish divorce

Dublin, 27 November
A narrow majority of voters approved limited no-fault divorce in the Irish Republic in a referendum held two days ago. A recount last night established that a majority of 9114 out of 1.63 million votes approved the lifting of the constitutional ban on divorce that has been in place since 1937. A Roman Catholic organization has announced it will challenge the result, claiming that the government interfered in the democratic process by using I£500,000 of public money in support of a "yes" vote in favour of lifting the ban. No-fault divorce will now be available from next year for couples who have lived apart for four of the previous five years.

Ten life terms for killer Rosemary West

Rosemary West with her husband Frederick West.

Winchester, 22 November
Rosemary West, convicted of 10 murders including those of her daughter and stepdaughter, was today sentenced to 10 terms of life imprisonment. Handing down the sentences, Mr Justice Mantell said "if attention is paid to what I think, you will never be released". Most of the killings took place in the 1970s; police are still seeking information on nine other young

women, missing after visiting or lodging with Mrs West, now 41, and her husband Frederick at 25 Cromwell Street, Gloucester, where many of the known victims' remains were found. Fred West, 53, hanged himself while in custody at Winson Green Prison in Birmingham on 1 January this year; he had been charged with the 10 murders of which his wife was convicted as well as two others.

First privatised trains

Britain, 5 February

The first privately run British passenger trains for almost 50 years went into operation today as South West Trains and Great Western, holders of the first two franchises to be awarded under the government's rail privatisation programme, began services. But a third service – on London, Tilbury, Southend Rail (LTS) – was cancelled amid allegations of ticketing fraud. The award of the first franchises, under the 1993 Railway Act, was announced on 19 December last year. Management buy-out teams were awarded the contracts for Great Western and LTS, while Perth-based bus company Stagecoach took the franchise for South West Trains. The British rail network was nationalised on 1 January 1948.

IRA blasts London Docklands

London, 10 February

The Irish peace process is in crisis after the IRA last night ended its 17-month ceasefire, exploding a large bomb in Docklands which killed two, injured 100 and caused an estimated £150 million damage. The bomb exploded at 7.01pm in an underground car park close to Canary Wharf and the Docklands Light Railway on the Isle of Dogs in east London. A one-hour warning was given, and in the statement the IRA said it was ending the ceasefire "with great reluctance".

The attack took most participants in the peace process by surprise. Only yesterday Sinn Féin president Gerry Adams declared that the ceasefire was "total and permanent". Today Adams refused to condemn the attack, blaming the British government and Unionist leaders for having rejected "an unprecedented opportunity for peace". British prime minister John Major called the bombing an "appalling outrage", which he said confirmed "the urgent need to remove illegal arms from the equation". Irish prime minister John Bruton condemned "without reservation" the return to violence.

Massacre in the classroom

Dunblane, 14 March

In a horrific and seemingly random attack, a former Scout leader walked into Dunblane Primary School in Perthshire yesterday morning and opened fire on a class of 29 five- and six-year-old children, killing 13 children and their teacher and injuring 15. Thomas Hamilton, a 43-year-old who was forced to quit the Scouts in 1974 over sexual abuse allegations, then turned one of his four handguns on himself and committed suicide. Three of the wounded children later died in hospital. Police said the attack seemed to be "totally random" although some reports suggest that Hamilton may have borne a grudge against the community in which there were complaints about the way he ran his youth club. Today, amid calls for tighter restrictions on the possession of handguns, the government announced an inquiry into the incident under Scottish judge Lord Cullen.

A poignant moment following the Dunblane tragedy.

Newbury bypass protesters evicted

Newbury, 29 February

Bailiffs today moved in to start evicting protesters blocking the construction of a road bypass to the west of Newbury in Berkshire. The proposed route of the new road will run through environmentally important areas and 12 archaeological sites, and for seven weeks a core of protesters have obstructed contractors, who were due to start work on 10 January. Local dignitaries including Lady Barber, the local Conservative Party chairman, and celebrities including Sir Terence Conran and Sir Andrew Lloyd Webber have joined protests. On 11 February 7000 people expressed their opposition to the bypass by walking part of the route. But Newbury's Liberal Democrat MP David Rendel says the great majority of people from this market town are in favour of the bypass.

Protesters blocking a Newbury road.

7 March. Genetically identical cloned sheep Megan and Morag are introduced to the world.

European Commission bans British beef

Brussels, 27 March

The European Commission today imposed a total ban on the worldwide export of British beef and many beef products. The ban, recommended by the EU veterinary committee two days ago, comes in the wake of scientific findings that human cases of the fatal Creutzfeldt-Jakob Disease (CJD) may be linked to consumption of beef derived from cows infected with "mad cow disease" or bovine spongiform encephalopathy (BSE). BSE is thought to be connected to the use of parts of sheep carcasses in cattle feed; a BSE epidemic in British beef herds peaked in 1992. Today's decree spells financial ruin for British beef farmers, who insist their meat is safe. They point out that the CJD cases studied by the scientists occurred before new, stricter guidelines on the parts of cattle used in beef products were introduced between 1988 and 1989.

Euro 96 – when football came home

London, 26 June

England's footballers and fans have suffered an agonising déjà vu, losing the semi-final of a major tournament to Germany on a penalty shootout for the second time in six years. Tonight in the semi-final of the European Championships at Wembley Stadium, England scored first but drew 1-1 after extra time with the Germans and lost 6-5 on penalties. Gareth Southgate of Aston Villa missed the crucial spot-kick. Memories of West Germany's similar triumph on penalties in the semi-final of the 1990 World Cup made the pain worse. Tonight disgruntled and drunken fans are fighting in the streets, but until now England's hosting of the Euro 96 Championships has been an unexpected success.

The team started slowly, disappointingly drawing 1-1 with Switzerland, but after a 2-0 victory over Scotland, England picked up momentum and the English seemed to unite behind their footballers, daring to believe that they might win their first major football trophy since the 1966 World Cup. In the Final Group A match, England thrashed the Dutch team 4-1, then edged past Spain in the quarter finals, winning 4-2 on penalties after a 0-0 draw. But the resolute Germans stood in the way and shattered the dream. Germany now face the Czech Republic in the Final on 30 June and are favourites to win.

Charles and Diana divorce

London, 28 August

The troubled marriage of the Prince and Princess of Wales ended quietly this morning. Following the announcement of the couple's separation in December 1992, Diana said that she did not want to divorce, but in the wake of public admissions of infidelity by both husband and wife, the Queen is believed to have demanded that the marriage be terminated. Buckingham Palace has announced that the Princess – who according to some reports received £17 million in the divorce settlement – is to lose her official title of Her Royal Highness; she will be known as Diana, Princess of Wales. The couple will share care of their sons, Princes William (14) and Harry (11).

10 July. President Nelson Mandela of South Africa with Betty Boothroyd, Speaker of the Commons, during his visit to the UK.

Irish peace talks

Gerry Adams (pointing) as he was refused entrance to Stormont Castle.

Belfast, 10 June

Talks on the future of Northern Ireland opened at Stormont Castle today but representatives of republican Sinn Féin were excluded until the renewal of the IRA ceasefire. In a protest dismissed by British prime minister John Major as "grandstanding" Sinn Féin president Gerry Adams attempted to lead party delegates into the talks but was turned away. Major described the negotiations as the "best opportunity for peace in the last 25 years", but they stalled almost at once when Unionist leaders refused to accept former US senator George Mitchell as chairman. Mitchell had served as chairman of the international decommissioning panel which reported in January this year, and in the light of that report, Unionists alleged that he was not impartial.

Shakespeare's Globe Theatre opens

London, 21 August

A £30 million recreation of William Shakespeare's Globe Theatre, built near the River Thames just 200 yards from the site of the 16th-century original, admitted its first paying audience last night. They came to see a production of the Bard's *The Two Gentlemen of Verona*. Made in the authentic Elizabethan style, the circular building has a thatched roof and open-air yard where some of the audience will stand in imitation of the "groundlings" of Shakespeare's day. Performers have to make do without stage lights or scenery and with few props.

The recreated Globe Theatre built on the south side of the River Thames.

A grieving nation bids Diana farewell

London, 6 September
Britain today led the world in mourning the death of Diana, Princess of Wales, as her state funeral was held in Westminster Abbey. Thousands who had camped out overnight watched as the princess's coffin, draped in the Royal Standard on a horsedrawn gun-carriage, was taken in a two-hour ceremonial procession from Kensington Palace, her west London home, to the Abbey. Millions more watched on television. An unprecedented outpouring of grief has swept the nation in the six days since Diana, 36, was killed in a road accident in Paris.

Diana died at about 4am on 31 August of injuries sustained when the Mercedes limousine in which she was travelling crashed at 85mph in the Pont de l'Alma road tunnel near the River Seine. Her friend Dodi Fayed, 42-year-old son of Harrods department store owner Mohamed Al Fayed, and the vehicle's French chauffeur, Henri Paul, died in the smash. Paparazzi photographers were chasing the Mercedes on motorcycles when it crashed. In London mourners gathered at Kensington Palace within hours of the news of her death. All week they came to honour her memory, leaving a mountain of floral tributes in their wake.

Today's funeral was attended by 1900 invited guests, many drawn from the Princess's Christmas card list. Celebrities such as popstar George Michael, Hollywood director Steven Spielberg and operatic tenor Luciano Pavarotti attended alongside state figures including Prime Minister Tony Blair, former Archbishop of Canterbury Robert Runcie and US First Lady Hillary Clinton. During the service Diana's brother, Earl Spencer, provoked

The coffin of Diana, Princess of Wales, is carried out of Westminster Abbey.

astonishment by launching a thinly veiled attack on the Royal Family in his tribute to the "unique, complex, extraordinary and irreplaceable" Diana. Referring to Buckingham Palace's decision to strip Diana of the title Her Royal Highness when she was divorced from Prince Charles last year, he said she had shown that "she needed no royal title to continue to generate her particular brand of magic" and he pledged that he and other members of the Spencer family would try to protect the "souls" of Diana's sons, Princes William and Harry, from being "simply immersed by duty and tradition". Afterwards Diana's coffin was driven to a burial site on the Spencer family estate of Althorp. As the convoy travelled northwards, thousands of mourners lined the roads, many hurling wreaths at the passing hearse.

Prince Charles and Princes William and Harry look at the floral tributes.

Scientists unveil lamb cloned from adult sheep

Ian Wilmut, who cloned the sheep.

Edinburgh, 23 February
The science fiction scenario of cloning humans from a single cell came a step closer today. Last year scientists here revealed that they had cloned twin sheep – Megan and Morag – from an embryo cell; today scientists at the Roslin Institute and PPL Therapeutics unveiled another sheep, Dolly, the first mammal cloned from an adult animal. Dolly was cloned from a cell taken from the udder of a Finn Dorset sheep and is genetically identical to the animal from which she was grown. The breakthrough raises the prospect of the mass production of farm animals using a cell from a single, particularly fine specimen such as a prize bull or pig. The scientists said there was "probably no technical reason" why the technique could not be used to reproduce humans, but current regulations forbid experiments in the area.

New Labour victorious

Westminster, 2 May

The rejuvenated Labour Party swept to power in yesterday's general election, bringing to an end 18 years of Conservative government. Tony Blair, 43, becomes the youngest prime minister since 1812 and presides over a majority of 179 seats in the House of Commons. The Conservatives' standing was badly undermined by allegations of corruption. Several leading Conservatives including Foreign Secretary Malcolm Rifkind and Defence Secretary Michael Portillo, widely tipped to be the next party leader, lost their seats. Neil Hamilton, one of the MPs accused of accepting financial rewards in return for asking parliamentary questions, was defeated by former BBC reporter Martin Bell, who stood on an independent "anti-corruption" platform. This morning Blair hailed "a vote for the future" and declared: "we can put behind us the battles of this past century and address the challenges of the new century".

Sinn Féin builds electoral momentum

Dublin, 7 June

Sinn Féin won its first ever seat in the Dáil yesterday, taking 2.5 per cent of first preference votes in the Irish general election. The result comes in the wake of the party's twin electoral successes last month. In the British general election on 1 May the party's president, Gerry Adams, and deputy leader, Martin McGuinness, were elected as Westminster MPs, but because both refused to swear the required oath of allegiance to the British crown they did not take up their seats. Then in the Northern Ireland local elections on 22 May, Sinn Féin won 16.9 per cent of the vote and received 74 seats. The overall results of the Irish general election were inconclusive. Bertie Ahern, leader of Fianna Fáil, is looking to form a coalition government with the Progressive Democrats.

British flag taken down in Hong Kong

The official handover ceremony as Hong Kong returns to Chinese rule.

Hong Kong, 1 July

After 155 years as a British colony, Hong Kong was returned to Chinese control at midnight last night. Yesterday Governor Chris Patten left his official residence in Government House and was ceremonially presented with the Union Jack that had flown above it. In the evening Prince Charles, Mr Patten, Prime Minister Tony Blair and Chinese President Jiang Zemin attended farewell ceremonies including a banquet and lavish firework display at Victoria Harbour. After the Prince and Mr Patten left aboard the royal yacht *Britannia*, businessman Tung Chee-hwa was sworn in as chief executive of the new administration.

Country protesters invade London to support fox-hunting

London, 10 July

An army of protesters from rural areas across Britain descended on central London today for a "countryside rally" to protest at proposals to ban fox-hunting. An estimated 100,000 gathered in Hyde Park for the speeches. It was a deliberately cross-party affair. Conservative leader William Hague attended and heard Labour's Baroness Mallalieu declare that if there is a battle over foxhunting "the countryside will fight and the countryside will win".

Welsh and Scots to have own assemblies

Cardiff, 19 September

Welsh voters yesterday narrowly approved the new Labour government's plans to create a representative assembly in Cardiff. 50.3 per cent voted in favour of the devolved assembly and 49.7 per cent against – a majority of less than 7000 in a total vote of 1,112,117. The result follows a more decisive vote in Scotland on 11 September, when 74.3 per cent voted in favour and 25.7 against the creation of a 129-member Scottish parliament. The Scots also approved by 63.5 to 36.5 per cent proposals to give their parliament powers to vary the main UK rate of income tax by three per cent in either direction. The Westminster government has announced that legislation will be introduced before the year's end and the assemblies will be established in 1999.

Blair meets with Sinn Féin

Belfast, 13 October

Tony Blair met and shook hands with Gerry Adams at Stormont Castle today, in the first encounter between a British prime minister and a Sinn Féin leader since the signing of the Ango-Irish treaty in 1921.

11 March. Sir Paul McCartney after receiving his knighthood from the Queen.

21 January. British fashion designer John Galliano (centre) after the Christian Dior collection show at the Paris Fashion Show.

Westminster, 29 January. Tony Blair announces an enquiry into the 30 January 1972 "Bloody Sunday" events in Londonderry.

London, 3 February. The FT-SE 100 index closes at a record high of 5,612.8; the companies on the index are valued at more than £1000 billion for the first time.

London, 1 March. Some 250,000 pro-hunting country-side campaigners march through the centre of the city.

Belfast, 23 March. Sinn Féin rejoins multi-party talks following its exclusion on 20 February.

Britain, 31 March. RAF nuclear bombs are withdrawn from service. Britain's only nuclear weapons are now submarine-launched Trident missiles.

France, 30 June. England's footballers bow out of the 1998 World Cup after losing 4-3 to Argentina on penalties following a thrilling 2-2 draw.

N. Ireland, 1 July. David Trimble is elected leader of the new Assembly.

London, 30 July. The conviction of Derek Bentley for the 1952 murder of a policeman is rescinded posthumously. Bentley was hanged in 1953.

Ireland, 6 August. Irish Olympic swimming champion Michelle de Bruinis (née Smith) is banned for four years for allegedly tampering with a urine sample.

Tehran, 24 September. The *fatwa* imposed on author Salman Rushdie following the publication of his novel *The Satanic Verses* is lifted.

London, 18 October. Former Chilean dictator Augusto Pinochet is arrested at a London clinic. He may be extradited to Spain to face charges of murder and torture.

London, 22 October. The Office for National Statistics reveals that the nation's birth rate has fallen to its lowest level since records were first kept in 1841: 1.73 children per family in 1998 compared to 2.82 in the mid-1960s and 4.8 in 1875.

Westminster, 16 November. Agriculture minister Nick Brown announces £120 million emergency aid for farmers.

Dublin, 26 November. Tony Blair is the first British prime minister to address both Irish Houses of Parliament.

Dome on course for great day out

Greenwich, 22 June

Tony Blair hailed the £758 million Millennium Dome in southeast London as "a symbol of Britain's creativity and imagination" as he visited to celebrate completion of the roof's highest point. The Dome has been erected on a former gas-works site to be the centrepiece of Britain's millennium celebrations in 2000. Today's tour of the site also marks the first anniversary of the beginning of construction. Blair told cheering workers: "It is on time, on track and on budget", before expressing his hope that the curious building, which will be filled with attactions, would provide "the greatest day out on Earth in the year 2000". There has been criticism of the project, and a recent survey found that almost twice as many youngsters would choose to see in 2000 in Times Square, New York, than at the Dome.

Tony Blair at the Dome.

The Millennium Dome at Greenwich, London.

End of Cornish tin mining

Cornwall, 6 March

Britain's – and Europe's – last working tin mine, the South Crofty near Redruth, closed today. The 800m (2600ft) mine has been working since the 16th century and tin has been mined in Cornwall for 3000 years. Only 15 years ago the Cornish tin-mining industry employed 20,000, but the collapse in tin prices led it to financial ruin.

War veterans jeer Japanese Emperor

London, 26 March

British World War II veterans today made a passionate but orderly protest as Japan's Emperor Akihito was driven down the Mall to Buckingham Palace as part of a four-day state visit. Hundreds turned their backs as his carriage passed, while others shouted abuse or made obscene two-finger gestures. The men, many of whom had been incarcerated in Japanese prisoner-of-war camps, are demanding a formal Japanese apology and compensation for wartime brutality. Tonight at a state banquet the Emperor said he felt "deep sorrow and pain" for those who bore the scars of their suffering in World War II, but stopped short of the formal apology the veterans are seeking.

'Slaughter of the innocents' as Omagh car bomb kills 28

The devastation caused by the bomb attack in Omagh town centre.

County Tyrone, 15 August

A car bomb attack aimed at disrupting the Northern Ireland peace process today killed 28 and injured 220 in the market town of Omagh. A misleading coded warning 40 minutes before the attack indicated that the bomb was hidden in the courthouse, leading police to begin evacuation towards the other end of the street, where the explosives were in fact hidden. The bomb is thought to have been planted by a republican splinter group, the Real IRA. The attack has been condemned by Sinn Féin, the IRA and another splinter group, the Continuity IRA, who denounced the "absolute inhumanity" of the "slaughter of the innocents".

Breakthrough in Anglo-Irish peace talks

Belfast, 10 April
An end to three decades of conflict in Northern Ireland is in sight tonight after multi-party negotiations at Stormont Castle bore fruit in an agreement for peace. British prime minister Tony Blair declared "Courage has triumphed" while his Irish counterpart Bertie Ahern said: "This is a day we should treasure, a day when agreement and accommodation have taken the place of difference and division". The deal proposes a 108-member Ulster assembly and a 12-minister executive, as well as cross-border bodies to establish links between Northern

Ireland and the Irish Republic and a Council of the Isles to link the Irish bodies to Westminster and the new assemblies in Wales and Scotland. The Irish government will withdraw its constitutional claim to Ulster. A controversial clause will release hundreds of paramilitary prisoners within two to three years.

The deal, signed on Good Friday, will be put to the vote in referendums in both parts of Ireland on 22 May. John Hume, leader of the nationalist Social Democratic and Labour Party, said: "I think that for all our people Good Friday will be a very good Friday".

Ireland says 'yes' to peace

Belfast and Dublin, 22 May
Voters in Northern Ieland and the Irish Republic yesterday gave emphatic approval to the Good Friday Agreement, establishing a framework for peace in Ulster. The "yes" vote in support of the agreement was 71.12 per cent in Northern Ireland and 94.39 per cent in the Irish Republic. The result followed an intense four-week campaign, with Tony Blair making three visits to Northern Ireland.

Hereditary peers to leave House of Lords

Westminster, 14 October
Labour is following through on its 1997 election pledge to remove the voting rights of hereditary peers in the House of Lords. Lady Jay of Paddington, Government leader in the Lords, announced today that a bill in the next parliamentary session will remove hereditary peers' 700-year-old right to sit and vote in the upper chamber and that a Royal Commission will report on options for longer-term reform.

25 June. The Queen opens the new £520million British Library at St Pancras in London. The Library used to be part of the British Museum.

Crowd cheers rare England victory

Mike Atherton (left) and Alec Stewart during their winning run.

Headingley, 10 August
It has been an agonising 13-year wait for England's long-suffering cricket fans, but today they got what they wanted: an England victory in a full five-Test series. It was the first since 28 December 1986. Before a partisan 10,000 crowd England won the Fifth Test against South Africa by 23 runs to take the series 2-1 with two Tests drawn. Captain Alec Stewart said: "We played exceptionally well throughout the series and today we

deserved to win". There was controversy over umpiring decisions that handed England a number of disputed leg-before-wicket dismissals but South Africa captain Hansie Cronje refused to blame his side's defeat on them. Mike Atherton, England captain for five years, scored 493 runs over 10 innings – average 54.77 – and was named England's man of the series. Bowlers Darren Gough, Angus Fraser and Dominic Cork also starred in this rare triumph.

Nobel Peace Prize

John Hume (left) and David Trimble.

Oslo, 16 October
The 1998 Nobel Peace Prize has been jointly awarded to John Hume, 61-year-old leader of the nationalist Social Democratic and Labour Party, and David Trimble, 54-year-old leader of the Ulster Unionist Party, for their roles in the Northern Ireland peace process.

Beef ban is lifted at last

Brussels, 23 November
European Union agriculture ministers voted this morning to lift the 32-month-old ban imposed on British beef exports because of fears that "mad cow disease" – or bovine spongiform encephalopathy (BSE) – might be connected to cases of Creutzfeldt-Jakob Disease in humans. The lifting of the ban is subject to approval by the European Commission after Britain has completed a cull of 4000 calves born to BSE-infected cows and EU inspectors have approved hygiene standards at selected British abattoirs. The BSE crisis has cost the British economy an estimated £4.6 billion and ruined the livelihoods of many farmers. The government knows that a great deal of work needs to be done to restore the standing of the beef industry. There is still opposition within Europe: Germany voted against and France abstained in today's vote.

Wedding breaks with royal tradition

The Earl and Countess of Wessex outside St George's Chapel.

Windsor, 19 June

Prince Edward, the Queen's 35-year-old youngest son, today married Sophie Rhys-Jones, 34, in St George's Chapel, Windsor Castle.

Planned as an informal occasion with a minimum of state pageantry, it was dubbed the "people's wedding" because 8000 members of the public were admitted by ticket to the castle to see the couple. A further 15,000 waited outside to watch the bride and groom's 5-km (3-mile) post-ceremony procession through Windsor in a horse-drawn carriage. An estimated global TV audience of 200 million tuned in to watch the ceremony. Earlier the Queen had announced that the couple were to become the Earl and Countess of Wessex and that after her death and that of his father Prince Philip, Edward would assume Philip's title of Duke of Edinburgh. Ms Rhys-Jones, who works in the public relations industry, did not want to become a princess as she wished to avoid comparisons with the late Diana, Princess of Wales. Earlier this month *The Sun* newspaper earned a stern rebuke from the Press Complaints Commission for publishing an old topless photograph of Sophie Rhys-Jones.

London police charged with 'racism'

London, 24 February

A judicial enquiry into the police investigation of the 1993 murder of black Londoner Stephen Lawrence today reported that there was "institutional racism" in the Metropolitan Police. Sir Paul Condon, Metropolitan Police Commissioner, rejected calls for his resignation while admitting that the police and criminal justice system had let the Lawrence family down and that he felt a "sense of shame".

Lawrence was stabbed to death in south London on 22 April 1993 and although the police arrested five white youths as suspects and charged two of them, prosecutors dropped the case because of lack of evidence. Lawrence's parents failed in a private prosecution against the youths in 1996. Home Secretary Jack Straw said that the police would for the first time be made accountable under race relations legislation.

Sean Connery at the opening of the Scottish parliament.

Scottish, Welsh assemblies open for business

Edinburgh, 1 July

In a formal opening ceremony, the Queen today presented the official mace to the 129 members of Scotland's first parliament in 292 years. She celebrated the "grit, determination, humour, forthrightness and above all strong sense of identity of the Scottish people". Presiding Officer Lord Steel of Aikwood addressed the monarch by the ancient title "Queen of Scots". In Cardiff, the new Welsh National Assembly, opened by the Queen and the Prince of Wales on 26 May, assumed its full powers today.

TV's Jill Dando murdered

London, 26 April

BBC TV personality Jill Dando was shot dead this morning outside her west London home by an unidentified gunman. Neighbours found her drenched in blood on the doorstep of her house in Fulham just after 11.30am. Attempts to resuscitate her failed, and she was taken to hospital, where she was declared dead at 1.03pm. The cause of death was a single gunshot to the head. Dando had won many fans and admirers, most recently as presenter of the BBC's popular Crimewatch programme. Today flags were flown at half-mast at the BBC. Police have found no motive for the attack.

4 Aug. Queen Elizabeth the Queen Mother celebrates her 99th birthday.

Hereditaries bid Lords farewell

Westminster, 11 November
Time was called on more than 700 years of parliamentary tradition as the bill abolishing the right of hereditary peers to sit in the House of Lords was made law. The 751 hereditary peers were a majority in the outgoing 1330-member House of Lords, and for most of them it was their last day in the upper chamber of parliament. But 92 of the hereditaries have had a stay of execution. They were elected in a ballot to sit alongside a majority of appointed "life" peers in an interim 670-member House of Lords until the reforms of the upper chamber are completed.

Paddington rail crash kills 27

The site of the crash near Paddington Station, London.

London, 6 October
Two trains collided at high speed near Paddington Station yesterday morning, killing at least 27 and injuring more than 100. The 8.06am train from Paddington to Great Bedwyn, Wiltshire, was cut in two when it collided with the incoming express from Cheltenham, Gloucestershire, at 8.11. Many suffered horrific burns as a vast fireball engulfed parts of the wreckage. People nearby said they heard trapped passengers screaming for help. Paddington station was closed and emergency centres set up. As 70 firemen and 35 ambulance crews began the harrowing rescue operation, the railway authorities said the final death toll could be higher still. A public outcry has been fuelled by suspicions that in the last three years privatised rail companies have compromised passenger safety by refusing to spend money on improved signalling.

New beginning in Ireland

Belfast, 2 December.
The Good Friday Agreement was formally enacted today as powers were passed from Westminster to the new Northern Ireland executive and the Dublin government withdrew its territorial claim to Northern Ireland. Prime Minister Bertie Ahern said "every Irish person is entitled to feel a great sense of pride today". The Northern Ireland Cabinet met before TV cameras at Stormont Castle. It is clear that problems still lie ahead, notably over the issue of decommissioning weapons. David Trimble, Ulster Unionist Party leader and First Minister of the executive, said that the Cabinet meeting was "very constructive". A hopeful sign came tonight with the IRA announcement that it has appointed a representative to enter discussions with the body set up under General John de Chastelain to facilitate arms decommissioning.

Total eclipse of the sun

Three stages in the eclipse of the sun.

Devon and Cornwall, 11 August
Around 1.3 million people packed into the southwest corner of England this morning to see Britain's first total eclipse of the Sun since 1927. But for most the view was spoiled by gloomily familiar British weather of heavy clouds and rain – and thousands of wraparound cardboard spectacles designed to protect the eyes while viewing the eclipse were discarded virtually unused. Some of the eager hordes enjoyed glimpses of the Sun's dramatic departure and reappearance, which lasted two minutes from 11.11am; all reported that even beneath thick cloud cover the sudden cold and descent of total darkness was impressive. Further north in the British isles, clearer skies gave people a better view, but of a partial eclipse. Some Britons, perhaps expecting the British weather to do its worst, had travelled abroad to view the event, which was also visible from parts of the European mainland.

British soldiers enter Kosovo as bombing ends

Yugoslavia, 12 June
British troops including the SAS, Paras and Gurkhas entered the Serbian province of Kosovo in Yugoslavia today after NATO ended its 78-day bombing campaign against the regime of Yugoslav president Slobodan Milosevic. NATO launched the air onslaught on 24 March in the face of his refusal to call off campaigns against ethnic Albanian separatists in Kosovo. On 9 June Milosevic's generals agreed to withdraw army and special police units from Kosovo within 11 days, paving the way for a 51,000-strong peacekeeping force, including American, Russian and British soldiers, to enter the province.

26 May. Manchester United win the European Cup, beating Bayern Munich 2-1, with goals by Sheringham and Solskjaer.

Lasers and lightshows, beacons and cricket bats

The Millennium Dome, the centrepiece of the UK's official celebrations, was opened by the Queen at 11.45pm on 31 December. The building itself, the zones inside (and the extension to the Jubilee underground line to transport visitors to the Dome from central London) were all completed in the nick of time.

A carnival, Blueprints for Paradise, entertained the 10,000 invited guests in the Millennium Dome shortly after midnight. Earlier, the Queen and Prime Minister Tony Blair had joined the guests in singing Auld Lang Syne.

The £780 million Millennium Dome in Greenwich, south-east London, grew from plans for an exhibition to celebrate the millennium first mooted in 1994 under the Conservative government of John Major. When the Labour Party was elected in 1997, it took the project on. The Dome, essentially a vast tent hung from 12 poles, contains 14 pavilions or "zones" including a Mind Zone, a Learning Zone, a Faith Zone and a Play Zone. It was promoted enthusiastically by Prime Minister Tony Blair as "a great British achievement", but ran into difficulties on its opening night, New Year's Eve 1999, when the gala ceremony was marred by organizational problems that left scores of invited guests queueing for hours to collect their tickets or pass through security. Some press reviews of the Dome's exhibits were lukewarm and initial ticket sales disappointing, but many visitors expressed delight. As 2000 began, the Dome faced a mighty challenge to meet its break-even target of 12 million visitors in the year.

– all have their place in Britain's millennium party

Millennium fireworks dispel the darkness behind Manchester Town Hall as part of the city's celebrations. Elsewhere in the city a crowd of 12,000 revellers turned out for a free concert in Castlefield starring Ian Brown, former singer of the Stone Roses, and in a lighthearted showpiece event a "millennium bug" fought against local celebrities.

The first cricket match of 2000 took place in Hambledown, Hampshire, just six minutes into the new year.

During celebrations in Exeter, Devon, a chicken puppet "laid" a metal egg containing pages inscribed with the wishes of local schoolchildren for a better world in the new millennium. Later the "chicken" met a fiery end.

In Cardiff a winter fairground attracted thrillseekers, while Welsh band the Manic Street Preachers drew 57,000 to the city's Millennium Stadium for a free concert. Some 10,000 young people descended on Tenby, west Wales, for a rave.

In crowded cities and deserted beauty spots,

The "Angel of the North", the 208-ton sculpture near Gateshead by Antony Gormley, welcomes the first sunrise of the new millennium. Made of weather-resistant steel, the Angel stands 66ft high and has a wingspan of 178ft.

Fireworks cascade behind the London Eye, a giant ferris wheel on the south bank of the River Thames, a little downstream from Big Ben. Last-minute safety concerns meant that the wheel did not operate as planned on 31 December.

Far from the partying crowds, the prehistoric sanctuary of Stonehenge in Wiltshire bears serene witness to the first dawn of AD 2000. A group of Druids were on hand to mark the event by dancing around the standing stones.

A storm of fireworks above Edinburgh Castle drew gasps from crowds in Princes Street Gardens. The city attracted 200,000 people – half from abroad – to its millennium bash, and partygoers were still dancing in the streets at dawn.

Britons welcome the dawn of a new age

In Centenary Square, Birmingham, Sir Cliff Richard fires a laser to light the Flame of Hope beacon. The flame will remain alight throughout 2000. The crowd later sang along to Sir Cliff's hit pop version of The Lord's Prayer.

The people of Northern Ireland looked forward to a brighter future following the progress towards peace in 1999. Two fifteen-year-olds who lost loved ones in the bombing of Omagh in August 1998 lit a millennium beacon in Belfast.

The year 2000 got off to a bracing start for a few hardy folk who braved the icy waters of the Firth of Forth at South Queensferry, near Edinburgh, on 1 January in the annual "loony dook" charity fundraiser.

Bristol hosted a lantern procession and laid on a superb firework display above the Industrial Museum. The Millennium Commission handed out around £5 million to help with the costs of the Big Party across Britain.

In Newcastle crowds were entertained by a string quartet suspended from a crane and by giant Geordie puppets, including one of England football captain Alan Shearer. At midnight fireworks illuminated the Tyne Bridge.

The century's statistics

Every ten years a census is taken of population and housing in the UK, providing a striking cross-section of British society. The last census was taken on 21 April 1991 and the next one is planned for April 2001. Where appropriate, corresponding figures for the Irish Republic have been included.

Population

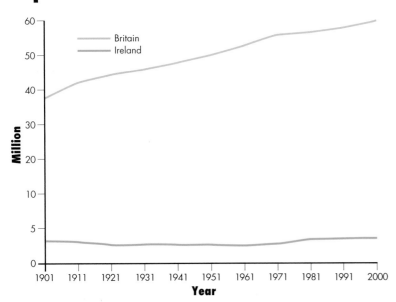

British population explosion
Britain's population at the 1991 census (57,808,000) was more than one and a half times larger than in 1901 (38,237,000). The

Irish population, however, has hardly changed at all. In the UK 89.4% live in urban areas and 10.6% in rural parts; Irish figures are 58% urban, 42% rural.

Births, deaths and marriages

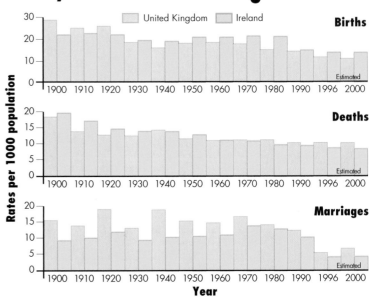

Matters of life and death
For much of the century the Irish birth rate was higher than that in the UK. Latest figures show that the average number of births per

childbearing woman is 1.7 in the UK and 1.8 in the Irish Republic. The marriage rate has fallen in both countries, but is holding firm at the century's end.

Labour force

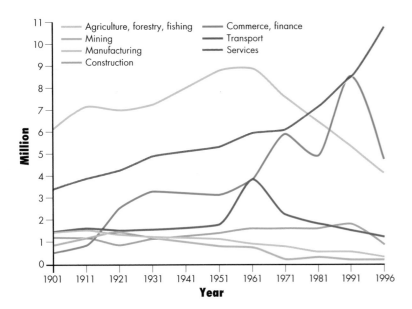

Changing job patterns
After 1961, the numbers employed in manufacturing industry saw a sharp decline while the service sector took off. Mining and farm-

ing endured a steady, less dramatic decline across the century; the transport sector enjoyed a boom in the postwar decades, but then settled back to near its 1901 level.

Unemployment

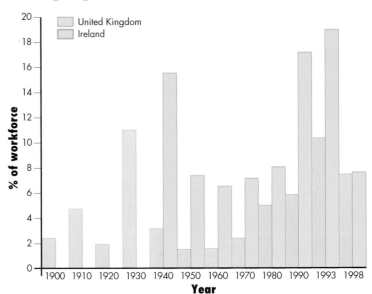

Human cost of boom and bust
In terms of the percentage of people out of work, the economic downturn of the early 1990s was nearly as bad as the more cele-

brated Depression of the 1930s. In the Irish Republic, where early 1990s unemployment was very high, figures are not available before 1940.

Transport

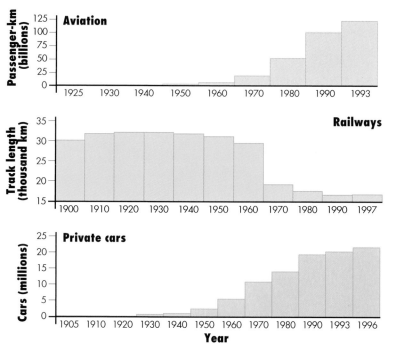

Gross Domestic Product (GDP)

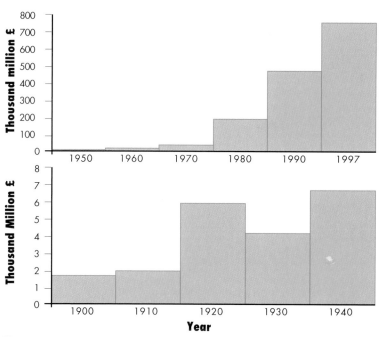

The rise of the car

The rapid fall in the length of the UK's rail network (the result of the 'Beeching' closures) closely matches the steep increase in the number of private cars on British roads. According to mid-1990s figures, there are 366,999km (228,042 miles) of paved roads in the UK. There are 57 UK airports.

Economic growth

Gross Domestic Product measures the total value of goods and services produced in the country, excluding income from overseas investments. The graphs above show GDP at current prices, ie not adjusted for inflation, which has at times been exceptionally severe, most recently in the 1970s.

Total crime

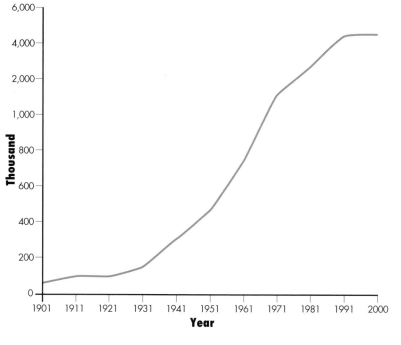

Types of crime

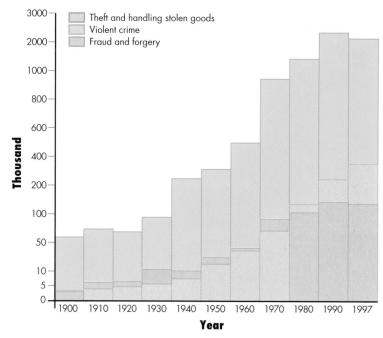

Criminal growth

The Home Office statistics above are for the UK only. The total number of reported crimes in the UK rose very steeply from just 77,934 in 1900 to 4,598,327 in 1997. Recently, drug trafficking offences more than doubled between 1991 (around 11,000) and 1997 (over 23,000).

'Hidden' offences

It is impossible to know how many crimes were committed but never reported. The violent crime figures, for example, include sexual offences such as rape, incest and indecent assault, which – because of changing social attitudes – were far more likely to be reported in the 1990s than in 1900.

Robert Cecil, Lord Salisbury

Lived: 3/2/1830–22/8/1903
Born: Hatfield, Hertfordshire
Died: Hatfield
Party: Conservative
First elected as MP: 1853
Terms as Prime Minister:
1885–6, 1886–92, 1895–1902
Oversaw: partition of Africa

Arthur James Balfour

Lived: 25/7/1848–19/3/1930
Born: Whittingehame, Scotland
Died: Woking, Surrey
Party: Conservative
First elected as MP: 1874
Term as Prime Minister: 1902–5
Oversaw: "Entente Cordiale"
with France

Henry Campbell-Bannerman

Lived: 7/9/1836–22/4/1908
Born: Glasgow
Died: London
Party: Liberal
First elected as MP: 1868
Term as Prime Minister: 1905–8
Oversaw: 1906 Trades Disputes
Act

Herbert Henry Asquith

Lived: 12/9/1852–15/2/1928
Born: Morley, Yorkshire
Died: Sutton Courtenay, Berkshire
Party: Liberal
First elected as MP: 1886
Terms as Prime Minister:
1908–10, 1910–15, 1915–16
(Coalition)
Oversaw: 1911 Parliament Act

David Lloyd George

Lived: 17/1/1863–26/3/1945
Born: Manchester
Died: Ty-newydd, Caernarvonshire
Party: Liberal
First elected as MP: 1890
Terms as Prime Minister:
1916–19 (Coalition),
1919–22 (Coalition)
Oversaw: Irish independence

Andrew Bonar Law

Lived: 16/9/1858–30/10/1923
Born: Kingston, N.B., Canada
Died: London
Party: Conservative
First elected as MP: 1900
Term as Prime Minister: 1922–3
Oversaw: official creation of Irish
Free State

Stanley Baldwin

Lived: 3/8/1867–14/12/1947
Born: Bewdley, Worcestershire
Died: Astley, Lancashire
Party: Conservative
First elected as MP: 1906
Terms as Prime Minister:
1923–4, 1924–9, 1935–7
Oversaw: abdication crisis

James Ramsay MacDonald

Lived: 12/10/1866–9/11/1937
Born: Lossiemouth, Scotland
Died: at sea, sailing for S. America
Party: Labour (left party 1931)
First elected as MP: 1906
Terms as Prime Minister: 1924,
1929–31 (both Labour), 1931–5
('National' government)

Arthur Neville Chamberlain

Lived: 18/3/1869–9/11/1940
Born: Birmingham
Died: Heckfield, near Reading
Party: Conservative
First elected as MP: 1918
Term as Prime Minister:
1937–40
Oversaw: start of World War II

Winston Leonard Spencer Churchill

Lived: 30/11/1874–24/1/1965
Born: Blenheim Palace,
Oxfordshire
Died: London
Party: Conservative
First elected as MP: 1900
Terms as Prime Minister:
1940–5 (Coalition), 1951–5
(Conservative)

Clement Richard Attlee

Lived: 3/1/1883–8/10/1967
Born: Putney, London
Died: Westminster
Party: Labour
First elected as MP: 1922
Term as Prime Minister: 1945–51
Oversaw: creation of welfare state

Edward Richard George Heath

Lived: 9/7/1916–
Born: Broadstairs, Kent
Party: Conservative
First elected as MP: 1950
Term as Prime Minister: 1970–4
Oversaw: British entry to EEC

Robert Anthony Eden

Lived: 12/6/1897–14/1/1977
Born: Windlestone, Co. Durham
Died: Alvediston, Wiltshire
Party: Conservative
First elected as MP: 1923
Term as Prime Minister: 1955–7
Oversaw: Suez crisis

Leonard James Callaghan

Lived: 27/3/1912–
Born: Portsmouth, Hampshire
Party: Labour
First elected as MP: 1945
Term as Prime Minister: 1976–9
Oversaw: "Winter of discontent" 1978–9

Maurice Harold Macmillan

Lived: 10/2/1894–29/12/1986
Born: London
Died: Birch Grove, Sussex
Party: Conservative
First elected as MP: 1924
Term as Prime Minister: 1957–63
Oversaw: Profumo scandal

Margaret Hilda Thatcher

Lived: 13/10/1925–
Born: Grantham, Lincolnshire
Party: Conservative
First elected as MP: 1959
Terms as Prime Minister: 1979–83, 1983–87, 1987–90
Oversaw: Falklands war 1982

Alexander Frederick Douglas-Home

Lived: 2/7/1903–9/10/1995
Born: London
Died: Coldstream, Scotland
Party: Conservative
First elected as MP: 1931
Term as Prime Minister: 1963–4

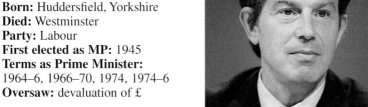

John Major

Lived: 29/3/1943–
Born: London
Party: Conservative
First elected as MP: 1979
Terms as Prime Minister: 1990–2, 1992–7
Oversaw: UK–Irish peace initiative in N. Ireland

James Harold Wilson

Lived: 11/3/1916–24/5/1995
Born: Huddersfield, Yorkshire
Died: Westminster
Party: Labour
First elected as MP: 1945
Terms as Prime Minister: 1964–6, 1966–70, 1974, 1974–6
Oversaw: devaluation of £

Anthony Charles Lynton Blair

Lived: 6/5/1953–
Born: Edinburgh
Party: Labour
First elected as MP: 1983
Term as Prime Minister: 1997–
Oversaw: Good Friday Agreement

The House of Windsor

Princess Alexandrina Victoria of Hanover, descendant of George I (1714–27), the first Hanoverian King of Britain, acceded to the throne on 20 June 1837 and ruled as Queen Victoria for more than 60 years. During World War I her grandson George V, faced with strong anti-German sentiment in Britain, changed his German surname from Saxe-Coburg-Gotha to Windsor. In 1936 King Edward VIII elected to abdicate rather than give up the love of American divorcée Wallis Simpson; the reigning monarch, Queen Elizabeth II, has enjoyed a long and fruitful reign but in the 1990s endured the divorce of her three eldest children amid a storm of media gossip and speculation that appeared to undermine the popularity of the Royal Family.

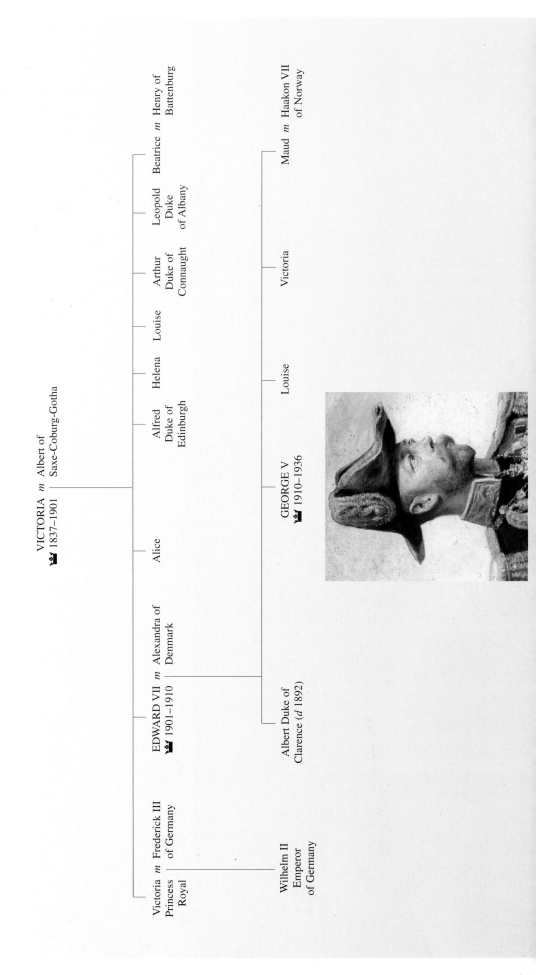

VICTORIA *m* Albert of
1837–1901   Saxe-Coburg-Gotha

EDWARD VII *m* Alexandra of
1901–1910   Denmark

Alice

Alfred
Duke of
Edinburgh

Helena

Louise

Arthur
Duke of
Connaught

Leopold
Duke
of Albany

Beatrice *m* Henry of
Battenburg

Victoria *m* Frederick III
Princess   of Germany
Royal

Albert Duke of
Clarence (*d* 1892)

GEORGE V
1910–1936

Louise

Victoria

Maud *m* Haakon VII
of Norway

Wilhelm II
Emperor
of Germany

Victoria of Hesse, *m* Louis of Battenberg
daughter of Queen
Victoria's daughter, Alice

Louis Earl Mountbatten (*d* 1979)

Alice *m* Prince Andrew of Greece

GEORGE V *m* Mary (May) of Teck (*d* 1953)
♚ 1910–1936

George *m* Princess Marina of Greece
Duke of Kent (*d* 1942)

John (*d* 1919)

Henry Duke of Gloucester (*d* 1974)

Mary *m* Henry Earl of Harewood

EDWARD VIII *m* Wallis Simpson (*d* 1972)
♚ 1936

GEORGE VI *m* Elizabeth Bowes-Lyon
♚ 1936–1952

Margaret *m* Antony Armstrong-Jones Earl of Snowdon (*div* 1978)

David Viscount Linley

Sarah

ELIZABETH *m* Philip Mountbatten Duke of Edinburgh
♚ 1952–

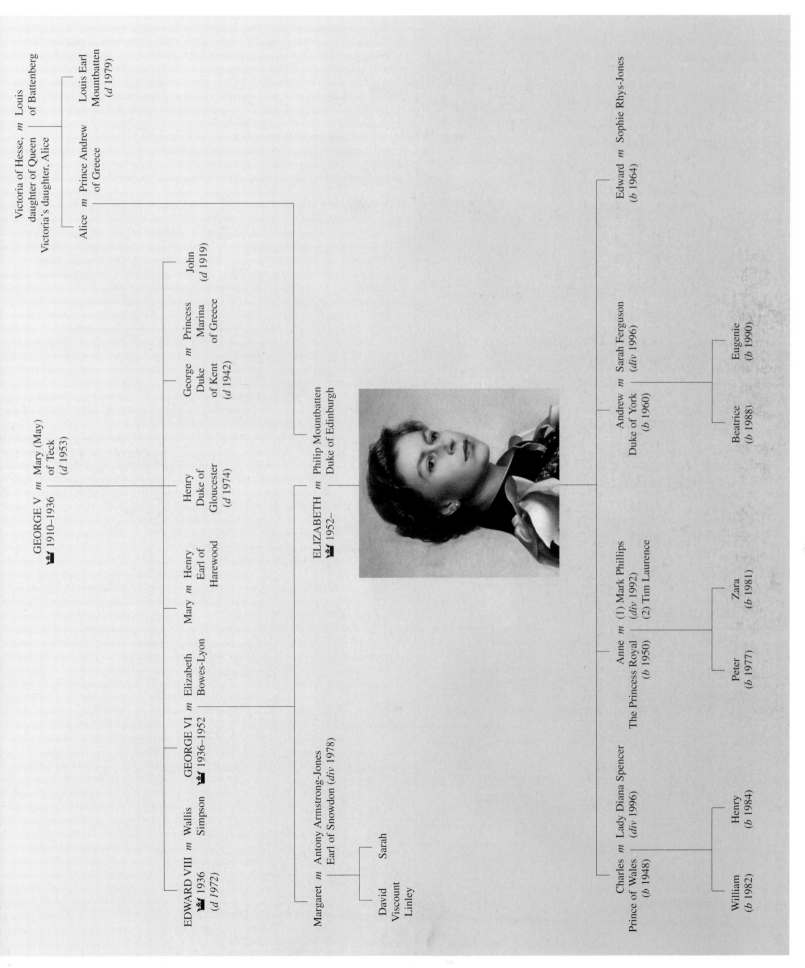

Edward *m* Sophie Rhys-Jones (*b* 1964)

Andrew *m* Sarah Ferguson (*div* 1996)
Duke of York (*b* 1960)

Beatrice (*b* 1988)

Eugenie (*b* 1990)

Anne *m* (1) Mark Phillips (*div* 1992)
The Princess Royal (*b* 1950) (2) Tim Laurence

Peter (*b* 1977)

Zara (*b* 1981)

Charles *m* Lady Diana Spencer (*div* 1996)
Prince of Wales (*b* 1948)

William (*b* 1982)

Henry (*b* 1984)

231

235

236

238

Picture credits